THE PRAEGER HANDBOOK
OF HUMAN RESOURCE
MANAGEMENT

The Praeger Handbook of Human Resource Management

Volume 1

Ann Gilley
Jerry W. Gilley
Scott A. Quatro
Pamela Dixon

Westport, Connecticut
London

Library of Congress Cataloging-in-Publication Data

The Praeger handbook of human resource management / edited by Ann Gilley ... [et al.].
  p. cm.
  Includes bibliographical references and index.
  ISBN 978–0–313–35015–3 ((set) : alk. paper) — ISBN 978–0–313–35017–7 ((vol. 1) : alk. paper) — ISBN 978–0–313–35019–1 ((vol. 2) : alk. paper)
1. Personnel management. I. Gilley, Ann Maycunich. II. Praeger Publishers. III. Title: Handbook of human resource management. IV. Title: Human resource management.
HF5549.P73 2009
658.3—dc22   2008034634

British Library Cataloguing in Publication Data is available.

Library of Congress Catalog Card Number: 2008034634
ISBN: 978–0–313–35015–3 (set)
      978–0–313–35017–7 (Vol. 1)
      978–0–313–35019–1 (Vol. 2)

First published in 2009

Praeger Publishers, 88 Post Road West, Westport, CT 06881
An imprint of Greenwood Publishing Group, Inc.
www.praeger.com

Printed in the United States of America

The paper used in this book complies with the
Permanent Paper Standard issued by the National
Information Standards Organization (Z39.48–1984).

10 9 8 7 6 5 4 3 2 1

For my family and friends, who inspire me daily—especially my husband, Jerry and my mother, Connie. And for those who guide me in spirit—Ann, Richard, Sig, and Bert.
   Ann Gilley

For my best friend, Ann, and for our girls—Lakota Sioux, Pepper Lee, and Abby Rose. You are the sweetness in my life.
   Jerry W. Gilley

First, I must acknowledge my colleagues and co-editors Jerry Gilley, Pam Dixon, and especially Ann Gilley. Ann, you took on an incredibly complex project and brought it to a successful completion, and managed to remain gracious in the heat of the battle. Thanks for the opportunity to contribute to the project.
I also wish to acknowledge the academic leadership at Covenant College, specifically my Department Chair Chris Dodson, for ensuring that I had adequate course release time to take on this project.
Lastly, I dedicate my efforts on this book to my wife Jamie, and to the "Quattro, Quatro" kids—McKenna, Keaton, Hallie-Blair, and Hudson. You are the "face of God" to me.
   Scott A. Quatro

For my mother, Mary, who taught me the meaning of perseverance, sacrifice, creativity, and generosity.
   Pamela Dixon

Contents

VOLUME ONE

Preface

One of the most overused and abused phrases uttered by managers is that "employees are our greatest asset." Although many organizations' annual reports and mission statements tout the importance of employees, most fail to "walk the talk," which reveals a definite disparity between the perceived importance of employees and their treatment. In reality, physical facilities receive better care and attention than most employees. As a result, organizations fail to maximize the potential of their human capital. Creativity, responsiveness, and quality suffer as the untapped talent within employees goes to waste and their growth and development are ignored. Effective managers align human resource management with their organization's strategic goals and objectives. How? Read on!

HUMAN RESOURCE MANAGEMENT

First, it is important to distinguish between two often misunderstood terms. Human resources is frequently the department within an organization charged with administrative duties such as payroll and benefits. *Human resource management* (HRM) is a dynamic and evolving practice used by leaders and managers throughout a firm to enhance productivity, quality, and effectiveness. It is the goal of this book to provide a resource through which organizational leaders and managers may understand the field of HRM and grasp its simplicity. It is within this simplicity that an appreciation of the complexity of HRM can be realized. This book provides an overview of the field and practice of HRM.

We have tried to clarify and simplify HRM so that it becomes less complicated to the newcomer. If, after studying the following chapters, readers feel better able to understand the field, its components, roles, areas of practice, unique competencies, and strategies for improving performance within organizations, then the book has indeed accomplished its mission. Ultimately, our goal is to provide the details, descriptions, and facts necessary to enable HRM professionals to develop strategies for becoming more effective professionals.

Regardless of one's orientation, this book will serve as a reference for HRM professionals and managers interested in a better understanding of the principles and practices of HRM. The question remains, *What is human resource management?* Given the complex nature of the practice of HRM, a simple definition is made even more difficult due to the rapidly changing nature of the field. However, the very term "human resource management" provides us with clues as to its meaning. Let us examine the terms "human resources" and "management" more closely.

What Are Human Resources?

Today's organizations consist of three types of resources: physical, financial, and human. *Physical resources* are machines, materials, facilities, equipment, and component parts of products, which are often referred to as *fixed organization assets.* Physical resources are important to the health of the organization because they provide it with stability and growth opportunities. Also, because they are tangible and can be seen, physical resources provide the public with assurances of quality as well as a measure of the organization's success. Buildings are an example of this type of resource.

The *liquid assets* of an organization refer to its *financial* resources. These include cash, stocks, bonds, investments, and operating capital. Similar to physical resources, financial resources are vital to the organization's ability to react to opportunities for growth and expansion, which reflect its overall financial stability and strength. This is determined by comparing the assets (physical and financial) with the liabilities (debts) of the organization. A positive outcome reveals *net worth,* which is the figure that investors and financial organizations use to assess the financial health of an organization.

Human resources refer to the workers employed by an organization. Unlike the typical, straightforward, standard measures used to value fixed and liquid assets, organizations lack widely acceptable means by which to value the contributions of their employees. For example, employees cannot be depreciated like physical resources and, more importantly, are seldom reflected in the net worth of an organization. However, employees are a greater asset than physical or financial resources, for the talent of employees is what determines an organization's success. Unfortunately, organizational board members and leaders often overlook this fact because employees are not used to reflect the organization's prosperity. Forward-thinking leaders of firms recognize the value of their employees and consider them in their asset portfolios. As a result, many recognize the importance of the HRM function and realize that improved knowledge, competencies, skills, and attitudes are necessary to improve the overall success of the organization.

The cost of recruiting, hiring, relocating, training, and orientation is one helpful measure available to companies to determine the importance of their employees. The collective knowledge, competencies, skills, and attitudes of the members of the organization are another measure. These intangibles have value. Obviously, a well-trained, highly skilled, and knowledgeable employee is more valuable to an organization than one who is not. This value manifests itself in increased quality, productivity, effectiveness, efficiency, and customer service.

What Is Management?

Examining the critical components of management frames the process of improving the success of an organization. The management process involves a group of similar activities performed by a manager, regardless of the type and size of the organization. These activities are planning, organizing, staffing, and controlling:

- Planning charts a course of action for the future, aiming to achieve a consistent, coordinated set of operations that yields desired results. Planning is the primary task of management and administrators, occurring prior to other manual activities as they determine the framework for their execution.
- Organizing is based on the goals and objectives established through the planning process, reflecting the thinking on the structure of and relationship among the various parts of the

HRM function and those of the organization. A classic discussion of organizing includes division of labor, authority, span of control, and structure of the organization (formal and informal).

- Staffing supplies qualified employees needed to run a planned and organized system, fulfill its mission, and achieve its objectives. Staffing includes recruiting, selecting, placing, appraising, and compensating employees.
- Controlling is the process that checks performance against standards, making certain that goals and objectives are being met. Controlling involves training, coaching, and regular checks of progress aimed at keeping the organization and its members on track.

What Is Human Resource Management?

Human resource management refers to activities and tasks useful in maximizing employees' performance. *Human resource management,* therefore, includes the recruitment, selection, placement, motivation, appraisal, development, communication with, utilization, and overall accommodation of employees to achieve organizational goals.

At the unit/departmental and individual levels, managers hold two primary responsibilities—improve and manage performance. At the unit/departmental level, managers engage in planning, teambuilding, and performance management activities to improve current and future performance. At the individual performer level, managers coach, appraise, motivate, and collaboratively develop career and professional development plans that enhance employee talent and career opportunities. The activities at the departmental and individual performer levels are known as *human resource development* actions.

At the division and corporate levels, managers participate in organizational development, change management, and strategic planning to enhance an organization's productivity and effectiveness. These efforts lead to organizational renewal, which is a firm's ability to reinvent itself and remain competitive. In summary, then, we can define HRM as the process of facilitating organizational performance, productivity, and change through organized (formal and informal) interventions, initiatives, and management actions in order to enhance a firm's performance capacity, capability, competitive readiness, and renewal.

ORGANIZATION OF THIS BOOK

This book is arranged by major topic sections. Part I includes entries related to Human Resource Practices, including recruiting and selection, employee development, performance management, compensation, benefits and insurance, and employment law. These topics, such as human resource planning and coaching, and the numerous laws impacting workers, are critical for managers and HRM professionals at all levels.

Part II, Organizational Issues, focuses on leadership and strategy, organizational development and change, and organizational behavior. Each entry in this section covers issues that profoundly impact an organization's direction and functioning, including strategic planning and change, innovation and competitiveness, and the organizational behavior issues (such as culture and teambuilding) that enhance or impede firm success.

Part III, General HR Issues, addresses concerns that are common to all firms at all levels and thus are critical components of HRM practice. Documentation, forecasting, job design, and safety are examples of covered topics. This section also includes entries on recent business and societal concerns impacting businesses, such as homeland security, international HR, metrics, safety, work-life balance, and workplace violence.

Part IV, HR Policy, includes discussions of and suggestions for guidelines and standards common to many firms. Employee policy handbooks often detail subjects such as dress codes, overtime, disciplinary procedures, Internet/email restrictions, flex-time, security, travel, and telecommuting, to name a few.

Parts V and VI include an abundance of resources for the manager and HRM practitioner. Resources include a sampling of related articles, books, Web sites, and organizations, along with checklists, sample forms, and other tools useful in managing human resources.

OUTCOMES OF HRM IN ORGANIZATIONS

Traditionally, the human resource department has been responsible for providing services such as compensation and benefits management, administration of personnel records and activities, compliance and outplacement services, employer relations, training and development, staffing and recruiting, and payroll management. These services continue to be vitally important to organizations. Forward-thinking organizations have expanded human resource services to meet the constantly growing needs of the organization and its members. Expanded service offerings such as coaching and developmental appraisals enable managers to lay the foundation needed to build a developmental culture within their organizations.

Effective managers provide development initiatives, performance coaching and appraisal activities, and serve the needs of tomorrow's organization. Expanded services such as these focus on satisfying the needs and wants of both internal and external constituents by providing added value, the result of interaction and facilitation of desired organizational goals and objectives. Within organizations, these actions promote changes such as enhanced communications, employee growth and development, and exemplary performance.

HRM activities, to be effective, adhere to a set of guiding principles that serve the organization and bring about the change necessary for continuous personnel growth and development. These guiding principles include

- focusing on important organizational processes such as facilities and resource management;
- learning through collaboration and teamwork;
- enhanced commitment to employees while meeting organizational needs; and
- measuring the value of HRM activity.

These guiding principles provide direction and focus while establishing a value-based approach critical to creating a productive, developmental culture and work climate.

One of the primary benefits of HRM involves having the right people in the right place at the right time interacting with the right leadership. Consequently, it is important to select and develop leaders, managers, and employees who possess the talent necessary to meet the goals and objectives facing the organization now and in the future. Specific strategies that bring about desired results include

- improving organizational effectiveness and responsiveness through people and processes, and
- building competencies in people and the organization.

To create competitive advantage through people and processes, human resource oriented organizations adopt the principles and practices that enable them to treat their employees as their most valuable component in achieving greater success.

Each approach nourishes an organization's capability through state-of-the-art human resource practices. Building competencies in people and organizations requires managers as HRM professionals—in concert with organizational leaders and HR practitioners—to focus on enhancing human resource principles, policies, and practices. Organizations that proactively focus on principles, policies, and practices to improve their responsiveness, enhance organizational renewal, and increase their overall performance capacity and capability will meet their strategic goals while providing rewarding career opportunities to a reservoir of highly talented personnel. Effective managers accept the challenges of and responsibilities for HRM by demonstrating that their employees are indeed the organization's greatest asset. HRM enables leaders and managers to lay the foundation for ever-increasing organizational success.

Part I
Human Resource Practices

Chapter 1
Recruiting and Selection

Staffing: An Overview

Staffing is one of the most fundamental and essential sources of an organization's financial performance and attainment of its long-term goals. According to Paul Austermuehle, senior vice president with the Bernard Hodes Group:

> Staffing is a mission-critical process that supports the organization's business model and strategic objectives.[1]

One of the underlying suppositions for an effective staffing program is that coherent and cohesive processes are needed to drive the staffing strategies from requisition to hire. Recruiting and selection are two essential elements of an overall process that should be viewed as a core competency that helps the company achieve its competitive advantage. The following are the critical success factors of the process:

1. Employer Branding
2. Business Staffing Plan
3. Sourcing
4. Recruiting and Selection
5. Hiring
6. On-boarding
7. Metrics and Implementation

Dave Ulrich,[2] noted professor at the University of Michigan's School of Business and codirector of the university's Human Resources Executive Education programs, states that the HR function must be focused on the creation of value. Therefore, staffing should also focus its activities and energies on this imperative. It must deliver products and services that are value-added in the eyes of all internal clients such as hiring managers and other HR partners. It starts with creating repeatable processes, deliverables that are created in conjunction with the customer. Shared responsibilities are defined that lead to the customer realizing the strategic importance of Staffing and how each player is accountable for the successful execution of the process.

By Ulrich's definition, staffing then becomes a "center of expertise," a function that is comprised of subject matter experts that understand how to combine the ensemble of critical success factors mentioned above to source and recruit the best-in-class candidates.

According to Karen Hart, also a senior vice president of the Bernard Hodes Group, the core of a successful recruitment program is a process that lends itself to efficiencies and economies of scale. She adds:

> This process should utilize but not be crippled by technology, should include a high level of customer service to both the candidate and the internal customers (HR team and hiring managers), and should be seamless in its scope. A periodic review of this process can result in elimination of redundancies, better utilization of staff, better response times, and better hires.[3]

Employer Branding

Austermuehle indicated the following regarding employer branding:

> The brand is best characterized as the relationship between an individual and the organization. It is described in a way that outlines how the relationship works and how each party benefits from their mutual commitment.

Austermuehle says that the staffing and marketing functions usually develop the descriptors of the brand together. They then identify key brand messages that apply to current employees, prospective employees, and, often, former employees who would be welcomed back to the organization. The messages should convey important information about how the employee best contributes to the business' strategic goals and what they can expect in return. This kind of message is often described as an employee value proposition. While there is usually one broad brand description, there can be several value propositions—each targeted to subsets within the talent community. This enables the company to hire people who fit to the culture regardless of their work function, area of expertise, or level of experience.

Overall, excellent companies attract excellent people. A durable brand in the marketplace results in a durable brand in the labor market. If quality is a hallmark of the company, it will attract quality people.

Business Staffing Plan

The business staffing plan (BSP) is an integral part of the organization's strategic business plan. The plan entails identification of the current and future skill sets and number of employees needed to deliver new and improved products and services to the company's customers. The BSP should be reviewed and updated on a quarterly basis to maintain is relevance and reliability.

The initial step in the planning process is to evaluate the characteristics of the current workforce in relationship to the needs identified in the BSP. It then compares the current staff with the desired future workforce to highlight shortages, surpluses, and competency gaps.

A list of questions to use during the BSP discussions is provided in the table on the next page.

Sourcing

Sourcing is basically finding the candidates of choice to satisfy the BSP requirements. It is the most important step in the staffing process. It should be initiated once the workforce

---

Questions to Ask during HR Staffing Planning Discussions

1. How is your industry changing? What demands will this place on your staff requirements?
2. What distinctive core competencies are linked to your organization's competitive advantage? How will these be sustained?
3. What new customer requirements and expectations will significantly shape your needs?
4. What new market penetrations will demand increased staff?
5. What new products will be or need to be introduced to meet strategic objectives? How will this impact the competency requirements of your staff?
6. What competitors are attractive to the talent you wish to hire? Who is attracting our talent away from us and why?
7. What customer contracts will justify additional staffing? When will these take effect? What success have you had in converting contractors to full time staff? How is this practice integrated into your business strategy?
8. What new data/assumptions have changed since our last meeting?
9. What are your cost/benefit hiring experiences?
10. Assuming that we will source effectively according to talent competencies, what values/beliefs do you need in the new hires?
11. What services do you need from HR in the staffing planning process?
12. What "applicant-friendly" recruiting strategies would make this business attract the kind of candidates you desire?
13. How effectively does your business employ the succession planning process in you hiring strategies?
14. How will turnover and retirements affect your staffing requirements?

---

plan has been finalized and then become an ongoing process that is refined once the periodic review of the BSP is completed.

Under most circumstances, internal searches should be conducted as the first priority for sourcing candidates for the BSP requirements. This can be accomplished using the key talent inventory maintained by human resources. Once this is completed, the external search can be initiated. Key external techniques include online job boards, traditional media advertising, career fairs, campus recruiting, international recruitment, rightsizing companies, diversity associations and conferences, and agencies and/or search firms. These practices will generate real-time candidates.

The company may have to invest in sourcing methods that focus on passive candidates, ones who are not actively searching for another job. This pool of talent is generally the best qualified and worth the time and energy to find. The list of techniques includes cold calling, researching industry journals, employee referrals, networking, and executive recruitment agencies.

Recruiting and Selection

Recruiting is selling the candidates on the personal and professional value of the opportunity presented to them. Recruitment can be handled in house or outsourced to a recruitment agency. After the application process opens, the candidate pool is narrowed based on skill sets, salary requirements, geographic location, experience, etc. External recruiting costs (or sourcing costs) include any initiative used to identify or attract candidates, including employer branding.

Selection of the best candidate can be achieved through many interviewing techniques. Behavioral interviewing is one of the most popular and provides an in-depth look into the prospective new hire's ability to handle multifaceted situations. Another tool is the panel or group interview. This provides the hiring team with an understanding of the applicant's capability to handle challenging and potentially stressful situations and is used primarily for managerial position candidates.

The ultimate goal of the recruiting and selection process is to find the most appropriate fit, for the candidate as well as the company.

Hiring

Hiring is a series of transactional events and is contingent upon successful completion of the following: background checks with appropriate law enforcement agencies, educational and employment verification and references, and physicals and drug testing (where necessary and/or required by state or federal law). Documents typically completed on the first day of employment include employee confidentiality agreements, relocation expenses agreements, payroll enrollment, employment eligibility, and the selection of medical, dental, and/or life insurance options.

On-boarding

On-boarding is an essential program that encompasses the employee's entire first year of employment with the organization. On-boarding processes are intended to make the individual's integration into the new environment as seamless and smooth as possible. It is a period of time to energize the new employee in order to lay the foundation for a productive and rewarding tenure with the organization. Successful on-boarding programs also entail assigning the new employee a mentor who acts as a confidant and counselor. Hence, on-boarding can be viewed as a solid retention tool as well.

Metrics and Implementation

The company should create an automated resume and applicant tracking system to manage all phases of staffing's responsibilities.

Use a "Balanced Scorecard" to track and measure the following:

1. Cycle time to fill positions.
2. Quality of hire as defined by the hiring manager.
3. Quantitative statistics that comprise the cost-per-hire:
   a. Fixed-overhead sourcing (agency, advertising, Internet posting costs) and recruiting (applicant travel, lodging, meals, rental car, etc.) expenses.
   b. Signing bonuses.
   c. Relocation and other hiring expenses such as visa preparation costs, medical exams, etc.

Successful implementation of the staffing model is best achieved by creating processes that are repeatable and used consistently by all concerned. Doing so provides the opportunity to identify/track costs mentioned above and establish the appropriate metrics for gauging real fiscal responsibility. This will then validate staffing's value proposition.[4]

Conclusion

Staffing can be viewed as a human resource center of excellence that keeps the organization supplied with the human assets it needs to continuously move ahead and maintain its competitive posture in the market place. Sourcing generates the slate of qualified talent that can be accessed by recruiters and their customers, the company's hiring managers. Repeatable processes, aligned with the business's overall human asset plan and integrated into the company's balanced scorecard, can facilitate the achievement of this imperative. The bottom line is to have the right people, at the right place, at the right time, and at the right price.

NOTES

1. Paul Austermuehle, senior vice president, Bernard Hodes Group, interview by authors, January 21, 2008.
2. David Ulrich, *Human Resource Champions* (Boston: Harvard Business School Press, 1997).
3. Margie Kasse, vice president, Health Care Division, and Karen Hart, senior vice president, Health Care Division, Bernard Hodes Group, interview by authors, January 15, 2008.
4. Ulrich, *Human Resource Champions.*

Fred Miles and Douglas Maxwell

ABILITY INVENTORIES

Over the past three decades, the process of assessing employee skills and abilities has evolved. Managers and human resource personnel have begun to use technology to assist in the analysis of employee skills, which has led to the development of knowledge management (KM) initiatives. Knowledge management involves several systems used to manage information about the intellectual capital within the organization. The organization usually has knowledge management database (KMD) software to analyze employee abilities and performance. This database allows managers and human resource personnel to easily track information about employees. In most cases, KMD systems have a varying range of sophistication depending on the size and needs of the organization. The use of this technology has revolutionized the notion of analyzing employee ability through a database system. Furthermore, such technology allows managers to make wise decisions about hiring, placement, and promotion.

Introduction

Ability inventories are assessments used to measure an employee's level of proficiency relative to pre-defined skill sets. Inventories are administered to measure the abilities of each employee. Inventories are usually based on performance standards for specific job tasks. The data from these inventories are uploaded and housed in the organization's KMD. Managers and human resource personnel can access the information to make data driven decisions about employee hiring, promotion, training and employee placement. When used correctly, ability inventories serve as a powerful tool for managing employees and meeting organizational objectives.

Uses of Ability Inventories

Organizations that use inventories realize the benefits of the tool. The data from inventories, accessed through KMDs, makes the process of decision making and managing employees much easier. Moreover, many possible uses of ability inventories exist. Below are a few possible applications of ability inventories to employee management.

Employee Hiring and Selection

Managers and human resource personnel can use ability inventories to enhance the hiring process for applicants. Inventories allow managers to rate resumes of applicants for the skills necessary to perform job tasks. In addition, data from inventories provide the manager with an analysis of each applicant's potential for hire. In short, ability inventories ease the process of selecting the right person for the job.

Training

Ability inventories provide managers with a detailed assessment of an employee's proficiency in predetermined performance standards. Inventories can be used on an ongoing basis to measure each employee's skills, knowledge, and abilities to perform job tasks. Consequently, data from the inventories aid the development of performance plans based on employee needs for growth. Data allows the efficient use of training dollars to provide employees with developmental activities relevant to needs.

Succession Planning

Ability inventories can be used as an effective strategy to implement succession planning. In most cases, inventories are automated and housed in a KMD located on the organization's intranet. Managers use the KMD to query inventories and identify employees who qualify for future positions. In addition, employees with strong potential can be matched with mentors to encourage their growth and development. In the long run, inventories allow managers to prepare employees to meet the future needs of the organization, while avoiding any interruption of business processes when a seasoned employee leaves.

Project Management

Data from ability inventories facilitate the decision-making process about implementation as new strategic initiatives arise. The organization's KMD can be queried to determine if the skills are available to implement the initiative. If a lack of skills exists, managers determine the development necessary to implement the initiative. Another aspect of project management is using inventories to select team members who possess the skills and attributes needed to complete the assigned task. Proper selection greatly increases the team's ability to complete projects on time and within budget. All in all, inventories serve as a powerful tool to aid the completion of organizational projects and initiatives.

CONCLUSION

Over the years managers and human resource personnel have worked to improve the process of assessing employee skills. Powerful tools such as KMD have allowed organizations to use data from Ability Inventories to measure employee's skills. Such processes have provided managers with the ability to quickly assess skill sets relevant to strategic organizational needs. Finally, such assessments aid the process of making data driven decisions about employee hiring, promotion, training, and employee placement.

Derrick E. Haynes

ASSESSMENT CENTER

An assessment center may be either a physical location or a methodology used for the human resource function of deciding who to select or promote to a position, diagnosing the relative strengths or weaknesses for an individual in work-related skills as an antecedent to development, or developing job-relevant or job-specific skills for a position either an individual currently has or to which the individual has the potential to be promoted. An assessment center will typically utilize multiple evaluation techniques, designed and tailored to expose behaviors considered relevant to the critical aspects of the position. By observing a participant's behavior under simulated conditions, a valid picture can be developed regarding how the person would actually perform in the position.[1]

Historical Background

Assessment centers trace their lineage to the War Office Selection Boards used by the United Kingdom during World War II. This was in response to the large proportion of officers selected for promotion being "returned to unit" as unsuitable. The old system, which relied upon criteria such as social and educational background and "exceptional smartness," was overhauled with an assessment center approach that sought to evaluate characteristics more relevant to the tasks and behaviors of military officers. The new system was deemed successful, as a substantial drop in officers being "returned to unit" was realized.[2] In the United States, assessment centers were utilized by the Office of Strategic Studies to select spies during World War II. The activities, which included group exercises (many with strenuous physical requirements), stress tests, and an interrogation of an "escaped" prisoner, were an attempt not only to assess the separate components, but to delve into the personality and character of each participant under very stressful conditions.[3]

In 1956, AT&T became the first private-sector organization to employ assessment centers. As a result of the AT&T Management Progress Study, assessment centers were incorporated into longitudinal research for individuals entering management positions in Bell Telephone operating companies. Career progress was charted accordingly.[4] Over the next decade, large organizations such as IBM, Sears, General Electric, and J. C. Penney created assessment centers closely modeled after AT&T.

Assessment centers today bear many of the characteristics of their predecessors, and have a rich body of scholarly research and documented practice to guide their continued growth and development. Additionally, the challenges and opportunities impacting assessment centers are truly global, as evidenced by the annual International Congress on Assessment Center Methods meeting, which has convened annually since 1973.

Common Features and Exercises

An assessment center will typically involve six to 12 participants, or "assessees," three to six assessors (middle-level managers or human resource staff members) who are trained to observe and evaluate the behaviors and abilities of each participant, and an administrator from the assessment center organization. The location of the assessment center will usually be away from the organization, such as a hotel conference center. The time required for each participant to complete all exercises and simulations is typically one to three days, with assessors then sharing observations. All behaviors as documented by the assessors are integrated through a consensus discussion process, led by the assessment center administrator. Each participant then receives a written report containing objective information relating to their performance, either from the administrator or one of the assessors.[5] The simulations and exercises in which each participant engages may include any of the following:

— **Leaderless Group Discussion**—A group of four to eight participants solve an assigned problem or problems together within a specified time frame. Written recommendations are often expected that have been fully endorsed by all exercise participants.
— **In-basket or In-box**—Although the terms themselves are something of an anachronism, this exercise presents each participant with memos, letters, reports, announcements, requests, and irrelevant information in a multitude of formats (voice mail, fax, e-mail, paper, etc.). The participant must then evaluate the various pieces of information and schedule meetings, delegate tasks, write correspondence, etc., all within a relatively short time period.
— **Written Case Analysis**—Each participant reads about an organizational problem and is required to prepare a set of recommendations for superiors to consider towards a resolution. The problem can be tailored either to assess more general abilities or to evaluate specific skills, depending upon the needs of the sponsoring organization.
— **Oral Presentation**—Each participant makes either a short speech or a longer, formal presentation on a topic of interest. Various presentation aides may be incorporated, including flip charts, overhead projectors, or slides. This simulation may alternately be combined with the written case analysis, as well.
— **Interview Simulation or Role-play Exercises**—The participant talks with one or more persons who may assume the roles of a subordinate, colleague, superior, or client. In all cases, the person being interviewed, or "role player," has been trained to act in a standardized manner towards the participant. Typically, the resolution of a problem is discussed, and the participant is observed by one or more assessors.[6]

Additional activities may also include a business game, background interview, cognitive ability or personality test, and oral fact finding. An integrated exercise, termed "A Day in the Life," may also be incorporated into the assessment center.

Fairness, Objectivity, and Legal Issues

In comparison with other selection methodologies, assessment centers are perceived as more fair and objective when factors such as gender, race, and age are included. The *Guidelines and Ethical Considerations for Assessment Center Operations* states that participants are to receive feedback of results,[7] as this serves to validate the credibility of an assessment center. Individuals should have a high level of confidence that results were obtained in an objective, accurate, and fair manner.

Federal courts not only view assessment centers as valid and fair, but have often mandated assessment centers when more conventional selection instruments have exhibited bias or other such problems.[8] By emphasizing actual behavior, as opposed to psychological constructs, assessment centers have gained acceptance and legitimacy in a wide variety of selection applications.

NOTES

1. William C. Byham, "What Is an Assessment Center?—Section 1: How an Assessment Center Works," in *The 34th International Congress on Assessment Center Methods,* http://www.assessmentcenters.org/articles/whatisassess1.asp (accessed October 30, 2007).

2. Liam Healy & Associates, "Assessment and Development Centres," http://www.psychometrics.co.uk/adc.htm (accessed November 2, 2007).

3. Douglas W. Bray, "Centered on Assessment," in *The 34th International Congress on Assessment Center Methods,* http://www.assessmentcenters.org/articles/centeredonassess.asp (accessed October 30, 2007).

4. Bill Waldron and Rich Joines, "Introduction to Assessment Centers (Assessment Centers 101). A Workshop Conducted at the IPMAAC Conference on Public Personnel Assessment, Charleston, SC, June 26, 1994." http://www.ipmaac.org/files/ac101.pdf (accessed November 2, 2007); and Bray, "Centered on Assessment."

5. Waldron and Joines, "Introduction to Assessment Centers (Assessment Centers 101)"; Raymond A. Noe, John R. Hollenbeck, Barry Gerhart, and Patrick M. Wright, *Human Resource Management* (New York: McGraw-Hill, 2003); Byham, "What Is an Assessment Center?"

6. Noe, Hollenbeck, Gerhart, and Wright, *Human Resource Management;* George C. Thornton III and Deborah E. Rupp, *Assessment Centers in Human Resource Management* (Mahwah, NJ: Lawrence Erlbaum Associates, Inc., 2006).

7. International Task Force on Assessment Center Guidelines. "Guidelines and Ethical Considerations for Assessment Center Operations." *28th International Congress on the Assessment Center Methods* (May 2000). http://www.assessmentcenters.org/pdf/00guidelines.pdf (accessed November 2, 2007).

8. Byham, "What Is an Assessment Center?"

Steven J. Kerno Jr.

BACKGROUND INVESTIGATION

Selecting the right new employees is a critical success factor for any contemporary organization. HR must ensure that all selection processes are thorough, consistent, accurate, decisive, and legally defensible. Indeed, one recent study found that the top 10th percentile of organizations calculate the average cost of turnover (including all position classifications, from nonexempt labor roles to exempt senior executive roles) to be in excess of $40,000 per employee.[1] Thus, it becomes clear that including a background investigation in the selection process for new employees is a wise investment of HR's time and resources.

Typical Methods and Components of Background Investigations

Most background investigations are contracted to third-party vendors to ensure consistency and objectivity, as well as to create some level of an "arms-length" relationship between the employer organization and the background investigation process. Also, the highly repetitive, specialized, labor-intensive, and administrative nature of the tasks further builds the case for outsourcing this process.

The following components are typically included in a thorough background investigation:

• Professional references—Typically conducted by internal HR staff, this is often the most valuable source of information regarding the established pattern of behavior of a prospective employee, but also the most difficult from which to solicit objective information. This is because most professional references provided by candidates are predisposed to provide a positive reference. This is the most common component of background investigations to be conducted by internal HR staff, as opposed to being conducted by an outsourcing partner given the organic nature of the dialogue, and related qualitative information that often surfaces during a reference-related discussion.

• Work history—Typically outsourced to a specialized vendor, this involves verifying previous employer organizations, dates of employment, and titles. Gaps of employment are included/identified as well.

• Educational history—Typically outsourced to a specialized vendor, this involves verifying institutions attended, dates of attendance, and diplomas, certifications, and/or degrees conferred.

• Criminal history—Typically outsourced to a specialized vendor, this involves investigating previous criminal activity/convictions via publicly available records.

• Credit history—Typically outsourced to a specialized vendor, this involves investigating credit history via publicly available records.

Negligent Hiring and Background Investigations

Given that the doctrine of negligent hiring has caused the courts to more regularly hold employers responsible for harmful employee acts in the workplace if a reasonable background investigation was not conducted, the importance of conducting thorough background investigations has grown. This requires that HR strike a tenuous balance between the prospective employee's right to privacy and the employer's legal responsibility to, in good faith, provide a safe work environment.[2]

See also Staffing: An Overview; Selection; Negligent Hiring; Privacy Act; Fair Credit Reporting Act

NOTES

1. Carla Joinson, "Capturing Turnover Costs," *HR Magazine,* July 2000, 107–19.
2. "SHRM Board Approves Investment Advice, Safety, and Reference Check Positions," *HR News,* May 2002, 11.

Scott A. Quatro

BEHAVIOR INVENTORY

According to Merriam-Webster, an "inventory" consists of a list of traits, preferences, attitudes, interests, or abilities used to evaluate personal characteristics or skills. Behavior inventories are found in various disciplines, such as psychology, education, and the social sciences. Examples of specific behavior inventories might include creative behavior inventories, reading behavior inventories, abuse behavior inventories, social behavior inventories, and group behavior inventories. In human resources, behavior inventories can "focus on how people behave and can be graded"[1] and therefore, specific inventories can be used in recruiting and developing staff. One specific inventory that can be used in human resources is the work behavior inventory (WBI).

Work Behavior Inventory

Work behavior inventories are assessments that measure work-related behaviors essential for successful employment. A WBI can provide information on individuals' personal style of behaving at work. By assessing work styles of both applicants and employees, WBI assessments can allow employers to objectively match people to jobs.[2] WBI instruments include a number of subscales to assess factors such as personality factors, social skills, leadership styles, emotional intelligence, cooperativeness, work quality, work habits, and self-presentation.[3] WBI assessments are frequently "normed" against other professionals and managers who have completed the inventory. They can also include information on the accuracy of each individual's responses (people tend to overreport or inflate their responses) and whether or not scores should be interpreted cautiously or adjusted to reflect a more accurate representation.[4]

WBI assessments can be used to focus and guide leadership development, to pinpoint specific strengths of individuals, and to identify areas for further training and skill development. For individuals, WBI assessments can help to identify the kind of work environment that will allow them to be most successful and can also help to guide career choices and career transitions.[5]

Organizations interested in obtaining WBI assessments can work with industrial and organizational psychology or human resources consulting firms, associations, and university programs that have expertise in the development and validation of WBI assessments. Sources can be found online, such as the Association of Behavior Analysis International, the Society of Human Resource Management, the Society for Industrial and Organizational Psychology, or governmental agencies such as the Office of Personnel Management. Further, journals such as *Personnel Psychology* will provide peer-reviewed research results regarding the various types and applications of behavior inventories.

See also Assessment Center; Talent Inventory

NOTES

1. Christopher Rowe, "Clarifying the Use of Competence and Competency Models in Recruitment, Assessment and Staff Development," *Industrial and Commercial Training* (1995): 12.

2. Human Resources Consultants, Inc., http://www.hrconsultants.com.

3. Jimmy Choi and Alice Medalia, "Factors Associated with a Positive Response to Cognitive Remediation in a Community Psychiatric Sample," American Psychiatric Association, http://psychservices .psychiatryonlie.org/cgi/content/full/56/5/602 (accessed October 13, 2007); and Human Resources Consultants, Inc.

4. Leadership Coach Academy, http://www.leadershipcoachacademy.com/WBI_Sample_Report.pdf (accessed October 13, 2007).

5. Ibid.

Lynda Kemp

CAMPUS RECRUITING

Many employer organizations utilize college and university campus recruiting as a primary means of attracting large numbers of candidates with generally high levels of promise. Indeed, according to the National Association of Colleges and Employers, direct-from-campus hiring is expected to increase by 16 percent in 2008, creating intense competition for college graduates.[1]

Primary Motivations for Campus Recruiting

Many HR-centric organizations place campus relations and college/university recruiting at the top of their list of strategic priorities. Most of *Fortune* magazine's Most Admired Corporations and 100 Best Companies to Work for in America strongly emphasize direct-from-campus hiring for exempt, professional roles.[2]

The following justifications are typically provided by those employers that invest heavily in college/university relations and recruiting programs:

- Intellectual capacity—college graduates have the highest level of overall intellectual capacity. Despite common perception, less than 30 percent of the adult U.S. population over the age of 25 have earned an undergraduate degree, and less than 12 percent have earned a graduate degree. Thus, the competition among employer organizations for these "best and brightest" potential employees is fierce, indeed.
- Intellectual curiosity—college graduates are more likely to pursue lifelong learning. And as the United States moves to a more knowledge-based economy (67.8 percent of 2006 GDP was generated by services-based industries), the intellectual curiosity of employees will continue to increase in importance.
- "Big five" personality characteristics—college graduates are more likely to exhibit the "big five personality traits," namely sociability, agreeableness, conscientiousness, emotional stability, and openness to new experiences. These traits have been demonstrated to be relevant to most work settings, especially for managerial and leadership roles.[3]
- High potential—college graduates are more likely to perform at high levels and to advance to senior-level roles. Thus, employer organizations that invest heavily in college/university recruiting do so with an eye towards long-term retention, development, and leadership succession from the ranks of their direct-from-campus hires.

Campus Relations and Management Trainee Programs

As discussed above, many of the HR benchmark organizations in U.S. industry make significant investments in campus recruiting. Such investment often involves a dedicated campus relations team charged with cultivating a talent pipeline from selected target campuses. Additionally, many of these organizations hire large numbers of direct-from-campus candidates into formal management/leadership development trainee programs. These programs typically involve one-to-three-month rotations through several staff units (i.e., HR, brand management, finance) and/or line units (i.e. manufacturing, store operations, field sales) for up to 18 months before a new hire is permanently placed into a formal role. While this requires a significant up-front and ongoing investment, a strategic HR perspective demands viewing such an investment in light of the significant, long-term return realized in the form of increased human/social capital.

See also Staffing: An Overview; Recruiting; Selection; Employment Testing

NOTES

1. "Job Outlook 2008," National Association of Colleges and Employers (September 2007).

2. http://money.cnn.com/galleries/2008/fortune/0802/gallery.mostadmired_top20.fortune/index.html and http://money.cnn.com/magazines/fortune/bestcompanies/2008/snapshots/1.html (both accessed April 1, 2008).

3. Lewis R. Goldberg, "An Alternative 'Description of Personality': The Big Five Structure," *Journal of Personality and Social Psychology* 59 (December 1990): 1216–29.

Scott A. Quatro

EMPLOYEE REFERRAL PROGRAMS

Employee referral programs (ERPs) expand the organization's talent pool, which can positively impact the company's financial performance. ERPs should be viewed as strategic business initiatives aligned with the organization's overall strategic business objectives and supported by the organization's senior leaders.

Dr. John Sullivan, professor of human resource management in the College of Business at San Francisco State University, has prepared an extensive list of key elements necessary for a world-class ERP.[1] Sullivan comments that a world-class employee referral program should include the following ensemble of critical success factors:

1. Identify that the overall objective of the ERP is to become a "best-in-class" program that attracts the highest quality candidates for key positions.
2. Define specific start and end dates for the program.
3. Design repeatable processes to facilitate and support speed of execution.
4. Develop a minimum number of rules that are easy to follow and that allow all associates to participate.
5. Process critical skills resumes expeditiously to ensure they are given the appropriate attention and emphasis.
6. Automate the program for ease of access and use, and permit employees to track the progress of their referrals.
7. Create promotional campaigns that address ongoing needs as well as high-priority requirements.
8. Provide rewards, financial and otherwise, that are paid expediently and that are commensurate with the level of importance of the positions to be filled.
9. Design the program to support the on-boarding process to take advantage of ties between the employee and the referred candidate to achieve the retention of the referred candidate as a "long-term" employee.
10. Design and deliver training programs to educate all employees who manage the program, and those employees eligible to participate, about the program's principles of engagement and the roles and responsibilities of all concerned.
11. Design and implement measurement criteria that track costs, cycle time, and percentage of ERP hires. Then, build metrics into the hiring manager's performance goals.

Advantages of ERPs

Sullivan's premise is that the most successful programs reduce staffing costs, decrease cycle time, and improve the quality of hiring decisions. He stresses that there are additional benefits of solid and productive programs. These include increased offer-to-accept ratios, improved morale and employee pride, and influencing a more effective utilization of the staffing department's time and resources.

The Bernard Hodes Group, one of the world's preeminent recruitment, communications, consulting, and talent acquisitions firms, suggests organizations can create an ERP that is regarded as an organizational core competency, and provides a competitive advantage by looking no further than its own employees when seeking top talent. Margie Kasse and Karen Hart, senior consultants for the organization, stated the following regarding ERPs:[2]

"Quality ERP programs, whether print or online, will consistently deliver candidates who:

- Are less expensive to recruit
- Are more qualified, and recommended
- Are less likely to turnover
- Are already familiar with your business
- Have a tendency to be more loyal
- In most cases, do not require relocation
- Are more likely to accept offers
- Require less time to hire
- Increase hiring managers satisfaction"

Another advantage of employee referrals is found when the initiative gives support to building and enhancing organizational culture. Similar values and beliefs within the current employees beget similar values and beliefs in the referred candidates. With a successful hire, organizational behavioral expectations are reinforced by the actions of the current employees. Positive employee engagement results in increased quality and productivity. The bottom line on an ERP is that a successful program has the potential to increase financial performance.

R. Wayne Moody[3] describes *employee enlistment* as a new employee referral strategy. Moody states that this is not the same as asking for referrals from employees. Rather, each associate is challenged to become a recruiter and is provided with "business cards" that can be distributed anywhere the employee goes. The cards do not contain names or positions, as is customary, but have a simple message such as: "We are always looking for great _____. For more information, log on to our Web site." The intent is to make others aware that the organization is truly interested in having people apply.

Disadvantages of ERPs

An organization that relies heavily on employee referrals runs the risk of possibly hiring individuals that may be too similar to the existing talent base. This could result in not bringing "new blood" with "new ideas" into the organization.

Another possible disadvantage can be found in the 2006 EEOC Compliance Manual that provides guidance on the prohibition of discrimination as defined in Title VII of the 1964 Civil Rights Act. It cautions that reliance on word-of-mouth programs such as employee referrals may generate candidates that do not necessarily reflect the diverse nature of the labor market.

Conclusion

Employee referral programs are superb talent acquisition tools but must be created and managed using best practices as derived from sound benchmarking strategies. Care should be given to ensure that senior staff actively supports this initiative. The program should be designed and implemented as an ongoing resource that survives the fluctuations of economic conditions and business needs. Periodic audits and appropriate use of metrics are vital for the program's effectiveness, longevity, and viability.

NOTES

1. John Sullivan, "Assessing Employee Referral Programs: A Checklist,"Electronic Recruiting Exchange (September 12, 2005), http://www.erexchange.com/articles/db/87C8B60EA1A4450BB3BF 26AC12AO4C6.asp (accessed January 11, 2008).

2. Margie Kasse, vice president, Health Care Division, and Karen Hart, senior vice president, Health Care Division, Bernard Hodes Group, interview by authors, January 15, 2008.

3. R. Wayne Moody, *Human Resource Management,* 10th ed. (Upper Saddle River, NJ: Pearson Prentice Hall, 2005).

Fred Miles and Douglas Maxwell

EMPLOYMENT TESTING

In today's job market, employers are looking for any edge they can obtain to build the most productive and cohesive work force. One way that firms are trying to gain a competitive advantage is through the use of employment testing.

Employment testing enables organizations to enhance their selection, placement, training and development, coaching, promotion, career guiding, and program evaluation practices, to name a few. A host of tests and resources are available to companies, including tests of knowledge, skills, and abilities that reveal a candidate's intelligence or mental ability, decision-making style, physical speed or strength, work style, values, ethics, salesmanship, approach to groups/teams, overall personality, etc.

Employment tests, like all assessment tools, are subject to errors in measurement and interpretation. Although tests may help organizations' selection of more qualified candidates, they reveal a limited picture—at a point in time—of an individual's overall ability. For these reasons, employment tests should comprise a component of the selection process and not provide the entire basis of the employment decision.

Legal Issues

Over the last 25 years, employment testing has grown in popularity as a substantial tool used to find the best "fit" among potential candidates. Some sources say that 55 percent to 65 percent of businesses are now using skills testing as a substantial part of the interview process. There are issues that human resources personnel need to consider, however, such as the Uniform Guidelines on Employee Selection and relevant employment laws such as Title VII of the Civil Rights Act of 1964 and the Americans with Disabilities Act of 1990.

Uniform Guidelines on Employee Selection

The EEOC, Civil Service Commission, Department of Labor, and Department of Justice have adopted uniform guidelines on the use of tests and other employee selection procedures that are used as a basis for employment decisions (e.g., hiring, firing, promotion, demotion, etc.). In essence, any selection procedure that adversely impacts the hiring, promotion, or other employment opportunities of an individual or group due to race, gender, or ethnicity is considered discriminatory and in contrast to the Uniform

Guidelines unless the procedure or practice has been validated in accordance with the guidelines. If two or more valid selection procedures are available to a user with a legitimate interest, the procedure that has a lesser adverse impact should be used. Further, employers are required to maintain records revealing the impact of tests and selection procedures on protected groups, along with specifics regarding candidates' gender, race, and ethnic group.

Civil Rights Act of 1964—Title VII

Title VII of the Civil Rights Act of 1964 was enacted to eliminate the use of discrimination in hiring practices. It says, in part, that it is:

> unlawful for an employer to refuse to hire any individual, or otherwise discriminate against any individual with respect to his . . . employment, because of race, color, religion, sex, or national origin.

Hiring once could be done, legally, based on the outcome of any test—until the court case of *Griggs v. Duke Power Co.* In this case, the U.S. Supreme Court found that Duke Power Company was using an "employment test" to weed out minorities. Duke Power had a "skills test" that measured one's aptitude in math, English, reading, and problem solving. Management at Duke Power knew that minorities did not have the same educational opportunities as Caucasians (due to segregation in schools) and would not perform well on their test.

Justice Burger's opinion said:

> *On the record before us, neither the high school completion requirement nor the general intelligence test is shown to bear a demonstrable relationship to successful performance of the jobs for which it was used. Both were adopted, as the Court of Appeals noted, without meaningful study of their relationship to job performance ability.*

Based on the Supreme Court's decision, legislation was drafted that detailed permissible uses of employment testing. Any test that is administered in the selection process must have a justifiable link to job function and skills. The test and its results must stand up in court on this point.

Americans with Disabilities Act of 1990

Another piece of legislation that affects employment testing is the Americans with Disabilities Act of 1990 (ADA). The act prohibits discriminating against qualified applicants based on a variety of disabilities. The act, among other things, requires the need for validity in employment testing. Tests must have one or more of the following:
• Content validity—the test is a representative sample of performance in some defined area of job-related skills, knowledge, or abilities.
• Construct validity—the test must illustrate relevant skills of the job.
• Criterion-related validity—the criteria on the test must be statistically linked to job success.

Controversy with Employment Testing

One of the more controversial areas in job testing concerns law enforcement. Let us look at two examples.

If one applies to be a dispatcher at a local Colorado police department, one must pass several tests. Most of those tests are easily defended as being pertinent to the job (e.g., polygraph, oral board interview, etc.). All applicants of the department's dispatch center must also take a computer test that measures the ability to multitask. The test taker will have to enter information into a computer while answering phone calls. This test is a good measure of one's ability to prioritize and complete important procedures.

This computer test easily fits into both the content validity and construct validity models because the tasks to be completed are directly job related. One needs to be able to multitask and communicate; these are skills that are important in the position.

Another example of an employment test is the "job functions test" that police officers must perform annually in the department. During this test, an officer must perform the following functions:

- Exit a patrol car
- Scale a chain-link fence
- Crawl under a table
- Climb through a window
- Run up a flight of stairs
- Identify a "suspect" by the description given to the officer before leaving the car
- Drag a 120-pound dummy 10 feet across a line in 64 seconds or less.

This test fits the "construct validity" and "criterion-related validity" models. Previously, the department held officers to a fitness standard called the Cooper Fitness Test. Although this test measured the overall fitness of an officer (a 1.5-mile timed run and pushups and sit-ups in a minute) at no point would an officer run a mile and a half during his or her job function; thus the test failed to pass any of the three validity tests and was removed as a requirement.

CONCLUSION

There are many things that a human resources professional must consider when conducting employment testing. One must weigh the legal ramifications with the proven validity of a test in predicting success in a job.

Matt Springer

INTERVIEWING

Job Interviews

While many types of interviews exist, perhaps the most common is the interview for a job. Interviews are all about the presentation of a candidate. The first impression is the most important, and people often make bad impressions due to poor interviewing skills and improper preparation. Interviews are often stressful for candidates, and those who do not interview as well as others may lose out on opportunities at which they would otherwise excel. Likewise, candidates who interview well have a better chance of obtaining the job, though they may not always be the most qualified. Interview etiquette is essential for those who are job hunting. The range of questions an employer can ask is broad, but not endless. Legalities prevent employers from asking personal questions such as issues regarding disabilities, religion, and marital status, unless these questions are demonstratively job-related. Asking candidates open-ended questions such as "Why do you want to work here?" often prove to be more successful than yes-or-no questions, as the employer will get a better sense of the candidate.[1]

Behavioral and Situational Job Interviews

A contemporary trend in interviewing is employing behavioral and situational interviewing. Questions in these types of interviews allow the candidate to provide more information and allow the potential employer to gain a better sense of how the employee may perform. Rather than asking general questions about the candidate's background, employers in behavioral and situational interviews probe as to how the candidate has managed and/or would manage particular situations. The ultimate goal of employing such an interviewing methodology is to improve the validity (accuracy) of the interview as a selection tool. The more accurate the interview data, the better the hiring decision,[2] and it is believed that "behavioral and situational interviewing is 55 percent predictive of future on-the-job behavior, while traditional interviewing is only 10 percent predictive."[3] Such statistics become even more compelling when considering that job interviews are the sole and/or most highly emphasized selection tool utilized by most employers.

Payless ShoeSource has long utilized behavioral and situational interviews as a key means of ensuring sound hiring decisions. Delineated below is an illustrative example of both a behavioral and a situational question asked of candidates for store manager positions with the firm:

- Behavioral interview question example—"Please think of a specific example from your past professional experience where you demonstrated the ability to develop a team. Once you have thought of this example, I would like for you to tell me about in great detail." This statement sets the context for a lengthy dialogue (often up to 20 minutes in length) about the core job-related competency (in this case, team building) for which the candidate is being screened.
- Situational interview question example—"Assume that you have just witnessed an employee stealing money from the cash register. I would like for you to tell me in great detail how you would handle this situation." This statement sets the context for a lengthy dialogue (often up to 20 minutes in length) about the core job-related competencies (in this case, conflict resolution and assertiveness) for which the candidate is being screened.

Once the context is set via these behavioral and situational questions/scenarios, the interviewer then probes deeply for detail, using open-ended follow-up questions and statements such as:

- "Tell me more about that."
- "How did that make you feel?"
- "What was the end result?"
- "Why did you do that?"
- "What would you do next?"

In the end, behavioral and situational interviewing methods result in much richer job-related dialogue, leading to more insight into a candidate's past experience via behavioral questions (i.e., "tell me what you did"), and future potential via situational questions (i.e., "tell me what you would do").

Interviewing for Data Collection

Interviews are the most common tool for gathering and analyzing data in organizational development. Often organizations "need a snapshot of what is presently being done, rather than simply jumping in and changing the process pell-mell."[4] Interview data gives management clear descriptions of employee needs and wants. Data collection interviews can be done in groups or individually. Interviews are subjective and respondents may be swayed by the way a question is worded. Interviews can be time consuming but have proven to be effective for gaining organizational development-related insight from employees.[5]

Exit Interviews

Exit interviews are another important tool in data collection, and are conducted when an employee leaves an organization. These interviews are designed to provide feedback on why the employee is leaving and what improvements can be made. Exit interviews are typically done in a one-on-one, face-to-face setting. This often deters employees from being as honest as they would like to be. Additionally, employees often feel that the interview will be of no value since he or she is leaving anyway. Nonetheless, exit interviews are important as they can potentially "improve a company's inner workings, and maybe even help colleagues."[6]

See also: Staffing: An Overview; Background Investigation; Selection

NOTES

1. Charles Fleischer, *HR For Small Business* (Naperville, IL: Sourcebooks, Inc., 2005).
2. Wendel Williams, "Behavioral Interviewing Can Be Accurate, but Only When Done Right," *Experience,* August 17, 2006, http://www.ere.net/articles (accessed March 1, 2008).
3. Katharine Hansen, "Behavioral Interviewing Strategies For Job Seekers," *Quintessential Careers,* January 1, 2008, http://www.quintcareers.com/behavioral_interviewing.html (accessed March 1, 2008).
4. Jack Orsburn and Linda Moran, *The New Self-Directed Work Teams,* 2nd ed. (New York: McGraw-Hill, 2000).
5. Thomas Cummings and Christopher Worley, *Organization Development and Change,* 8th ed. (Mason, OH: South-Western, 2005).
6. Jared Sandberg, "Ah, the Exit Interview: Free at Last, Is It Smart to Really Be Candid?" *Wall Street Journal Online,* May 26, 2005, http://208.144.115.170/columnists/cubicleculture/20050526-cubicle.html (accessed March 1, 2008).

Meghan Clarisse Cave

JOB DESCRIPTION

A job description states what is involved in performing a particular job. It identifies the duties, responsibilities, and working conditions of a particular job. This information is of great value to the jobholder and the employer. It establishes expectations for job performance and minimizes misunderstandings that can occur between these two parties. Furthermore, job descriptions provide essential information for human resource management functions such as recruitment and selection, performance appraisal, legal compliance, and career planning.

Job Description: Contents

Job descriptions can vary considerably regarding how much detail they contain. There is no customary written format for job descriptions, although they usually will have the same format within the same company. Most job descriptions, however, will provide certain types of information. Job descriptions typically contain sections that include the following types of information: job identification, job summary, responsibilities and duties, working conditions, relationships, standards of performance, and job specifications.[1]

Job Identification and Job Summary

In the *job identification* section of a job description, the following information may be given: the job title, the job code or identification number, the FLSA status of the job (exempt/nonexempt), the department or division where the job is performed, the location of the job, the immediate supervisor's title, the grade or level of the job, its EEOC classification, the date the job description was last revised, the effective date of the job description, and who approved the job description as well as the date of approval. A job description should also contain a *job summary*. The job summary provides an overall description of the job and include its major functions, activities, and tasks. A job summary should provide a brief, yet clear, picture of what is involved in performing the job.

Responsibilities, Duties, and Working Conditions

A job description should have a section listing the *responsibilities and duties* of the jobholder. This section will list the job's major duties and responsibilities, with a brief description for each. Often these will be listed in order of importance, along with the weight or value of each duty. The value of each duty is often expressed as a percentage of time devoted to it. It is also important for a job description to mention the *working conditions* of the job, especially when these conditions may be hazardous (e.g., noise levels, temperature levels, risk of electric shock). Additionally, some jobs may require working with physically demanding tools, machines, and other equipment.

Relationships, Standards of Performance, and Job Specifications

Sometimes a job description will include information about the *relationships* associated with a job. This information will describe to whom the jobholder reports, whom he or she supervises (if applicable), and with whom the jobholder works inside and outside of the organization. These details should allow one to see how the job relates to other jobs within the organization.

Some job descriptions also may contain a section about *standards of work performance.* This information will state the level or degree of performance expected with the job's major duties and responsibilities. This might pertain to performing tasks within certain time periods, achieving specific targets, producing a limited number of errors, etc. Lastly, the *job specifications* section of a job description will state the knowledge, skills, abilities, and other characteristics required to perform the job. Specific qualifications and experience might also be included in this section. Although the job specification may be included as part of the job description, it may also be an entirely separate document.

Although few job descriptions will contain all of the details given above, most will contain at least three parts: the job title, a job identification section, and a job duties section.[2]

Additionally, because the format and length of job descriptions can vary so greatly, they may not present information in the same order or with as much detail as discussed above. To help organize and classify jobs, the U.S. Department of Labor published the *Dictionary of Occupational Titles* (DOT). This book held detailed descriptions of about 20,000 jobs in a standardized format. The DOT helped establish some consistency in job titles and descriptions across the United States. The Department of Labor replaced the DOT with the Occupational Information Network database, called O*NET (http://online .onetcenter.org/). This online database includes all of the information from the DOT as well as job descriptions for thousands of more jobs.

Job Description: Influence on HRM Functions

Job descriptions provide essential information for human resource management (HRM) functions such as recruitment and selection, performance appraisal, and career planning, and they also assist in Americans with Disabilities Act (ADA) compliance.[3]

Recruitment and Selection, and Performance Appraisal

Job descriptions play a crucial role in helping HR managers achieve their *recruitment and selection* goals. In terms of recruitment, job descriptions help shape the job advertisement or posting that is used to attract potential job applicants. If the job advertisement is poorly designed and does not accurately reflect the job description, HR managers will end up with applicants who are unqualified for the job. Badly written job descriptions may also cause problems in the selection process because it may not be clear what type of selection tools (e.g., selection tests) should be used. An organization's *performance appraisal system* is another major area of HRM directly related to job description. You cannot accurately appraise the performance of a jobholder without having a specific description of what he or she is expected to do. Job descriptions identify the key duties and responsibilities that management will analyze when evaluating and rewarding employee job performance.

Career Planning and ADA Compliance

Job descriptions can assist individuals with their *career planning*. For example, by reading descriptions of jobs they could apply for in the future, individuals can determine what knowledge, skills, and abilities they need to develop to achieve their career goals. Accurate job descriptions will help them seek the training and mentoring necessary to perform these jobs in the future. Through this process, individuals can pursue a series of jobs that will shape their desired career paths. Job descriptions can be very helpful in achieving *ADA compliance*.[4] According to the ADA, job descriptions must take into account the needs of disabled workers. Job descriptions must specify the physical demands and requirements of the work entailed. Additionally, the ADA requires that job descriptions state the environmental conditions of the work to be performed (e.g., exposure to dangerous conditions). If they are written well, job descriptions can offer legal protection and support when accommodations are provided to disabled jobholders.

See also Job Design; Job Analysis

NOTES

1. Gary Dessler, *Human Resource Management* (Upper Saddle River, NJ: Pearson Prentice Hall, 2005).

   2. George Bohlander and Scott Snell, *Managing Human Resources,* 14th ed. (Mason, OH: Thomas South-Western, 2007).
   3. Marie Gan and Brian H. Kleiner, "How to Write Job Descriptions Effectively," *Management Research News* 8, no. 28 (2005): 48–54.
   4. Gan and Kleiner.

Michael J. Gundlach and Suzanne Zivnuska

JOB POSTING

A job posting refers to communicating the profiles of either vacant or available positions existing within an organization to allow those seeking jobs to apply.[1] Job postings are alternately referred to as listings, announcements, and notices. Job postings can be made available to both those internal and external to the organization, depending upon the firm's overall recruitment strategy, the availability of qualified candidates, and the costs associated with such efforts. Since internal and external job postings possess certain characteristics that should be considered before pursuing either, each shall be examined separately.

Internal Job Postings

Internal job postings, by definition, exclude anyone who currently is not employed by the organization. They may be communicated by internal job bulletin boards available to all employees, on a restricted basis for certain middle and upper management positions, or online via a company's intranet. The applicants for internal job postings are likely to have greater knowledge regarding the firm and its activities and the nature of position duties and responsibilities (reducing the likelihood of inflated job expectations) than are external potential candidates. These factors contribute to the likelihood of finding a candidate more quickly and less expensively through the utilization of internal job postings. Internal job postings may include more targeted and specific information such as pay grade, human resource or hiring manager contact information, and posting and unposting date, in addition to a description of responsibilities, skills, education, and experience necessary. Internal job postings also may offer a cash bonus to anyone who refers a candidate for a position that requires advanced or specific skills that are difficult to find, if the person referred is successfully hired. Even if a position is also communicated through external sources, any applicants from within the organization often are given first consideration.[2]

External Job Postings

External job postings may be utilized by an organization for entry-level positions and occasionally for highly specialized or upper-level management positions for which there are insufficient qualified internal candidates.[3] External job postings also allow an opportunity to hire people who have more current or relevant knowledge, skills, experiences, and ideas as they relate to the organization's markets or how it conducts business. There are many ways an organization can communicate job postings externally, and the choice will impact such factors as the number of applicants, their qualifications or suitability for the position in question, and the likelihood that applicants will accept a position, if one is offered.[4]

Job postings have traditionally been communicated through advertisements in newspapers and journals or periodicals. With the increased prevalence of the Internet, organizations now commonly post their openings to the company Web site, to job banks and job boards, and with trade associations and societies.[5] Additionally, for positions requiring a highly specialized or unique skill set or for mid- to top-level management, organizations may utilize the services of an executive search firm or "headhunter." A company may post a certain critical position with a headhunter, who often has a large (and private) database of individuals to access, many of whom may not even be searching actively for a new position.[6]

External job postings will often need to communicate more information than internal ones, since applicants may not be as familiar with the organization. This may include the job title, the department or division, its geographic location, the starting salary or wage, appropriate contact information for interested applicants, and descriptive information such as the products or services the organization derives its revenues from, appropriate accreditations or memberships (e.g. ISO9000, QS9000, Fortune 500, S&P 500), and perhaps a statement to encourage minorities, handicapped individuals, or veterans to apply.

Gaining a Competitive Advantage

Since job postings, particularly those where an organization is soliciting external candidates, often have an impact on the knowledge, skills, and other characteristics such as minority status or gender of those who apply, companies should be mindful of tailoring their communications appropriately. Companies that are aware of a possible image problem or perception among certain segments of the population need to be particularly careful or sensitive to the concerns of members of these groups, and the possibility that additional resources may be required to encourage their application. Conversely, companies are often able to more effectively attract talent when jobs are posted in novel or unusual ways. For example, when Ben & Jerry's, a manufacturer and distributor of premium ice cream and similar products, needed to conduct a search for a new CEO in the early 1990s, they invited customers to participate in a contest titled "Yo! I Want to be CEO!" Applicants were invited to submit a 100-word essay and the lid of their favorite Ben & Jerry's flavor.[7] The favorable press coverage generated, coupled with the socially conscious nature of the company, have allowed Ben & Jerry's to gain a competitive advantage in the marketplace for its corporate parent, Unilever.[8]

See also Employment Agencies, Search Firms, and Headhunters; Selection

NOTES

1. "Job Listing," HR World, http://www.hrworld.com/dictionary/job-listing/ (accessed December 10, 2007).

2. Raymond A. Noe, John R. Hollenbeck, Barry Gerhart, and Patrick M. Wright, *Human Resource Management* (New York: McGraw-Hill, 2003); James A. Breaugh, *Recruitment: Science and Practice* (Boston: PWS-Kent, 1992).

3. Noe, Hollenbeck, Gerhart, and Wright, *Human Resource Management.*

4. Breaugh, *Recruitment: Science and Practice.*

5. "Job Searching," About.com, http://jobsearch.about.com/od/joblistings/Job_Listings.htm (accessed December 11, 2007).

6. Steve Brooks, "Getting a Hand Hiring Top Talent," *Restaurant Business,* October 2007, 22–26; Claire Gagne, "Search & Employ," *Canadian Business,* January 16, 2006, 62–63.

7. Ross Sneyd, "Yo! Ben & Jerry's Scoops Up a New CEO after Contest," *Chicago Sun-Times,* February 2, 1995.

8. "Our Brands," Unilever Web site, http://www.unilever.com/ourbrands/ (accessed December 13, 2007).

Steven J. Kerno Jr.

NEGLIGENT HIRING

Employers run a risk of liability for negligent hiring. The duty stems from the common law duty to provide a safe workplace. Negligent hiring is a potential cause of action based in tort law.[1] Employers face liability if they expose a customer, employee, client, or other to injury caused by an employee. Employers must exercise reasonable care to investigate a potential employee's fitness for the job he or she will perform. The elements of a cause of action for the tort of negligent hiring are: selection of an employee who is not capable to perform the work and the employee's actions, while working, caused the foreseeable harm.

Cause for Concern

Human resource practitioners and those involved in the hiring process must have a thorough understanding of the job description. Everyone involved in the hiring process must understand the degree of foreseeable danger involved in the work that the potential employee will perform. For example, if the employee will have foreseeable contact with customers, then you should examine the job candidate's background for any criminal convictions related to assault and similar offenses.

Preventing Liability

An employer has a duty to provide a safe workplace. The employer's obligation extends to customers, clients, and any other visitors to the work site. Therefore, employers should complete background checks on all employees. At a minimum, the background check should include having the candidate complete an application, checking references, and perhaps checking for criminal convictions. In situations in which the employee will serve in a position exercising discretionary care of people or money there should be calls to references (both listed in the candidate's resume and not listed) and a check of both criminal and credit histories. Employers are wise to make and document reference checks consistently on all potential employees.

Protecting Privacy

Contrasted with the duty to provide a safe workplace is the duty of the employer to protect the privacy of employees. Employers may be liable for defamation when they provide inaccurate information about current or former employees. Thus, an employer must balance the need to protect the privacy of all employees with the need of the potential employer of that employee to avoid potential harm. Many employers are adopting policies of answering minimally intrusive questions: the fact of the employee's employment, title, and the dates of employment. In cases where there is a documentation of dangerous behavior, release of information must be evaluated on a case-by-case basis.

See also: Fair Credit Reporting Act; Recruiting; References

NOTE

1. Rest. 2d Torts, Sec. 314 *et. seq.*

Laura Dendinger

POLYGRAPH TEST

A polygraph is a member of the larger domain of machines commonly known as "lie detectors." In familiar usage, polygraph refers to a machine that simultaneously records the heart rate, breathing rate, and electrical resistance at the fingertip (caused by changes in sweat production) of a person being interrogated; some polygraphs also record muscular activity. These physiological responses are graphically recorded and juxtaposed in real time with the questions being asked.

Under stressful circumstances, physiological changes, such as those measured by a polygraph, differ from normal. Theoretically, a skilled operator/interrogator can reliably elicit and detect these physiological changes in response to specific questions such that he can identify which questions and/or answers cause stress to the person being questioned. Then, if the stressful questions and answers correlate with a particular theme of interrogation the assumption is that the interrogee's answers are less than truthful.

The U.S. Congress enacted the Employee Polygraph Protection Act of 1988[1] (EPPA). The act states:

> The term lie detector includes a polygraph, deceptograph, voice stress analyzer, psychological stress evaluator, or any similar device (whether mechanical or electrical) that is used, or the results of which are used, for the purpose of rendering a diagnostic opinion regarding the honesty or dishonesty of an individual.

The EPPA significantly restricts the use of polygraphs in the work place for testing of employees or prospective employees and provides for severe penalties (up to a $10,000 fine and liabilities from private civil action) for any use outside of its very specific exemptions. Any consideration of polygraph utilization should be carefully investigated for legality and appropriateness of situation.

Employee Rights, Restrictions, and Exemptions under the EPPA

Exemptions to the EPPA, noted in the following section, do not apply unless a host of requirements are met during each phase of the test.

All Phases

The examiner may not conduct a polygraph test if a physician provides sufficient written evidence "that the examinee is suffering from a medical or psychological condition or undergoing treatment that might cause abnormal responses during the actual testing phase." An examinee may not be asked any question not provided in writing prior to the test, any degrading or needlessly intrusive questions, or any questions concerning religious beliefs or affiliations, racial beliefs or opinions, political beliefs or affiliations, sexual behavior or orientation, or union beliefs, opinions, or affiliations.

Pre-test Phase

Reasonably before the test the prospective examinee must be notified in writing:
• Of the date, time, and place of the examination
• Of the right to have representation present
• Of the nature and characteristics of the machine to be utilized and the tests to be conducted
• Whether the examination area is equipped in any manner that would allow for monitoring or observing (e.g., with a camera or two-way mirror)
• That the session may, with mutual knowledge, be recorded by either party
• That any admission of criminal activity may be reported to appropriate authorities
• That the examinee may review all questions to be asked
• That the examinee may terminate the test at any time

The examiner must also sign a written notice informing the examinee:
• That the examinee cannot be required to take the test as a condition of employment
• That any statement made during the test may constitute additional supporting evidence for the purposes of an adverse employment action
• The legal rights and remedies available to the examinee if the polygraph is not conducted in accordance with this act
• The legal rights and remedies of the employer under this act

Post-test Phase

Before any adverse employment action, the employer shall further interview the examinee on the basis of the results of the test, and provide the examinee with a written copy of any opinion or conclusion rendered as a result of the test, and a copy of the questions asked during the test along with the corresponding charted responses.

Exceptions to the EPPA

With respect to lie detector statutes, any state or local law or any collective bargaining agreement that is more restrictive than the EPPA takes precedence.

The EPPA does not apply to "federal, state and local governments and any political subdivision of state or local government." Significantly, the *federal government* may perform polygraph testing on certain employees of contractors to several federal agencies, but the exemption does not necessarily allow the *contractor* to perform the tests. Some of the specific employees affected by these exemptions are experts or consultants with access to top secret information or with intelligence or counter-intelligence functions with the Department of Defense, National Security Agency, Defense Intelligence Agency, Central Intelligence Agency, or Federal Bureau of Investigation.

Private-sector exemptions include security services such as armored car personnel, alarm system installers, security personnel charged with protecting currency, precious commodities, or negotiable instruments, and "facilities, materials or operations having a significant impact on the health and safety" of the public, such as: electrical and nuclear power facilities, public water supplies, shipping and storing of radioactive or toxic material, and public transportation.

Also exempted are manufacturers, distributors, and dispensers of Schedule I, II, III, or IV controlled substances if the prospective employee will have direct access to the controlled substance or if a current employee is tested in connection with an ongoing investigation as described below.

Section 7.d. of the EPPA, Limited Exemption for Ongoing Investigations, allows an employer to request that an employee submit to a polygraph test if the employer provides a written statement to the employee that describes the specific incident that is being investigated, including that the ongoing investigation involves economic loss or injury to the employer's business, that the employee had access to the property that is the subject of the investigation, and a reasonable explanation for implicating the employee.

Examiner Requirements

Polygraph examiners must be licensed and bonded. The EPPA places restrictions on examiners regarding the maximum number of exams performed per day (five), the minimum duration of exams (90 minutes), and the content of examination reports.

Disclosure of Information

Unless otherwise specified in writing by the examinee, the examiner may not release information obtained during an exam except to the employer who requested the exam, legal authorities or government agencies in accordance with due process, or, of course, the examinee. Employers are similarly restricted from disclosing information from a polygraph exam.

Employers are required to display an EPPA poster, distributed by the Department of Labor, where employees and prospective employees can readily see it. The notice can be downloaded from http://dol.gov/esa/regs/compliance/poster/pdf/eppabw.pdf.

NOTE

1. Public Law 100-347, 100th Cong. (June 27, 1988). *Employee Polygraph Protection Act of 1988,* 29 USC 2001.

Martin Kollasch

RECRUITING

Any business or organization that employs workers requires having some form of recruitment process. This process involves understanding the staffing needs of the organization, and then attracting the most qualified candidate for the position. Hence, a primary purpose of the human resources department is to ensure the organization has a collection of reasonably qualified applicants available for review when a vacancy may occur.[1]

Internal vs. External Recruiting

An organization really has two main sources of recruiting personnel for any vacancy or newly created position, either internal or external. It is often desirable to fill higher positions by promoting from within, or to utilize existing employed and experienced talent to fill vacancies. However, it is also advantageous to recruit externally when it becomes necessary to employ candidates with technological expertise that the organization may be lacking. Additionally, while entry-level positions are logically filled from external sources, bringing in outsiders can often improve the organization by gaining new ideas or new ways of conducting business.[2]

There are distinct advantages to internal recruiting that are worth considering. First, it is more economical to recruit from within, and second, there is usually a better knowledge of internal applicant skills and abilities over an unknown external applicant. A third advantage is that having an internal policy of promoting from within will also enhance organizational commitment and motivation towards job satisfaction. A downside to internal recruiting is that if the strategy involves change, some entrenched managers and employees may not be as willing to embrace change, and thus the old way of doing things may be the preferred style.[3] Outside of the benefit of new ideas and thinking being brought into the organization, another advantage to external recruiting is the potential of acquiring talent that will help bring the organization into competitive advantage. Some of the disadvantages of external recruiting is that it is generally much more time consuming and costly to recruit outside talent. It takes time and resources to acquaint the new employee with organizational tasks and required skills. Additionally, introduction of new personnel may have an impact on cohesion and morale within the ranks, and finally, typically there is less information available on the external candidate. Therefore, more assessment is needed during the initial days of employment.

External Recruitment Sources

There are a myriad of ways to recruit externally. The most common and least expensive method is the unsolicited application in which job seekers apply to the organization by walking in the door and completing an application, or by submitting a resume. Often considered by many an internal method, employee referrals are sometimes implemented where the organization asks for qualified friends or family members. This has the advantage of generally increasing job tenure and reducing employee turnover.

Typically, external recruitment takes place when the organization actively seeks outside the boundaries of the organization. Throughout the years, a common method has been to advertise in local newspapers, magazines, and trade journals. This approach affords the opportunity to target specific job markets or geographical areas. Additional coverage can be supplied via local radio stations and television or cable networks to draw from a larger geographical area. Since this method of recruiting is fairly expensive, the job criteria needs to be narrowly defined in an attempt to attract only the most qualified candidates.

A more popular method in recent years is to contract with employment agencies or search firms that actively seek and screen potential candidates who meet the specific requirements of the organization. There are two basic types of employment agencies; one is funded by the public in the form of a state employment agency, and the other is a private firm that specializes in providing candidates. Either will screen potential candidates during the selection process so as to refer only the most qualified candidates to the parent organization. Within the realm of private employment agencies, two types are present. One provides the service for the organization requiring the candidate to pay for the employment services; and the other provides the service free to the candidate while billing the organization if the candidate is hired.

Another popular method used by many organizations is the college campus visit, or the job fairs that universities hold during the year by inviting organizations searching for entry-level employees. One other very successful technique for organizations to attract college candidates is via the internship program, in which the organization will employ a college student to learn that particular business and establish a long-term relationship.

Thanks to recent technology, one of the more recent methods for recruiting now is the World Wide Web. Many people are now using electronic job boards such as Monster.com, Careerbuilder.com, and the like to post their resumes for prospective employers to view. Thus, employers are able to manually scan or use software to search, review, and screen potential candidates.[4] At the same time, many employers are e-recruiting through their own Web sites to receive resumes and online applications for screening through an automated database that focuses on key words. Other employers are accepting only resumes and electronic applications at their own Web sites. For these employers now using e-recruiting techniques, a large database sorts and screens potential employees, while at the same time applicant tracking facilitates the ability to categorize candidates by various criteria. One advantage to applicant tracking software is the ability to hone in on certain characteristics so that an organization may target more diverse candidates to build diversity within the organization.

Regardless of the recruitment method used, each has the final goal of selecting the right candidate for a position the organization needs filled.

NOTES

1. H. John Bernardin, *Human Resource Management: An Experiential Approach,* 4th ed. (Boston: McGraw-Hill, Irwin, 2007).

2. James G. Meade, *The Human Resources Software Handbook: Evaluating Technology Solutions for Your Organization* (San Francisco: Jossey-Bass/Pfeiffer, 2003).

3. Raymond A. Noe, John R. Hollenbeck, Barry Gerhart, and Patrick M. Wright. *Human Resource Management: Gaining a Competitive Advantage,* 4th ed. (Boston: McGraw-Hill Irwin, 2003).

4. Ibid.

Frank E. Armstrong

REFERENCES

References are commonly used by organizations as one of the selection methods for screening prospective employees. References are typically supplied by the person being interviewed, and can include current and former bosses, coworkers, customers, vendors, colleagues, and college professors.[1] References can also include reference letters, which are prepared recommendations from people who may be very difficult to contact for a variety of reasons (relocation, frequent travel or job changes, etc.). It is important to develop an action plan to maximize the value of contacting and speaking directly with the references a prospective employee may provide.

Considerations When Contacting References

References provided by a potential employee should be able to convey a sense for how well the person will "fit" into the new organization, be able to identify and describe relevant job skills and abilities, and supply documented records and other such objective information. Additionally, checking references can save a company time, money, and public embarrassment, should the position be public in nature and scope, and representative of the organization or institution in general. A recent example of insufficient reference checking includes the hiring, and subsequent forced resignation five days later, of George O'Leary as the head football coach at the University of Notre Dame. O'Leary was found to have falsified both his academic credentials from the State University of New York at Stony Brook, as well as his performance as a scholar-athlete at the University of New Hampshire, on an application for employment.[2] The following guidelines should facilitate this process:

— *Obtain permission before contacting*—An applicant must grant permission before a firm contacts either present or former employers.[3] This can be addressed by including a reference check release or permission form with any application materials. Additionally, previous employers may require applicant approval before the release of any information.
— *Contact the reference prior to asking questions*—Doing so allows the reference individual an opportunity to schedule a future time and location, if necessary, to ensure the confidentiality of responses.[4] It also should facilitate a conversation in which miscellaneous intrusions or time constraints are less of an issue. Also, some employers have policies that prohibit the dissemination of any reference information of a subjective nature and will provide only job titles held, dates of employment, salary history, and other such information that has been documented.[5] Should this occur, it may be necessary to contact the applicant for an alternate, or, if multiple reference names have been provided, to use another.
— *Prepare questions beforehand*—Depending on the nature of the position, questions should be tailored to ensure that relevant job-related information is obtained and that no questions are asked that might elicit personal facts or characteristics. A good strategy is to compile a reference check questions sheet and to begin by asking more open-ended questions, to develop and encourage dialogue with the reference individual. Possible subject areas for questions are as follows:
  ○ What duties did the person perform while employed?
  ○ How would you describe the person's work performance or progress?
  ○ How did the person compare with coworkers regarding work performance?
  ○ If given the opportunity, would you reemploy the person? If no, why not?
  ○ What strengths did the person exhibit as an employee? What limitations or weaknesses?[6]
— *Stick to the script*—If any information is offered by the reference that does not pertain to the applicant's knowledge, skills, job performance, or other such qualifications, it should be ignored. Further, be aware of any subjective statements that could be considered discriminatory.[7]
— *Check more than one reference*—Although this may slow down the hiring process, it is well worth the extra effort. Additionally, some organizations have adopted the practice of requesting many references—sometimes as many as 12—to overcome the fact that the first few typically have the most positive information to report about the candidate.[8]

Consequences for Failing to Check References

Failing to properly check the references provided by a prospective employee, other than increasing the possibility of an embarrassing situation for higher-profile positions, can also leave an employer vulnerable to a more serious, time-consuming, and costly situation—a negligent hiring claim. U.S. courts have ruled that employers have a responsibility to check criminal records for employees where contact with the public regularly occurs. Also, damages against firms are being awarded when negligence in performing a reasonable search into the potential employee's background is proven.[9]

See also: Background Investigation; Negligent Hiring; Selection

NOTES

1. "Employment References—How to Get and Provide References for Employment," About.com: Job Searching, http://jobsearch.about.com/od/referencesrecommendations/a/referencetips.htm (accessed December 20, 2007).

2. "Short Tenure—O'Leary Out at Notre Dame after One Week," CNNSI.com, College Football, http://sportsillustrated.cnn.com/football/college/news/2001/12/14/oleary_notredame/ (accessed January 2, 2008).

3. "Guide to Checking Job References," Work.com,http://www.work.com/checking-job-references-107 (accessed December 18, 2007).

4. "Do You Know Who You Are Hiring? Don't Forget the Reference Checks!" *Leading Edition: E-Newsletter for Purdue University Supervisors,*http://www.purdue.edu/hr/LeadingEdition/LEdi_1003_ref_check.htm (accessed January 2, 2008).

5. "Employment References—How to Get and Provide References for Employment."

6. Purdue University, "Staff Recruitment and Selection—Procedures Manual," http://www.purdue .edu/humanrel/contribute_pdf_docs/staffhire2005.pdf (accessed January 2, 2008).

7. "Do You Know Who You Are Hiring? Don't Forget the Reference Checks!"

8. Raymond A. Noe, John R. Hollenbeck, Barry Gerhart, and Patrick M. Wright, *Human Resource Management* (New York: McGraw-Hill, 2003).

9. "Do You Know Who You Are Hiring? Don't Forget the Reference Checks!"

Steven J. Kerno Jr.

RESUME

Potential employees will document their past job experiences and skills with a document called a resume. The typical resume will list the job candidate's educational background, work history, relevant skills, career objective, and references. Candidates typically list their name, address, and contact information in the heading of the resume. The listing of the candidate's name at the top of the document assists the computer in alphabetizing candidates when resumes are scanned into the computer for analysis and storage.

Many times, candidates introduce themselves by listing an overall career objective. This way, the potential employer is able to identify the applicant's focus area. What the candidate lists after the objective depends on his/her station in life. Candidates that have recently completed their education will typically list their educational achievements first. Candidates who have some related work experience will open their resume by listing their employment starting with the most recent.

Resumes, in conjunction with applications, are used as initial screening devices. The resume is reviewed to determine the degree to which an applicant meets the minimum requirements of the job. HR professionals will look at job titles and experience from previous jobs in order to determine job functions performed. Action verbs such as "managed," "coordinated," or "analyzed" provide insight into the skills, abilities, and strengths of the applicant.

Beyond the minimum qualifications, the resume provides insight into major accomplishments, which should be written as quantitative outcomes (e.g., 15 percent productivity increase). This provides insight into how an applicant contributed to the success of previous employers. In addition, a resume can represent an applicant's fit based on its look and feel. If the job to be filled requires attention to detail, creativity, or sales, then the resume should match the characteristics desired. In other words, the resume should be detailed, creative, or oriented toward selling.

Types of Resumes

Generally, candidates will limit resumes to one to two pages. There are two basic ways to format a resume: the (preferred) chronological approach and the functional approach. Regardless of the format, HR should be able to review the resume and pick out applicable information quickly. On average, less than 40 seconds is dedicated to scanning a resume. Therefore, a resume should have adequate white space in margins and between sections; appropriate use of bullets, bold and italicized text, and indents.

Chronological Approach

Candidates using a chronological style of resume will follow a chronology to list their work experiences, starting with the most recent. Human resource practitioners prefer this style of resume. It is easier for the reader of a chronological resume to find a gap in the time sequence that might indicate a period of unemployment. Also, a recruiter is able to trace the career path of a potential employee in terms of increasing responsibility.

Functional Approach

Candidates using a functional style of resume group work experience by job function, such as "sales" or "marketing." This style of resume lends itself to a potential employee who is changing fields or has a career path that is not readily apparent from the combination of jobs.

Available Technology

More companies are moving towards soliciting online applications. Firms are able to process the data from online applications to sort them based on objective criteria, such as a requisite certification or degree. There are also advantages for potential employees submitting online applications. The candidates can enter more information online, as brevity is not as important. Also, potential employees will lengthen resume data as more companies scan the documents into the computer for analysis.

Resume Content

When reviewing a resume, HR should remember that the resume is essentially a marketing tool for applicants. The applicant will, to the greatest extent possible, provide information that paints a positive picture. Therefore, it is in the organization's best interest to use the resume as a basis for interview questions that will probe and elicit details regarding the applicants work experience. Further considerations include gaps in job history, frequent job changes, varied experiences and industries, and typing errors.

Gaps in Job History

HR should watch for gaps in job history. If gaps exist, then questions during an interview should determine the reason for the gaps. Gaps may consist of family obligations or education, which are reasonable. However, if the reason indicates the applicant could not find work, this could be a red flag.

Frequent Job Changes

Numerous job changes could suggest a lack of commitment, inability to strive toward long-term goals, or dissatisfaction on the part of past employers with the applicant's work. All reasons suggest that you may spend money on training only to have the employee leave the company soon after she is hired.

Varied Experiences and Industries

While relevant experience is important, HR should not pass over applicants with varied experience or education outside the organization's industry. Considering an applicant who has experiences, accomplishments, and/or skills that were applied outside the industry may be an advantage because the applicant may provide new perspectives and creative solutions to projects.

Typing Errors

A resume that contains typing errors suggests carelessness. If the applicant does not give the necessary level of attention to their resume, you cannot be sure that they will give it to their work.

Conclusion

Resumes are an important component to the selection process. As an initial screening device, the resume will enable HR to determine to what degree an applicant meets the minimum requirements of the job. Effective resumes are formatted appropriately, contain relevant content, and convey the degree to which an applicant is a good fit for a given job.

See also: I-9 Forms; Interviewing; Record Retention Laws

NOTE

1. "Résumé," *Dictionary of Human Resources and Personnel Management* (2006), http://www .credoreference.com/entry/6511733 (accessed March 13, 2008).

Laura Dendinger

SELECTION

Effectively selecting new employees into an organization is among the most important of all organizational initiatives. The cost impact associated with poor selection processes and related decisions is sobering, with some studies indicating a bottom-line impact of up to $200,000 per departing employee.[1] Clearly, selection must be positioned as a key strategic priority for any firm intent upon achieving sustainable high performance. HR professionals must lead the charge in this regard.

To this end, the selection process must include careful consideration of interviews, tests, and references as selection mechanisms. Further, each of these predictors must be developed and employed with the goal of maximizing the consistency (i.e., reliability) and accuracy (i.e., validity) of the process and related hiring decisions, so as to better ensure both the legality and strategic value-added of the organization's staffing function.

Interviewing and Selection

Interviewing is the most commonly employed selection mechanism. Unfortunately, it is also the most erroneous. Too many organizations overemphasize interviews as selection predictors, and conduct interviews in a faulty manner. Traditionally unstructured and personally customized (by the interviewer) interviews are very subjective. In order to improve both the consistency and accuracy of interviews, many organizations are increasingly taking the following steps:

1. Structured interviews—developing and consistently employing structured interview guides.
2. Behavioral questions—including behaviorally based interview questions that probe deeply for job-related details and experience from a candidate's past. These questions essentially ask a candidate, "Tell me, in great detail, what did you do?" in relationship to a specific accomplishment from their past that is directly related to the job for which the candidate is being considered.
3. Situational questions—including situationally based interview questions that probe deeply for job-related details in a hypothetical context. Such questions essentially ask a candidate, "Tell me, in great detail, what you would do?" in relationship to a contextually bound competency or ability that is directly related to the job for which the candidate is being considered.
4. Training interviewers—ensuring that all interviewers are trained in conducting structured interviews that include behavioral and situational questions.

Combined, these steps go a long way towards minimizing the risks associated with the inherent subjectivity and related inconsistency and inaccuracy of traditional interviews.

Testing and Selection

Another critical selection mechanism is candidate testing. Common tests include work sample tests, general intellectual capacity tests, manual dexterity tests, drug tests, and personality tests. The latter has become more common as organizations increasingly prioritize organizational culture fit in the selection process.[2] Common personality tests employed in this vein include those based on the Myers-Briggs Type Indicator (MBTI) and Big-Five Personality Dimensions constructs.

Background Investigation and Selection

Lastly, background checks allow an organization to investigate the employment, education, and criminal history of a candidate. This has become an increasingly challenging task for organizations to perform, as fewer and fewer past employers are willing to divulge performance-related information relative to candidates. However, it has concurrently become an increasingly important task as the doctrine of negligent hiring has evolved, which holds employer organizations potentially liable for illegal employee actions in the workplace. At a minimum, it is incumbent upon a hiring organization to verify dates of employment and job titles with past employers, verify educational records including graduation date(s) and degree(s) conferred, and to investigate criminal records.

Legal Compliance and Selection

It is important that organizations conduct all of the above outlined selection steps with a keen eye towards compliance with EEO-related statutes. Central to this is ensuring the job-relatedness of all selection mechanisms. This can be demonstrated via either content validity (i.e., requiring a manufacturing candidate to complete a manual dexterity test because such skills are clearly related to performing the job), or empirical validity (i.e., demonstrating a positive correlation between candidate scores on a manual dexterity test and subsequent, longitudinal performance ratings in the job should those same candidates indeed be hired). In general, the more accurate a selection mechanism is (i.e., demonstratively job related) the more valid it is as a predictor of job performance, and hence the more legally defensible it is as a basis for unbiased hiring decisions.

In rare circumstances, selection processes may, with impunity, systematically enforce what is in effect "legal discrimination" in favor of candidates that are members of specific protected classes. For example, the Hooters restaurant chain has successfully defended its right to require that all successful wait staff candidates be female. Hooters has demonstrated via several court actions that having an exclusively female wait staff is a business necessity given the mission and business model of the firm, and hence that being female is a bona fide occupational qualification (BFOQ) for a wait staff position in a Hooters restaurant.

Strategically Focused Selection

Perhaps most important in today's competitive environment is the need for an organization's selection process to reinforce the accomplishment of strategic objectives. And perhaps the Hooters example (although arguably quite provocative) is a prime case of a firm doing exactly that. Hooters has effectively developed and operationalized a selection process that, through extensive interviewing and testing, enables the firm to consistently and accurately hire successful "Hooters Girls." The process even involves situational interview questions that probe a candidate's willingness to be subject to "potentially offensive verbal banter" with Hooters patrons. In the end, it can be argued that such selection steps are integral to Hooters success given the firm's business model, and give evidence to the strategically-focused nature of the firm's selection process.

See also: Staffing: An Overview; Background Investigation; Employment Testing; Interviewing; HR Strategy

NOTES

1. Carla Joinson, "Capturing Turnover Costs," *HR Magazine,* July 2000, 107–19.
2. David E. Bowen, Gerald E. Ledford, and Barry R. Nathan, "Hiring for the Organization, Not the Job," *Academy of Management Executive,* November 1991, 35–51.

Scott A. Quatro

TALENT INVENTORY

Talent inventory is a critical human resource planning activity that enables HR professionals and managers to identify human resource capacity and capabilities. It provides a wealth of information useful in forecasting human resource requirements and matching them with human resource strategies. These activities also identify the organization's strengths and weaknesses, its opportunities and threats, and the quantity and quality of human resources within the firm.

Talent inventory can be defined as an organization's effort to identify the skills, knowledge, and abilities of their current employees.[1] Talent inventories enable HR professionals and managers to identify employee proficiencies and establish a reliable baseline for organizational productivity, performance, and quality management. Once established, performance management strategies and employee development plans can be established. Such decisions can be made regarding the aggregate competencies of employees as well as on an individual basis. Furthermore, decisions can be made about future external recruiting efforts necessary to improve skill and knowledge gaps and to improve the human capital capacity of the organization.

As a result, talent inventories reveal employees':
- Specialized training
- Current employment information
- Significant work experiences
- Educational background (including degrees, licenses, or certifications)
- Language skills
- Growth and development plans (past and present)
- Professional association leadership
- Work history
- Special contributions
- Major accomplishments
- Key attributes, strengths, and special skills
- Aspirations
- Motivators and de-motivators
- Development opportunities
- Awards received[2]

Such information helps organizations develop profiles of their employees' capacity and capabilities. Accordingly, the purpose of a talent inventory is to determine the current human resource capacity and capabilities and compare it to estimated labor requirements at some future date.[3]

Talent inventories also identify needed competencies, key positions, and high potential employees. Competencies include the following:
- Knowledge, skills, abilities, attitudes, and attributes of employees
- Role-specific competencies of employees
- Core competencies that are linked to strategic goals
- Gaps in employees' knowledge, skills, abilities, attitudes, and attributes, which equal development opportunities

Key positions refer to critical roles in the organization in which specialized skills are needed to remain competitive. Further, such positions require ongoing developmental and learning activities. Finally, talent inventories require an individual talent assessment of all high performing and high potential employees.

Forecasting Human Resource's Capabilities and Capacity

It is critical that organizations identify the current and future quantity and quality of human capital. This is needed for organizations to remain competitive, flexible, and agile.

This is likened to a professional baseball, football, or basketball franchise that anticipates its future human resource needs to remain competitive. The franchise must forecast the future strengths and weaknesses of the team, project departures of key players, assess its bench strength, anticipate changes in competition, blend the team with a mix of veterans, young players, and rookies, determine when certain players can be used, identify which players have developed well enough to play every day, and have key backups in vital positions. In short, a well-developed talent inventory is greatly influenced by future HR requirements of the organization, requiring HR professionals and managers to analyze their situation carefully and make projections accordingly.

Forecasting includes the external and internal supply of labor and the aggregate external and internal demand for labor.[4] External supply refers to the labor market as a whole while internal supply refers to the conditions inside the organization. Each of these components must be carefully examined by HR professionals and managers to accurately project the quantity and quality of future human resources.

NOTES

1. Jerry W. Gilley and Ann Maycunich, *Beyond the Learning Organization: Creating a Culture of Continuous Growth and Development through State-of-the-Art Human Resource Practices* (Cambridge, MA: Perseus Publishing, 2000), 62.

2. Ibid.

3. Jerry W. Gilley, Steven A. Eggland, and Ann Maycunich Gilley, *Principles of Human Resource Development,* 2nd ed. (Cambridge, MA: Perseus Publishing 2002).

4. Jerry W. Gilley and Ann Maycunich Gilley, *Strategically Integrated HRD: Six Transformational Roles in Creating Results Driven Programs* (Cambridge, MA: Perseus Publishing, 2003).

Jerry W. Gilley and Paul Shelton

Chapter 2
Employee Development

Employee Development: An Overview

Employee development has emerged, in part, out of training in organizations. Training is much more limited in terms of scope and overall impact on an organization. The content of training programs can lose relevance quickly; it is typically a one-time event, whereas development is ongoing and topical. The shift from training to development reflects a growing awareness of the strategic implications of human resources.

Purpose of Employee Development

Employee development serves two purposes: (1) improving organizational performance, and (2) developing the employee. In both instances, learning is central. More specifically, learning capability is the foundation from which both organizational performance and individual growth are realized. The major drivers for the increased emphasis on learning capability include the need for (1) continuous improvement, (2) innovation, and (3) continuous adaptation.

Continuous Improvement. Continuous improvement is a concept that grew in momentum with the implementation of total quality management (TQM) in the 1980s, which places emphasis on feedback and measurement to increase performance. The process has been labeled single loop learning,[1] and the focus is on learning to get better at current work processes through incremental improvements over time.

Innovation. Being first to market with a new product or service enables an organization to attain a competitive advantage. To do so requires innovation. Innovation is realized through creative problem solving and learning—learning new ways of understanding or reconfiguring concepts and ideas.

Continuous Adaptation. The degree to which an organization has a competitive advantage derives from learning to respond or adapting to external market conditions, including customer needs, new competitors, and new technology.

Types of Employee Development

Employee development places emphasis on formal education, job experiences, assessment centers, and mentoring and coaching programs; all aimed at developing competencies that are directly related to future contribution to an organization. Because it is future-oriented, the learning that takes place may not necessarily be related to an employee's current position in the organization. Rather, development prepares employees for future jobs.

Formal Education.   Formal education can take place off-site as part of university degree programs, or on-site through "corporate universities," which will typically involve lectures by business experts or senior executives in the organization, simulations, or adventure learning.

Job Experiences.   Experience on the job is made up of working through problems, decision making, interpersonal relationships, and task management. Development through job experiences occurs when employees are faced with new tasks or challenges on the job—where the employee must stretch his skills (forced to learn new skills) or apply current knowledge in a new way. Formal programs that support this type of development include job enlargement, job rotation, transfers or promotions, or temporary assignments and projects.

Assessment.   Assessment involves collecting information and providing feedback about performance, skills, and behaviors on the job. There are various methods and instruments that can be used, including personality assessments, psychological tests, in-basket exercises, and leaderless group discussions.

Mentoring and Coaching Programs.   Mentoring, either one-on-one or with a group, has been shown to be a highly effective way to develop employees. A mentor is an experienced senior employee who works one-on-one with a less experienced employee (protégé). Effective mentoring relationships are ones that are based on shared interests, values, or similar personalities.

Coaching consists of a manager or peer who works with an employee to develop skills and provide feedback. Coaches can work one-on-one with employees, or provide information and resources in order to support the employee learning on her own.

Conclusion

Most organizations use the development methods described in this article. Regardless of the approach, employees need a development plan that outlines the type of development needed, goals, and a way to measure improvement or growth. The most effective development plan involves identifying and tailoring the plan to the employee's needs, and puts the control of development in the employee's hands.

NOTE

1. Christopher Argyris, "Single-Loop and Double-Loop Models in Research on Decision-Making," *Administrative Science Quarterly* 21 (1976): 373–75.

Pamela Dixon

ACTION PLAN

An action plan is a way to make sure an organizational (or team or individual) goal is made concrete. An action plan describes the way an organization will use its strategies to meet its goal. Action planning is the process that guides the day-to-day activities of an organization or project. It is the process of planning what needs to be done, when it needs to be done, by whom it needs to be done, and what resources or inputs are needed to do it. It is the process of operationalizing strategic objectives, which is why it is also called operational planning. The design and implementation of the action plan depends on the nature and needs of the organization. Middle and frontline managers use action plans to achieve the organization's goals and objectives.

What Should Be in an Action Plan?

An action plan clearly delineates the *why, what, who, when* , and *necessary resources* relative to the plan, as outlined below:

WHY is this action being carried out? The goal statement is listed as the first item on the action plan worksheet. Clearly defined goals help communicate to all relevant organizational members why certain steps are being undertaken and what the organization hopes to accomplish after the steps are completed.

WHAT actions or critical steps (objectives) will occur? Before steps are detailed, agreement is reached about a strategy for arriving at the desired result. One way organizations do this is through brainstorming possible options, writing them up on a flip chart, and making a decision as to which make the most sense. The decision is made by assessing the advantages and disadvantages of each option and comparing the options against appropriate criteria such as: alignment with the organization or general project approach, employee or staff capacity to use a strategy, cost, and timing. Each critical step or task is outlined to break the goal down into individual components. The goal becomes easier to manage when it is broken into smaller steps. The critical steps are detailed to help plan for obstacles or barriers that might arise during each action step.

WHO will carry out these steps or actions? Identifying who will be responsible for carrying out each step makes it clear who should be included and who is responsible for making decisions if any decisions are required. The key question here is: Who should participate in and be responsible for actions in the action planning process? Effective action plans identify who specifically is responsible for carrying out an activity and the degree of authority that goes with the responsibility. Organizations that successfully use action plans recognize there is no use in saying that someone is responsible for putting together a report by a certain date unless he has the authority to insist that contributors give him their contributions by a certain date.

The decision on who should be responsible for a particular activity takes the following into account: the experience, skills, capabilities, and confidence needed to do the task; who has time to do the task when it needs to be done, as well as the ability to do it; and the willingness of someone to do a job or learn a job. Of course, there will always be some tasks no one is too keen to do, but it does help if people see a task as naturally falling into their work (for example, an accountant says she will do the budgeting), or someone is interested in a particular task or tasks. Even if someone is not fully competent and experienced, if he is willing to be coached and mentored it may be worthwhile to invest a bit of extra time in making him the responsible person, as a longer-term investment in development.

In the action planning process, the need to establish who is responsible for getting a task done does not mean that other people won't also be involved. At the team level, there may be a need to spell out exactly what this means in more detail.

WHEN will these actions take place, and for how long? A timeframe for the actions is developed and increases the likelihood that individuals will work more efficiently. The timeframe also helps to better strategize each sequence of steps to reach the completed target date. Sequencing is the key when it comes to planning the time needed for an action plan: doing things in the right order, and making sure that actions do not get held up because something that should have been done earlier has not been done, and is now holding up the whole process. When the action planning process is complete, it is useful to do a summary of the time plan, both as a checklist and to help employees to see at a glance when the busiest periods are likely to be and to prepare for them in advance.

WHAT RESOURCES are needed to carry out the steps? Resources can include money, time, people, locations, events, etc. Resources also refer to both internal to the organization and external—those resources that are not a part of the organization but that may be required or helpful for carrying out the action step. What all this usually means is money. Looking at the inputs required is necessary in order to work out the financial cost. In most instances, the bottom line will be a financial cost of some kind to the organization or project.

The action planning process identifies what is likely to incur costs, and then the activity is carefully budgeted. The budget summarizes the financing resources that are needed in order to carry out the action plan. This budget then is incorporated into the overall project budget or, if the budget already exists, compared with allocations for the relevant line items or budget areas. A budget cannot be prepared until there is an action plan.

In summary, then, action planning is the process in which organizations plan what will happen in the project or organization in a given period of time, and clarify what resources are needed to make it possible.

See also Strategic Planning

Ronald R. Sims

APPRECIATIVE INQUIRY

Appreciative inquiry (AI) is a perspective, a mindset, and a systematic process of creating positive change in organizations. AI is a systemwide, participative approach to identifying what is present at the positive core of a human system that creates optimal performance within an organization. *Appreciation* is that which is increasing in value or affirming past and present strengths or successes. *Inquiry* is being curious, exploring or asking questions. Therefore, appreciative inquiry is an approach to organizational development that asks questions about what is already working well within an organization to bring about positive change. Appreciative inquiry was founded in 1980 by David Cooperrider and Suresh Srivastva of Case Western Reserve University.[1]

Appreciative Inquiry vs. Problem Solving

The term appreciative inquiry was coined by David Cooperrider, who challenged the traditional problem-solving approach to performance improvement and proposed a new paradigm of looking at an organization's strengths and building on what is already working well within the organization. Appreciative inquiry differs from the problem-solving approach as follows:[2]

- Appreciate *what is* vs. identifying the problem
- Imagine *what might be* vs. conducting a root cause analysis
- Determine *what should be* vs. brainstorming solutions
- Create *what will be* vs. developing an action plan

The Five Principles of Appreciative Inquiry

Appreciative inquiry is based on the following five principles:[3]

The Constructionist Principle—This principle states that individuals create their own reality, and an organization's reality is created through the consensus of its individuals through conversations of what they believe to be true and anticipate the future to be.

The Principle of Simultaneity—This principle contends that inquiry is intervention, and that the questions we ask determine what we discover.

The Poetic Principle—Organizations must be studied as social systems. Just as a poem is open to interpretation, so is a human organization, and organizations have a choice on what to focus on with regard to their human experience. Finding themes is the key to identifying the organization's real capabilities.

The Anticipatory Principle—Similar to the placebo effect, this principle contends that the future that organizational members anticipate is the one they create. The images of the future determine their current behavior.

The Positive Principle—Focusing on past successes and building on what works is more effective for positive organizational change than focusing on the problem.

The Appreciative Inquiry Process

The four core processes of appreciative inquiry are[2]

1. *Definition*—Choose the positive as the focus on inquiry.
   Since human systems grow in the direction of what they study, the *definition* phase includes identifying an affirmative focus for the inquiry. This is often identified with the executive or leader of the change initiative. This phase also includes creating the interview questions and determining participation.
2. *Discovery*—Inquire into exceptionally positive moments and locate themes that appear in the stories.
   The *discovery* phase brings a group of stakeholders together to interview each other eliciting positive stories of past and present successes to build positive energy. During this phase, participants identify themes that appear in the stories that help them build consensus on the positive core of the strengths of the organization.
3. *Dream*—Create shared images of a preferred future.
   The *dream* phase engages participants to envision what is possible for the future of the organization. This phase often includes drafting a possibility statement that summarizes the organization's vision and purpose and experiencing what this future would look, feel, and be like if the shared positive experiences were the norm in the organization.
4. *Design and Delivery*—Innovate ways to create that future.
   The *design and delivery* phase, sometimes referred to as *Destiny,* includes participants identifying innovative ways to create the future through inspired individual and organizational commitments to develop strategies and systems that build off the positive core of the organization.

NOTES

1. David Cooperrider and Suresh Srivastva, "Appreciative Inquiry in Organizational Life." *Research in Organizational Change and Development* 1 (1987): 129–69.

2. Magruder Watkins, Jane and Bernard Mohr. *Appreciative Inquiry* (San Francisco: Jossey-Bass/Pfeiffer, 2001).

3. Ron Zemke, "Don't Fix That Company! Appreciative Inquiry in Organization Development." *Training* 36 (1999): 26.

Dean Savoca

BURNOUT

Burnout is a state of physical, mental, or emotional exhaustion, or negativity toward one's job. An employee experiences burnout when something causes continuous stress at work and the employee does not perceive that he or she has the personal capacity to effectively deal with the situation.

Symptoms

Symptoms of burnout vary among individuals but often include stress, illness, diminished productivity, tiredness, higher rates of absenteeism, interpersonal conflicts, and substance abuse. Burnout is more common in the service professions than in other professions,[1] although in all professions it is associated with low employee buy-in, which can lead to diminished productivity or high turnover; both of which impact the bottom line of the company and, in many instances, customer satisfaction. Young, talented employees with great future potential are reporting burnout early in their careers.[2] As the epidemic of burnout continues to grow, it is costing U.S. companies an estimated $200 billion every year in reduced productivity, accidents, absenteeism, turnover, and insurances expenses.[3]

Causes

The cause of burnout varies among individuals, but several common themes provide insight into the elements that are consistently found in burnout research. Organizations that promote workaholic behaviors, either directly or indirectly, will experience higher levels of burnout during a time when "growing demands for productivity, meeting bottom line requirements, and a push toward greater efficiencies" are driving organizational culture.[4] Working extremely long hours on a regular basis, large amounts of travel, and a large number of direct reports can directly contribute to increased levels of employee burnout. Technology creates another element that challenges employees: constant availability. With the evolution of the BlackBerry, an employee is often expected to be continuously available to clients and superiors, which can lead to burnout. In industries with frequent layoffs and turnover, the constant concern and fear of losing one's job also contributes to feelings of burnout.

One last and widespread contributor to burnout is managerial malpractice in the building of manager-employee relationships. "As a result of managerial malpractice, employee morale and productivity remain low, which leads to poor-quality products and services, and higher costs."[5] In these situations, feelings of helplessness and frustration can be overwhelming and potentially lead to burnout symptoms.

Strategies for Preventing Burnout

The best way to manage burnout is to prevent it from occurring in the first place. Prevention measures can be taken at the organizational level as well as the personal level.

Following are suggestions for each category. Because organizational situations and individuals are so incredibly diverse, there is no one-size-fits-all answer. Each situation will demand a unique combination of strategies to prevent burnout.

Organizational Strategies for Preventing Burnout

- Have managers focus on results and allow the process to be less micromanaged.
- Measure productivity by outcomes instead of the number of hours an employee is at the office. Take care not to reward workaholic behaviors.
- Provide mentor programs to support young talent and those newly promoted to positions of higher responsibility.
- Focus on the strengths of employees and align them with the needs and profit goals of the organization.
- Encourage individuals to develop themselves. Provide emotional intelligence, professional development, and career development opportunities for employees.
- Provide critical employee feedback and allow employees to provide feedback of managerial practices.

Individual Strategies for Preventing Burnout

- Develop professional networking.
- Achieve and maintain work/life balance and seek opportunities to continue to improve your understanding of how to balance the demands of your career and your personal life.
- Focus and build on your strengths so that they align with the needs of your employer and work to promote these strengths.
- Expand your marketability and take charge of your personal career development. This will help develop a sense of security and minimize anxiety and anger during times of high turnover.
- Accept mentor programs, professional development, career development, and emotional intelligence development from your employer and/or the community.
- Provide honest, useful feedback when your organization requests it. Listen carefully to feedback provided to you.

See also Career Resource Centers; Managerial Malpractice

NOTES

1. Dana Yagil, "The Relationship of Service Provider Power Motivation, Empowerment and Burnout to Customer Satisfaction," *International Journal of Service Industry Management* (2006): 258.
2. Lara Ashworth, "Insights," *People Management,* January 25, 2007, 57.
3. Joseph Jordan, "Beating Burnout," *Chemical Engineering* (1999): 133.
4. "Beware the Dangers of Being an 'Extreme' Organization," *HR Focus,* April 2007, 10.
5. Jerry Gilley, "Taming the Organization," *Human Resource Development International* (2001): 217.

Teresa Dwire

CAREER PLANNING AND DEVELOPMENT

Many employees feel trapped, stagnated, or overlooked in their present assignments. Deriving little pleasure from one's work contributes to increased stress and poor performance. Dissatisfied workers often do not work up to their full potential and may fail to meet expectations. Some have lost their professional mission in life, or they have been unable to identify their vocational purpose. To further complicate matters, some organizational leaders and managers are reluctant to approach employees about performance problems. They hold their breath, look the other way, cross their fingers, and hope that somehow the situation will work itself out. In short, many performance problems are career related.

Organizational leaders who accept responsibility for establishing career development programs and organizing career planning efforts contribute to employees' success. The overall success of both individuals and organizations depend on organizational leaders' ability to create career development program policies, allocate financial resources, provide opportunities for collaboration and integration, and advocate the importance of career development. Effective career development agents provide guidance and information regarding the impact and importance of career development, exhibit leadership and expertise in creating career development activities, and serve as a liaison between employees and the organization.

Barriers to Career Development

Career development requires change; thus, organizational leaders need to help employees address it accordingly. It has been suggested that "people resist [change] not out of spite but out of fear...some people will fight back when they believe that the change [career development] threatens their own best interest."[1]

Several common concerns about career development are often expressed by organizational leaders. They are:

- We cannot promote everyone, so why raise unrealistic expectations?
- We have a space on our performance appraisal forms to indicate what career plans our employees have, and our organizational leaders are supposed to discuss these career plans with their people. What else is there to do?
- What if employees "develop" in ways that would not be useful to the organization?
- We do not have the staff needed to implement career development.
- We are sure it would be nice, but we cannot afford it.
- If we develop our employees, they will just jump ship to other organizations.
- We already have a career development program.
- We have a lot of internal courses and a generous tuition reimbursement program, and employees do not even take advantage of these now.
- Organizational leaders are technical people—they are not good at career development.[2]

Organizational leaders' support and the identification of the needs of individual career development address the above concerns. Effective career development advocates identify the people who have a stake in the outcome of career development and explore the existing career development resources within the organization. Additionally, they ascertain employee commitment to career development activities along with the steps needed to gain support or acceptance.

What Is Career Development?

Career development has been an accepted developmental strategy within organizations for several decades.[3] Career development programs communicate strong employer investment in their personnel, something organizations want in order to maintain a positive recruiting image. As such, successful career development programs are integrated into the organization.

Career development can be defined as an organized, planned effort comprised of structured activities or processes that result in a mutual career plotting effort between employees and the organization.[4] Within the system of career development, employees are responsible for career planning, while the organization is responsible for career management. These two separate but related processes combined form career development, a partnership between the organization and its individual employees.

Career development allows and encourages personnel to examine future career paths. Career development programs help individuals analyze their abilities and interests in order to better match their personal needs for career development with the needs of the organization. Organizational leaders can improve employee attitudes toward work, work satisfaction levels, efficient allocation of human resources, and loyalty among personnel.

A marriage between employer and employee is essential in career development. In this process, organizations engage in developmental planning, which is the process of assessing appropriate goals and objectives, along with the proper allocation of physical, financial, and human resources. Concurrently, employees are encouraged to engage in career/life planning, which includes analysis of personal goals and competencies and a realistic evaluation of future opportunities. Both organizations and their personnel need to conduct three types of analyses:

- *Needs analysis* refers to the examination of personal and organization needs.
- *Skills analysis* refers to the evaluation of an individual's competencies while the organization examines the competencies required within each job classification and those needed throughout the organization.
- *Potential analysis* is conducted when both individuals and the organization project their future competency requirements and determine areas of deficiency or weakness.

These evaluations determine the "matching process" between individual and organization. Organizational leaders can then blend career information (employee) with developmental plans (educational organization) to improve the matching process. This also provides valuable insights for future implementation of career development activities by organizations and their employees.

Several benefits and limitations of collaborative career development have been identified.

Benefits

- The organization has a record of employees' interests, mobility, and goals.
- Information can be available in a database for selection decisions and HR planning, taking each individual's input into account.
- Development needs of the group reveal opportunities for training curricula and development planning options organization-wide.
- Development plans can be a measure of individual involvement in one's career management.
- Community pressure for greater responsiveness and quality requires everyone to upgrade skills and keep them current; an annual development plan is a means of accountability.
- An ongoing emphasis can be maintained by requiring an updated development plan annually as a basis for career discussions.

Limitations

- Employees may not be open about career development goals and plans in an environment devoid of trust. They may write what they think should be written, rather than what they want.
- Shared goal information must be administered, whether on paper copies or in a database. If a database is to be kept, who enters and modifies the data?
- The purpose of shared information from employees must be clearly communicated. Will it be used for staffing decisions? For HR planning? For training needs assessment? Without a perceived benefit to leaders, faculty, and staff, this becomes one more administrative requirement.[5]

Successful career development programs require organizations and their personnel to work together as a team. Organizational leaders are responsible for management of career development programs, including identification and facilitation of the development activities deemed appropriate. Familiarity with a variety of career development theories aids program development and selection of appropriate activities.

Organizational leaders and employees must accept ownership of and responsibility for their own career and personal growth. Organizations do their part by providing the resources and support necessary for success. The most effective career development programs enjoy board member support and align individual needs with those of the organization.

Purpose of Career Development

Organizations implement career development programs to develop and promote employees from within, encourage commitment and loyalty, improve morale and motivation, and reduce turnover. Demonstrating the organization's commitment to personnel improvement, growth, and development increases organizational success.

Six integrative activities can be adopted by organizational leaders: (1) forecasting future organization needs, (2) utilizing performance appraisals, (3) job announcements and postings, (4) career pathing for employees, (5) training and development, and (6) the creation of consistent compensation practices.

Effective career development programs account for the diversity of people, use methods other than the traditional classroom training approach, and focus on long-term results. For best results, organizational leaders encourage employees to identify their needs and career goals and plan career development activities accordingly. To ensure success, we offer several guidelines:

1. Start small and design a specific program in response to a particular need.
2. Integrate the program into ongoing personal activities or programs.
3. Obtain organizational leaders' support.
4. Encourage time management and lobby for support.
5. Develop an evaluation process and communicate measured results.
6. Continue to explore alternatives and maintain flexibility.[6]

Quite simply, successful career development is based on individualized needs and interests, remains flexible, incorporates appropriate evaluation procedures, and enjoys the support of organizational leaders.

Organizational leaders cannot assist employees adequately unless the organization offers the right kinds of challenging career development activities. Organizational leaders must also develop an appropriate awareness and appreciation of career development. Otherwise, career development will proceed in a piecemeal fashion.

Benefits of a Career Development System

Career development yields many benefits, including:
- Reduced turnover of highly skilled or experienced employees
- Revision of outdated expectations for career opportunities after flattening or reorganizing
- Motivated personnel who take responsibility for their own development and continue to add value
- Understanding by employees of the urgency to keep skills current
- Managers, employees, and organizational leaders' buy-in of the need for continuous learning
- Equal opportunity for minorities and women
- Organizational leaders who are convinced of the importance of developing their personnel
- A competitive organization through productive and motivated employees
- Flexible employees who can move out of functional "silos" or narrowly defined roles
- Matching of realities in the organization to recruiting promises
- Employees with meaningful development plans.[7]

To reap the benefits of career development, organizational leaders must relate to employees at all levels and cultivate individuals who are responsible for various career development roles—such as department supervisors, team leaders, and other informal leaders. In this way, career development becomes a vital part of individual and educational organizational enhancement. Simultaneously, organizational leaders emphasize the importance of career development to employees, inform and update others within the organization while serving as mentors and career counselors, and maintain a careful balance of facilitating, coordinating, and monitoring of career development activities.

Conclusion

Preparing employees for current and future job assignments requires managers to embrace career development programs. Career development is a process of creating a partnership between the organization and its personnel, enhancing their knowledge, skills, and abilities. Career development *is* a quintessential developmental activity of an organization. It allows for improved individual proficiencies while concurrently enhancing organization success.

Managers should understand that the primary purpose of career development is to help employees analyze their abilities and interests to better match personnel needs to the needs of the organization. Effective managers identify the factors in maintaining a successful career development program, recognize their general responsibilities in the area of career development, and isolate methods for improving the harmony between employees and the organization related to career development. Applying career development to the organization setting helps prepare organizations and their personnel to meet the challenges of a dynamic environment.

NOTES

1. Robert Maurer, *Beyond the Wall of Resistance: Unconventional Strategies that Build Support for Change* (Austin, TX: Bard Books, 1996).

2. Patricia Simonsen, *Promoting a Developmental Culture in Your Organization: Using Career Development as a Change Agent* (Palo Alto, CA: Davies-Black Publishing, 1997).

3. Jerry W. Gilley, Steven A. Eggland, and Ann Maycunich Gilley, *Principles of Human Resource Development,* 2nd ed. (Cambridge, MA: Perseus, 2002).

4. Ibid.

5. Simonsen, *Promoting a Developmental Culture in Your Organization.*

6. Gilley, Eggland, and Gilley, *Principles of Human Resource Development.*

7. Simonsen, *Promoting a Developmental Culture in Your Organization.*

Jerry W. Gilley and Ann Gilley

CAREER RESOURCE CENTER

Career resource centers, often referred to as career development centers, are a source of information, counseling, and development tools that help guide the formation of employee career planning. These range from a few books and videotapes underneath job postings to complex online resource centers, to external agency services and even outplacement resources. Companies have successfully used career resource centers for years. For example, Hewitt Associates has tracked growth for more than 15 years and has used a career development center to provide transition management, coaching, and outplacement as an element of their success.[1]

Reasons for Career Resource Centers

Career development is often considered the responsibility of the employee, and due to this, there are several reasons why organizations would be wise to provide career development resources to serve and attract employees. Current and future trends suggest that employees will change jobs more often than in previous years, and this means organizations will also be dealing with a growing amount of change. Additionally, there will be an increased demand for knowledge workers. When an organization provides career development resources, it is taking charge of developing the higher-quality, more flexible employees it will need.[2] Because organizational competition for talent will grow ever more fierce, career resource centers can be used to attract and keep talent, making strong career development centers an element that, in the eye of perceptive future employees, is an employer of choice above the organization's competition. In high-turnover industries, career resources are being provided as outplacement support, which directly benefits the organization by reducing stress and anxiety related to the concern of losing a job. When employees experience lower levels of stress and anxiety, they are less likely to demonstrate the symptoms of burnout, such as lower productivity, higher absenteeism, and increased reports of illness.

Considerations for Career Resource Center Development

Once an organization recognizes the benefits of career development centers, it has the option of outsourcing an agency or consultant that specializes in career development, or developing its own in-house services. When beginning the process of implementing career development, it is important to consider some of the changes in career development assumptions. For example, teaching no longer focuses on memorization in isolated situations, but is much more effective when information is connected with contextual situations and simulations that engage in higher-level problem-solving activities. Another change is that the focus is not just on academics, but also character development.[3] Also essential to career development planning is to consider how to integrate the following elements into the organization's career resource center. First, career development must be driven by business needs. It must be guided by a vision and philosophy of career development and supported by senior management. Communication and education are critical, and employees must hold responsibility for their own growth.[4]

Career Development and Technology

Another aspect of career development centers on technology. With global interdependence and ever-growing staffs, sometimes it is unrealistic to have a physical career resource that everyone in the company has access to. Many companies have developed online resources that include feedback, development planning, training, and career planning.[5] Although online resources lack the ability to address as many learning styles and needs as interpersonal teaching, it is a useful avenue for addressing the demands and realities of a global economy.

Conclusion

Implementing career development centers in an organization can be challenging and is often considered the HR effort that will last for only a brief time. When the decision to introduce a career development plan is put into place, it will take the follow-through and commitment of senior executives for it to be successful. Significant literature and numerous experts are available to help implement a solid career resource center that is beneficial to both the employer and employee. It is advisable to fully research and plan before implementing career development so that it has the greatest potential for success.

NOTES

1. B.G. Doyle, "Hewitt Associates: 15 Years of Growth and Innovation," *Caribbean Business* (2005): S3.

2. Jeanne Meister, "The Quest for Lifetime Employability," *Journal of Business Strategy* 19, no. 3 (May–June 1998): 25.

3. Rich Feller and Judy Whichard, *Knowledge Nomads and the Nervously Employed: Workplace Change and Courageous Career Choices* (Austin, TX: CAPS Press, 2005).

4. Peggy Simonsen, *Promoting Development Culture in Your Organization Using Career Development as a Change Agent* (Palo Alto, CA: Davies-Black Publishing, 1997).

5. Jacki Keagy and Jim Warner, "Creating a Virtual Career Development Center," *HR Focus,* October 1997, 11.

Teresa Dwire

COACHING

Why coaching? First, organizations face the same challenges today that they faced centuries ago: scarcity of resources (and corresponding battles), varying levels of individual talent, the need to improve performance, distribution complexities, competition, and so on. Organizations are facing constant and rapid change, which requires them to confront new challenges, provide quick innovative solutions, and manage talented employees.

Therefore, effective organizations adopt a strategy that helps them to institute and manage change, provide ongoing training, and model collaboration and team building.[1] They need managers who can model mastery, mold values, character, and commitment, and improve individual and team performance.[2] Finally, they need creative problem-solvers—ones who can assess and strategically deploy human talent and make quick and decisive decisions. Quite simply, organizations need their managers to developing coaching skills and abilities.

What Is Coaching

Coaching is a partnership that equips individuals with the tools they need to succeed. Most important, coaching enables people to develop themselves.[3] Additionally, coaching is a developmental process in which all employees grow and develop, improve their performance, and advance their careers. An old Chinese proverb states, *"give a man a fish, you feed him for a day; teach a man to fish, you feed him for a lifetime."* The same is true of the coaching process. Briefly, managers (as coaches) partner with employees in straightforward, honest, and collaborative exchanges regarding performance that focus on expanding excellence through individual learning, growth, and development. Coaching provides individuals with the ability to approach or react to opportunities, threats, and other events in a confident, reflective, powerful way.

Why Coach?

Skeptics claim that coaching is simply the newest management gimmick. Not true; presidents, monarchs, heads of state, world-class athletes, and performers have and continue to surround themselves with experts on whom they rely for advice, guidance, feedback, support, reinforcement, encouragement, challenge, confrontation, instruction, observation, and more. They realized that they cannot excel without the guidance of a coach, and many have credited coaches (whom they have also called mentors, sages, guides, or confidants) with contributing to their success.

Benefits of Performance Coaching

The benefits of coaching are numerous for employees, managers, and organizations.

Coaching Benefits to Employees

For the employee, coaching encourages challenges, opportunities, and growth. Coaching provides:

- A better relationship with one's manager, including appreciation of his or her expertise
- Improved self-esteem via challenging and rewarding assignments, positive feedback, and encouragement
- An environment that encourages growth and development
- Opportunities to develop to one's fullest potential
- Opportunities to influence the way in which one relates to work, the work environment, and the organization
- Greater job/career satisfaction
- Being treated as a human being with a complex set of needs and values, all of which are important in his or her work and life.[4]

Performance Coaching Benefits for Managers

Managers aid their organizations and personnel through coaching activities. In return, they reap the following benefits:

- A better understanding of their employees' skills, strengths, and areas needing development for current and future assignments; also enables succession planning
- Opportunities to better serve their personnel through learning facilitation, persuasion, mentoring, and leading
- Superior results through people (e.g., higher sales levels, better customer service, greater production, fewer errors, etc.)
- A more motivated and productive workforce
- Enhanced problem solving as a result of collaboration
- They are energized, motivated, and challenged to become the best managers/leaders they can be
- They take on increasingly difficult managerial assignments, which initiates change within the firm
- They are perceived as human beings rather than as resources in the productivity process
- They enhance their own interpersonal skills.[5]

Performance Coaching Benefits for the Organization

Ultimately, organizations improve as personnel improve. Just as a rising tide raises all ships, organizational benefits of coaching include:

- Better communications between and among leaders, managers, and personnel
- Improved performance and effectiveness
- Improved capability, which is a firm's ability to establish internal structures and processes that influence its members to create organization-specific competencies and, thus, enable the organization to adapt to changing customer and strategic needs
- Increased competitiveness through achievement of strategic goals and objectives
- Enhanced creativity, problem solving, and decision-making
- More accurate HR and succession planning (the result of assessment of talent, growth and development plans)
- Healthy employees who are more qualified to lead the firm to long-term success, the result of the aggregate growth, development, reflection, and renewal abilities of personnel
- Transfer of individuals' enhanced knowledge, skills, and abilities to the firm (organizational learning)
- Development and maintenance of the most important systems and linkages needed for improving performance, readiness, efficiency, and effectiveness
- Adaptation of developmental and leadership strategies that optimize the contributions of all employees
- Enhanced collaboration, teamwork, and the ability to capitalize on synergy to produce results
- Competitive advantage through people, which is nearly impossible for rivals to duplicate.[6]

Conclusion

The need for and benefits of coaching are clear. The times require it, organizations and their employees need it, and managers are capable of it.

See also: Mentoring; Performance Coaching

NOTES

1. Frederic M. Hudson, *The Handbook of Coaching: A Comprehensive Resource Guide for Managers, Executives, Consultants, and Human Resource Professionals* (San Francisco: Jossey-Bass, 1999).
2. Jerry W. Gilley and Nathaniel W. Boughton, *Stop Managing, Start Coaching* (New York: McGraw-Hill, 1996).
3. David B. Peterson and Mary Dee Hicks, *Leaders as Coaches: Strategies for Coaching and Developing Others* (Minneapolis, MN: Personnel Decisions International, 1996).
4. Jerry W. Gilley and Ann Gilley, *The Manager as Coach* (Westport, CT: Praeger, 2007).
5. Ibid.
6. Ibid.

Jerry W. Gilley

COMPUTER-BASED TRAINING

Computerization has transformed literally every segment of society—including education. Virtual campuses have provided people with educational opportunities that previously did not exist. Consider the following factors:

- Computerization affects the way almost every business operates—most households even have computers with Internet access.
- Globalization requires that organizations stay connected with information to remain competitive.
- The rate at which change is imposed upon business demands that employees keep their level of skill up to date.
- Investment of time and money are ever increasing challenges in an organization's ability to participate in the training and development process.
- Education—as an industry—is expanding its reach with nontraditional approaches to instruction through use of the World Wide Web and multimedia.

Computer-based training (CBT)—also know as "technology delivered training" or "computer assisted instruction"—is the vehicle that links all of these innovations and needs together.

The Fundamentals

Some historical accounts of the advent of computer-based training (CBT) divide the process into segments that mark distinctions in approaches to CBT over the years. Terms like "e-learning" and "performance era" highlight differences between how learning can take place and how knowledge can be assimilated. In an effort to produce a concise and operational definition of CBT, the various concepts will be combined as follows:

- Computer-based training refers to the process of delivering training or providing learning opportunities utilizing a computerized, electronic delivery system. This system can include, but is not limited to:
  - Stand-alone computer and video applications utilizing CDs, DVDs, and software.
  - Live audio and/or video feed providing real-time links to classroom instruction.
  - Computer applications that connect the user to a network or Internet stream. This could be live or preprogrammed.
  - Expert systems (specialized computer programs) that train themselves as business transacts within an organization. An example of this would be an inventory monitoring system

that can track sales volume, manage the reordering process, and provide updates to personnel as needed. In this case, the employees are both educated in the dynamics of business operations at the same time they participate in the continual updating of the system—a kind of reciprocal training.

More than a simple training process that occurs in front of a computer screen, CBT seeks to add value to the organization by utilizing existing technology to integrate new knowledge with mission-critical applications. This can range from an employee acquiring the skills to use word processing software, to designing an office automation system that teaches the employee as it is developed and updated.

Advantages and Disadvantages

When looking at technology as an instructional delivery system, it is important to consider its strengths and weaknesses. Advantages and disadvantages will have an organization-specific element, but there are general considerations when looking at the pros and cons of CBT. Some advantages:

- Flexibility—In terms of scheduling, CBT offers the organization and participants the ability to make the training work around their schedule. Often, live streaming can be scheduled according to availability. The pace of the training can also be controlled to allow students to learn at their own speed.
- Progress tracking/scoring—Since the training takes place on a computer, the system can track the students' progress and manage the grading. Additionally, management can view student progress and provide feedback.
- Utilization of expert instruction—People who serve in the capacity of trainers within an organization often must learn new topics to serve as instructors. This process is costly, time consuming, and lowers the quality of education due to the limitation of instructor expertise. In most cases, CBT brings people with high levels of experience and knowledge to the organization at a reasonable cost.
- Enhanced training capacity—Occasionally, there is a need to train large numbers of personnel in a short period of time. Traditional methods of training would make this task difficult, if not impossible. With CBT, the organization can utilize existing technology and flexible scheduling to minimize interruption to the daily operations of the organization.

As is the case with any system, there are disadvantages to CBT that should be considered. Some disadvantages include:

- Access to technology—Although most of the workforce today has access to a computer, there are several scenarios in which personnel do not. Some examples might include various medical personnel, people who are skilled in maintenance trades, operators in manufacturing facilities, and individuals who have never had the occasion to use a computer in their career.
- Lack of human interaction—Learning styles vary from person to person. Some individuals learn more efficiently when they interact with the instructor. Although CBT can be used in conjunction with a facilitator, it largely depends on the student managing the learning process alone.
- Students with limited computer aptitude—Low levels of computer literacy can create discomfort with participation in CBT. More importantly, the effectiveness of CBT for those individuals that feel compelled to participate might be lower than normal—and could potentially go undetected.

Considerations and Suggestions

When considering CBT as an option for your organization, ask the following questions:

1. What are the challenges facing your organization?
2. Who needs to be involved?
3. Is the content available, or can you create it?
4. Is the technology available, or can it be acquired?
5. Do the targeted learners have the skills necessary to benefit from CBT?

When you are satisfied with the answers to these questions, here are some suggestions on how to proceed:

1. *Work with established products and vendors*—Leverage their expertise.
2. *Try to start with "off the shelf" products*—These are less expensive and give you a chance to test the process of CBT before investing in a customized system.
3. *Gather as much information as you can before proceeding*—Learning from the experiences of others will keep you from repeating their mistakes.
4. *Make sure that your CBT programs are based around business results and business strategies*—Know that training is the appropriate intervention for the issue being addressed, and make sure the results are measurable.

Resources:

Oakes, Kevin. "Annual Pay and Compensation Report." *T+D* 57, no. 1, (2003): 64.
Wokosin, Linda. "FAQs about Your First CBT." *Intercom* 51, no. 9 (2004): 21–23.

Scott McDonald

CONTINUOUS IMPROVEMENT PLAN

Continuous improvement is a method of creating incremental change through the activities of individuals or groups typically focused on identifying and eliminating non-value-added processes, allowing organizations to operate more efficiently. Continuous improvement planning is the process of identifying and coordinating the incremental activities that support the improvement methodologies that organizations have identified as important to meeting their strategic objectives.

Continuous Improvement Methodologies

It is important to understand the difference between the continuous improvement process and other improvement initiatives that have been introduced to organizations over the past years. In today's organizations, when someone speaks of continuous improvement it is more than likely based on one of a number of different improvement methodologies that are currently being implemented throughout North America, Europe, and Asia in industries such as manufacturing, health care, service, construction, and beyond. Common names for these programs are Lean Manufacturing, Total Quality Management, Six Sigma, Toyota Production System, Theory of Constraints, Demand Flow Technology, and a number of other lesser-known names. Continuous improvement strategies are used in all of these methodologies as the core philosophy behind the success of the program.[1]

Continuous improvement is found within an organization's culture of dedicated, ongoing incremental improvement that is a natural, expected activity of all associates and directly tied to the strategic goals of developmental organizations. This is in sharp contrast to organizations that focus on large, project-based, or departmental-driven improvement initiatives that occur sporadically over a long period of time and are disconnected from any strategic objectives often found within traditional organizations.

The Origins of Continuous Improvement

One of the more common types of continuous improvement methods often referred to is the Plan, Do, Check, Act (PDCA) model that was introduced by W. Edwards Deming and Walter Shewart in the 1950s. This simple model is based on a continuous cycle of improvement and had its origins in quality control and production improvements.
- *Plan:* Based on the strategic objectives of the organization, identify the area, process, or activity that warrants improvement.
- *Do:* Implement the change.

- *Check:* Review the area, process, or activity that is being improved to ensure that the excepted objectives are met.
- *Act:* Upon completion of the improvement, review the actions taken, lessons learned, and initiate another improvement event that will continuously driving incremental improvement.

Initially, Deming introduced this model to the Japanese in an effort to assist with the rebuilding of their country after World War II. The Toyota Motor Company adopted these techniques early on and combined them with Henry Ford's mass production techniques to create what is now known as the Toyota Production System.[2] An integral part of their system is the use of Kaizen events that drive continuous improvement throughout their organization. These events have their foundations in the PDCA model. In the mid-1970s, General Motors, followed in later years by companies such as Motorola and General Electric, implemented improvement methodologies that have their roots firmly planted in the PDCA model.

Continuous Improvement Events

Continuous improvement activities are often referred to as rapid continuous improvement events (RCIs) and could be thought of as *the activity that provides the opportunity for continuous improvement to occur.* In other words, ideas turn into actions that produce results. The simplicity of the RCI event is the key behind its success. RCI teams typically consist of a

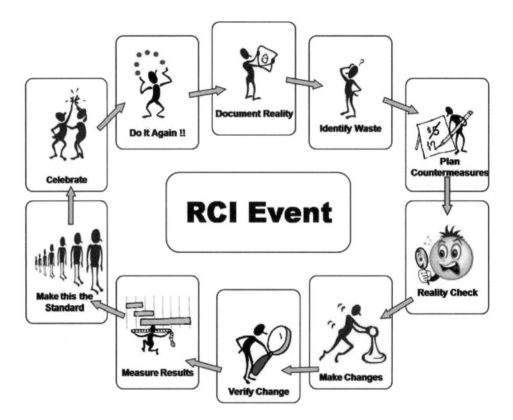

highly focused group of four to eight people, at least ⅓ from the area affected along with others that can provide additional perspectives. The team follows a methodical process of identifying the issues, determining and implementing solutions, and follow-up using a set of standard tools often defined by the improvement methodology (e.g., Lean Manufacturing, Total Quality Management, and Toyota Production System). The RCI event should have a very specific objective that is measurable, and the team can be held accountable for meeting at the end of the event. Most events are five days long, but can be shorter or longer depending on the overall objectives and availability of resources. In many smaller organizations where resources are limited there has been success in running two-day RCI events that are highly focused and result in amazing incremental improvement.

Regardless of the length, the key is to scope the event appropriately and keep focused on the overall strategic objectives of the organization. As mentioned previously, the incremental nature of improvements combined with the circular process of continuous improvement can at times make it feel as though there is very little improvement being made. The RCI event is one of a thousand steps often required to achieve true transformation. The scoping of the RCI event and ensuring that it ties back to the overall objectives of the organization is critical for successful events.

Continuous Improvement Planning

Determining the sequence and timing of the RCI events is dependent on the magnitude of the change and the urgency of meeting the strategic objectives. The idea behind the continuous improvement philosophy is that once the area, process, or activity has been improved, returning to the same area and improving it again and again will result in much greater gains than if the improvement was only completed once. Connecting these improvement events together in some sort of systematic sequence is often the task of the value stream manager or an individual who is able to dedicate her resources to understanding where the non-value- and value-added activities are occurring and their connection to the strategic objectives of the organization.[3] This individual will direct the RCI coordinators who reside in each division of an organization to schedule and scope RCI events according to the overall value stream. The RCI events are typically planned on a yearly basis and occur at least once a month in many organizations.

Continuous Improvement Culture

When you think of the word "culture," what is your definition? How would you define the culture of your organization? Do you think there are different cultures within your organization? Different cultures within a department? Chances are there are as many definitions as there are people. Culture is a difficult term to define because it is something one cannot touch or feel; instead, it is an idea or a way of thinking and acting. When the term "culture" is used in the work environment, a common definition is "the sum of peoples' habits related to how they get their work done."[4] If the culture is based on peoples' habits, then a large part of shifting or changing a culture has to do with being able to identify and change behaviors that result in new actions that eventually become habits. Keep in mind that *all* habits are not bad. When we are talking about understanding an organization's culture, a large part of the analysis consists of observing and documenting actions, then working toward the reshaping of people's behaviors that result in the creation of new habits. These habits result in measurable actions that are used to define the culture based on the vision, values, purpose, and goals of the organization. The continuous improvement culture could be defined as: *an organization that is continuously working toward identifying non-value-added activities and eliminating them from the process, leaving only value-added activities.*

NOTES

1. David Blanchard, "Lean Green and Low Cost: Census of U.S. Manufacturers," *Industry Week,* October 2007, 38.

2. James P. Womack, Daniel T. Jones, and Daniel Roos, *The Machine That Changed the World,* (New York: HarperCollins, 1991), 277.

3. Mike Rother and John Shook, *Learning to See* (Brookline, MA: The Lean Enterprise Institute, 1999), 7.

4. David Mann, *Creating a Lean Culture* (New York: Productivity Press, 2005), 3.

Kyle B. Stone

CORPORATE UNIVERSITY

Corporate universities have existed in the United States for more than 40 years.[1] A corporate university is the "formal entity associated with an organization that is chartered with providing employees with the skills and understanding they need to help the organization achieve its business objectives, both short and long term."[2] Corporate universities differ from traditional training and development functions in their close alignment with an organization's strategic goals and objectives. A corporate university can be "a centralized strategic umbrella for the education and development of employees." It can also be the "chief vehicle for disseminating an organization's culture and fostering the development of not only job skills, but also such core workplace skills as learning-to-learn, leadership, creative thinking, and problem solving."[3]

How Corporate Universities Differ from Training Departments

Corporate universities differ from training and development departments in their alignment with business strategy. One way to look at the difference is that training and development functions are "short-term, tactical, and narrowly focused," whereas corporate universities are "broader and more strategic."[4] A simple connection is not sufficient; virtually any course can be shown to have some connection to business objectives or strategy. To truly function as a corporate university, the following needs to occur: there must be "a major, direct connection to the business goals"; there must be "CEO-level awareness and support, if not direct involvement"; and courses must focus on more than building or improving professional skills of employees.[5]

What Should Corporate Universities Teach?

Conceptually, corporate universities should strive to have one of the following primary strategic focuses for their programs and curriculum:
• Initiative driven: focus on "*driving a corporate-wide initiative* or business plan or project."
• Change-management focused: focus on driving change or facilitating a transformation. process
• Leadership development driven: focus on developing managers and/or leaders.
• Business development driven: focus on developing business opportunities or exploring new possibilities.
• Customer/supplier relationship management orientation: focus on educating and managing the customer and supplier relationship.
• Competency-based/career development focused: focus on individual skill development and managing the career development process.[6]
A combination of any of these would be acceptable. Each of these strategic focuses, however, derives from the requirement that corporate universities have strong links to specific business strategies and goals.

Corporate University Structure

Physically, corporate universities come in many forms. When people hear the term corporate university, many think of "Hamburger U." With a dedicated building and dedicated staff, McDonald's Corporation's Hamburger University in Oak Brook, Illinois, is one of the world's best known corporate universities, providing training to more than 5,000 "students" a year.[7] For organizations without dedicated buildings, however, training occurs in a variety of ways: in a traditional classroom format, either on- or off-site; via satellite, bringing employees together from different locations simultaneously; as Web-based offerings, which allow for customization as well as performance measurement; and through virtual reality, where actual job duties can be mimicked virtually.[8]

Corporations, through their corporate universities, also partner with traditional educational institutions as a means of providing learning opportunities and training programs to their employees. For example, UnitedHealth Group and United Technologies partnered to offered MBA classes through Stanford University. UnitedHealth Group also partnered with Rensselaer Polytechnic Institute and other employers to deliver programs to employees through UnitedHealth's Learning Institute.[9]

Although the traditional definition of "university" pertains to degree-granting educational institutions, in recent years, the American Council of Education has begun to recognize, and grant credit for, some coursework and programs affiliated with corporate universities. At Hamburger U, for example, students in the restaurant manager and mid-management curriculum can earn credits toward a college degree through their course work. These credits are eligible to be transferred to other colleges and universities and applied toward a degree.

In another direction, many corporate universities are opening their doors to nonemployees—and charging tuition—as a tool for building relationships and enhancing effectiveness as well as a means of teaching their own strategies for success. Disney, for example, offers three-day professional development programs for nonemployee executives to help these executives "learn how to make magic in their own industries."[10]

The Future of Corporate Universities

Globalization, flattening of organizations, demographic shifts and loss of talent, technology, and other global business trends will continue to affect the way in which organizations must prepare their employees to remain competitive, the content of learning efforts, and the way in which knowledge and information are delivered. Increasingly, the purpose of corporate universities is shifting from being "a place to go," with structured program delivery occurring at a designated central location, to dynamic, "on-demand," and "constantly changing" operations that "come to you."[11]

Resources:
http://www.corpu.com/

NOTES

1. "Corporate Universities: First Lessons from a European Learning Group," *Journal of European Industrial Training* (2000): 50.

2. Global Learning Resources, Inc., "Corporate Universities Overview," http://www.glresources.com/ls_cu.php (accessed October 12, 2007).

3. Jeanne Meister, "Ten Steps to Creating a Corporate University," *Training and Development* (1998): 38.

4. Global Learning Resources, Inc., "Corporate Universities Overview."

5. Ibid.

6. Kevin Wheeler, "The Uses and Misuses of the Term Corporate University," (Global Learning Resources, Inc., 2003). http://www.glresources.com/dl_docs./uses_of_term_corp_univ.pdf (accessed October 12, 2007).

7. Hamburger University, McDonald's Web site, http://www.mcdonalds.com/corp/career/hamburger_university.html (accessed October 15, 2007).

8. Denise R. Hearn, "Education in the Workplace: An Examination of Corporate University Models," http://www.newfoundations.com/OrgTheory/Hearn721.html (accessed October 12, 2007)

9. Meryl Davids Landau, "Corporate Universities Crack Open Their Doors," *Journal of Business Strategy* (May–June 2000): 18.

10. Ibid.

11. Josh Bersin, "Death of Corporate University: Birth of Learning Services," Bersin & Associates, http://www.bersin.com/tips_techniques/05_nov_death_cu.asp (accessed October 13, 2007).

Lynda Kemp

CROSS-TRAINING

Today, organizations are always trying to accomplish more work with fewer workers. Therefore, one technique that helps to motivate and retain employees is known as cross-training. Cross-training, however, requires managers and HR professionals to replace their traditional idea of *one job per person* with a broader definition.[1]

Cross-training involves teaching an employee who was hired to perform one job function the skills required to perform other job functions.[2] It requires teaching employees the skills and responsibilities of another position in an organization to increase their effectiveness.[3] Cross-training is training someone in another activity that is related to his current work. The name comes from the fact that training is across a broader spectrum of the organization's work.[4] Cross-trained employees might focus their efforts on one process or could set up a systematic job-rotation plan and train workers to become proficient in a variety of functions.[5]

For some organizations with limited human resource capacity, cross-training enables operations to continue if a key employee requires a leave of absence. Such absence could produce disastrous consequences unless someone else is trained to conduct operations smoothly during an extended absence.[6] A temporary employee may not be the best solution if the job requires technical skill or an in-depth knowledge of the operations.[7]

Employees are a valuable asset; but since some organizations cannot afford to hire the appropriate number of employees, cross-training makes it easier to maximize employees' skills and talents in order to remain competitive. Investing in employees' is a critical strategy for retaining key employees, and in turn, employees are willing to learn new skills. Thus, employees will be more productive and loyal, and overall morale will improve.[8] Cross-training reveals that an organization has confidence in employees' skills and abilities. Consequently, firms are willing to provide workers with opportunities for career growth.

Benefits of Cross-training

Cross-training offers a number of benefits for organizations. As such, a well-designed cross-training program can help reduce costs, reduce turnover, increase productivity, and improve employee morale. Further, it provides greater scheduling flexibility, which could improve organizational efficiency and effectiveness and can provide greater job satisfaction among employees. Cross-trained employees usually feel that their jobs have been enriched, and they often suggest creative and cost-effective improvements that can lead to productivity gains that help firms stay competitive.[9] Cross-training also provides the following benefits:

- Prevents stagnation.
- Offers a learning and professional development opportunity.

- Rejuvenates all departments.
- Improves understanding of the different departments and the organization as a whole.
- Leads to better coordination and teamwork.
- Erases differences, enmity, and unhealthy competition.
- Increases knowledge, know-how, skills, and work performance.
- Improves overall motivation.
- Leads to the sharing of organizational goals and objectives.
- Helps patrons/customers/clients because employees are empowered to answer questions about the entire organization.
- Requires staff to reevaluate the reasons and methods for accomplishing their work; therefore, inefficient methods, outdated techniques, and bureaucratic drift are challenged, if not eliminated.
- Raises an awareness of what other departments do.
- Enhances routine scheduling with the ability to move employees throughout the organization.
- Increases coverage, flexibility, and ability to cope with unexpected absences, emergencies, illness, etc.
- Increases the "employability" of employees who have the opportunity to train in areas they were not originally hired for.[10]

Pitfalls of Cross-training

Cross-training can create a condition in which employees focus too much on acquiring new skills instead of becoming expert in their current position. It is also difficult to find new challenges once employees have *mastered* all cross-training opportunities, and can lead to high turnover of more experienced and seasoned employees due to the marketability of their skills.[11] Another disadvantage is trying to establish a program without taking a systematic approach.[12] Other potential pitfalls of cross-training include:

- Failing to include employees in planning the program.
- Trying to coerce the participation of reluctant employees.
- Failing to recognize the value of new skills with appropriate changes in compensation.
- Assuming that employees are familiar with the techniques needed to train others.
- Penalizing employees who take part in cross-training by not reducing their workload accordingly.[13]

Success Criteria

Gaining the full support of top management is one of the most important factors in the success of any cross-training initiative. Next, it is extremely important to communicate to employees that cross-training is not a management conspiracy designed to eliminate jobs, but that it is a benefit to all employees as well as the organization.[14] It is also important to involve employees who are already performing the job in the training process, which will allow experienced employees to share their thoughts and ideas on how to properly train others, and will help prevent them from feeling like their job may be in jeopardy.[15] Thus, the decision to cross-train should be considered carefully because there are many complex and uncertain factors, including:

- Labor dynamics
- Product dynamics

- Task heterogeneity
- Worker heterogeneity[16]

Effective cross-training programs are carefully planned and organized. Cross-training should not be implemented due to a sudden shortage of qualified employees. Cross-training, as in other forms of strategic intervention within organizations, should be planned and coordinated with clear outcomes in mind. Therefore, it is important to decide who will be eligible for training and if the training will be restricted within job classifications or open to other classifications. Managers and HR professionals will also need to determine whether cross-training will be administered internally or externally, and whether the training will be mandatory or voluntary. Some organizations have developed a task force consisting of both management and employees to identify the advantages and disadvantages of cross-training, determine the feasibility of setting up a program, identify the implementation issues, and establish a realistic schedule for each position.[17]

Employees must be made to feel that their efforts are being recognized for a cross-training program to be successful. Therefore, organizations need to address compensation issues before cross-training programs are implemented; thus, organizations must be willing to compensate employees for increasing their skills by instituting pay-for-skill or pay-for-knowledge programs.[18] Organizations also need to be willing to promote employees who learn new skills. Finally, cross-trained employees must be given the time they need to absorb new information. Accordingly, their workload should be reduced during the training so that they will not feel as if they are being penalized for participating in the program.

NOTES

1. Brian Gill, "Cross-Training Can Be a Win-Win Plan," *American Printer* (October 1997).

2. Lynda Rogerson, "Cover Your Bases," *Small Business Reports* (July 1993).

3. http://www.entrepreneur.com/encyclopedia/term/82142.html.

4. http://management.about.com/cs/peoplemanagement/g/crosstraining.htm.

5. Rogerson, "Cover Your Bases."

6. Thomas Love, "Keeping the Business Going When an Executive Is Absent," *Nation's Business* (March 1998).

7. Ibid.

8. Gill, "Cross-Training Can Be a Win-Win Plan."

9. Rogerson, "Cover Your Bases."

10. http://www.easytraining.com/crosstrain.htm.

11. http://www.industrialrelationscentre.com/employee-development/publications/current-issues-series/cis-cross-training-at-peace-river-pulp-a-case-study.pdf.

12. Rogerson, "Cover Your Bases."

13. Ibid.

14. Gill, "Cross-Training Can Be a Win-Win Plan."

15. Ibid.

16. http://www.allbusiness.com/human-resources/careers-career-development/585607-1.html.

17. Gill, "Cross-Training Can Be a Win-Win Plan."

18. Jerry W. Gilley and Ann Maycunich, *Beyond the Learning Organization: Creating a Culture of Continuous Growth and Development through State-of-the-Art Human Resource Practices* (Cambridge, MA: Perseus Books, 2000), 62.

Paul Shelton and Jerry W. Gilley

DELEGATION

Delegation is a primary responsibility of managers who are familiar with the organization and have the authority to redistribute job tasks, responsibility, and authority. Delegation requires trust in one's employees, confidence in their abilities, and an understanding of performance improvement's impact on an organization.

Delegation can be defined as appointing someone to operate on your behalf. It is simply assigning an employee a task or responsibility that is otherwise part of someone else's job.[1] Consequently, when managers delegate a work assignment to an employee, they remain accountable for the outcome. In other words, tasks and responsibilities may be delegated, but accountability cannot. Thus, accountability rests with the individual who was originally assigned the task or responsibility—typically the manager. Therefore, it is important to have an open, honest discussion about the accountability relationship that occurs as a result of the delegation. In this way, an employee knows exactly what she is accountable for, and to whom.

The following guidelines improve delegation activities:

1. *Decide what to delegate*—choose a job/task that is realistic yet challenging.
2. *Plan the delegation*—review all essential details and decisions, determine appropriate feedback controls, provide for training and coaching, and establish performance standards.
3. *Select the right person*—consider the employee's interests, skills, abilities, qualifications to complete the assignment, and what support or training is needed.
4. *Delegate effectively*—clarify the results expected and priorities involved, specify level of authority granted, identify importance of the assignment, feedback, and reporting requirements.
5. *Follow up*—insist on results but not perfection, demand timely performance reports, encourage independence, do not short-circuit or take back the assignment, and reward good performance.[2]

The delegation cycle begins by identifying tasks and responsibilities to be delegated. This often requires that the manager analyze jobs, determine which tasks are most appropriate for delegation, and clarify the expected results. Once identified, managers should meet with their employees to explain the work assignment rationale and allow workers to ask questions or share opinions.

Next, identify the level of authority being granted to an employee. In other words, this answers the question, "What authority can the employee exercise to accomplish the task at hand?" The authority granted in a delegation depends upon the employee's experience and the manager's confidence in the employee's skills and abilities. Confidence refers to the extent to which you trust the employee's abilities based upon the employee's performance history. Thus, the combination of confidence and experience determines the level of authority to grant.

A model illustrating this relationship places experience on a horizontal axis from limited-extensive and confidence on a vertical axis from low-moderate-high. The working model demonstrates five levels of authority placed according to ones level of experience (1–9) and the confidence others have in his/her abilities (1–9). The levels of authority are represented by:

1. Rookie (1,1)—limited experience, low confidence
2. Worker bee (5,5)—moderate experience, moderate confidence

3. New member (9,1)—extensive experience, low confidence
4. Rising star (1,9)—limited experience, high confidence
5. Partner (9,9)—extensive experience, high confidence[3]

When delegating tasks and responsibilities, it is important to identify the appropriate level of authority. Employee experience and your confidence in his or her skills and abilities determine which level of authority is granted. For example:

- **Rookie (1,1)**—At this level of authority, experience is limited and confidence is low. The employee gets the facts (e.g. gathers data, prepares data requests), although the coach decides what further actions are necessary. As the individual successfully completes assignments, the coach's confidence rises.
- **Worker Bee (5,5)**—Experience and confidence are both moderate. The employee decides the actions to be taken while the coach maintains veto power. This limits the employee's freedom until he has gained even more experience and the performance coach's confidence rises higher. Performance feedback and monitoring activities are still very important at this stage.
- **New Member (9,1)**—This employee's experience is extensive, although he has little or no firsthand knowledge of the employee and thus has little confidence. Therefore, allow the employee to handle the task while closely monitoring performance. Feedback is not as critical here because the individual has performed successfully in the past. Monitoring future performance is the best way of increasing one's confidence in the employee's skills and abilities.
- **Rising Star (1,9)**—At this level, experience is limited, although one has complete confidence in the "potential abilities" of the employee. Under this circumstance, work closely with the employee by training him, assigning tasks to be completed, and providing positive and constructive feedback about performance. Serving as a career advisor (for the performance coaching and management process role, see Chapter 3) is most appropriate when working with this type of employee.
- **Partner (9,9)**—At this point, experience is extensive and confidence is high. The employee is free to act and simply report results. Here the employee is operating on the manager's behalf, at the highest level of authority.[4]

A few moments should be spent with the employee discussing possible performance barriers once the most appropriate level of authority has been identified, Such a conversation gives an employee an opportunity to discuss more thoroughly the exact performance outputs expected.

NOTES

1. Jerry W. Gilley, Nathaniel W. Boughton, and Ann Maycunich, *The Performance Challenge: Developing Management Systems to Make Employees Your Organization's Greatest Asset* (Cambridge, MA: Perseus Books, 1999).

2. Jerry W. Gilley and Ann Gilley, *The Manager as Coach* (Westport, CT: Praeger, 2007).

3. Gilley, Boughton, and Maycunich, *The Performance Challenge.*

4. Gilley and Gilley, *The Manager as Coach.*

Jerry W. Gilley

EMOTIONAL INTELLIGENCE

The general construct of emotional intelligence (EI) is becoming widely known, appearing in popular books, journal articles, and magazines.[1,2] EI can best be explained as "people smarts," as opposed to "book smarts." EI is just one of the many elements that make each employee unique. With the popularity of EI, there has been a rush of competing models. To date, the majority of research has examined three competing models of EI. It is instrumental to understand the three models before making managerial decisions regarding EI.

Models of Emotional Intelligence

Ability-based Models

Emotional intelligence is defined as the "ability to monitor one's own and others' feeling and emotions, to discriminate among them, and to use this information to guide one's thinking and actions."[3] The model considers perceiving and regulating emotion, as well as thinking about feelings.[4] The ability model of EI consists of four branches, including perceiving, using, understanding, and managing of emotion. There is currently only one measure of EI ability. The Mayer Salovey Caruso Emotional Intelligence Test (MSCEIT) has 141 items and takes approximately 40 minutes to complete. The ability measure asks the participant to correctly answer questions. The measure produces four branch scores and an overall EI score. The ability model is theoretically distinct from traditional models of intelligence (e.g., verbal and quantitative) and provides essential information currently omitted from cognitive ability assessments.[5]

Mixed Models

The mixed model approach defines EI as effectively understanding oneself and others, relating well to people, and adapting to and coping with immediate surroundings to be more successful in dealing with environmental demands.[6] Mixed models overlap with dozens of other concepts because of their breadth of coverage, including such characteristics as motivation, personality, and psychological well-being. There are several mixed model self-report EI measures available today including the Emotion Quotient Inventory (EQ-i) and the Wong Law Emotional Intelligence Scale (WLEIS). These measures are relatively brief and easy to administer. Ability model researchers suggest that mixed models decrease the degree to which the components independently contribute to a person's behavior and general life competence because they include several nonability-based characteristics.[7] In general, mixed models assess so many different elements not related to cognitive intelligence that the results cannot be summative of EI.

Trait Models

Trait EI is defined as a grouping of emotion-related dispositions located at the roots of personality hierarchies[8] and as within employee consistency and between employee uniqueness in the capacity and willingness to perceive, understand, regulate, and express emotion in the self and others.[9] Trait models of EI "capture motivational aspects through personality components, which capture the 'can do' of EI, whereas personality captures the intrinsic 'will do.'"[10] EI as a personality domain is significantly related to several important life outcomes such as job satisfaction and turnover.[11] There are many measures of self-report trait EI, such as the Multitrait Emotional Intelligence Assessment (MEIA), the Schutte Self-Report Emotional Intelligence Test (SSEIT)[12] and the Trait Emotional Intelligence Questionnaire (TEIQue). Scores on measures of trait EI, including the MEIA and the TEIQue, are unrelated to nonverbal reasoning, which supports the view of EI as a part of personality rather than intelligence. Measures of trait EI should not be summed to produce an overall score. An overall measure of EI limits the role of EI in predicting variables. Trait models are best used in combination with ability models and do not illustrate EI ability while measured alone.

The three models presented have received considerable attention over the last 10 years. Models of EI are developing more salient definitions and measures, but to date, no model has been selected as the most predictive or reliable. It is best to use a combination of measures from different models to gain an accurate view of EI.[13]

What Does Emotional Intelligence Predict?

Several unjustified claims have been introduced to management concerning the predictability of EI. Researchers are conducting validation studies to test many of these claims. The results are promising, but not to the degree first suggested. Managers today can use EI as a predictor of leadership, job satisfaction, contextual behaviors, and performance.

The role of the leader in the organization is instrumental to success. Leaders continually interact with subordinates throughout daily tasks. Interpersonal interactions that involve emotional awareness and management have increased the quality of exchange.[14] Leaders that effectively read their subordinates' emotions and moods are better equipped to assign the most appropriate task at that time. Research illustrates that the EI of leaders is significantly related to the job satisfaction and contextual behaviors of their followers.[15]

Job satisfaction is the complex emotional reaction to the job. Employees with higher abilities of EI experience greater amounts of positive emotions, successful coworker interactions, and satisfaction compared to individuals low in EI.[16] People with higher job satisfaction exhibit sustained positive moods and an increase in extra-role behaviors. Thus, employees with high EI are more likely to perform extra-role behaviors because they have increased job satisfaction. Also, they can perceive and understand the emotional needs of their coworkers more than employees who are low in EI.[17]

Increased EI is negatively related to turnover intentions because emotionally intelligent individuals see themselves as a part of the organizational process. Problems and challenges within an organization are seen not as threats to emotionally intelligence employees, but as opportunities.[18] Opportunities create a niche for the emotionally intelligent employee because they are able to take advantage of the situation and increase positive emotions. Emotionally intelligent employees are more likely to sustain organizational challenges and not leave. Obtaining managers with high EI may positively impact later retention of valued employees.[19]

Employees with high cognitive ability have sustained levels of task performance regardless of EI. However, emotionally intelligent employees with lower cognitive ability have increased task performance compared to emotionally unintelligent employees with low cognitive ability.[20]

Conclusion

Managers have known for a long time that "people" smarts are important to several job relevant outcomes. It is no surprise that academics have now identified a construct that establishes "people" smarts known as EI. Although there is little concrete empirical evidence to illustrate the predictive ability of EI, there is promise. Utilizing EI for employee selection and promotion decisions may be premature, but EI measures should be used to aid decisions including team formation, leadership responsibilities, and task management. However, EI models not rooted in theory or selected for use because of popularity would not consistently or accurately predict outcomes. It is important to critically assess why an EI measure should be used, who created it, and what it predicts.

NOTES

1. John D. Mayer, Peter Salovey, and David Caruso, "Models of Emotional Intelligence," in *The Handbook of Intelligence,* ed. R.J. Sternberg (New York: Cambridge University Press, 2000), 396–420.

2. Daniel Goleman, *Emotional Intelligence* (New York: Bantam Books, 1995).

3. Peter Salovey and John D. Mayer, "Emotional Intelligence," *Imagination, Cognition, and Personality* (1990): 185–211.

4. John D. Mayer and Peter Salovey, "What Is Emotional Intelligence" in Peter Salovey and D. Sluyter (Ed), *Emotional Development and Emotional Intelligence: Implications for Educators* (New York: Basic Books Inc., 1997), 3–31.

5. Mayer, Salovey, and Caruso, "Models of Emotional Intelligence," 396–420.

6. Ibid.

7. Ibid.

8. K.V. Petrides and Adrian Furnham, "Trait Emotional Intelligence: Psychometric Investigation with References to Established Trait Taxonomies," *European Journal of Personality* 15 (2001): 4235–4448.

9. R.P. Tett, K.E. Fox, and A. Wang, "Development and Validation of a Self-report Measure of Emotional Intelligence as a Multidimensional Trait Domain," *PSPB* (2005): 859–88.

10. Ibid.

11. A. Furnham, and K.V. Petrides, "Trait Emotional Intelligence and Happiness," *Social Behavioral and Personality* (2003): 815–24.

12. Nicola S. Schutte, John M. Malouff, Lena E. Hall, Donald J. Haggeryy, Joan T. Cooper, Charles J. Golden, and Liane Dornheim, "Development and Validation of a Measure of Emotional Intelligence," *Personality and Individual Differences* (1998): 167–77.

13. Tett, Fox, and Wang, "Development and Validation of a Self-report Measure of Emotional Intelligence."

14. Chi-Sum Wong and Kenneth S. Law, "The Effects of Leader and Follower Emotional Intelligence on Performance and Attitude: An Exploratory Study," *Leadership Quarterly* (2002): 243–74.

15. Ibid.

16. Petrides and Furnham, 2001.

17. Abraham Carmeli, "The Relationship between Emotional Intelligence and Work Attitudes, Behaviors and Outcomes," *Journal of Managerial Psychology* (2003): 788–813.

18. Ibid.

19. Ibid., 403–19.

20. S. Cote and M. Miners, "Emotional Intelligence, Cognitive Intelligence, and Job Performance," *Administrative Science Quarterly* (2006): 1–28.

Dana M. Borchert

GOAL SETTING

Goal setting is the formal process by which employees establish their goals or objectives for a given performance period. Goals include: (1) the actions the employee is going to take,

(2) the outcome or targets the employee expects to achieve, and (3) the metrics that will allow the employee to measure his or her success (e.g., time, cost, quantity, quality, etc.).

Employees generally establish both performance goals and development goals. Performance goals identify the job functions employees are expected to perform to meet their job requirements. Development goals are designed to document what actions employees can take to assist them in improving their performance and in growing their skills and capabilities.

Setting Performance Goals

Goal setting is the first step in the performance process, during which the employee will establish his individual goals. This generally occurs annually, semiannually, or quarterly depending on the frequency of the performance cycle. During the performance planning process, the employee and her manager work together to identify potential performance and development goals for the employee to ensure that they are properly selected, aligned to the business strategy and goals, and clearly documented so that the employee and manager will know that success has been met.

Step 1: Identify the Goals. Identify, prioritize, and select the goals, ensuring that they align to and support the overall goals of the business. This step should begin with a review of the corporate goals and how they filter down to the individual employee-owner. The cascading process ensures that the employee understands the company's goals and that his individual goals align to and support the higher-level goals of the business. A manager should review the cascaded goals with the employee at the corporate, functional, and team levels to help the employee understand how the work she does every day supports the business.

Step 2: Document the Goals. Once company goals have been cascaded, the manager and the employee will work together to document the employee's individual performance goals for the year, so the employee knows specifically what is expected of him. Document the goals by creating a detailed, written description of each goal using the SMART acronym:

S = Specific: clear, unambiguous, straightforward, and understandable
M = Measurable: quantity, quality, time, money
A = Achievable: challenging but within the reach of a competent and committed person.
R = Relevant: relevant to the objectives of the organization so that the goal of the individual is aligned to the corporate goals.
T = Time bound—to be completed within an agreed time scale.[1]

Step 3: Plan. Create a plan for how the employee will achieve the goals.
• Identify the key projects or tasks that will help the employee achieve each of her goals.
• Determine which projects or tasks need to be completed sequentially/simultaneously and plan accordingly.
• For each project or task, describe measurable results or outcomes.
• Determine what resources (money, people, time, etc.) are needed to carry out each project or task.
• Establish a time frame for the completion of each project or task (include a start or finish date).
• Set up milestones along the way to review project completion and overall impact.
• Consider the potential obstacles that might confront each goal and its associated projects. Then, map out possible solutions for each obstacle.[2]

Step 4: Perform. Once the employee has documented goals it is time to deliver on them. Throughout the performance period, the employee should work according to the established performance plan, documenting achievements and completed milestones, tasks, and projects. The employee should keep the manager as well as other stakeholders informed of his progress.[3]

Step 5: Evaluate. Throughout the performance cycle, the employee and manager should meet to assess the employee's performance against the performance goals to ensure that she is on track and to gauge whether existing goals are still realistic, timely, and relevant.[4]

Setting Developmental Goals

Employee development goals are created as a part of the development planning process, which is a planned effort to grow the employee's professional capabilities so that the employee and the company become even more successful together. Development planning is a forward-focused conversation about how the employee can be successful in her current job, while simultaneously building capabilities for the future.

Employee development goals should be created using a similar process as performance goals. The employee and manager should work together to identify the employee's performance or skill gaps for his current position as well as for the employee's desired future position or career. The employee and manager should agree on the developmental priorities and set SMART development goals in order to enable the employee to improve or enhance her skills and abilities. The development goals should be tracked and evaluated in a similar fashion as performance goals to ensure that the employee is achieving his development goals.

NOTES

1. Michael Armstrong, *Performance Management: Key Strategies and Practical Guidelines* (London: Kogan Page, 2006).

2. Penny Locey and Linda A. Hill, *Harvard Business Online: Harvard Manage Mentor* (Cambridge, MA: Harvard Business School Press, 2001), http://ww3.harvardbusiness.org/corporate/Products-and-Services\reference\product-Harvard-managementor-overview.htm. Accessed October 2, 2001.

3. Ibid.

4. Ibid.

Stephanee Roessing

HUMAN RESOURCE DEVELOPMENT

The term "human resource development" (HRD) provides us with clues as to its meaning. Clearly, it is related to the development of people, but calling people "human resources" reveals an organizational orientation just as "financial resources" and "physical resources" do. Thus, HRD is about the development of people *within* organizations. Therefore, to properly define HRD, let us examine the terms "human resources" and "development" more closely.

All organizations consist of three types of resources:

• Physical resources are machines, materials, facilities, equipment, and component parts of products, which are often referred to as fixed assets.

- Financial resources refer to the liquid assets of an organization. They are the cash, stock, bonds, investments, and operating capital.
- Human resources refer to the people employed by an organization.[1]

There are several ways in which HR professionals and managers can determine the importance of human resources. First, HR professionals and managers consider the cost of replacing valuable employees. Such costs include recruiting, hiring, relocating, lost productivity, training, and orientation. Another consideration is the knowledge, competencies, skills, and attitudes of the human resources. HR professionals and managers need to place a value on these intangibles. Quite simply, a well-trained, highly skilled, and knowledgeable employee is more valuable to an organization than one who is not. This value is ultimately reflected in increased productivity, enhanced attitudes toward work and the organization, and efficiency. While organizations are aware of the value of human resources, they often fail to consider them in their asset portfolio. As a result, many do not realize that improved knowledge, competencies, skills, and attitudes are necessary to improve the overall efficiency and effectiveness of the organization. Consequently, they do not recognize the importance of HRD functions, nor value its contribution to organizational success.

What Is Development?

The term "development" requires addressing two questions:

1. What is meant by the development of employees?
2. What type of development really occurs within an institution?[2]

Development of human resources refers to the personal and professional advancement of knowledge, skills, and competencies. It also includes improved behavior of individuals within the organization, which reflects a focus on the individual and a philosophical commitment to the professional advancement of human resources within the organization. Continuous employee development benefits the organization through greater efficiency and more effective practices. Ultimately, development refers to the continuous improvement of an organization's culture through interventions that crystallize the firm's mission, strategy, structure, policies and procedures, work climate, and leadership practices.

Purpose and Mission of HRD

The purpose of HRD is to bring about the changes that cause the organizational and performance improvements necessary to enhance the organization. In short, HRD's function is used to *make a difference* in the way an organization and its employees operate. In other words, learning activities, career development systems, performance interventions, and change initiatives bring about improved on-the-job performance, reducing costs, improving quality, and increasing the competitiveness of the organization.[3]

Human resource development occurs when employees participate in activities (formal and informal) designed to introduce new knowledge and skills to improve performance behaviors. Unfortunately, on-the-job training is a hit-or-miss approach that sometimes results in inadequate or inappropriate knowledge, skills, and behaviors. Therefore, HRD refers to the introduction of organized learning, performance, and change activities designed to increase knowledge, skills, and competencies, and improve behavior.[4]

The mission of HRD is to provide individual development focused on performance improvement related to a current job and to provide career development focused on performance improvement related to future job assignments. The mission of HRD also is to develop performance management systems used to enhance organizational performance capacity and capability, and provide organizational development that results in both optimal utilization of human potential and improved human performance. Together, these enhance the culture of an organization, hence its effectiveness as measured by increased competitive readiness, profitability, and renewal capacity.[5]

Roles in HRD

These are the roles in HRD: managers/leaders, learning agents, instructional designers, performance engineers, and HRD consultants (performance and change agents).[6]

- Manager of an HRD function includes managing the organizational learning and performance management systems, planning, organizing, staffing, controlling, and coordinating of the HRD function, and providing strategic leadership.
- Learning agents (instructors) are responsible for identifying learning needs and developing appropriate activities and programs to address those needs, presenting the information that is associated with learning programs and training activities, and evaluating the effectiveness of the programs and activities.
- Instructional designers design, develop, and evaluate the learning activities. They are often the organization's media specialist, instructional writer, task analyst, and evaluator.
- Performance engineers conduct performance, causal, and root-cause analysis to determine current and desired performance.
- HRD consultants range from technical experts to facilitators who solve problems to bring about change.

These roles are used to execute the mission and purpose of the HRD function.

HRD Practice

Five fundamental areas of practice have emerged as essential in order to execute each of the four missions of HRD:

- Analysis—the identification of individual, business, performance and organizational needs through a variety of analysis activities.
- Instructional design—the design, development, and evaluation of learning activities and career development programs.
- Learning acquisition—the delivery and facilitation of instruction designed to improve employees' knowledge, skills, and abilities.
- Learning transfer—the activities required to make certain that learning and change are applied to the job.
- Evaluation—the examination of the changes in behavior and impact or learning, performance, and change interventions and initiatives.[7]

NOTES

1. Jerry W. Gilley, Steven A. Eggland, and Ann Maycunich Gilley, *Principles of Human Resource Development,* 2nd ed. (Cambridge, MA: Perseus 2002).

2. Ibid.

3. Ibid.

4. Ibid.
5. Ibid.
6. Ibid.
7. Ibid.

Jerry W. Gilley and Ann Gilley

INTERACTIVE VIDEO TRAINING (IVT)

Interactive video training (IVT) utilizes different technological mediums to blend interaction and video into a user-controlled episode.[1] IVTs are used in various training situations and can be a very important tool for the human resource manager (HRM). IVTs can be viewed in a hardcopy or online format. With an increase in broadband Internet speeds, many HRMs provide online training that can be viewed from work or home. The online format can also provide a necessary option for the employee who works remotely or travels often.

Principal Forms of Interactive Video

There are three different forms of interactive video training that can provide diverse experiences for the user. The first form is called customizable. Customizable IVTs allow the employee to modify options that play the video using the user's selections. The predefined options allow the user only to create a special performance of the video, not interact with the video when it is streaming. An example of a customizable video might be one that allows the employee to choose between different HR informational videos. An important option may allow a handicapped employee the ability to change font size or colors that assist with viewing of the video.

The second form is called conversational. Conversational IVTs allow the employee to interact with the video as if they were a part of the video. This form may allow the user to watch a video pertinent to a situation and then make a decision based on the facts presented in the video. A human resource example might be a video that attempts to train employees in a specific task like cardiopulmonary resuscitation (CPR).

The final form of IVT is called exploratory. Exploratory IVTs provide the employee with a fully interactive environment in which they may move through virtual surroundings or view any object in this environment. The object might be utilized by the video to provide suitable information to the user as they attempt to make decisions and interact with the virtual world.

Challenges of Using IVT

A current employee resource base may include individuals who do not have many technological skills. The younger generation is growing up learning how to use technology to communicate and learn, but the older generation has not had that preparation. This might create an uncomfortable situation for employees in that they might not interact correctly with a video, or it may prevent them from using this form of training tool. The HRM will have to assess this inability and either provide an alternate method or additional training as required.

Another challenge may be acquiring the needed technology to provide IVT within the company. Human resource budgets may prevent the HRM from purchasing either the videos or the equipment required to play the IVTs. Many IVTs can be a simple digital video disc (DVD) or video cassette that do not require a lot of high-priced equipment. But most of the time, exploratory or conversational IVTs that are used require a substantial amount of equipment to operate.

IVT can also introduce problems when dealing with handicapped employees. The nature of the IVT environment can prevent these employees from viewing, hearing, or even interacting with the IVT medium.[2]

Create, Manage, and Deploy IVT

Many companies provide an application to create, manage, and deploy one's own IVT. These applications can provide the HRM with a powerful tool that customizes a company's own IVT series. An example might be within a company that employs pilots or police officers. The HRM might develop an IVT that challenges the employee with different video segments of life-and-death situations that will cause the video to branch based on their decisions.[3] Many companies have governmental or corporate standards that need to be met, and customized IVT series might provide the assessment tool needed to comply with these standards.

Another option might be to purchase packages that provide specific training videos with special or limited customizable options. The HRM does not have to know how to create the video, as the package will provide a particular video with limited customized options that are set by the HRM before delivering the IVT to their employees.

NOTES

1. Kenneth C. Laudon and Jane P. Laudon, *Management Information Systems: Managing the Digital Firm* (Upper Saddle River, NJ: Prentice Hall, 2004).

2. Lucie Zundans and Natasha Wright, "Can Big Brother Watch? The Challenges of Interactive Video Teaching," paper prepared for the Australian Association for Research in Education Annual Conference Auckland, December 2002.

3. Thomas J. Donahue and Mary Ann Donahue, "Understanding Interactive Video," *Training and Development Journal,* December 1983.

Lori Nicholson

JOB SHARING

Job sharing involves two individuals who are responsible for the duties and responsibilities of one position within an organization.[1] This type of flexible work arrangement enables the pair to work a reduced number of hours during the week; and at the same time, it provides the organization with full-time coverage for that position. Job sharing is one of a variety of flextime options proliferating in the U.S. workforce today. Even though utilization of this flexible work arrangement is increasing, job sharing is viewed as the most challenging of all flexible work arrangements.[2] However, when implemented and maintained well, it has proven to be a beneficial option for both the employee and his respective organization.

This entry briefly explores the challenges involved in successful utilization of a job-sharing partnership. In addition, it will outline the benefits derived by the individuals and the organizations that utilize job sharing as a flexible work arrangement. Further, critical success factors that ensure successful partnerships will be discussed, and the implications for human resources departments as well as managers will be described.

Challenges

It has been suggested that job sharing is "the most complicated and problematic" of the flexible work arrangements.[3] It is seen as a challenging arrangement because of the complexity involved in terms of coordinating tasks in a transparent and seamless manner; gaining acceptance from internal stakeholders; sharing information; and relaying consistent messages (versus mixed) to coworkers, management, and clients. Overcoming these challenges requires that attention be paid to specific critical success factors necessary for successful implementation and maintenance of the job-sharing partnership.

Critical Success Factors

Several interdependent factors support the successful utilization of job-sharing partnerships. The factors viewed as most important include formal policies; managerial support and promotion; access to information and communication technology; planning; communication; and compatibility between the job-share pair.

Policies, Support, and Promotion

Support mechanisms such as clearly written policies outlining the criteria and procedures for a job-sharing partnership are critical. A commitment and endorsement by senior leadership is also important. Examples include communications promoting the use of job-share partnerships, such as articles describing success stories in the company newsletter; or job-share opportunities posted on an internal bulletin board, which also ensures equal access for all employees.

Technology

Information and communication technology (ICT) is a critical enabler to the coordination and transference of work between the job-share pair on a day-to-day basis.[4] ICT applications include Web portals, e-mail, and voice mail. Also, electronic documents (e.g., Microsoft Word) that are saved on a server or database are used to maintain daily logs that are written by and shared between partners.

The individuals within the partnership must execute tasks in a transparent and seamless manner. In order to accomplish this, utilization of technology is imperative. Further, the pair must devise and implement a well-thought-out work plan and integrate strategies for communication between the pair and with internal stakeholders, and the pair must be compatible.

Planning

Planning pertains to how the pair will accomplish their shared work. Coordinating work and sharing duties can be organized temporally or functionally.[5] If organizing the work by dividing time, the pair may work different part-time schedules each week, or alternate the number of hours worked on a monthly basis. Duties organized functionally consist of the pair taking responsibility for separate tasks. Regardless of how a work plan is executed, work coordination requires a high proficiency in communication skills and access to a variety of communication tools.

Communication

There are three primary aspects to communication that enable success in a job-share partnership: (1) information sharing between partners, (2) communication with organizational stakeholders (e.g., coworkers, management, and clients), and (3) feedback regarding performance.

Communication must be managed between the partners so that the coordination of work is transparent and seamless. The pair must know when and what kind of information the other partner will need at any given time. Using a web portal, e-mail, voice mail, or daily logs and maintaining copies of correspondence and meeting minutes will facilitate communication. Further, holding regular update meetings via phone, instant messenger, or face to face is essential for coordination of work, and will help to facilitate relationship building.

Communication with coworkers, management, and clients requires that the pair provide consistent information and reduce the potential of variations in the messages. Consistency is achieved by ensuring copious notes are completed in a daily log, information and documents are shared between the pair in a timely manner, gaining access to the partner who is not working (e.g., agreeing it is okay to contact the other in cases in which clarification is needed), and creating "scripts" for messages that are common in the position. For example, the pair may agree on a script to use when a coworker asks a follow-up question to one of the job-share partners from a prior interaction they had with the other partner. If the answer to the question is not known, the script may sound like, "I want to make sure I give you accurate information, so I will research it and call you back within the hour." Scripts lend credibility and consistency to the messages communicated to internal stakeholders.

Performance reviews communicate expectations for performance and outcomes, and describe the degree of success achieved. Reviews can be delivered by the supervisor one-on-one (separately) with individuals, the pair together, or a mixture of both. Even though some performance reviews occur annually, six-month reviews are common with job-sharing partners.

In general, agreement on how communication will be managed is essential to a successful working partnership. Agreement is easier when the pair is flexible, accommodating, and, above all, compatible.

Compatibility

Working in a job-share partnership requires that an individual is not only accountable for his own work, but for the work of his partner. A key factor of being successful in a job share is being in synch with one another, which requires sharing similar values and work styles.[6] Further, resolving conflicts quickly and effectively is necessary. This requires strong relationships built on trust, respect, and compassion. Developing a strong partnership requires hard work, time, and energy. For many job-share pairs, the benefits garnered through a job share partnership outweigh the extra time and energy required to make the partnership successful.

Benefits

Those working in a job-share partnership generally benefit from being able to support the demands of family or other facets of life, and the need or desire to work and grow in a career. Also, there are two primary benefits for organizations; retention, and the ability to leverage the intellectual capital of two, rather than one individual.

Work-life Flexibility

Working in a job-share partnership enables an individual to meet the demands of being a primary caregiver to his family, or demands from other facets of life (e.g., continuing education), and at the same time maintaining a career.[7] Women make up half of the workforce and are still, in many cases, the primary caregiver. In this light, it is easy to see why the majority of job-share partnerships consist of women. Further, older workers, regardless of gender, who are eligible for retirement are choosing to stay in the workforce; however, they are looking for a flexible work schedule that allows for a better balance between work and other facets of life. Job sharing is a flexible work arrangement that enables work-life flexibility.

Retention

While a challenging and successful career is important, many people are choosing to create a balance and give time and energy to other facets of their life. Rather than losing the talent because the design of a job does not allow for that balance, organizations are responding by offering flexible work arrangements, including job sharing. Retention of talent is of great concern to organizations because they require a highly skilled workforce in order to remain competitive in their respective industry. Job sharing is increasingly utilized by businesses as a viable retention strategy, and successful implementation and maintenance of job-share partnerships have demonstrated positive results.[8]

Leveraging Intellectual Capital

Job sharing capitalizes on the notion of intellectual capital, which is a combination of human capital (people) and social capital (interaction of people). From this perspective, knowledge sharing between the job-share pair and others in the organization is a value-added dimension based on the organization's ability to obtain and utilize the combined knowledge and experiences of the job-share pair. Further, the job-share pair will ultimately share knowledge with each other, learning from each other while working together, which further increases their value to the organization. The intellectual capital gained by utilizing job-sharing positions has great potential that can be tapped with the support of the human resources department and the manager of the job-share pair.

Implications for Human Resource Departments

A well-thought-out job-share design begins with examining whether or not the position can be shared, and ensuring there are two individuals with the same qualifications that can share the position. Human resources (HR) can assist with both the job design and the selection processes. Further, HR can provide guidance and tools for the job-share partners and their respective managers. Guidance includes how to build the relationship between the partners, how to organize work, and advising the manager on ways to manage performance and ensure that the intellectual capital garnered from the pair is fully engaged. HR will also work with the legal department to set up agreements, and establish the pay and benefits package.

Implications for Managers

Managers are aware of the benefits of retaining highly qualified employees, yet the mindset that job sharing is a viable option remains limited.[9] Through their dedicated time and effort, managers perform a critical role in ensuring that a job share is successful. Therefore, their buy-in is critical. Managing a job share position involves a higher level of complexity compared to a regular job. There is an increase in the amount of time to monitor the work, at least initially. Further, modifying communication (more e-mail versus face to face), and ensuring performance expectations are being met is required. The way a manager thinks about how work gets done will not necessarily be in line with how an effective job-share partnership works. Therefore, flexibility on the part of the manager and a willingness to change their frame of reference will be important. Finally, promoting the idea and communicating support for the partnership with management and other stakeholders is critical. Similar to the manager, the way other stakeholders think about how work gets done will likely be different from how an effective job-share pair works. Through their communicated support, the manager of the pair will influence how other stakeholders perceive the job share arrangement.

Conclusion

There are many challenges involved in successful utilization of a job-sharing partnership, as well as benefits derived by individuals and their respective organizations, critical success factors, and implications for human resources departments and managers. Job-sharing partnerships are not an easily executed flexible work arrangement, but mounting evidence suggests the extra time and energy involved in ensuring a successful partnership has great benefits for both the individual and the organization.

See also Flextime

NOTES

1. M. Branine, "Job Sharing and Equal Opportunities under the New Public Management in Local Authorities," *International Journal of Public Sector Management* 17, no. 2 (2004): 136–52.

2. C.M. Solomon, "Job Sharing: One Job, Double Headache?" *Personnel Journal* 73, no. 9 (September 1994): 88–94.

3. Ibid, 89.

4. Branine, "Job Sharing and Equal Opportunities."

5. S. Lewis, "Restructuring Workplace Cultures: The Ultimate Work-Family Challenge?" *Women in Management Review* 16, no. 1 (2001): 21–29.

6. Solomon, "Job Sharing: One Job, Double Headache?"

7. D. Pollitt, "Greater Flexibility and Better Work-Life Balance," *Human Resource Management International Digest* 11, no. 2 (2003): 14–16.

8. Ibid.

9. Lewis, "Restructuring Workplace Cultures."

Pamela Dixon

MASLOW'S HIERARCHY OF NEEDS

Abraham Maslow's hierarchy of needs theory has stood the test of time, as it was first formally introduced to business practitioners in 1965.[1] As a seminal theory, it has resonated across several academic disciplines and professional fields, including psychology, sociology, theology/religion, organizational behavior, and HR. It serves as an outstanding foundational construct for designing and operationalizing HR practices in line with fundamental human needs.

Maslow's Hierarchy and HR Practices

According to Maslow's research, universal human needs can be categorized as either *lower order* or *higher order*. The lower-order needs are physiological, safety, and social, while the higher-order needs are esteem and self-actualization. Maslow further argued that two key principles are operative for all human beings relative to the hierarchy. First, the *deficit principle* states that any satisfied need is no longer a felt motivator. Second, the *progression principle* states that once a need is met, human beings are motivated to satisfy the next highest need in the hierarchy. The relative needs can be further understood vis-à-vis various key HR practices/initiatives, as delineated below.

- Physiological—the lowest-order need. The obvious key HR connection point here is to ensure that the wages and benefits afforded to employees are such that their basic needs for food, shelter, and medical care will be adequately met. This underscores the importance of designing compensation systems, including job grades and pay ranges, that are externally and internally consistent and equitable, and in compliance with related compensation laws.
- Safety—the second-level need. The key HR connection point relative to safety needs is to ensure that the workplace in general, and the jobs in particular, are safe for employees. This highlights the need to ensure compliance with EEO-related statutes, as well as OSHA-related requirements. All employees must be protected from physical and emotional harm in the workplace.
- Social—the third-level need. The key connection points for HR are to ensure that employee acculturation is intentional, and employee relations are positive and proactively managed. Social capital is developed when the HR function develops and delivers a thorough new employee orientation program, and ensures that employee conflicts are addressed forthrightly.
- Esteem—the fourth-level need. The key HR connection relative to esteem needs is career planning and development. HR must ensure that all employees are viewed as assets that are worthy of ongoing investment, and allow for the development of individual career development plans for all employees. Related to this is the role of HR in developing and administering extrinsic rewards as recognition of outstanding employee performance.
- Self-actualization—the highest-order need. The key connection point for HR here is to ensure that as many employees as possible can identify with the larger mission of the organization, and how their individual contributions and unique value commitments fit into the larger whole. This involves treating employees as holistic beings and affording them significant autonomy and responsibility in performing their work.

Maslow's Hierarchy and Strategic HR

While all of the needs on Maslow's hierarchy are important for HR practitioners to be mindful of, in developed economies, the higher-order needs of esteem and self-actualization are most pressing. For example, the majority of employees in the United States are no longer motivated by lower-order needs, and hence are desirous of the sort of treatment mandated by a contemporary, strategic view of HR. Accordingly, many organizations in the United States have shifted the focus of their internal HR professionals and resources. These firms have begun to de-emphasize those activities more aligned with the lower-order needs (while still ensuring HR soundness in those areas, often via outsourcing partners focused on employment law compliance, employee wellness, and benefits administration), and instead have increasingly emphasized those HR activities more aligned with the higher-order needs. Arguably, a contemporary and strategic approach to HR mandates that U.S.-based organizations focus their internal HR resources in areas such as staffing, job design, training and development, and organizational mission alignment, in an effort to better meet the esteem and self-actualization needs of their employees.

See also Motivation; Job Satisfaction; HR Strategy

NOTE

1. Abraham H. Maslow, *Eupsychian Management* (Homewood, IL: Richard D. Irwin, 1965).

Scott A. Quatro

MENTORING

Mentoring occurs when one individual chooses or is asked to invest in or educate another individual for either personal needs or organizational performance management. Mentorship refers to a developmental relationship between a more experienced mentor and a less experienced partner, referred to as a mentee or protégé.

There are two types of mentoring relationships: formal and informal. Informal relationships develop on their own between partners. Formal mentoring, on the other hand, refers to assigned relationships, often associated with organizational mentoring programs designed to promote employee development. In well-designed formal mentoring programs, there are program goals, schedules, training (for mentors and mentees), and evaluation. Mentors inspire their mentees to follow their dreams.[1]

History

The word mentor has its origins in Homer's poetic epic, *The Odyssey.* In Homer's story, Odysseus, king of Ithaca, sailed off with his army to do battle in the Trojan War. Before leaving, Odysseus entrusted his faithful friend, Mentor, to care for and educate his son, Telemachus. The war lasted 10 years, and Odysseus's return trip took another decade. Meanwhile, back in Ithaca, noblemen were courting Penelope, the wife of Odysseus, in her husband's absence. Thinking that Odysseus would never return, these suitors wasted his possessions by staging numerous feasts and parties. Throughout all of this, Mentor faithfully performed his duties in caring for and educating Telemachus. His efforts were manifest in the young man Telemachus, who ultimately demonstrated he was worthy to be the son of Odysseus. Originating from this tale, the word mentor became synonymous with loyal and trusted friend, enlightened advisor, and teacher.[2]

Overview

Mentoring programs generally serve the following broad purposes:
- *Educational or academic mentoring* helps mentored people improve their overall academic achievement.

- *Career mentoring* helps mentored people develop the necessary skills to enter or continue on a career path.
- *Personal development mentoring* supports those mentored during times of personal or social stress and provides guidance for decision making.

What are some examples of mentoring programs? Traditional programs such as Big Brothers/Big Sisters have been joined by school-based programs, independent living skills programs, court-mandated programs, and recreational "buddy" programs. Religious institutions continue to play a leadership role, and corporations and social organizations now promote employee and member involvement.[3] Increasingly, older youth are encouraged to volunteer as part of their educational requirements.[4]

Mentoring is very similar to coaching. Coaching is a term used more often today in reference to a mentoring relationship. Both coaching and mentoring are processes that enable both individual and corporate clients to achieve their full potential. Coaching and mentoring share many similarities, so it makes sense to outline the common things coaches and mentors do, whether the services are offered in a paid (professional) or unpaid (philanthropic) role. They both:

- Facilitate the exploration of needs, motivations, desires, skills, and thought processes to assist the individual in making real, lasting change.
- Use questioning techniques to facilitate the client's own thought processes in order to identify solutions and actions rather than takes a wholly directive approach.
- Support the client in setting appropriate goals and methods of assessing progress in relation to these goals.
- Observe, listen, and ask questions to understand the client's situation.
- Creatively apply tools and techniques, which may include one-to-one training, facilitating, counseling, and networking.
- Encourage a commitment to action and the development of lasting personal growth and change.
- Maintain unconditional positive regard for the client, which means that the coach is at all times supportive and nonjudgmental of the client and their views, lifestyle, and aspirations.
- Ensure that clients develop personal competencies and do not develop unhealthy dependencies on the coaching or mentoring relationship.
- Evaluate the outcomes of the process, using objective measures wherever possible to ensure the relationship is successful and the client is achieving their personal goals.
- Encourage clients to continually improve competencies and to develop new developmental alliances where necessary to achieve their goals.
- Work within their area of personal competence.
- Possess qualifications and experience in the areas in which skills-transfer coaching is offered.
- Manage the relationship to ensure the client receives the appropriate level of service and that programs are neither too short nor too long.[5]

Insights from Research

While research on the effects of mentoring is scarce, some studies and program evaluations do support positive claims. In an evaluation of Project RAISE, a Baltimore-based mentoring project, it was determined that mentoring had positive effects on school attendance and grades in English, but not on promotion rates or standardized test scores.[6] Related to this, it was concluded that positive effects are much more likely when one-on-one mentoring has been strongly implemented. Another evaluation found that participants in various mentoring programs had higher levels of college enrollment and higher educational aspirations than nonparticipants receiving comparable amounts of education and job-related services.[75]

The primary duties of a mentor change over time. At any moment, mentoring duties may involve different facets of activity. Switching one's duties from mentor-advisor to mentor-confidant to mentor-critic might occur over the span of a day or even over a few hours. Being responsive to the necessity of changing one's mentoring demeanor requires critical personal attention and oversight.[8] Mentors and mentees or protégés should have a clear purpose and understanding for their mentoring relationship. Once established, there are many opportunities for both parties to benefit from the relationship.

NOTES

1. Wikimedia Foundation, Inc., http://en.wikipedia.org/wiki/Mentoring.

2. Virginia Commonwealth University, http://www.vcu.edu/graduate/pdfs/mentoring.pdf.

3. Michael Newman, *Beginning a Mentoring Program* (Pittsburgh, PA: QED Communications, 1990).

4. U.S. Department of Education, http://www.ed.gov/pubs/OR/ConsumerGuides/mentor.html.

5. The Coaching and Mentoring Network Ltd., Oxford, http://www.coachingnetwork.org.uk/resourcecentre/WhatAreCoachingAndMentoring.htm.

6. U.S. Department of Education.

Virginia Commonwealth University, http://www.vcu.edu/graduate/pdfs/mentoring.pdf.

7. Ibid.

8. Virginia Commonwealth University, http://www.vcu.edu/graduate/pdfs/mentoring.pdf.

Roger Odegard

MYERS-BRIGGS TYPE INDICATOR

The Myers-Briggs Type Indicator (MBTI), based on Carl Jung's theory of psychological types, is a personality questionnaire that is primarily concerned with the differences in people that result from where they like to focus their attention, the way they acquire information, the way they like to make decisions, and the type of lifestyle they adopt. The premise is that people have varying preferences, with each type having its own set of inherent strengths. There is no right or wrong to these preferences. They simply help us to understand ourselves and our behavior, as well as help us to understand and appreciate the differences in others.

The developers of MBTI were Katherine Cook Briggs and her daughter, Isabel Briggs Myers, who initially created the indicator during World War II. They believed that a knowledge of personality preferences would help women who were entering the industrial workforce for the first time to identify the sort of wartime jobs in which they would be "most comfortable and effective."[1]

While many academic psychologists have criticized the indicator in research literature, claiming that it "lacks convincing validity data,"[2] proponents of the test cite "unblinded anecdotal predictions of individual behavior."[3] Regardless, personality testing is an expanding $400 million industry utilized by almost half of all American companies, with the MBTI being the most popular assessment tool of its kind in the world with about

2.5 million tests being given each year.[4] Critics and supporters alike say that the MBTI endures because it does a good job of pointing out the differences between people, and as such is a valuable asset in team building and improving communication.

MBTI Type Preferences

There are 16 distinct and unique personality paths based on the concept of type preferences, in which MBTI asserts that individuals find certain ways of thinking and behaving easier than others. These psychological polarities are sorted into four opposite pairs that result into the 16 possible combinations. MBTI assumes that although each of us uses all eight of these parts of our personalities at least some of the time, we experience one part in each of the four pairs as more natural and comfortable. The more natural and comfortable parts of our personalities describes our *preferences*. Each preference is represented by a letter—namely, E or I, S or N, T or F, and J or P. A person's personality type is made up of a combination of these four preferences and is identified by the four letters representing them, which is referred to as *type*. For example, ENFP represents a type of personality that prefers extroversion, intuition, feeling, and perceiving. MBTI contends that if people understand their psychological preferences, with time, they can become more proficient with the opposite psychological preference and thereby more behaviorally flexible. The eight preference types that define MBTI are as follows:

The *E-I scale,* or *attitudes,* describes two opposite preferences for where attention is focused—the outer or inner world. Extroversion (E) is focused on the outer world where energy is derived from others. Introversion (I) is focused on the inner world where energy comes from within one's self.

The *S-N scale,* or *information-gathering functions,* describes opposite ways in which a person perceives or acquires information. The *Sensing (S)* function trusts information that is acquired in the present, tangible and concrete or information that is gathered by the five senses. In other words, you must experience it to be true. On the other hand, *iNtuition (N)* allows for going beyond and trusting information that is more abstract or theoretical. Reliance on this "sixth sense" shows the relationships, meanings, and future possibilities of new information.

The *T-F scale* is the *decision-making or judging function.* Both the Thinking and Feeling functions are based on data received from their information gathering functions (S or N). The *Thinking (T)* function emphasizes logic, analysis, and objective rational thought in decision making. The *Feeling (F)* function prioritizes human values, trying to determine the impact of decisions on others, while striving to achieve the greatest harmony.

The *J-P scale* is the *function of relating to the outside world.* Individuals have a preference of showing their Judging or Perceiving functions when dealing with the outside world. The person who prefers the *Judging (J)* function tends to be organized and orderly and makes decisions quickly with the information acquired through the T or P functions. The person who prefers the *Perceiving (P)* function tends to be flexible, adaptable, and keeps all options open as long as possible with the information that was acquired through either the T or P functions. So TJ types tend to show their logical side to the world, whereas FJ types appear as empathetic. Those types ending in P show the world their Perceiving functions—SP types appear concrete and solid, while NP types appear loose and abstract. P types appear to keep all matters and possibilities open.

The MBTI does not measure knowledge, skills, or abilities. Nor does it measure intelligence. Further, it is not intended to be used as a tool for employee selection, promotion, or assigning projects. Type preferences are considered to be polar opposites, and a precept of MBTI is that an individual fundamentally prefers one thing over another, not a bit of both. No one type is better than someone else's—just different. The belief is if a person understands his type preferences, he can approach work in a manner that best suits his style, including managing one's time, problem solving, best approaches to decision making, and dealing with stress. Knowledge of type can help a person deal with workplace culture, development of new skills, understanding participation on teams, and coping with change in the workplace.

NOTES

1. Isabel Briggs Myers with Peter B. Myers, *Gifts Differing: Understanding Personality Type* (Mountain View, CA: Davies-Black Publishing, 1995).

2. John Hunsley, Catherine M. Lee, and James M. Wood, "Controversial and Questionable Assessment Techniques," in *Science and Pseudoscience in Clinical Psychology*, ed. Scott O. Lilienfeld, Steven J. Lynn, and Jeffrey M. Lohr (New York: Guilford Press, 2004), 39–76.

3. Barbara Barron Tieger and Paul D. Tieger, *Do What You Are: Discover the Perfect Career for You through the Secrets of Personality Type* (Boston: Little & Brown, 1995).

4. Douglas Shuit, "At 60, Myers-Briggs is Still Sorting Out and Identifying People's Types," *Workforce Management* (December 2003).

Victoria T. Dieringer

NEW EMPLOYEE ORIENTATION

New employee orientation is the process by which organizations welcome new employees. New employee orientation, often spearheaded by a meeting with the human resources department, generally contains information about safety, the work environment, the new job description, benefits and eligibility, company culture, company history, the organization chart, and anything else relevant to working in the new company.

John Sullivan, head of the Human Resource Management Program at San Francisco State University, concludes that several elements contribute to a world-class orientation program. According to Sullivan, the best new employee orientation process:
• Has targeted goals and meets them.
• Makes the first day a celebration.
• Involves family as well as coworkers.
• Makes new hires productive on the first day.
• Is not boring, rushed, or ineffective, and uses feedback to continuously improve.[1]

Pre-Orientation Planning

Human resources professionals and line managers first need to consider key new employee orientation planning questions before implementing or revamping a current program. These are the key questions to ask:
• What things do new employees need to know about this work environment that would make them more comfortable?

- What impression and impact do you want to have on a new employee's first day?
- What key policies and procedures must employees be aware of on the first day to avoid mistakes on the second day? Concentrate on vital issues.
- What special things (desk, work area, equipment, special instructions) can you provide to make new employees feel comfortable, welcome, and secure?
- What positive experience can you provide for the new employee that she could discuss with her family at the end of the first day of work? The experience should be something to make the new employee feel valued by the organization.
- How can you help the new employee's supervisor be available to the new employee on the first day to provide personal attention and to convey a clear message that the new employee is an important addition to the work team?

Since first impressions are crucial, here are some tips for putting your best foot forward during an orientation session:

- Begin the process before the new person starts work. Send an agenda to the new associate with the offer letter so the employee knows what to expect. Stay in touch after he or she has accepted the position to answer questions. Make sure the new person's work area is ready for the first day of work.
- Make sure key coworkers know the employee is starting and encourage them to come to say "hello" before orientation begins.
- Assign a mentor, or buddy, to show the new person around, make introductions, and start training. Let the mentor have sufficient notice so they can make preparations. The mentoring relationship should continue for at least 90 days.
- Start with the basics. People become productive sooner if they are firmly grounded in the basic knowledge they need to understand their job. Focus on the why, when, where, and how of the position before expecting them to handle assignments or big projects. Don't overwhelm them with too much information.
- Provide samples about how to complete forms and the person's job description with the orientation packet.

An effective orientation program—or the lack of one—will make a significant difference in how quickly a new employee becomes productive and has other long-term impacts for your organization. The end of the first day, the end of the first week, the end of each day in your employment, is just as important as the beginning. Help your employees feel that you want them to come back the next day, and the next, and the next.[2]

New Employee Orientation Checklist

Welcome your new employee. Smile, and tell them you are glad that they have come to work in your establishment. You can make a big difference at this point. Show them around the facility, pointing out any important features along the way like emergency exits and hazardous areas, for example. Pretend you are showing a guest through your home. You want to make them feel comfortable and for them to relax as much as possible. Introduce them to people you meet along the way. Chances are your new worker will not be able to remember everyone's name when he is through with your tour, but you will at least have given other people the chance to learn who the new person is. As you introduce your new employee, explain what job he will be assigned and to whom he will be reporting. This will help existing employees mentally fit the new person into what they know of your organization.

Introduce your new employee to the supervisor to whom he will be reporting, if they have not already met. Show him the work station and where to get any supplies he might need. Talk briefly about important contacts he will want to remember, such as the person responsible for ordering supplies, the payroll person, and any others you feel are key to the operation.

Prepare a checklist of subjects that should be reviewed with each new employee and then set aside the appropriate amount of time so that can be done. Let everyone else know that you are not to be interrupted while you are orienting your new worker. You will want to convey to the new person that he is the most important item on your agenda at the moment.

Consider the following items for your new employee orientation:

- Personnel file contents
  - Job application or resume
  - Interview summary
  - Reference check information
  - Verification of any licenses or certifications required on this person's job (driver's license, teaching credential, broker's license, etc.)
- Complete necessary paperwork:
  - INS Form I-9, Employment Eligibility Verification
  - Employment agreement, if you use them
  - Receipt for their copy of your employee handbook
  - W-4 form for payroll withholding
  - Personal data sheet so you will have the information necessary on emergency contacts, home address and telephone number, Social Security number, etc.
  - Security or identification card information form
  - Benefit coverage election and beneficiary designation forms for your benefit programs that provide immediate eligibility for all employees.
- An explanation of the following practices and procedures you use in your organization:
  - Hours of work and attendance/tardiness policy
  - Payroll periods, when paychecks are delivered, and when the new employee's first check will arrive
  - Rates of pay
  - Overtime rules
  - Training or introductory employment period
  - Employee benefits for which they are or may become eligible:
    - Medical insurance
    - Sick leave
    - Vacation
    - Personal leave, jury duty, holidays
    - Pension programs, savings programs and/or stock plans
    - Life, disability, and accident insurance
    - Employee activities
    - Other benefits you offer and how much the employer will pay for each
  - Advancement or promotion opportunities and procedures
  - Employee suggestion plan
  - Parking arrangements
  - Union-related information if this person will be in a represented group
- Provide copies to the new employee of the following documents:

- Employee handbook
- Safety plan
- Annual report
- Employee newsletter
- Letter explaining COBRA (Consolidated Omnibus Budget Reconciliation Act of 1988) governing continuation of benefits following payroll separation
- Direct payroll deposit request
- Employee benefit booklet explaining each of the organization's offered benefits
- Show the employee any marketing or informational materials that are used with your customers or clients. Play any video or audio tapes you have prepared for employees or customers that explain what your organization is all about.
- Explain your organization's mission and its philosophy of doing business.
  "The way we do things around here..."
  "We believe that our customers are..."
  "Nothing is more important than..."

During your orientation discussion with the new employee, you want to take the opportunity to stress "how we do things around here." This is the best time for you to create the attitude you want your workers to have in performing their jobs. Remember that you can set the tone for the remainder of their employment with you. Make it positive and stress the things that are truly important to your organization. Give the employee opportunity to ask questions along the way.

Be sure you show your new employee where the required employment posters are located. If they are in a lunch room/break room, take the opportunity to explain the rules for use of that part of your facility. Make a special point of reviewing the organization's policy regarding sexual harassment.

How long should this process take? That depends on you and your organization. It will likely require an hour of your time at a minimum. It will be an hour in which to clarify important information and avoid misunderstandings that could take you many hours to correct later on. An hour making people feel welcome and important and giving them the information they need to succeed in your organization is indeed an hour well spent.[3]

NOTES

1. Susan M. Heathfield, "New Employee Orientation," *New Employee Orientation,* About.com, Human Resources, http://humanresources.about.com (accessed February 22, 2008).
2. "Employee Orientation: Keeping New Employees on Board," About.com, Human Resources, http://humanresources.about.com (accessed February 28, 2008).
3. William H. Truesdell, *New Employee Orientation: Starting Off on The Right Foot* (Walnut Creek, CA: Management Advantage, 1998).

Roger Odegard

ON-THE-JOB TRAINING

On-the-job training (OJT) may be broadly defined as an intervention undertaken within an employee's workplace to increase or to enhance individual knowledge, skills, and capabilities as he relates to his job.[1] The training is typically led by an experienced instructor or trainer, who may be a manager or supervisor, peer, or specialist in the activity or skill, and is designed to change targeted job behaviors. On-the-job training is normally integrated into an employee's "everyday" working conditions or physical environment, and utilizes the actual machinery, equipment, tools, documents, and other materials that are commonly used. The employee's goal is typically to display competence or sufficient mastery such that he may be assigned to work independently or with minimal supervision. The guiding philosophy of on-the-job training is that employees are capable of learning necessary job skills through observing other, more knowledgeable, or experienced persons, and by imitating or replicating their behaviors when and where appropriate.[2] Other terms that alternately may be used to refer to on-the-job training include job shadowing, job coaching, and hands-on training.

History

On-the-job training has, in some capacity, existed for centuries. The training required to gain entrance into many craft guilds during the Middle Ages required an extensive period of on-the-job training (also referred to as an apprenticeship, of which such training is an important component), including the production of a *masterpiece,* to demonstrate mastery of the skill or trade.[3] On-the-job training continued during the Industrial and Agricultural revolutions, as the need increased for skilled operators of technologically advanced machinery. Those individuals capable of mastering the unique skills necessitated by the new inventions and processes introduced during this period were often able to increase their standard of living.

Where Appropriate or Desirable

On-the-job training is appropriate and desirable for newly hired employees, when experienced employees are confronted with a situation requiring the updating or upgrading of their current skill set, when employees can be trained for positions where their skill set is applicable, when there is considerable overlap of responsibilities within a department or work unit (it may also be referred to as "cross-training"), or when employees are transferred or promoted to new positions.[4] On-the-job training is a critical component of a modern-day apprenticeship, which is a work-study training method that also incorporates classroom activities. Apprenticeships are particularly common among vocationally oriented jobs or skilled trades, including electrical work, carpentry, masonry, plumbing, tool and die, and others. On-the-job training has been increasingly used within other occupations, such as call center operators, retail salespeople, telemarketing, and computer-related administrative jobs, as well. Additionally, management trainees for many firms continue to receive much of their training while on the job. When certain skills that are unique to a position are necessary for its successful execution, and when the facilities and equipment are present on-site, it is likely the job is appropriate for on-the-job training.[5]

Factors Influencing the Effectiveness of On-the-job Training

The following list is intended to describe certain critical elements that, when properly accounted for, can significantly improve the overall effectiveness of an on-the-job training program.
— *Selection of trainers.* Individuals selected to conduct on-the-job training should possess expert knowledge of the skills and activities within their area of the training program.

Some organizations require trainers to complete intensive "train the trainer" programs, in which classroom training involving concepts and theory is integrated with the demonstration of proficiency with the tools, equipment, and machinery that employees will need instruction on.

— *Initial evaluation of employees.* Employees requiring training may have differing levels of literacy or skills pertaining to job content. As such, an evaluation of basic skills (reading, writing, arithmetic) may be necessary for entry-level type positions, while proficiency in different computer software or various job-related standards and practices may be more appropriate for positions requiring more specific or advanced knowledge.

— *Clear specification of training course content and anticipated outcomes.* Before deployment, training materials such as lesson plans, employee training manuals, applicable policies and procedures, checklists to chart progress, and trainer assignments should be clearly specified. Additionally, anticipated outcomes from the training, such as an improved safety record, improved employee retention, and greater workforce flexibility regarding job assignment should be stated, as there will likely be up-front costs associated with such an undertaking.[6]

— *Tailor rewards to successful training outcomes.* The phrase "What gets rewarded gets done" may be successfully tailored to employees regarding on-the-job training efforts. When significant milestones or levels of proficiency or competence are attained, employees should receive appropriate rewards to reinforce their continued efforts and progress. Rewards need not always be financial, either. Public recognition for a "job well done," when accompanied with genuine sincerity, can be much more effective than a bonus or raise, and is often remembered long after any financial compensation is received.

Expected Benefits

Adhering to on-the-job training and related programs does require considerable discipline on the part of management. The continued pressure on many organizations to reduce costs wherever and whenever possible can translate into reduced or scaled-back training options for employees. However, the work environment that on-the-job training often fosters is an ancillary benefit, with improved employee morale, productivity, and professionalism,[7] coupled with the continued skills shortage in many sectors of the economy, indicate that perhaps these organizations should reexamine the benefits, both short-term and long-term, of such programs. Finally, in companies having a large percentage of retirement-eligible employees, these workers could be deployed through coordinated on-the-job training efforts with new or recent hires to ensure that their knowledge and skills, sometimes collected over several decades, do not "walk out the door" when they do.

NOTES

1. CIPD, "On-the-job Training," http://www.cipd.co.uk/subjects/training/trnmthds/otjtrain.htm (accessed December 5, 2007).

2. Raymond A. Noe, John R. Hollenbeck, Barry Gerhart, and Patrick M. Wright, *Human Resource Management* (New York: McGraw-Hill, 2003).

3. Allen Farber, "Medieval Guilds and Craft Production," http://employees.oneonta.edu/farberas/arth/ARTH200/artist/guilds.html (accessed December 6, 2007).

4. Noe, Hollenbeck, Gerhart, and Wright, *Human Resource Management.*

5. U.S. Department of the Interior, "Personnel Manager—On-the-Job-Training (OJT)," http://www.doi.gov/hrm/pmanager/ed6b.html (accessed December 5, 2007).

6. CIPD, "On-the-job Training"; Noe, Hollenbeck, Gerhart, and Wright, *Human Resource Management;* Peter Zelinski, "Engineering Employees," *Modern Machine Shop* (August 2007): 88–95.

7. U.S. Department of the Interior, "Personnel Manager—On-the-Job-Training (OJT)."

Steven J. Kerno Jr.

PERFORMANCE AIDS

A performance aid, also known as a job aid, is a tool to assist an employee in completing a task. It is intended to ease correct completion of a job that is (1) immediately accessible, (2) instructional, (3) sufficiently descriptive, and (4) concise.[1] Performance aids are typically found in the form of checklists, help menus, templates, charts, and so forth. Performance aids help employees quickly and correctly complete a job task without having to memorize all of the steps of the task. The performance aid must be descriptive enough to effectively explain the task without being so verbose as to slow down the performer. Performance aids are not the same as formal education—rather, they are quick tools to use in place of, or to augment, formal education.

Why Are Performance Aids Important?

Learners Want Instant Access

As adults age, they have a greater affinity toward self-directed learning.[2] That is, adults want (and can) learn without direction from an instructor. Moreover, employees are beginning to expect that organizations allow and encourage them to learn at will, which enables them to more efficiently obtain new knowledge, skills, and attitudes.[3] Performance aids are a quick and easy way to provide vast amounts of accurate and helpful information to employees.

Educators Want Cheaper Solutions

Performance aids are designed to assist an employee with completing a job. Some research suggests that we should train an employee only when the employee does not know how to do the job.[4] Classroom training is costly and often overkill for what might easily be accomplished with a performance aid. Because performance aids are simpler mechanisms than training, they cost a lot less to build.

When Should Performance Aids Be Used?

Perfection Is Paramount

In situations in which tasks are complicated and exact performance is essential, a performance aid may be an appropriate tool to assist the employee in correctly completing the task.[5] For example, patients would find it unacceptable to get an infection in the hospital if a step was missed in the cleaning of their wound. Of course, if the task is too complicated to be simply explained in a performance aid, additional education and tools may be needed or the content may need to be divided into subtasks.

Repetition Is Rare

If a job task is infrequently performed, a performance aid is a helpful memory-jogging tool.[6] When a task is rarely performed, people have a difficult time remembering how to complete it—especially if that task is complicated. In that situation, having a checklist or some other form of performance aid is a good way to reinforce correct task completion. If the learner must do the task solely from memory, a performance aid is not appropriate and full training is required.

Resources Are Limited

When employees need to be taught something, educators can create training or job aids to impart this information. However, if there is little time or money to prepare the education, a performance aid is a cost-effective method because it is faster and easier than training and development.[7]

Speed Is Secondary

Tasks that must be completed very quickly may not allow the employee the time needed to refer to a performance aid.[8] For example, a paramedic cannot take the time to refer to a performance aid when CPR is needed. In this situation, a performance aid is not appropriate; rather, the employee needs to memorize the task steps, which may require training.

Environment Is Fitting

If a task is completed in a fast-paced, dangerous, confined, or somehow difficult work environment, a performance aid may not be appropriate.[9] Performance aids are effective only when the employee can easily access and refer to them. For example, a telephone pole worker cannot easily access an instruction manual while hanging from a pole.

How to Create a Performance Aid

Identify the Content

Just like training and development, performance aid creation should start with an in-depth look at what must be conveyed. Once the need for a performance aid has been determined, start by narrowing down the content you *want* to teach down to the content you *need* to teach. This may be done by writing the objective of the content, defining how you want learners to practice that objective, analyzing audience needs, and then asking yourself if knowing the objective alone provides enough information for the learner to complete the task.[10] That is, what else does the learner need to know in order to accomplish the objective? It is imperative that *only* the needed content be included in a performance aid, not tangential content.

Determine Format

Once performance aid content has been identified, determine the best format.[11] For example, if the task requires sequential performance, you might consider a checklist or flow chart. A task that requires complex decision making may benefit from a decision table or algorithm. When the task requires differentiation between elements, you may consider a matrix. In any event, determining the format will help organize information for your performance aid.

Create the Performance Aid

Developing the performance aid may be a fairly simple step if you have adequately analyzed and planned your solution. Creativity and innovation on the part of the designer often enhance the learner's experience.

Test and Improve

The performance aid should be tested in the real environment with individual employees, whose use of the aid without assistance should be observed.[12] Only after the employee has finished using the performance aid should you ask her thoughts and opinions regarding improvement. After incorporating improvements, continue the testing process until satisfied the performance aid accomplishes its objective.

Maintain

Periodically checking the performance aid ensures that it is still useful and accurate. Set up a maintenance cycle with all performance aids to remind you to check them on a regular basis (e.g., annually). Performance aids that are no longer being used should be improved or archived. Outdated performance aids do not improve performance and can actually lower results. For example, consider a salesperson who sells a discontinued product because an outdated product list was used. Ensure that content is accurate and up to date.

NOTES

1. Joseph Harless, "Guiding Performance with Job Aids," in *Introduction to Performance Technology,* ed. Martin Smith (Washington, DC: National Society for Performance and Instruction, 1986).

2. Malcolm Knowles, *The Modern Practice of Adult Education: From Pedagogy to Andragogy,* 2nd ed. (New York: Cambridge University Press, 1980).

3. Harriett Hankin, *The New Workforce.* (New York: AMACOM, 2005).

4. Robert F. Mager and Peter Pipe, *Analyzing Performance Problems,* 3rd ed. (Atlanta, GA: Center for Effective Performance, 1997).

5. William J. Rothwell and H.C. Kazanas, *Mastering the Instructional Design Process,* 2nd ed. (San Francisco: Jossey-Bass, 1998).

6. Ibid.

7. Ibid.

8. David E. Ripley, "Harless on Job Aids," in *Performance Engineering at Work,* ed. Peter Dean, 2nd ed. (Washington, DC: International Society of Performance Improvement, 1999).

9. Ibid.

10. Robert F. Mager, *Making Instruction Work,* 2nd ed. (Atlanta, GA: Center for Effective Performance, 1997).

11. Ripley, "Harless on Job Aids."

12. Ibid.

Kevin F. Preston

PERFORMANCE COACHING

Performance coaching gives managers the opportunity to share their perspectives of their employees' performance and discuss methods of improvement. In this way, performance coaching serves a vital function within the organization. At the core of performance coaching lies the concept of *feedback.* Accordingly, performance coaching is an ongoing minute-by-minute, day-by-day feedback opportunity that provides managers an opportunity to create action plans that improve employee performance. Additionally, performance coaching is specific and timely in order for employees to make the types of corrections and improvements required to bring about desired business results.

Many employees fail to perform adequately due to barriers that prohibit exemplary performance. Performance coaching:
- Provides assessment of employees strengths, weaknesses, and areas for improvement.
- Frames plans for growth and development.
- Encourages feedback for improvement.
- Helps isolate performance obstacles and formulate strategies for overcoming them.[1]

As a result, employees participate in discussions that improve the work environment and general conditions under which they are asked to perform.

Principles of Performance Coaching

Three fundamental principles explain most employee behavior and why managers fail to secure the results they desire. These principles include:

1. Performance/reward disconnect—failing to perform adequately because there is no correlation between their performance and that rewarded by the organization.
2. Performance whitewashing—failing to communicate which results are the most important or treating all performance results the same.
3. Inspection failure—failing to inspect their employees' work.[2]

Performance/Reward Disconnect

Some managers demonstrate the concept of team building and invest much time and money training their people in the skills, knowledge, and practice of self-directed work teams. However, they continue to compensate their employees for individual performance. Thus, performance behaviors that an organization desires are ignored or punished in the workplace.

Performance Whitewashing

Performance whitewashing occurs when managers fail to communicate their expectations and the outcomes required of their employees. Such behavior confuses employees and causes them to prioritize results according to their own perspectives, which may or may not align with organizational expectations. Correction requires managers to determine and express which results are truly important and which are less so. These priorities must be communicated to employees and rewarded accordingly.

Inspection Failure

Many managers have little time to review or inspect employees' performance. Consequently, employees are on their own to produce results they perceive to be important to the organization. Employees must know what is important and that their managers will be inspecting performance outputs. Thus, effective managers link expectations with inspection, which can occur during performance coaching.

Prepare for a Performance Coaching Episode

Effective managers examine their strategies to create an environment conducive to the sharing of information and ideas. In fact, every performance coaching episode has an opening, body, and conclusion. Careful planning of the approach includes climate-setting comments designed to reduce stress for both parties along with a brief overview of the agenda.

To improve the outcome of performance coaching, effective managers decide the best time and place for the exchange to take place. The primary focus of the meeting entails consideration of items to be discussed and the manner in which they will be handled. Planning the conclusion and follow-up activities guarantees closure for both parties. Further, planning the conclusion helps to emphasize the importance of continuous review and reinforcement of the agreed-upon action plan.

For the best results, schedule the meeting when and where both parties can spend quality time together without distraction, interruption, or interference. The setting should be a neutral, private room or office, off-site if necessary. The location should allow both parties to be alone together without distractions. Some employees may be reluctant to share their opinions openly and honestly without sufficient privacy.

Effective managers properly prepare the meeting room to create an environment that encourages the free exchange of ideas, suggestions, and opinions. The environment should allow both parties to function as equals in discussions, via tactics such as placing chairs side by side and having beverages or snacks available. Such a trust-building and confidential meeting makes employees feel valued; strengthening positive feedback while fostering an air of "working together" to improve performance or manage deficiencies.

The following general guidelines will help prepare for the actual performance coaching exchange. These guidelines help establish an environment that exudes respect for individuals and their contributions. They also serve as a reminder of the participatory emphasis of performance coaching exchanges, reinforcing their developmental nature. To ensure successful performance coaching activity, managers should:
- Establish and maintain rapport with their personnel.
- Explain clearly the purpose of the interview.
- Encourage employees to share their opinions and ideas.
- Listen actively, without interruption, to employees' opinions and ideas.
- Avoid confrontation or arguments that lead to negative or destructive discourse.
- Focus on performance, not personalities.
- Confront; do not criticize or blame.
- Focus on future performance, not past performance.
- Emphasize individual strengths as well as areas needing improvement.
- End the interview on a positive note.
- End the interview when all parties reach agreement.[3]

Why Performance Coaching Fails

Performance coaching occasionally fails to yield positive outcomes because managers focus on personal characteristic and personalities rather than performance. Another reason for disappointing outcomes is because some managers focus too much on employees' past actions instead of focusing on future performance. Although past performance *does* provide a means of sculpting and structuring the future, a manager's attention should be on future performance behaviors.

Conclusion

Performance coaching provides individuals with feedback on their performance. Coaching is useful in helping employees recognize their strengths and achievements over a specific period of time, and identify areas where they can continue to grow and develop. Employees are able to define performance goals for a specific period of time and to review the "match" between the organization's expectations and those of the employee. Performance coaching helps managers make decisions regarding the performance of employees and aids in construction of developmental and career planning activities that improve their productivity.

Managers and employees should work closely together during a performance coaching. This requires creating a partnership focused on identifying the strengths and weaknesses of the employee and the creation of an action plan that builds on strengths and manages weaknesses. A mutually beneficial partnership allows both parties to build a trusting, collaborative relationship that helps individuals identify performance development opportunities. In this way, managers solicit the involvement and support of employees in their growth and development, which addresses one of the primary reasons why institutions fail to achieve desired performance results. Moreover, managers will enjoy better outcomes when employees willingly participate in their own action planning.

See also Coaching; Mentoring

NOTES

1. Jerry W. Gilley and Ann Gilley, *The Manager as Coach* (Westport, CT: Praeger, 2007).
2. Jerry W. Gilley, Nathaniel W. Boughton, and Ann Maycunich, *The Performance Challenge: Developing Management Systems to Make Employees Your Organization's Greatest Asset* (Cambridge, MA: Perseus Books, 1999).
3. Gilley and Gilley, *The Manager as Coach.*

Jerry W. Gilley and Ann Gilley

PRODUCTIVITY IMPROVEMENT PLAN

Improving productivity means increasing efficiency, output, or yield. Productivity improvement plans address obtaining increases by eliminating wasted steps, decreasing the need to rework a step or streamline the process. A Google search of the phrase "productivity improvement plan" provided 2.14 million hits. There is much to say about this topic. Checking ABI/Inform, an online database, provided a list of 9,976 scholarly journals, trade magazine articles, and newspaper articles related to productivity. The mechanisms often mentioned to improve productivity are lean enterprise, six-sigma, Baldrige criteria, and benchmarking. These are all useful; however, cultural issues typically need to be addressed first. If the culture of the organization is one in which problems are hidden and the messenger is shot, then adding improvement tools should not be the first step. Below is a story to help explain the system perspective based on the Baldrige criteria.[1]

Andrew and Digby have been friends since college. Both went on to have successful careers, and each manages an organization but in different fields. Andrew's attitude toward his employees is influenced by Theory Y, which states people are influenced by higher-order needs. Digby embraces Theory X, believing that people are motivated by basic needs. Both executives have been successful, so they never examined the influence of their own beliefs.

Both are experiencing tough competition and are talking to each other more often to get feedback. Andrew explained the elements of his beliefs, Theory Y.

- "People will exercise self-direction and self-control if they are committed to the objectives of the task."
- "The average person can learn and even seek responsibility."
- "The ability to make innovation decisions is widely dispersed throughout the general population and is not necessarily the sole province of those in management positions."[2]

Because Andrew believes people come to work wanting to make a contribution and do a good job, he looks at practices, procedures, and systems to see why things go wrong. Digby's attitude encompasses the ideas that people are lazy and need to be watched. When problems occur, Digby wants to blame someone.

This distinct difference in attitudes espoused by each executive could also be viewed under the lens of intrinsic and extrinsic motivation. "The most important act that a manager can take is to understand what it is that is important to an individual. Everyone is different from everyone else. All people are motivated to a different degree, extrinsically and intrinsically. That is why it is vital that managers spend time to listen to an employee to understand whether he is looking for recognition by the company or by his peers, time at work to publish, flexible working hours, or time to take a university course. In this way, a manager can provide positive outcomes for his people and may even move some people toward replacement of extrinsic motivation with intrinsic motivation."[3]

Once Andrew understood his friend's belief of theory X, he shared the management grid, contained in Table 2.1, with him. This grid shows the characteristics of progression from a traditional organization to one demonstrating performance excellence.[4]

Often, executives in the *Traditional* stage think their problems will go away "if only they could get good workers." Contests are held between employees, departments or divisions to try to motivate people. "Extrinsic motivators...are not only ineffective but corrosive. They eat away at the kind of motivation that *does* produce results."[5] Problems are fixed when the customer complains. A study done by the Technical Assistance Research Program (TARP) reported that only 5 percent of dissatisfied customers complain to top management, 45 percent complain to an agent or frontline representative such as a hotel desk clerk, and 50 percent encounter a problem but never complain. Oftentimes, a customer who encounters a problem will go elsewhere for the product or service in the future.

In the *Awareness* stage, the leadership realizes that the rules of the game have changed and what achieved success in the past will not necessarily provide success in the future. The battle cry of organizations in this stage is "if only suppliers and manufacturing would do their job, we would not have these problems." Organizations in this stage know they need customer, employee, and supplier input, but they may not be good at obtaining it or using it.

Businesses at the *Improving* stage are doing very well. They recognize that one of the roles of leadership is to remove the roadblocks that keep people from doing a good job. New ideas are sought, and employees continually improve processes. There are positive trends in data tracked, and comparisons to industry leaders show the company to be one of the leaders. Internal improvements made correlate well with improved customer satisfactions so the teams are working on the correct processes.

Table 2.1

Category	Traditional	Awareness	Improving	Outstanding
Leadership	• State lofty goals • Motivating people is the solution • Delegate improvement activities • Business units compete with one another	+ Mission/vision statement includes all stakeholders + Recognize procedures and practices cause most variation	+ Open to new ideas from others, including other organizations + Consider whole system + Remove barriers that rob people of pride in work	+ Leadership highly visible and a role model of ethical behavior + Leadership acts as a coach + Good corporate citizen + Ongoing communication
Measurement, Analysis, and Knowledge Management	• Fight fires • Key product and service features are tracked in addition to financial data • A lot of data, little information	+ Root cause analysis prevents reoccurrence • Some useful visual displays of data • Track opportunities per 1,000	+ Value-added reports and graphs + Data are tracked in all areas of business including support (accounting, purchasing, etc.) + Track opportunities per million + Aware of best practices globally	+ Extensive depth and breadth of information + Ready access to information throughout the organization + Positive correlation between internal measures and customer satisfaction + Understand why best practices have worked at other organizations
Strategic Planning	• There is a business plan • Optimization occurs within a department	+ Progress to business plan is reviewed + Business plan is updated annually • There is a plan for business excellence	+ Business plan and performance excellence plan are one + Plan includes stretch goals • Plan covers one-to-two-year horizon • Cross-functional input to plan but limited scope	+ Business plans include performance excellence goals and strategies + Customers, suppliers, and employees provide input to plan + Resources are provided to achieve goals + Short- and long-term views + Total system is optimized
Workforce Focus	• Training is offered to employees • There is a suggestion box	+ Employees on problem-solving teams • Increased focus on obtaining more suggestions • Mass training	• Employees are told they are empowered + Training is just-in-time + Employees are involved in process analysis and improvement + There are opportunities for teams and individuals to contribute + Employee satisfaction levels show positive trends	+ Internal supplier-customer relation + Employees feel and act empowered + Culture supports use of new skills + Employees feel their ideas are important + Employee satisfaction, attendance, and turnover levels are outstanding

Process Management	• Improvement effort is focused on manufacturing of product or delivery of service • Receiving inspection	• Quality is owned by manufacturing • Control charts are used to maintain some processes • End-of-line inspection is the safety net • Inspection of supplied material occurs if there has been a recent problem	• Some prevention activities • Motto is "if it ain't broke, don't fix it" + Key processes throughout organization identified, studied, and improved + Process control and improvement in support areas + Suppliers are part of the team	+ Prevention and elimination of waste + Robust designs not sensitive to expected variation + Process control and improvement + Reduced cycle time + Supplier certification + Assessments done on processes and systems
Results	• Data are available to those that ask	• Some data tracked in support areas	• Data on key processes throughout the organization show mostly positive trends • Some comparisons to industry norms	+ Three-to-five-year trends show continual improvement + One of the leaders according to data for product, service, and response time throughout organization
Customer and Market Focus	• Take care of customer problems • Track customer satisfaction by "looking in the rearview mirror" only (e.g., market share) • Assume silence means satisfaction	• Guarantee is typical for industry • There is a customer satisfaction survey	• Listen to customers • Satisfy the customers • Have service standards + Customer has easy access to organization + Frontline employees have current information and make things right for the customers • Positive trends in customer satisfaction	+ Lead the customer regarding the art of the possible + Commitments to customers lead the industry + Delight the customers + Customer problems are rare, but when they occur, correction is prompt + One of the leaders in customer satisfaction, loyalty, and market share.

Key: + indicates attributes that should be carried forward to achieve and sustain outstanding status.

The *Outstanding* stage reflects excellence in everything the company does. The leadership is visible and is a good role model for the expected behavior. Cooperation among employees and department is valued. The customers' future requirements are anticipated and created by the company. We did not ask for a fax machine or antilock brakes, but proactive companies developed them and created a new need. An organization at this stage is a workplace of choice.

Digby now realizes he is entrenched somewhere between the *Traditional* and *Awareness* stages, whereas Andrew's organization is firmly in the *Improving* stage. When Digby started using Andrew as a sounding board, he was hoping there was something he could have his employees do that would improve the competitiveness of his company. Maybe he could ask everyone to develop a flowchart of their process or something like that. He heard flowcharts are powerful. (For basic improvement tools, see GOAL/QPC or Langley). Digby was disappointed to hear that first he had to look himself in the mirror and realize how his underlying beliefs have had a negative impact on his company. Change was needed, but it started with him examining his behavior. At first, Digby was disappointed that he was the one that needed to change, but then he started to get excited. His friend Andrew agreed to coach him in his leadership style and help him on the journey.

Resources:

Brassard, Michael, ed. *The Memory Jogger: A Pocket Guide of Tools for Continuous Improvement and Effective Planning,* 2nd ed. Salem, NH: GOAL/QPC, 1985.

Langley, G., K. Nolan, T. Nolan, C. Norman, and L. Provost. *The Improvement Guide.* San Francisco: Jossey-Bass, 1996. TARP presented at Quest for Excellence IV Conference, Washington, DC.

NOTES

1. NIST National Institute of Standards and Technology, *Criteria for Performance Excellence* (2007), http://www.quality.nist.gov/Business_Criteria.htm (accessed August 13, 2008).

2. A.D. Shriberg and R. Kumari, *Practicing Leadership.* (Hoboken, NJ: John Wiley & Sons, Inc., 2005), 77.

3. W.E. Deming, *The New Economics for Industry, Government, Education.* (Cambridge, MA: Massachusetts Institute of Technology. 1993), 1115.

4. M.S. Heaphy and G.F. Gruska, *The Malcolm Baldrige National Quality Award: A Yardstick for Quality Growth* (Reading, MA: Addison-Wesley Publishing Co., 1995), 24–25.

5. Alfie Kohn, *No Contest* (Boston: Houghton Mifflin, 1986), 60.

Maureen S. Heaphy

PROFESSIONAL CERTIFICATION

Society expects practitioners of all disciplines to be professional and competent. There are many ways to identify and determine competence today. One approach, professional certification, has been used to describe a process that is said to separate individuals who are competent from those who are less competent. It is viewed as a vital part of the evolutionary process of professionalization because it focuses attention on the competencies that constitute an occupation, including human resource management (HRM).[1] Competencies are used to define an emerging field and provide guidance to its practitioners in conducting self-assessment activities useful in continuous learning. They also provide information for academic and professional preparation programs for HRM program development, and can aid employers in identifying qualified practitioners. Additionally, perhaps the most important aspect of professional certification is that it communicates clearly to practitioners the expectations of the profession, enabling them to perform their roles and tasks within the profession more effectively.[2]

The identification of competencies unique to the field of HRM sets it off from others in the eyes of the public. It also aids HRM practitioners in focusing on, studying, and improving those competencies, which may lead to the development of variations or more sophisticated practices.

Identified competencies are helpful to HRM practitioners and the field in six different ways. They will provide:

- Experienced professionals with a tool for self-assessment and professional growth.
- A common set of concepts and vocabulary that will improve communication among professionals and other professional groups.
- The academic and professional preparation programs with information for program development.
- A basis for a potential certification program.
- Aid to employers in identifying qualified applicants.
- A basis for defining an emerging field of study.[3]

Accordingly, the Society for Human Resource Management (SHRM), American Society for Training and Development (ASTD), International Society for Performance and Improvement (ISPI), and American Payroll Association (AMA) have each developed specialized certification programs. Finally, in 1985, a nonprofit organization, the International Board of Standards for Training, Performance, and Instruction (IBSTPI), was created for the purpose of continuing certification research, competency development and validation, and consulting services.

Characteristics of a Profession

Research has identified eight essential interrelated characteristics vital to a profession. Of course, the degree of importance of the different characteristics varies from occupation to occupation. The eight characteristics include:

1. A code of ethics
2. An organized and accepted body of knowledge
3. Specialized skills and identified competencies
4. Minimum education requirement for members
5. Certification of proficiency needed for before members can achieve professional status
6. An orderly process in the fulfillment of responsibilities
7. Opportunities for the promulgation and interchange of ideas among members
8. Demands of acceptance of the disciplines of the profession, realizing that the price of failure or malpractice is to be "out" of the profession[4]

Purpose of Professional Certification

Since professional certification is primarily viewed as an impetus to professional development, it encourages practitioners to achieve high standards and it encourages the field of HRM to focus the use of resources in order to assist them in doing so. Thus, the identification and advancement of professional competencies is the primary purpose for

professional certification. Secondary purposes include:
- Avoiding external regulation
- Enhancing prestige of the field
- Stabilizing individual job security
- Increasing the influence of societies and associations on the profession
- Protecting the public, clients, and employers
- Improving academic programs
- Assisting in hiring practices
- Recognizing practitioner achievement
- Enhancing the field[5]

Regardless of the expressed purpose for certification, its significance lies in the fact that individuals, in preparation for certification, are required to increase their knowledge and ability, and that, rather than the designation itself, is its greatest benefit. Self-improvement is satisfying to the individual and increases one's sense of worth, which is a benefit to employers. Ultimately, it increases the quality of the product and services in HRM.

Qualification Criteria Utilized to Develop Professional Certification Programs

In a study of 70 associations and societies that maintain certification programs, 10 qualification criteria were identified as the most important when evaluating applicants for certification. They are:

1. Professional experience
2. Successful completion of written examinations or work projects
3. Completion of a program of study
4. Current employment in the respective field
5. Successful completion of a professional examination
6. Membership in a professional association or society
7. Completion of additional training and/or continuing education
8. Evidence of ethical behavior
9. Personal and professional references
10. Successful completion of an oral evaluation and/or interview[6]

Most of these criteria are being used by each of the HRD-related societies previously identified as having a specialized professional certification program.

For specific information regarding the exact requirement of each of the four HRM-related certification programs, please visit their respective Web sites listed in the Resources section:

Resources:

American Payroll Association
 http://www.asisvcs.com/publications/pdf/189900.pdf.
 American Society for Training and Development
 http://www.astd.org/NR/rdonlyres/7B0E3A00-9C07-400D-9BE1-1649BB8B9BD4/0/CPLP
 _Candidate_Bulletin_FINAL012308.pdf.
 International Society for Performance and Improvement
 http://www.certifiedpt.org/index.cfm?section=apply.
 Society for Human Resource Management
 http://www.hrci.org/hrci_files/_items/hrci-mr-tab2-1329/docs/2008%20cert%20handbook.pdf.

NOTES

1. Jerry W. Gilley and Steven A. Eggland, *Principles of Human Resource Development* (Reading, MA: Addison-Wesley Publishing Company, 1989).

2. Jerry W. Gilley and Michael W. Galbraith, "Examining Professional Certification," *Training and Development Journal* 40, no. 6 (June 1986): 60–61.

3. Barry B. Bratton and Michael Hildebrand, "Plain Talk about Professional Certification," *Instructional Innovator* 25, no. 9 (December 1980): 22–24, 49.

4. W. E. Scheer, "Is Personnel Management a Profession?" *Personnel Journal* 43, no. 5 (May 1964): 225–62.

5. Gilley and Eggland, *Principles of Human Resource Development.*

6. Ibid.

Jerry W. Gilley and Paul Shelton

SOCIALIZATION

Completion of candidate interviews should lead to the selection of the most qualified candidate(s). However, one consideration should be addressed prior to extending a job offer—the socialization process. Socialization can be defined as a process by which organizations bring new people into the culture.[1] Examining socialization more closely reveals that placement and orientation as well as the characteristics and phases of socialization are critical to the future success of the employee. This prevents a mindset in which employees are left on their own to sink or swim within the muck and mire of organizational culture.[2]

Placement

Placement is the process of introducing new employees to their coworkers, supervisor, managers, and organizational leaders, which is sometimes referred to as the career path identified by the employee and/or the organization. Thus, the first few days on a new job can be very difficult. Effective organizations understand the complexity of personal integration on the job and provide "support" employees to make introductions and provide overviews of the workplace, and so forth. Sometimes mentors are provided to help with long-term indoctrination and growth and development activities.

Managers and HR professionals determine how well the candidate's personality, career objectives, values, beliefs, and attitudes align with those of the organization. Accordingly, the organizational culture is one of the first determinants of the socialization process.[3] Thus, new employees adopt a set of basic assumptions that enable them to invest, discover, or develop an understanding of the organizational environment. These assumptions are deeply embedded and transmitted through such mechanisms as the following:

- Formal statements of organizational philosophy
- Material used during recruiting, selection, and socialization of new employees
- Promotion criteria
- Stories, legends, and myths about key people and events
- What leaders pay attention to, measure, evaluate, control, and reward[4]

Therefore, it is critical to determine the cultural match between new employees and the organization. New employees must possess the values, beliefs, and attitudes necessary to assure acceptance within the firm. If these values, beliefs, and attitudes are absent, a mismatch will occur that results in negative outcomes for both the employee and organization.

Orientation

Organizations that fail to prepare new employees for the organization and their respective coworkers will bring on a condition known as *employment shock*—the psychological gap between what new employees expect and what they find.[5] To avoid this adverse condition, organizations conscientiously use orientation training programs that familiarize new employees with their roles and responsibilities, the organizational system, its expectations, performance standards, performance output requirements, reporting relationships, growth and development requirements, and growth and enhancement practices used to ensure organizational renewal and competitive readiness.[6] Employee turnover and the cognitive dissonance associated with unresolved expectations can be greatly reduced when such programs are used.

Phases of Socialization

Three phases of socialization predominate within organizations: *anticipatory socialization, accommodation socialization,* and *role management.*[7] Each phase requires different activities and undertakings to increase an employee's chances of enjoying a successful career within an organization.

Anticipatory Socialization

When employees first join an organization, they typically pose two questions:

1. What will it be like to work for the firm?
2. Are they suited to the jobs available within the firm?

Each question should be addressed by the organization prior to hiring the individual, since first impressions are typically lasting ones. Thus, employees will feel a heightened sense of satisfaction and loyalty if addressed correctly.

Accommodation Socialization

The second phase of socialization occurs after an employee becomes a member of the organization. It is a period in which employees discover the organization and its jobs as they really are, and in time, employees become competent performers on the job and active participants within the firm. This is sometimes referred to as the probationary period, and can be very stressful for most individuals. Four common activities constitute the accommodation phase:

1. Establishing new interpersonal relations with both coworkers and managers
2. Learning the tasks required to perform the job
3. Clarifying one's role within the organization via formal and informal groups
4. Evaluating one's progress toward satisfying demands of the job and the role[8]

If things are positive during this phase, employees will feel a sense of accomplishment and acceptance by coworkers and superiors while gaining confidence in performing their jobs.

Role Management Socialization

Role management refers to the conflict that occurs once an individual has been fully integrated into the organization. Conflict may involve interpersonal relationships with coworkers or managers, inadequate development opportunities, insufficient job assignments, job performance, misinterpretation of rules or regulations, and so on. Regardless, role management socialization refers to the organization's ability to address and resolve conflicts between employees and the firm.[9] Unresolved or negative resolution may cause resentment, poor attitudes, or lukewarm cooperation on the part of new employees, while successful resolution results in reinforcement of positive organizational perceptions. Effective organizations focus on resolving conflict in a positive way to enhance relationships and build organizational esprit de corps.

Characteristics of Effective Socialization

Some organizations are more effective in socializing employees into their culture than are others. Effective organizations understand the importance of recruiting employees using effective job interviewing techniques followed by selection and placement using realistic career path projections. Accordingly, they address and resolve the issues most concerning employees prior to joining the organization.

Effective organizations focus their attention on enhancing employee socialization by providing five different but impactful activities, including:
• Tailor-made and individualized orientation programs
• Social and technical skill training
• Performance evaluations designed to provide supportive and accurate performance feedback
• Challenging work assignments that stretch an employee's abilities and talents
• Demanding but fair managers who practice effective performance coaching techniques[10]
Each of these activities retain and develop new employees while reducing tension and conflict within the organization.

Conclusion

Organizations that adopt effective socialization practices and policies understand fully the damage caused by conflict. As a result, these organizations encourage managers and HRD professionals to be proactive in socializing employees, communicating the unique elements of the organization's culture, and helping resolve conflict early in a new employee's tenure with the firm.

See also New Employee Orientation

NOTES

1. James L. Gibson, John M. Ivancevich, James. H. Donnelly, and Robert Konopaske, *Organizations: Behavior, Structure Process,* 12th ed. (New York: McGraw-Hill, 2007).

2. Jerry W. Gilley and Ann Maycunich, *Organizational Learning, Performance, and Change: An Introduction to Strategic HRD* (Cambridge, MA: Perseus Publishing, 2000).

3. Wayne F. Cascio, *Managing Human Resources: Productivity, Quality of Work Life, Profits* (New York: McGraw-Hill, Inc., 2005).

4. Ibid.

5. Gibson, Ivancevich, Donnelly, and Konopaske, *Organizations: Behavior, Structure Process.*

6. Jerry W. Gilley, Steven A. Eggland, and Ann Maycunich Gilley, *Principles of Human Resource Development,* 2nd ed. (Cambridge, MA: Perseus Publishing, 2002).

7. Gibson, Ivancevich, Donnelly, and Konopaske, *Organizations: Behavior, Structure Process.*

8. Ibid.

9. Gilley, Eggland, and Gilley, *Principles of Human Resource Development.*

10. Ibid.

Jerry W. Gilley

TRAINING

Training is the process of obtaining knowledge, skills, and/or abilities needed to carry out a specific activity or task. Identifying individual and company-wide training needs is a first step to increasing productivity and performance, creating sustainable value from human capital, and retaining talented employees.[1] This entry discusses organizational trends that have an impact on training, specifically the acquisition and keeping of key talent, training and delivery methods, and transferring skills.

Acquiring and Retaining Key Talent

Acquiring and keeping key talent ranks high on the list of concerns of senior leaders in organizations. Organizational success is directly related to acquiring and retaining talent. Increased global competition and a projected lack of available talent make acquiring and retaining talent a challenging task. Approaches to overcome these challenges include succession planning, leadership and employee development, and career planning.[2]

All of the above-mentioned approaches support cultivating a supply of internal talent to meet the needs of an organization. Training is a key ingredient in all of the approaches, both formal and informal training (e.g., projects and developmental assignments on the job). With the soaring costs of searching for and hiring new employees, it is prudent for organizations to assess their internal talent and cultivate that talent for future needs.

Training Delivery Methods

Training methods vary greatly, so it is essential to get the right combination to ensure the highest possible rate of learning and the subsequent return on investment. Organizations should identify the training method that best fits their employees' learning styles, be flexible enough to allow for changes when needed, and ensure that the training can be transferred into everyday job skills. Regardless of the method used, ensuring that training is effective is the primary goal. To start, answer the following questions:

• What is the primary purpose of the training?
• What are the learning objectives?
• Which organizational objectives and/or strategies is the training going to impact?
• Is senior level management supportive and/or involved?
• Where will the training be held, and is it centrally located?
• What are the costs associated and subsequent measures to determine overall effectiveness?

Once variables such as these have been addressed, the organization will be in a better position to implement training.

In addition to the traditional training methods used, such as formal presentations and print distribution, there are a number of methods that have shown higher success rates in terms of learning and transferring skills back to the job. These include experiential-based training, Web-based training (WBT), and 360-degree programs.

Experiential-based Training

Experiential-based training has evolved from classroom training, placing a heavier emphasis on an individual's taking action as part of the learning process. Participants are given opportunities for hands-on learning. Games, writing assignments, exercises, and challenge courses are options used to give participants a chance to discuss points of view and to try out new skills. Debriefing at the conclusion is a vital part of experiential training because it draws together everything the participant has learned at that particular session.

Web-based Training

Web-based training, or e-learning, engages the employee through opportunities for discussion and group participation, which are experienced without the employee leaving their computer terminal. The multimedia-rich environment has proven beneficial for learning as well as efficient delivery of training materials.

360-Degree Feedback

Three-hundred-sixty-degree programs are used for training or career development. Feedback is the essential component used to evaluate an employee's behavior and skills on the job. Information is gathered from several sources, including those people who have direct contact with the employee (e.g., coworkers, customers, or boss). Once feedback is provided, developmental goals and an action plan are created to enhance or build upon current skill sets.

Transferring Skills

With the increase of global competition for workers, it cannot be overstated how critical training has become. Organizations need to ensure that training endeavors are effective. In other words, the new knowledge and/or skills are transferred directly to the job, and employees are applying what they learned on the job.

Integrating HR processes such as compensation, learning management, and performance management will ensure training is transferred to the job. Integrating these processes helps set clear performance goals for the employee after the training, provides a financial reward, and helps to enhance ownership on the part of the training participant. Further, supervisors who follow up with employees with on-the-job coaching and mentoring will increase the likelihood that new skills transfer directly to the job.

Many challenges are looming ahead for the U.S. labor force. More and more, it has become imperative to retain current workers and continue to build upon the talent and skills of those workers. Developing and maintaining a comprehensive training program will ensure that organizations have the talent they need now and in the future.

See also Computer-Based Training; Interactive Video Training; Training Evaluation

NOTES

1. Bruce Pfau and Ira Kay, "Playing the Training Game," *HR Magazine,* 2002.
2. Susan Melsinger, "Talent Management in a Knowledge-Based Economy," *HR Magazine,* 2006.

3. Nancy R. Lockwood, "Talent Management: Driver for Organizational Success," *SHRM Research Quarterly* (2006),http://www.shrm.org (accessed January 2008).

Robin R. Labenz and Pamela Dixon

TRAINING EVALUATION

Countless HR thought leaders have vigorously proposed the merits of building learning organizations that are committed to making substantial investments in training.[1] They have done so on the grounds that organizations that invest in training and that learn better and faster than do their competitors achieve stronger long-term performance. Such an argument is compelling indeed, especially given the pace of change in today's marketplace.

The Case of "Big Blue"—Training-related Investment at the "Twelfth Hour"

Consider, for example, the case of IBM. In the mid-1990s, "Big Blue" was faced with the very real possibility of permanently losing its blue-chip status as one of the benchmark firms in American industry. The firm had relied too heavily and too narrowly on its core competencies in hardware manufacturing, research and development, and administrative discipline, and as a result had literally missed the shift from "big machines" (mainframes) to "smaller machines" (servers and PCs) and bundled IT services. Fortunately, the board of IBM saw the writing on the wall before it was too late, and brought in Lou Gerstner, a marketer from Nabisco, as CEO. Gerstner's challenge was less associated with embracing the need for IBM to learn (and learn fast) as an organization, but more so with leveraging the newfound knowledge that was generated via the learning that he catalyzed as the new leader intent on taking the firm in a critical new direction. The means by which he codified this shift towards learning was heavy investment in HR practices focused on the following training-related corporate priorities and initiatives.

1. *Learning-centric Performance Management.* Organizations intent on leveraging increasing organizational knowledge must first catalyze and reinforce learning at the individual employee level. They do so by building specific and measurable learning objectives into their performance appraisal tools and process, and orienting these learning objectives towards critical business needs. IBM's Gerstner started here by ensuring that the performance management process for the firm shifted towards the measurement of employee learning as a key assessment component, especially for those employees in leadership roles. And these learning objectives were articulated to specifically reinforce the marketing and systems thinking knowledge and skills necessary to compete in the new IT market.

2. *Cross-functional and Cross-divisional Team Structures.* In addition to fostering increased learning at the individual employee level, organizations must employ cross-functional and cross-divisional team structures as much as possible, for both temporary project and permanent operational purposes. Doing so ensures that individual employee learning is not only enhanced, but shared with others on a regular basis. Gerstner ensured that these types of team structures, essentially unheard of in the traditionally compartmentalized IBM of old, were immediately put in place. Such teams eventually became the means through which IBM offered bundled IT services alongside hardware components, and led the drive towards increased services revenue for the firm as a whole. Today, an increasingly significant portion of IBM's revenues are generated by intangible IT services (bolstered by the mid-2002

acquisition of PricewaterhouseCoopers' consulting business) offered to clients via cross-functional and cross-divisional teams. It is somewhat ironic and perhaps even nostalgic to remember that IBM stands for "International Business Machines," given this fundamental shift in their business model.

3. *A Shared Corporate Knowledge Bank.* Despite the shift to a increasingly services-based business model, IBM still produces machines—and they use them to house their shared corporate knowledge bank. This database allows IBM associates anywhere in the world to share and access the best practices of the firm. And the expectation within the firm is that they will do so on a regular basis.

Combined, these three training-related infrastructure components enabled IBM to measure and reward individual employee learning, foster team learning, and codify the increased knowledge associated with that learning. The end result of investing in these training-related initiatives and priorities at IBM speaks for itself—the firm is once again considered to be at the leading edge not only of the IT industry, but of American industry as a whole.

Training Best Practices

Perhaps the single biggest constraint regarding investment in employee training is the risk involved. Put simply, employees are not "owned" by an organization. Thus, investing in employees is inherently risky. Despite this, the best performing organizations make employee training and development investment a priority, rightly recognizing that such investment leads to competitive advantage. This involves the training best practices of plan, do, check, and act.[2] The above-outlined case study of IBM can be further illuminated via this framework.

- *Plan*—Gerstner clearly understood the strategic value of training initiatives. Perhaps even more importantly, he ensured that the training initiatives outlined at IBM during the early stages of his CEO tenure were tightly aligned with the IBM's strategic shift from hardware manufacturing to integrated IT services.
- *Do*—IBM employed several pedagogical and training design approaches to ensure that learning transfer (from classroom to the conference room) was maximized.
- *Check*—Gerstner understood the critical interdependency that exists between training and performance management. Thus, he ensured that the IBM performance management and appraisal system evaluated employees based at least in part on the basis of whether or not they demonstrated the new skills and behaviors associated with recently completed training and development programs.
- *Act*—Gerstner reinforced, sustained, and advanced the ongoing importance of training as a key to sustained competitive advantage for IBM. The firm did so by rewarding employees from a compensation standpoint at least in part based on the training components of performance appraisals. Additionally, the corporate knowledge bank championed by Gerstner further solidified the importance of training by ensuring that tacit individual employee learning was codified and shared with the larger organization.

Levels of Training Evaluation

Clearly, the IBM case reflects a keen understanding of the critical interdependencies that exist between training, performance management, and compensation. Such systemic design of HR practices is critical to the widely embraced, hierarchical training evaluation construct that considers the reaction, learning, behavior, and results levels of training evaluation.[3] Once again, the above outlined case study of IBM can be further illuminated via this framework:

1. *Reaction*—the first level of training evaluation. At IBM, Gerstner ensured that all participants in formal training sessions/workshops completed evaluative questionnaires immediately upon completing the session/workshop. These questionnaires included assessment of participants' reactions to the instructors, facilities, and general usefulness of the session/workshop content.
2. *Learning*—the second level of training evaluation. Gerstner ensured that "graded" simulations and exercises were part of every management training session/workshop at IBM. These simulations/exercises involved participants receiving real-time, evaluative feedback from both instructors and colleagues.
3. *Behavior*—the third level of training evaluation. As outlined above, Gerstner ensured that employee behavior vis-à-vis the training initiatives was evaluated via IBM's performance management process, and reinforced via IBM's compensation system. In short, IBM employees were evaluated and compensated at least partially based upon their demonstration of the skills and competencies addressed in the training sessions/workshops that they had attended.
4. *Results*—the fourth and highest level of training evaluation. In the end, it can be argued that IBM recovered from the brink of being delisted by the New York Stock Exchange at least in part due to the heavy investment that Gerstner catalyzed in organization learning and related training initiatives.

See also Employee Development: An Overview; Training; Learning Organizations; Needs Analysis

NOTES

1. Jerry G. Gilley and Ann Maycunich, *Organizational Learning, Performance, and Change* (Cambridge, MA: Perseus Publishing, 2000); David Ulrich and Wayne Brockbank, *The HR Value Proposition.* (Boston: Harvard Business School Press, 2005).

2. Judy D. Olian, Cathy C. Durham, Amy L. Kristof, Kenneth G. Brown, Richard M. Pierce, and Linda Kunder, "Designing Management Training and Development for Competitive Advantage: Lessons from the Best," *Human Resource Planning* 1 (1998): 20–31.

3. David Kirkpatrick, "Four Steps to Measuring Training Effectiveness," *Personnel Administrator* (November 1983): 17–28.

Scott A. Quatro

Chapter 3
Performance Management

Performance Management: An Overview

The performance challenge facing every organization is to develop management systems that make employees the firm's greatest asset. Designing, developing, and implementing an organization-wide performance management process links performance to the organization's strategic goals and objectives, constituent needs and expectations, and employee compensation and rewards. Applying the concepts, principles, and ideas of the performance management process at both the organizational and individual levels promotes maximum efficiency and performance throughout the firm.

Many ineffective organizations use an outdated, overly simple performance management process in which: (1) they identify and assemble the material resources required for employees to perform the job; (2) workers engage in activities to complete tasks; and (3) employers assess employees' performance and allocate compensation and rewards.[1] This simple process has its roots in the Industrial Revolution of more than a hundred years ago, when supervisors needed a fast, efficient way to manage a multitude of workers often performing similar routine manufacturing tasks. Today's sophisticated workforce demands more of its managers.

The dilemma facing many organizations is their ignorance regarding how to manage performance, develop people, or create initiatives and techniques that enhance effectiveness. Quite simply, how can companies transform their leaders, managers, and employees into high performers who are their greatest asset? This requires creating a performance management system that allows organizations to prepare for growth, achieve their strategic goals and objectives, and enhance organizational capability and competitiveness.

Successful performance management initiatives mandate significant change in organizational philosophy, operations, and strategy. This monumental effort requires firm leaders to sponsor and embrace change, since they are responsible for the performance of their organization and its employees. This section explores the specifics and challenges of performance management, including evaluations, feedback, performance analysis, motivation, retention, and more.

Improving Performance Management

Organizations have, over the years, learned much about human productivity, employee work and motivation, components of supervisor effectiveness, and the impact of organizational leadership and support with respect to performance management. As a result, more contemporary models of effective performance management have evolved. These models incorporate numerous human resource management theoretical frameworks, such as goal setting, motivation, coaching, feedback, and rewards.

Effective performance management techniques are applicable at the organizational, departmental (business process), and individual levels.

Organizational Level. The primary aim of performance management at the organizational level is achievement of strategic goals and objectives. Common organization goals and objectives include increases in sales, customer satisfaction, or profits; greater community involvement; higher rankings or perceived quality compared to competing firms; and so forth.

Department (Business Process) Level. No department or division is an island—all interact with or support others. Every job interacts with others at the business process or departmental level (e.g., finance, human resources, admissions, counseling, accounts payable, etc.).[2] Establishing goals for each process, function, and department collectively helps the organization meet the needs and expectations of its internal and external stakeholders.

Identifying interfaces between these business processes to reduce breakdowns or isolate potential improvements improves organizational efficiency and overall performance. In turn, organizations are able to uncover related opportunities for individual employee performance improvement, growth, and development.

Individual Level. Employees execute the tasks and assignments required to meet individual, departmental, and organizational responsibilities. Although

> the organizational and business process levels may be architectural masterpieces, if performers cannot execute efficiently and effectively, performance quality and outputs will be negatively affected. Unless organizations create conditions by which their employees can produce adequate products and services, organizational process goals will be jeopardized.[3]

Individuals are the heart of any organization—we do the work! Hence, the discussion that follows focuses on performance management at the individual level.

With an understanding that firm supervisors and managers possess diverse backgrounds typically *not* in human resource management, we will expand on the six-step contemporary system of performance management mentioned earlier in order to provide a systematic, comprehensive, in-depth approach useful to all. We suggest an enhanced performance management system that consists of the following 11 steps.

1. Identify stakeholder needs and expectations
2. Link the job to the organization's strategic goals and objectives
3. Provide resources
4. Establish preliminary job-related performance goals
5. Hire/promote/select qualified performers
6. Establish employee-specific performance goals
7. Develop performance standards and expectations
8. Coach and provide feedback
9. Conduct developmental evaluations
10. Create performance growth and development plans
11. Link compensation and rewards to individual goals, growth, and development.

Roles in Performance Management

Performance management forces organizational leaders to assume additional roles and their related responsibilities: champion for change, performance management advocate, and performance coach.

Change Champion. Improving performance within organizations requires firm leaders to accept their role as its champion, identifying key success details for building performance capacity. Seven critical factors of success build capacity for performance management and improvement.[4] Firm leaders must:

1. Lead performance management and improvement initiatives
2. Mobilize commitment for performance management and improvement
3. Modify initiatives and structures to support performance management and improvement
4. Monitor employee progress through performance management initiatives
5. Make performance management last by reinforcing and rewarding employee growth and development
6. Create a shared need for performance management and improvement
7. Shape a vision for performance management and improvement initiatives

Effectively sponsoring change requires a basic understanding of the nature of change and the human response to it. The nature of change may be categorized by type:[5]
- *Micro changes* are small, manageable, common transitions, such as adopting a new instructional method, adding new software to one's computer, or participating in graduate studies.
- *Organizational changes* are large-scale transitions that affect interactions, reporting relationships, and responsibilities. Examples include organizational reorganization or merging of departments.
- *Macro changes* are massive transitions that alter one's life or change ones assumptions, values, or beliefs. The events of September 11, 2001, for example, represent a macro change for millions of people.

Micro change occurs when "I" change; organizational change is when "we" change; macro change involves "everyone." Although the term *macro* sounds extensive, it seldom occurs; but when it does, it dramatically affects our lives. Such change alters the way we think and behave forever.

Human begins are inherently resistant to change, and often fear it. We are more comfortable and inclined to embrace the known, familiar, and routine, even when change may be in our best interest. Change can be frightening, particularly when it forces us out of our comfort zone or area of expertise, or exposes us to potential failure. Change champions understand our reactions to change and set up conditions for employee success. They provide individuals with abundant communications, tools, and support to help workers integrate change into their organizational lives. Ultimately, the keys to successful change management are understanding, communication, and support.

Performance Management Advocate. Effective firm leaders serve as advocates during the performance management process, acting as guides, providing and interpreting information, identifying problems, facilitating solutions, and evaluating outcomes. Advocates are proactive "scouts" who pioneer ways the organization can successfully implement the process.[6] As scouts, firm leaders focus on the success of performance management, acting as change ambassadors within the firm. Advocates for performance management demonstrate vision, possess credibility with other decision makers and stakeholders, and ask the organization to take risks that may seriously impact its future.

Performance Coach. Employing performance management requires a dramatic shift in the role of the firm leader to that of performance coach. Coaches are responsible for establishing rapport with employees, encouraging face-to-face communications, being active participants with employees rather than passive observers, and engaging their listening, questioning, and facilitation skills to achieve desired organizational results.

As discussed earlier, performance coaches engage in four distinct roles (trainer, mentor, confronter, counselor). As such, performance coaches' responsibilities are varied and ever-changing, depending on the situation. They function as cheerleaders, listeners, feedback providers, motivators, advisors, and so forth.

Conclusion

Organizations are systems operating on three distinct levels: organizational, departmental (business process), and individual. Each level requires evaluation based on its goals, design, and management practices. Although it is often more expedient to view organizational management from a macro level, the performance challenge is best addressed by applying the principles and concepts of the performance management process at the individual level. This process offers a long-term approach that enables firm leaders, managers, and employees—in spite of their different perspectives—to develop a common view of the organization and its future.

Performance management is a comprehensive, systematic process that benefits all organizational levels and employees by enhancing individual and collective performance. Performance management is comprised of goal setting, establishing related standards and expectations, performance coaching, developmental evaluation, creating growth and development plans, and linking compensation and rewards to individual growth and development.

NOTES

1. James Fuller and Jeanne Farrington, *From Training to Performance Improvement: Navigating the Transition* (San Francisco: Jossey-Bass, 1999).
2. Geary A. Rummler and Alan. P. Brache, *Improving Performance: How to Manage the White Spaces on the Organizational Chart* (San Francisco: Jossey-Bass, 1995).
3. Jerry W. Gilley, Nathaniel W. Boughton, and Ann Maycunich, *The Performance Challenge* (Cambridge, MA: Perseus Books, 1999), 42.
4. David Ulrich, *Human Resource Champions* (Boston: Harvard Business School Press, 1997).
5. Daryl R. Conner, *Managing at the Speed of Change* (New York: Villard Books, 1992), 79.
6. Jerry W. Gilley and Ann Maycunich Gilley, *Strategically Integrated HRD,* 2nd ed. (Cambridge, MA: Perseus Publishers, 2003).

Ann Gilley and Jerry W. Gilley

DEVELOPMENTAL EVALUATIONS

One of the most important activities that organizations can do to improve productivity, performance, and quality is to conduct regular (monthly, quarterly, semiannual, or annual) performance appraisals with every employee. Performance appraisals, sometimes called performance reviews, give managers the opportunity to judge the adequacy and quality of employees' performance useful in adjusting compensation levels and create professional development plans aimed at improving future performance. Unfortunately, the term "performance appraisal" restricts the manager's ability to work collaboratively with employees in their development. This is because the term "appraisal" often is perceived negatively, which can create defensiveness on the part of employees when engaging in the review process. To overcome this problem, we refer to performance appraisals as developmental evaluations.[1]

Developmental evaluations are an excellent way to analyze employee performance and make recommendations for improvement. Many employees fail to perform adequately due to barriers that prohibit exemplary performance.[2] Developmental evaluations help isolate these obstacles and formulate strategies for overcoming them.

The principal purpose of a developmental evaluation is to assess the employee's strengths and weaknesses. In this way, developmental evaluations provide managers with opportunities to analyze employees' knowledge, skills, and attitudes, and to determine those areas of excellence or needing improvement. These evaluations also present opportunities for managers and employees to discuss current and future developmental goals and objectives, and how employees plan to achieve them. Most importantly, developmental evaluations are a vehicle for discussion of future growth and development activities that will enhance employees' abilities and competencies as well as advance their careers.[3]

At the core of every developmental evaluation lies the concept of feedback. In this way, developmental evaluations and performance coaching are very similar activities. The fundamental difference between the two is that performance coaching is an ongoing minute-by-minute, day-by-day feedback opportunity, while developmental evaluations are designed to be formal, summative evaluations. In some respects, both performance coaching and developmental evaluations are designed to achieve the same goals—the creation of growth and development plans that improve employee performance. Accordingly, developmental evaluations are specific and timely in order for employees to make corrections and improvements required to bring about desired business results.

Without corrective and meaningful feedback needed to make appropriate performance adjustment, employees will be "flying blind" without any kind of assistance from their manager or the organization. Consequently, they will make decisions regarding their performance without adequate data. Absent such informative data, employees will make mistakes, which could have disastrous outcomes. Fortunately, developmental evaluations give managers the opportunity to share their perspectives of their employees' performance and discuss means of improvement. In this way, developmental evaluations serve a vital function within the organization.

Types of Developmental Evaluations

Managers can use one of five different types of development evaluations to improve employees' performance. Each of these five differ in application, focus, purpose, manager's role, employee's role, and power distribution. The types of developmental activities include:

• Work planning and reviews are used to direct, control, and improve performance. Their focus is on an employee's current job and is designed to manage workflow by objectives and results. Work planning and reviews are characterized by discussions between managers and employees about the goals and objectives employees are attempting to achieve, and the results they are attempting to accomplish.

- Compensation reviews are intended to motivate employees by rewarding past efforts and identifying future compensation and reward potential for upcoming performance. The focus is upon identifying the compensation and rewards an employee will receive as a result of meeting or exceeding performance standards. They are characterized by review of salary structure, merit increases, bonuses, benefits, and nonmonetary rewards that are appropriate based upon an employee's past and anticipated future performance.
- Developmental planning's purpose is to improve employees' knowledge, skills, and attitudes. The focus of this evaluation is on skill building, and is characterized by preparing self-improvement and personal growth activities and action planning. As a result, agreed-upon growth and development plans begin to surface.
- Career planning is the process of establishing individual career objectives for employees and creatively developing long-term developmental activities to achieve them. Career planning differs from growth and development plans in the time frame encompassing maximization of knowledge, skills, and abilities. In short, career planning is a long-term process of charting an employee's career, while growth and development plans help improve employee production immediately.
- Human resource planning is designed to maintain organizational continuity vis-à-vis human resources over an extended period of time, focusing on career pathing, succession planning, and blending high potential career actions. Human resource planning remains largely the exclusive domain of managers and executives, with limited solicited employee input. Ultimately, the final human resource determination lies with the organization.[4]

Examination of each of the five unique developmental evaluation activities reveals that they are conducted for very different reasons while focusing on distinct activities and outcomes. Further, each of the five developmental evaluations is a separate developmental evaluation opportunity and should not be used in combination, as their purpose differs greatly.

Unfortunately, the most common evaluations that are mistakenly combined are those of work planning and compensation review. Given that work-planning evaluations are conducted to direct, control, and improve performance, they should not be combined with discussions related to an employee's compensation and rewards. Compensation and reward evaluations should be separate activities used to reward employees for past performance achievements and motivate future accomplishments. Mistakenly, these two separate, distinct reviews are completed in combination. Thus, employees enter into the developmental evaluation process solely interested in the identification of their future compensation and rewards. This bias often prevents open, honest discussions about current or future performance and prohibits an in-depth analysis of strengths and weaknesses. Employees enter this evaluation process anticipating the amount of salary increase or potential bonuses to be received as a result of their performance. Thus, it is inappropriate to combine them, as their individual effectiveness is weakened.

Conclusion

Developmental evaluations provide employees with feedback on their performance, help recognize their strengths and achievements over a specific period of time, identify areas where they can continue to grow and develop, define performance goals for the next 6–12 months, and review the "match" between the organization's expectations and those of employees. Quite simply, developmental evaluations help organizations make decisions regarding the performance of employees and aid in construction of developmental and career planning activities that enhance their work.

See also Performance Coaching; Performance Appraisals

NOTES

1. Jerry W. Gilley, Nathaniel W. Boughton, and Ann Maycunich, *The Performance Challenge: Developing Management Systems to Make Employees Your Organization's Greatest Asset* (Cambridge, MA: Perseus Books, 1999).

2. Jerry W. Gilley, *Improving HRD Practice* (Malabar, FL: Krieger Publishing Co, 1998).

3. Jerry W. Gilley and Ann Gilley, *The Manager as Coach* (Westport, CT: Praeger, 2007).

4. Jerry W. Gilley and Joe Davidson, *Quality Leadership* (New York: Wm. M. Mercer, 1993).

Jerry W. Gilley and Ann Gilley

EVALUATION

One of the most important and powerful components of HRM practice is that of evaluation. Evaluation should be a daily practice presiding over each component of HRM practice, including selection and recruiting, employee development, organizational and needs analysis, the performance management process, compensation and reward system, HR practices, policies, and procedures, and organizational development and change management initiatives. As an operational approach: evaluate, evaluate, evaluate. When uncertain of usefulness, effectiveness, or credibility: evaluate. Then and only then will HRM professionals be able to determine the viability, reliability, and utility of HR programs, activities, partnerships, initiatives, interventions, practices, and processes.

Evaluation is a process, not an event, that involves all key decision-makers, stakeholders, and influencers, and should be influenced by a clear understanding of the organization's performance and business needs, as well as its strategic goals and objectives.[1] As a process, evaluation is used to measure every aspect of the HRM function. Accordingly, it should measure the HRM philosophy and practice, as well as the impact and utility of strategic business partnerships.

During the evolution of the HRM function, evaluation displays the distinctive characteristics of each phase. During the activity phase of HRM (see the entry on HR Strategy), the majority of evaluation occurs at the completion of programs and/or tranactions. However, as HRM crosses over the line of demarcation from an activity to a results orientation, which is the value-added phase, the evaluation process changes dramatically. Now evaluation becomes a tool for measuring performance improvement and the impact of various interventions, initiatives, partnerships, and strategic practices throughout the organization. Consequently, evaluation captures the scope, depth, and degree of impact HRM professionals and their interventions and practices have on the organization.

The Evaluation Process

Regardless of the type of evaluation completed, the evaluation process consists of six steps, each of which is essential and based upon the previous steps. Quite simply, the evaluation process compares results with objectives. The six steps include:

1. Collecting data
2. Analyzing data
3. Interpreting and drawing conclusions from the data
4. Comparing conclusions to stated objectives
5. Documenting results
6. Communicating results to key decision-makers, stakeholders, and influencers.[2]

A variety of data collection techniques are used during the evaluation process, including questionnaires, interviews, focus groups, organizational reports and records, pretests and posttests, and management's perception of change. Each of these techniques can be used to collect the data necessary to draw conclusions and make recommendations to stakeholders and decision-makers.

To improve the accuracy of the evaluation process, HRM professionals should use an intervention analysis worksheet. This is a simple, straightforward guide designed to capture more salient information regarding the impact of any HRD intervention or initiative. An intervention analysis worksheet incldues the following information:

• What is the name of the intervention or initiative?
• What organizational change took place? Have performance skills, knowledge, or business results changed or improved as a result of the intervention or initiative?
• What on-the-job performance behaviors changed as a result of the intervention or initiative? What were the organizational benefits as a result of the intervention or initiative?[3]

Such tools helps HRM professionals capture information that can be used to improve interventions and initiative as well as improve their implementation. Further, the information gathered can serve as the foundation for individual interviews and focus group activities. The definitive benefit of the intervention outcome analysis tool is that it allows HRM professionals the opportunity to discuss their interventions or initiatives with key decision-makers, stakeholders, and influencers and gather their perceptions, opinions, and points of view. Such an engagement can only help improve the image and credibility of HRM professionals within the organization.

Validity, Reliability, and Utility

Since the accuracy of evaluation results impact image and credibility of HRM professionals, they must be accurate. Therefore, the three criteria of validity, reliability, and utility should be used to measure the effectiveness of an evaluation.

Validity

Validity is concerned with the extent to which an evaluation measures what it is supposed to measure.[4] Accordingly, evaluations should be more objective as they attempt to isolate and control independent variables (things that affect the outcome[s] of the evaluation), which can alter the evaluation's accuracy. Three types of validity relevant to HRM evaluations are content, predictive, and concurrent validity.

Content Validity. Content validity is used to ensure that evaluations represent specific competencies, performances, and skills that reflect actual practice. Therefore, HRM professionals must guarantee that the questions used to assess employee performance or level of competence accurately measure real-life events when constructing an evaluation. Content validity ensures that evaluations test *real-life practices* under circumstances and conditions similar to those encountered on the job. When evaluations are developed in such a way as to achieve this end, they will be meaningful as well as useful.

Predictive Validity. Predictive validity refers to an evaluator's (HRM professional) ability to predict future performance.[5] It assures that the evaluations used accurately reflect what an employee accomplishes on the job. Two types of data are involved:
• The results of an evaluation
• Individual performance on the job
If the evaluation has high predictive validity, an employee scores high on an evaluation and performs at a high level on the job. Evaluations exhibiting this type of validity serve as the foundation for predicting future performance and organizational outcomes, which become valuable information for supporting the utility of HRM interventions, initiatives, and practices. Such outcomes, again, are useful in improving the image and credibility of HRM, its programs, and professionals.

Concurrent Validity. Concurrent validity is used to determine whether or not evaluation results provide an accurate estimate of present performance.[6] As with predictive validity, concurrent validity involves the relationship between the evaluation and some other measure. For example, comparing the results of a written test with that of performance observations enables HRM professionals to test the accuracy of each evaluation technique. A strong correlation (relationship) in results allows for use of the most cost-efficient evaluation technique, since either one can predict on-the-job performance accurately.

Reliability

Consistency and stability of an evaluation indicate its reliability.[7] It could be said that an evaluation is reliable if results are consistent and scores do not change significantly over time, which is known as test/retest reliability.[8] Evaluations are also considered reliable if scores do not change a great deal when different variations of the same evaluation are used. In other words, if the order of questions used during a focus group or an interview varies from evaluation to evaluation, but the evaluation includes the exact same questions and the results are similar, the evaluation is considered reliable. This is referred to as equivalent form reliability.

Utility

Evaluation must also be easy to use while being valid and reliable. Accordingly, HRM professionals must consider ease of scoring, distributing, administering, and interpreting various evaluations prior to selecting the most appropriate form. Additional factors influencing utility include evaluation subjectivity, comparability of scores and performances, and cost.[9]

Conclusion

Evaluation is the key to reflective insight and continuous improvement. Without evaluation, HRM professionals will never truly know how well they are performing or how they are perceived within the organization. Failure to evaluate is equivalent to HRM malpractice and deception. Further, evaluation is a state of mind, not a technique, and should guide everyday practice and activities. Consequently, it provides invaluable information that can only help improve the image and credibility of the HRM function within the organization.

NOTES

1. Jerry W. Gilley, Steven A. Eggland, and Ann Maycunich Gilley, *Principles of Human Resource Development,* 2nd ed. (Cambridge, MA: Perseus 2002).

2. Ibid.

3. Ibid, 388.

4. Ibid.

5. Ibid.

6. Ibid.

7. Ibid.

8. Ibid.

9. Ibid.

Jerry W. Gilley and Ann Gilley

EXIT INTERVIEW

An exit interview occurs between an employer and employee when the employee has given notice to terminate employment. Long considered perfunctory, exit interviews can be a strategic tool that can help employers reduce turnover, increase retention, and hire more strategically in the future. Exit interviews can yield information that allows employers to more proactively manage their employees.

When to Interview

There is some debate as to when to conduct an exit interview; therefore, employers should consider their specific needs when determining what works best for them. Options include: right after an employee announces his resignation, midway through the notice period, a few days before the employee leaves, when an employee returns to collect a final paycheck or turn in his uniform, or two to seven weeks after an employee has left.

Each option has its strengths and weaknesses. Conducting the interview early on provides the opportunity to counteroffer, especially if the purpose for leaving is strictly financial.[1] Waiting for several weeks after an employee gives notice allows for an employee to address the multitude of HR actions that generally occur (i.e., benefits, insurance, workload transitions, etc.) during one's final days. Time in between allows employees to deal "with their own cognition about why they are leaving."[2] Generally, however, conducting an exit interview during an employee's final week or last day is discouraged, as the employee is usually focused more on the transition and less on the reasons why.

How to Interview

Interviews can be conducted in person, via a paper survey, or by using an electronic survey on the Internet. Many of the Web-based interviews provide greater anonymity and confidentiality, and can often interpret data as well.[3] Interviews can be conducted by internal HR professionals, or employers can elect to use outside sources (which may be perceived as more neutral). Exit interview forms should be consistent across the company.[4] Increasingly, employers are looking to technology to automate the exit interview process.[5]

However an employer chooses to conduct an interview, a few basic guidelines should be followed. Always give advance notice to the employee that he will be asked to conduct an exit interview. Interviewers should be respectful, considerate, and appreciative of the outgoing employee's time and input; interviewers should not be defensive. Finally, information gathered at an exit interview should be kept confidential, and the former employee should be made aware of this.[6]

Why Interview

Exit interviews can yield valuable information into the current operations of a company that can lead to positive change.[7] Employers should strive to learn as much as possible about why employees leave so that changes can be implemented to decrease turnover and increase retention.[8] Also, departing employees often want to "help" those who stay behind by offering constructive comments that might result in improved work situations.[9] Employees should be informed that information gathered may be used to make concrete changes in the future.[10]

Exit interviews can inform future hiring decisions. Some employers use the information gathered at exit interviews to create preferred candidate profiles. Others have developed databases of insights, focusing on trends and patterns in the information rather than single anecdotes.[11] Examples of changes that have been made as a result of exit interviews include changes in supervisor training, changes in incentive programs, and changes in pay packages.

What to Ask

Exit interviews should seek to understand workers' motives, attitudes, and insights. Interviewers should "avoid being too general or asking leading questions."[12] Open-ended questions will allow employees to speak from their own experience. Interviewers should listen carefully, probe for greater detail, not make assumptions, and avoid arguing with the interviewee. Interviewers should strive to "keep the interview going in as positive a direction as possible" and worry about "validating and analyzing" the information later.[13] Questions an interviewer might ask include:

- If the CEO left unexpectedly today and you were put in charge, what are the first things you would change?
- What could have changed six months ago that would have prevented you from looking for a new job?
- If you were not looking, what factors tipped the scale when an opportunity came up?
- Who do you think is next to resign? And why?
- If one person from the firm would cause you to think twice about leaving, who would that person be?
- Why did you not leave us sooner than now?
- How did your manager communicate your responsibilities? Do you think he or she was fair and reasonable?
- Describe any areas of conflict that have affected either your performance or morale, or that you believe affected other employees.[14]

NOTES

1. Scott Westcott, "Goodbye and Good Luck," *Inc.*, April 2006, 40.

2. "How New Style Exit Interviews Can Help You Reduce Turnover," *Human Resource Department Management Report*, April 2005, 2.

3. Ibid.

4. Margaret Macafee, "...Conduct Exit Interviews," *People Management,* July 2007, 42.

5. "How New Style Exit Interviews Can Help You Reduce Turnover," 2; and Kathy Gurchiek, "Execs Take Exit Interviews Seriously," *HR Magazine,* January 2007, 34.

6. Westcott, "Goodbye and Good Luck," 40.

7. Terry McKenna, "How to Conduct Exit Interviews," *National Petroleum News,* May 2007, 23.

8. Don H. Harris, "The Benefits of Exit Interviews," *Information Systems Management,* Summer 2000, 17.

9. Harris, "The Benefits of Exit Interviews," 17, and Westcott, "Goodbye and Good Luck," 40.

10. Westcott, "Goodbye and Good Luck," 40.

11. Ibid.

12. Harris, "The Benefits of Exit Interviews," 17.

13. Ibid.

14. Westcott, "Goodbye and Good Luck," 40.

Lynda Kemp

FEEDBACK

Feedback is the sharing of observations about job performance or work-related behaviors. The goal is to achieve work objectives by reinforcing or changing behavior.[1]

Feedback can be given upward, downward, and laterally, by an employee to his/her manager, direct reports, or peers. One of a manager's most important responsibilities is to provide actionable feedback to his/her direct reports to enable them to build on their strengths, address areas in need of development, and achieve their performance goals.

Benefits of Effective Feedback

Providing timely and actionable feedback to the employee has many benefits. Feedback:
- Reinforces appropriate behaviors
- Aids an employee in correcting inappropriate or ineffective behaviors
- Ensures the employee has a clear understanding of his/her manager's expectations
- Provides clear direction to the employee for improving his/her work performance
- Encourages and supports employee development
- Promotes constructive communication between the manager and the employee.

Giving Effective Feedback

In order for feedback to have a meaningful and positive impact on the recipient, it is important that the giver of the feedback follow some general guidelines.

1. *Give feedback as close to the performance event as possible.*[2] To have the greatest impact, the feedback should be given to someone soon after you have observed his/her performance. This will allow the person to recall the specific situation and his/her actions and put the feedback in the proper context.

2. *Address behaviors and actions, not personality.* Avoid accusations and personal attacks such as "You did...," and "Why did you...?" which lead to resistance and resentment. Instead, focus on behaviors and consequences, such as "Arriving 15 minutes late delays the team and hinders its productivity."

3. *Balance the good with the bad.*[3] Too much of anything can be a bad thing, including critical feedback. Try to balance criticism with positive feedback whenever possible. Let the person know what she is doing well as well as what performance she needs to improve. This may not always be realistic, but if the giving of feedback is generally balanced, the receiver will be more likely to accept critical feedback when it is given. An effective strategy is to start with a positive observation, provide the critical feedback, and end with a positive comment.

4. *Be sure that the intent in giving feedback is to be helpful, and not punitive, and that the person knows it.*[4] A part of giving effective feedback is establishing a trusting relationship with the recipient. It is critical that the recipient of the feedback trust that the feedback is being given as a means to help him be more successful.

5. *Make sure the feedback is concrete and specific.*[5] When giving feedback about a person's performance, it is important to provide meaningful and actionable feedback to him. This can be done by providing the specific details of the situation that was observed, the actions that the person took, and the results that these actions had on the person's performance. By providing specific examples of demonstrated behaviors to the person and the results that his behaviors and actions had on performance and the business, the giver of the feedback can coach the recipient on why/how those actions led to a positive or negative outcome.

6. *Ensure that the feedback is actionable.*[6] Feedback should be given about actions or behaviors that a person can change or enhance. Giving feedback or criticism about a person that cannot be changed (e.g., someone's height) is not helpful, as they cannot take action on this feedback.

7. *Avoid making sweeping generalizations.*[7] As mentioned before, providing specific examples of actions or behaviors is essential; sweeping generalizations, such as "You always..." or "You never..." can put the recipient of the feedback on the defensive and cause the feedback to go unheeded and unaddressed.

8. *Provide examples of appropriate performance.*[8] Identify the change that must occur in terms of steps to be followed or other specific ways to improve knowledge, skills, or performance.

9. *Review the downside of continuous poor performance.*[9] The employee must clearly understand the consequences of poor performance, and that change must occur.

10. *Check for agreement/understanding and establish a commitment for next steps.* Once the feedback has been given, the giver should confirm that the recipient understands the feedback that has been given. If the giver of the feedback is the recipient's manager, then it is appropriate for the manager and the employee to discuss what steps the employee should take to act on this feedback and by when. The manager and the employee should then commit to a date when they will meet to check in on the commitment for action.

11. *Express confidence in the employee's ability to improve.* All employees possess areas of strength. Offer support and share your confidence in the employee's ability to be a valued member of the organization.

NOTES

1. *Harvard Business Online: Harvard Manage Mentor* (Cambridge, MA: Harvard Business School Press, 2001).

2. Terry R. Bacon, *Effective Coaching* (Durango, CO: International Learning Works, 1997).

3. Ibid.

4. Ibid.

5. Ibid.

6. Ibid.

7. Ibid.

8. Jerry W. Gilley, Nathaniel W. Boughton, and Ann Maycunich, *The Performance Challenge* (Cambridge, MA: Perseus Books, 1999).

9. Ibid.

Stephanee Roessing

FORCED RANKING EVALUATION

Forced ranking is a form of evaluating employee performance within an organization. Organizations such as General Electric, Ford, PepsiCo, Cisco, Sun Microsystems, and other Fortune 500 firms use a form of forcefully ranking the performance of their employees relative to a peer group.[1] Other euphemisms for this approach include vitality curve, quartile ranking, up or out policy, rank and yank, top grading, differentiation, and laddering.[2] GE is probably the most widely known for its forced ranking system.

Forced ranking systems are very appealing from an executive point of view. It forces organizations to invest in top performers and to coach lower performers to either improve or allow the employee to move on to another organization that would fit that employee better, by giving the employee feedback that is honest and consistent. The belief is that if you continually invest in the best performers, then you increase the performance potential of the organization. The process involves systematic and rigorous assessments that managers perform at regular intervals during the year.[3] The assessments are usually along a competency-based evaluation approach in which employees are assessed based on their ability to master certain defined job-critical skills. Those employees are then compared to others within their peer group.

The Basics

How does forced ranking really work? Given the nature of the system, assessments and assessment tools are very important. Subjectivity is something that can undermine the entire system. Ideally, forced ranking maintains a level of transparency that allows employees to determine their development needs with the mentoring of their supervisor in order to improve performance. In actuality, forced ranking evaluates one individual's performance against the performance of another or others, creating a relative rather than an absolute measuring device. Three of the most popular ways to compare employees is through "group order ranking, individual ranking, and paired comparisons."[4]

With group order ranking, all employees are placed into a particular classification, such as top one-fifth or second one-fifth. Often used for admitting students into higher education, this evaluation technique places students into segments of the total population. When managers use this type of ranking, all of their subordinates are ranked. For instance, if a manager has 25 subordinates, then five would be in the top one-fifth while five would be in the bottom one-fifth.

Individual ranking orders employees from best to worst. The approach assumes that there are equal differences between each employee, such as the difference between the first and second employee is the same as the difference between the 21st and 22nd.[5] The goal is a clear ordering of employees from the best performer to the lowest performer.

A paired comparison identifies each employee with every other employee and rates each as either the superior or weaker member between the pair. The employee is provided a summary of ranking derived from the total superior scores received. Although this method is administratively cumbersome, it ensures that every employee is compared against every other.

Ford Motor Company utilizes a group order ranking by dividing all 18,000 employees into groups of 30 to 50 employees. Their system defines that 10 percent receive an "A," 80 percent receive a "B," and 10 percent receive a "C." C players, as this group has become known, are restricted from pay increases, and if they sustain C ratings for two consecutive years, they are either demoted or terminated. Many "self-select" out of the organization as a result of these rankings. General Electric has a similar well-known program, in which the breakdown is 20 percent, 70 percent, and 10 percent. The focus in both these scenarios is to keep and reward the top performers while removing the bottom groups. Performance is believed to be built by virtue of raising the standard every year and increasing quality within the organization by removing those who are not in line with expectations.

Pros and Cons

Proponents of forced ranking suggest that the true cost of keeping low performers are great, and actually weaken the company.[6] A study on profit growth within one company showed that "A managers grew profits on average 80% in one company and 130% in the other, while C managers achieved no profit growth."[7] Other arguments are that by keeping low performers in a role, they are occupying a role that is then not available to an A player or a high performer, thus limiting the advancement of the very people whom the organization wants to retain. Those who are asked to report to a C player are believed to be subjected to limited learning opportunities, are held back from being able to make a strong contribution, and ultimately may leave out of frustration that advancement is not available.

On the other side of the argument, some scholars argue that performance within a forced ranking system neglects to take into consideration that there is not necessarily a normal distribution curve in performance and potential of employees.[8] It has been suggested that to gain a normal distribution, a sample size that is typical in teams (in the tens) is not large enough to make the assertion that individuals within a forced ranking system have been randomly sampled (usually in the thousands). This undermines the belief that a forced ranking system maintains objectivity. The argument continues that if hiring and development practices are effective, then there should be no need to identify later that there are average and poor performers.[9] Another difference in opinion is the belief that given certain dynamics of teams, a forced ranking system can actually serve to shroud low performers if they are in a low-performing team. Is it the same to remove the worst employees from a high-performing team as it is to not remove the best employees from a team of bad performers?[10] Additionally, ranking individuals against each other in an environment where team work is valued sends a contradictory message.

Identifying Performance

In "A New Game for C Players," the authors conducted a study in which only 16 percent of managers strongly agreed that their company knew who the higher and lower performers were in the senior ranks.[11] This issue is compounded at the line level, where a supervisor may have 20 or 30 subordinates to review. Critical to a forced ranking process is the ability to review and rank employees within the underpinnings of fairness.

The process that accompanies a forced ranking system is detailed and rigorous. Implementation of a forced ranking system takes on an added requirement because they can be grounds for wrongful termination or EEO-related lawsuits on the basis of a disparate impact if not implemented properly.[12] The goals of most performance appraisal processes are to:

- Help or prod supervisors to observe their subordinates more closely and to do a better job coaching.
- Motivate employees by providing feedback on how they are doing.
- Provide backup data for management decisions concerning merit increases, transfers, dismissals, and so on.
- Improve organization development by identifying people with promotion potential and pinpointing developmental needs.
- Establish a research and reference base for personnel decisions.[13]

Implementing a forced ranking system in an organization requires that care is taken to inform and train employees. Several "to-dos" are identified in IOMA's Report on Managing Customer Service:

- Give employees notice of the new policy.
- Clearly communicate objectives and measurable expectations, and involve the employee in goal setting.
- Provide accurate feedback as often as possible.
- Ensure evaluations contain concrete examples of good and bad performance [so that you can] avoid claims of biased stereotypes.
- Monitor your results to see whether your decisions are having a lopsided effect on the basis of age, race, gender, etc.
- Train managers on how the system is supposed to work, and be prepared to bring them back periodically for refresher training.
- Build quality-control checkpoints into the process to ensure quality of the performance reviews, quality of feedback to employees, avoidance of rater bias (e.g., leniency/strictness, halo effect, etc.), and compliance with relevant regulations and other legal considerations.
- Obtain regular feedback from employees on the effectiveness of the process and their perceptions of the system's fairness.
- Permit employees to challenge their performance ranking through internal dispute mechanisms. [14]

Conclusion

Clearly, there are perils to implementing a forced ranking process in any organization. Understanding the culture of the organization, and what limits of change the organization can handle, would be important when advising executives on the prudence of such measures. The executives may likely be enamored with the idea on some level. Harnessing the hidden potential in the existing talent will continue to be at the forefront of conversation in the coming years as organizations try to utilize every advantage within reach. It is within management and HR's ability to direct and foster appropriate tools for capturing the hidden organizational talent and potential. Kelly Holland reported in the *New York Times* in September 2006:

> It is instructive to note that critics of performance reviews have been around for a very, very long time. When the Wei dynasty in China rated the performance of its household members

in the third century A.D., the philosopher Sin Yu noted that "an imperial rater of nine grades seldom rates men according to their merits, but always according to his likes and dislikes."[15]

Whether it is with forced ranking or with another tool, known or unknown today, performance management is a concept that will change and adjust to market conditions, but will likely be around in perpetuity.

See also Human Capital; Performance Management: An Overview

NOTES

1. Sundararaman Ramesh, "What Value Does an Employee Add?" *IIMB Management Review* 16, no. 2 (2004): 21–27.

2. Ibid.

3. Stephen P. Robbins, *Organizational Behavior,* ed. Jennifer Glennon, 10th ed. (Upper Saddle River, NJ: Prentice Hall, 2003), 503–4.

4. Ibid.

5. Ibid.

6. Beth Axelrod, Helen Handfield-Jones, and Ed Michaels, "A New Game Plan for C Players," *Harvard Business Review* (January 2002): 80–88.

7. Ibid.

8. Ramesh, "What Value Does an Employee Add?"

9. Ibid.

10. Ibid.

11. Axelrod, Handfield-Jones, and Michaels. "A New Game Plan for C Players."

12. "Forced Rankings: Today's Performance Reviews Are Taking a More Serious Tone,"*IOMA's Report on Managing Customer Service* 11 (2001): 5.

13. Kelly Holland, "Performance Reviews: Many Need Improvement," *New York Times,* September 10, 2006, http://www.nytimes.com/2006/09/10/business/yourmoney/10mgmt.html?ex=1315540800&en=f9bf772cdd74e62e&ei=5088&partner=rssnyt&emc=rss (accessed March 18, 2008).

14. "Forced Rankings: Today's Performance Reviews Are Taking a More Serious Tone."

15. Holland, "Performance Reviews: Many Need Improvement."

Lisa Scott Brinkman

MOTIVATION

Employee motivation must be a central and overarching focus for HRM. The reality is that the direction, level, and persistence of effort demonstrated by employees is directly impacted by their individual and aggregate motivation levels. It is clear that the highest performing firms have highly motivated employees, and HRM functions that design and operationalize HRM practices are undergirded by a sound understanding of motivation theory. Ultimately, all motivation theories are grounded in a baseline understanding of the role that both extrinsic and intrinsic rewards play in affecting employee motivation levels.[1]

Extrinsic Rewards and HR Practice

An extrinsic reward is a motivational stimulus provided by someone else. In short, it is a reward that comes from outside the employee, and is thus offered to the employee as incentive for certain behaviors. Extrinsic rewards are valued outcomes for a job well done. Several key truths relative to HRM practice and extrinsic rewards can be delineated.

- *Reward alignment*—in order for extrinsic rewards to be motivating, they need to customized to the aggregate organization. For example, the employees at Google are corporately motivated through challenging, broad-based assignments, whereas the employees at Mary Kay are corporately motivated via lavish public recognition ceremonies and rewards such as the coveted pink "career car." From a strategic HRM perspective, the key is to use the chosen extrinsic rewards to reinforce the desired employee behaviors, which in turn are aligned with the firm's overarching strategic objectives. At Google, these desired behaviors include collaboration and creativity, which are central to achieving strong performance in the IT industry. At Mary Kay, the desired behaviors are independence and entrepreneurialism, which are central to success in the direct-selling industry.
- *Reward attractiveness*—in order for extrinsic rewards to be motivating, they need to be customized to individual employee preferences. At Google, individual employees are afforded the flexibility of choosing which assignments to take and which to pass on. At Mary Kay, while the pink "career car" may be the ultimate reward and the color is nonnegotiable, recipients in the United States can choose from several makes and models, including a Saturn Vue, a Pontiac Vibe, and a Cadillac CTS. Or recipients can even choose a cash equivalent reward instead of the car.
- *Reward consistency*—in order for extrinsic rewards to be motivating, they must be consistently awarded. That is, once the organization and the HRM function have delineated the formal guidelines (as at Mary Kay) or even the informal, shared cultural expectation (as at Google) relative to the rewards, it is imperative that they be consistently administered. Imagine the impact if Mary Kay decided in a particular year to eliminate the "career car" award due to "unforeseen business challenges." The result would be significant erosion of motivational pull that had built up over many years (the first pink car reward was given to high-performing employees in 1969), and may never be fully recovered. Amazingly, many firms do exactly this when faced with financial pressures.

Intrinsic Rewards and HRM Practice

An intrinsic reward is a self-administered motivational stimulus. In short, it is a reward that comes from inside the employee, and is thus experienced by the employee as a natural by-product of performing certain tasks/jobs. Intrinsic rewards are valued emotional states experienced in relationship to the job itself. Intrinsic motivation and rewards are affected primarily via job design and ongoing career development. Specific intrinsic rewards include feelings of competence, personal development, and autonomy. Both Google and Mary Kay have designed jobs and related career development programs to reinforce these key emotional states throughout their employee ranks.

See also Performance Management: An Overview; Promotion; Job Satisfaction

NOTE

1. Edward E. Lawler, "The Design of Effective Reward Systems," in *Handbook of Organizational Behavior,* ed. Jay W. Lorsch (Englewood Cliffs, NJ: Prentice-Hall, 1987), 255–71; Edward Deci, *Intrinsic Motivation* (New York: Plenum Publishing, 1975).

Scott A. Quatro

PERFORMANCE ANALYSIS

Performance analysis is a formalized feedback activity designed to provide individuals with valuable information regarding the quantity and quality of their performance.[1] They help managers make difficult decisions regarding their employees' futures, and is useful in conducting performance appraisals, compensation reviews, career planning, and human resource planning. Performance analysis provides an opportunity for employees to create action plans to overcome performance deficiencies while building upon strengths and managing weaknesses.[2]

Performance analysis can be a formal or informal feedback process that helps organizations transform their employees into their greatest assets. These formal and informal feedback approaches enable employees to develop strategies for their continuous improvement, which ultimately leads to improved organizational responsiveness, quality, efficiency, and effect. Performance analysis is designed to provide individuals with valuable information regarding the quantity and quality of their performance. They help organization leaders and managers make difficult decisions regarding their employees' futures, and are useful in conducting work planning and review activities, compensation reviews, career planning, and human resource planning. Performance analysis provides a forum in which employees create action plans to overcome performance deficiencies while building upon strengths and managing weaknesses.

Performance analysis is also an examination of the knowledge, skill, abilities, and attitudes of employees, their current and future career goals and objectives, and the "match" between employees and organizational expectations. Such an analysis also helps determine how employee performance helps the organization achieve its strategic goals and objectives. Accordingly, performance analysis exposes performance problems and identifies solutions and opportunities for employee growth and development.

Critical Questions

Performance analysis discloses the existing and desired conditions surrounding an employee's performance. As a result, performance analysis answers the following key questions:

1. What results (performance outcomes) are being achieved?
2. What results are desired?
3. How large is the performance gap?
4. What is the impact of the performance gap?[3]

In preparation for a performance analysis, managers address a number of their own questions. Each will help set the stage for a substantive, outcome-based analysis and help provide a complete and comprehensive depiction of an employee's current performance and what prevents optimal performance from happening. Some of the questions include the following:

1. Have I compared the individual's performance outputs and activities with identified performance standards?
2. For what specific performance outputs or activities may I praise the employee?
3. In what specific areas do I want the employee to improve?
4. Can I support my evaluation of the person's performance with facts?

5. What specific improvement(s) do I want to see as a result of the evaluation meeting?
6. What kind of professional development activities can I offer my personnel?
7. What kind of follow-up do I have planned?
8. What type of action plan would I recommend for this individual?[4]

Evaluating the Performance Analysis Process

As a way of determining the effectiveness of performance analysis, it is critical to evaluate the process. This evaluation will also identify areas of improvement. Several important questions frame this evaluation:
- Did the performance analysis achieve its purpose?
- Did I help my employee examine her performance?
- How could I have made the analysis more productive?
- What changes could I have made in my approach to achieve a better outcome?
- What items or subjects could I have discussed that were omitted?
- What unnecessary items could I have omitted from the discussion?
- What did I learn about my skills and abilities?
- What did I learn about my employee that I did not know before?
- Do we (organization leader and employee) have a better understanding of each other as a result of the appraisal?
- Do I feel that I am able to conduct my next appraisal more effectively?
- What did I learn about my interpersonal skills (e.g., questioning, listening, handling difficulties)?[5]

Each of these questions provides managers with an opportunity to reflect upon the performance analysis process, its outcomes, and the employer-employee relationship that has been enhanced as a result.

See also Developmental Evaluations; Performance Appraisals

NOTES

1. Jerry W. Gilley and Ann Maycunich, *Organizational Learning, Performance, and Change: An Introduction to Strategic HRD* (Cambridge, MA: Perseus Publishing, 2000).

2. M. Buckingham and C. Coffman, *First, Break All the Rules: What the World's Greatest Managers Do Differently* (New York: Simon and Schuster, 1999).

3. William Rothwell, *Beyond Training and Development: State-of-the-art Strategies for Enhancing Human Performance* New York: AMACOM, 1996.

4. Ibid. 13.

5. Jerry W. Gilley, Nathaniel W. Boughton, and Ann Maycunich, *The Performance Challenge: Developing Management Systems to Make Employees Your Organization's Greatest Asset* (Cambridge, MA: Perseus Books, 1999).

Jerry W. Gilley and Ann Gilley

PERFORMANCE APPRAISALS

A performance appraisal is the process by which an organization assesses the job-related performance and development of its employees. The process is twofold: (1) rating performance against company-set standards, and (2) providing feedback as to quality of work performed.

Purpose of Performance Appraisals

The purpose of performance appraisals is to maximize employee performance. By assessing the strengths and weaknesses of its employees, an organization can create goals to develop the most effective, highly skilled, productive, and satisfied workforce.

Performance Appraisal Benefits

There are many benefits to conducting performance appraisals for managers and individual employees, as well as their departments and the organization as a whole. They are:
- Improved communication between managers and employees
- Motivated employees who perform/produce at a higher level
- Creation of short- and long-term goals (individual, department- and company-wide) and monitoring of progress toward previously set goals
- Identification of training needs
- Heightened sense of accountability, empowerment, teamwork, and loyalty
- Increased promotion and retention rates
- Validation for rewards/pay increases
- Documentation of ongoing performance issues for legal reasons

Performance Appraisal Frequency

Formal performance appraisals are most commonly conducted once per year. However, a continuous feedback approach, whereby the employee receives updates on a regular basis (either formally or informally), is the most effective means of keeping tabs on performance and helping employees improve. With continuous feedback, there are no "surprises" at the formal appraisal meeting.

Many organizations also use a probationary appraisal for assessing new-hire performance. This appraisal is usually done within several weeks or months of an employee's hire date. Passing a probationary appraisal is often a condition of continued employment and can also be used as a benchmark for benefit administration (e.g., time off and insurance benefits).

Some organizations use what is considered a "warning" appraisal for specific instances of poor performance. When performance or behavior is particularly egregious, the employee is given a warning or ultimatum to immediately improve performance or change a behavior. If immediate improvement is not seen, termination is usually the consequence.

Performance Appraisal Methods

Many different approaches to conducting performance appraisals exist. The size and culture of an organization affect what type of appraisal system is used and how often an appraisal is done (most often once a year). The resources necessary to implement a formal system can be extensive; creation of forms, analysis and dissemination of information, filing, etc., can be time consuming and costly. However, once in place, a process can be maintained with little manpower.

The appraisal can take an informal or formal approach. Informally, performance is casually discussed and documentation is kept to a minimum. In a formal approach, performance is discussed in an appraisal meeting in which key performance indicators are thoroughly documented (usually on a standard form). Some of the most common performance appraisal methods are:

- *Performance-based*—the manager rates specific job related requirements associated with an employee's position. Identifying where an employee falls on a "below expectations" to "exceeds expectations" scale is a quick way to accurately assess performance. This method involves filling out a standard rating-scale form, which can make the process fairly fast and simple. In order to be fair and equitable, the job-related requirements that are measured must be the same for all employees who hold the same position.
- *Top-down*—several management-level members rate the performance of an employee.
- *Upward*—the employee rates the performance and effectiveness of the manager.
- *Peer review*—peers and team members rate the employee's performance. Care must be taken in choosing unbiased peers, and the manager must decide how much weight is given to each peer's feedback in order to reach a fair result. Choosing someone in competition for a promotion or pay raise may lead to flawed feedback. This method can be used when a manager has limited contact with the employee.
- *Self-assessment*—employees rate their own performance. A self-assessment can be implemented into all performance appraisal methods.
- *360-degree review*—this method relies on feedback gathered from people throughout an organization, and at varying professional levels, who have worked with the employee. This includes the manager, peers, and customers (both internal and external).
- *Continuous feedback*—the appraisal process is conducted more than once per year (usually 2–4 times). This allows for constant monitoring, communication, feedback, and modification of performance and goals.
- *Narrative*—an essay-type evaluation of performance is written by the manager. This can be used alone, but is most often used to supplement the standard rating form. This can be a very subjective means of evaluation, with the writer often discussing more personality-based traits of the individual versus measurable job skills. It can be used as a way to "soften the blow" of a less than favorable appraisal. The effectiveness of a narrative is directly related to the writing skills of the manager. If used alone, it does not allow for a rating comparison of several employees.
- *Follow-up reviews*—continuation of the appraisal process when training/development opportunities are scheduled, short-term goals are evaluated/changed, and progress is discussed. Follow-up reviews are often conducted within several weeks of the main appraisal meeting.

Pitfalls

Some common mistakes that managers make during the appraisal process are:
- Not having a clear description of a job's specific requirements, or not having agreement between the employee and manager about the specific job related requirements that are being rated.
- Rating immeasurable or irrelevant characteristics such as popularity or personality, instead of measurable performance indicators.
- Giving a "middle of the road" rating to a poor performer in order to avoid conflict.
- Conducting the appraisal with little or no input from the employee.
- Rating "instances" of performance, not performance over the entire rating period.
- Receiving feedback about the employee from inappropriate people.
- Retaliating against an employee who has "gone against" the manager.

- Holding past performance/behavior either for or against the employee; letting past performance distort perception of an employee's performance in the current appraisal period.
- Not following up with the employee regarding any unresolved issues stemming from the appraisal meeting.
- Not following through with training/development needs that were recognized in the appraisal process.

Types of Documentation

Although the most commonly used type of appraisal documentation is a standard rating-scale form, narratives and electronic appraisal forms are gaining popularity:

- *Rating form*—a standard rating-scale form that lists job-related requirements and skills is filled out for the performance appraisal period.
- *Narrative*—an essay-type evaluation of performance is written by the manager. This allows for more flexibility to discuss performance issues and behaviors that are not covered on a standard rating form.
- *Electronic appraisal*—an electronic or online system is used to track ratings, instead of a paper form. This allows for easy analysis and editing of collected data. Using electronic media can be a time- and money-saving opportunity, but should not be used to avoid a face-to-face discussion with an employee.

See Also Developmental Evaluations; Performance Management Systems; Performance Analysis; Performance Standards

Resources:

DelPo, A. *The Performance Appraisal Handbook: Legal and Practical Rules for Managers.* (Berkeley, CA: Nolo, 2005).

Performance-Appraisals.com. http://www.performance-appraisals.com.

Society of Human Resource Management. http://www.shrm.org.

Wilson, P. *Performance-Based Assessments.* (Milwaukee, WI: ASQC Quality Press, 1995).

Jennifer A. Majkowski

PERFORMANCE CONSULTING

Performance consulting is the process of closing the gap between current performance and desired performance within an organization. This process includes identifying the root cause, proposing and implementing performance improvement solutions, and evaluating results. The purpose of performance consulting is to help organizations achieve their business goals by improving performance results. The results improvement process[1] summarizes the systematic approach in which performance consulting operates:

1. Desired Results Determined and Project Defined
   This phase includes determining where is the gap in results and defining a project to close the gap.
2. Barriers Determined and Changes Specified
   This phase includes identifying why the gap in results exists, the barriers to achieving the desired results, and determining what changes are necessary to close the gap.
3. Changes Designed, Developed, and Implemented
   This phase includes how to close the gap—the designing, developing and implementing the potential changes to close the gap in results.

4. Results Evaluated and Maintained or Improved

This phase includes determining if the gap in results was closed, monitoring the changes, evaluating their impact, and modifying the changes to close the gap in results.

Levels of Performance Consulting

Performance consulting focuses on three levels of the organization including organizational level, process level, and job level. The organizational level includes understanding the organizational system and processes and identifying which processes are impacting the lack of performance. The process level includes analyzing the processes and determining which job functions are critical to improving performance. The job level includes analyzing job outputs, identifying gaps in desired performance, and proposing potential solutions to close the gap.

Performance Consulting Client Types

Performance consulting includes identifying and managing four client types—decision makers, stakeholders, influencers, and scouts.[2] Performance consulting includes understanding each of these client types' needs and how they influence an effective performance improvement initiative. Decision makers, typically executives, have the final approval on the project and are most concerned with the bottom-line financial impact of an intervention. Stakeholders are ultimately responsible for the implementation of the intervention and are accountable for its success. Influencers are clients who do not have authority to approve an intervention, but do influence the decisions made by decision makers and stakeholders. Scouts serve as guides to provide information that supports a successful change initiative.

Performance Consulting Process

While there are numerous performance consulting models, the performance technology model[3] summarizes the key elements of the performance consulting process, including performance analysis, cause analysis, intervention selection, and evaluation. Performance analysis identifies the gap between desired and actual performance levels through analyzing organizational objectives, capabilities, structure, and culture as well as external factors. Numerous data collection methods can be used, including interviews, focus groups, observation, and review of organizational data. The cause analysis identifies the potential causes of the performance problem and determines the underlying root cause and obstacles to performance. The intervention selection includes working collaboratively within the organization to determine the potential solutions, assigning resources, and creating action plans to implement the intervention. Lastly, evaluation includes assessing the effectiveness of the intervention and determining what changes are necessary to continue the performance improvement process.

Performance Consulting Approach

Performance Relationship Map

This is a tool to help understand human performance within the organization. It identifies a specific business goal and looks at current employee performance versus desired performance and current operational results versus desired operational results to achieve the goal. It also identifies factors (external) and forces (internal) that are affecting performance.

Performance Analysis

This includes working with the client to understand the business need, performance problem, and desired outcomes and to determine the criteria of how to measure success. Information is gathered through interviews, focus groups, organizational data, and observation to understand the organizational system.

Developing Models of Performance

This step identifies best practices and competencies to achieve performance results. Best practices are determined by talking with employees who are top performers. Competencies are identified by reviewing the knowledge, skills, and attitudes necessary to be successful in a job. Criteria is determined to measure performance results and environmental factors impacting performance are identified.

Identifying Actual Performance and Factors Impacting Performance

This step includes identifying the problem and determining and analyzing the specific factors and causes for the problem. A performance assessment is created to determine the gap in performance and gain agreement on the actions to solve the problem. This step also identifies the factors impacting performance or root cause, which may include employee knowledge, skills, abilities, behaviors, motivation or environment.

Implementing Performance Improvement Interventions

Implementation of an intervention closes the performance gap in order to achieve the business goal(s). This includes identifying the performance improvement intervention to address the root cause of the performance problem.

Measuring Results

Measuring the results of the actions based on the set criteria and reporting these effectively is the last step in the performance consulting process.[4]

NOTES

1. Geary Rummler, *Serious Performance Consulting* (Silver Spring, MD: International Society for Performance Improvement, 2004).

2. Jerry Gilley and Ann Maycunich, *Organizational Learning, Performance and Change* (Cambridge, MA: Perseus Publishing, 2000).

3. William Deterline and Marc Rosenberg, "Workplace Productivity: Performance Technology Success Stories," *International Society for Performance Improvement* 25 (1992): 21–22.

4. Dana Robinson and James Robinson, *Performance Consulting: Moving Beyond Training* (San Francisco: Berrett-Koehler, 1996).

Dean M. Savoca

PERFORMANCE MANAGEMENT SYSTEMS

Performance management systems guide, motivate, control, and develop personnel behavior and talent toward achievement of desired individual and organizational objectives.

Many organizations are ignorant with regard to motivating, managing performance, and developing people so that they become the organization's greatest asset. Effective performance management systems enable individuals to maximize their potential while organizations build a dynamic, highly functioning workforce prepared for change, growth, and the challenges of a globally competitive environment.

Individual Performance Management

Those responsible for leading and managing others possess diverse backgrounds typically *not* in human resource management or development. In fact, many supervisors and managers are largely unprepared for the rigors of developing others. New supervisors often express shock at the complexity and requirements of managing others' performance.

Performance management is a systematic process that, once mastered, may be applied across cultures, industries, departments, jobs, and people. Steps in performance management are:

1. Link the job to the institution's strategic goals and objectives
2. Hire/promote/select qualified performers.
3. Establish employee-specific performance goals.
4. Develop performance standards and expectations.
5. Coach and provide feedback.
6. Conduct developmental evaluations.
7. Create performance growth and development plans.
8. Link compensation and rewards to individual goals, growth, and development.[1]

Performance management demands that supervisors and managers possess a host of broad skills, specifically, interpersonal/communications, technical, and strategic skills. Effective managers partner with their employees, working closely to identify areas of strength and opportunities for improvement, coaching, growth, and development of both parties. Technical skills are necessary to establish appropriate goals and standards during the training and coaching phases, as employees look to their supervisors to model best practices. Strategic skills enable managers to link individual jobs and compensation to broader organizational initiatives.

Organizational Performance Management

Performance management systems are effective processes across all levels of an organization—from executive to front line. Poor performance—that which has fallen below acceptable standards—typically occurs due to lack of appropriate performance management. All too often, organizations respond to an individual's unacceptable performance via reprimands, training, job reassignment, negative performance reviews, or other negative consequences.

Organization-wide performance management systems reduce poor performance while creating cultures of teamwork, partnering, trust, communications, and continuous improvement. Organization-wide systems require:

• Senior management support and involvement
• Resource allocation
• Training for and commitment from all supervisory and managerial staff
• Ongoing development of all new and existing supervisory and managerial staff

Benefits of Performance Management

In reality, performance management is everyone's responsibility—and everyone benefits. The specific benefits of performance management are numerous for employees, management, and the organization.

For individual employees, performance management:
- Eliminates unrealistic career expectations, particularly when organizations face cutbacks, flattening, or reorganization.
- Motivates employees, who take responsibility for their own growth and development.
- Helps individuals understand the urgency of keeping skills and abilities current.
- Creates meaningful growth and development plans.
- Increases involvement in decision making.
- Enhances promotion opportunities (as their skills improve).

For supervisors and managers, performance management:
- Encourages their continuous support of learning, growth, and development.
- Helps supervisors and managers develop their staff.
- Enhances their interpersonal relationship skills.
- Helps supervisors match organizational realities to recruiting promises.
- Cultivates flexible employees who are capable of moving out of narrowly defined tasks and into functional roles.
- Develops specific performance goals and objectives for their staff in support of organizational strategies.

For organizations, performance management:
- Reduces turnover of highly skilled employees by providing environments conducive to growth and development.
- Assists human resource planning.
- Enhances organizational responsiveness and competitiveness through productive, motivated employees.
- Increases commitment from employees at all levels.
- Improves individual performance that contributes to the greater good.

Ineffective Performance Management

For many, performance management is an alien term. All too often, supervisors' and employees' limited exposure to performance management surfaces during the formal performance appraisal, which is rarely understood to be an essential component of strategic performance management. What *prevents* institutions from engaging in formal, systematic performance management? Reasons include, but are not limited to:
- Supervisors/managers/organizations do not realize they need a performance management system.
- Supervisors and managers do not know how to design and implement performance management systems.
- Supervisors/managers' backgrounds are not in human resource management; thus they are not trained in effective performance management techniques.
- Time constraints.
- Union interference.[2]

Employee evaluations traditionally are conducted on an annual basis, use simple appraisal forms, and often provide individuals with their only source of *formal feedback* regarding their efforts. The traditional evaluation process has been widely criticized as:

- Retroactive, focusing on past performance (which cannot be changed) instead of future, long-term improvement.
- A one-sided, biased portrayal of another's performance (and often by a supervisor/manager unskilled in evaluating the work of others or the use of the appraisal forms).
- Not timely—annual reviews are insufficient gauges of one's daily work.
- Too simplistic and not representative of the complexities of many positions.
- Inconsistent—the quality of performance appraisals varies from supervisor to supervisor, department to department, and institution to institution.
- Incomplete—lacking forward-looking employee performance growth and development plans.
- Lacking motivational components.
- Often combined with the compensation and reward discussion, which dilutes the focus on organizational goals.
- Erroneous in the assumption that all employees know exactly what they are supposed to do, when, how, and to what level of quality.[3]

Improving Performance Management

Performance management systems enhance the performance of individuals and thus that of their organizations. Improving performance and its management requires commitment and support of all organizational players, particularly management. Senior management is responsible for reducing any barriers (e.g., ignorance, egos, lack of resources, organizational inertia, poor communications) that inhibit establishment of a performance management system. Doing so will unleash the potential of all employees, which ultimately benefits the firm.

See also Coaching; Compensation; Strategic Communications

NOTES

1. Jerry W. Gilley, Nathaniel W. Boughton, and Ann Maycunich, *The Performance Challenge: Developing Management Systems to Make Employees Your Organization's Greatest Asset* (Cambridge, MA: Perseus Books, 1999).

2. D.B. Peterson, and M.D. Hicks, *Development First: Strategies for Self-development.* (Minneapolis: Personnel Decisions International, 1995).

3. M.J. Rosenberg, "Human Performance Technology: Foundation for Human Performance Improvement. In *The ASTD Models for Human Performance Improvement: Roles, Competencies, and Outputs,* ed. William Rothwell (Alexandria, VA: American Society for Training and Development, 1996).

Ann Gilley and Jerry W. Gilley

PERFORMANCE STANDARDS

For years, managers have struggled with the process of achieving high levels of performance from their employees. Improving employee performance lies in the development of strong performance standards. Such standards establish a clear process for the employee to follow to perform job tasks and enable the manager to provide feedback, coaching, and evaluation of performance. Performance standards are developed from well-written job descriptions that clearly define the tasks necessary to perform a job. To standardize job descriptions, many organizations seek guidance from business-specific professional associations that develop industry-wide standards for performance. As organizations continue to refine the process of defining job tasks and refining job descriptions, employee performance will continue to improve.

Understanding Performance Standards

To understand performance standards, the needs of the organization, leadership, managers, and employees must be examined. Each need contributes to the formation and implementation of performance standards. For the purposes of this entry, performance standards are defined as "the quantifiable measures that define the criteria for performing tasks to be completed by employees."[1] Generally, performance standards can be split into two categories; activity-based, and productivity performance standards. Activity-based performance standards relate to the types of tasks performed by the employee. Examples of activity-based standards include: typing reports, answering phones, processing claims, responding to e-mails, and other related duties. In contrast, productivity performance standards are directly related to the quality and quantity of work employees are expected to complete. Examples of productivity performance standards include: process 100 claims with less than a 5 percent error rate, recruit 35 employees by the end of the quarter, and sell 15 products per shift.

Benefits of Performance Standards

Well-developed performance standards benefit the organization at both the macro and micro levels. They also increase the satisfaction and productivity of employees. Below is a list of some of the benefits that occur from the use of strong performance standards.

- Standards create common expectations for performance throughout the organization, building a culture of employees who have the same understanding of performance expectations.
- Performance standards provide structure and order to the organizational culture.
- Organizations use standards to set expectations for performance that support its strategic goals and objectives.
- Standards protect organizations from frivolous lawsuits based on managerial malpractice.
- Employees have a clear understanding of the expectations necessary to perform job duties when performance standards are used.
- Managers are able to provide quality feedback, based on the framework provided by performance standards.
- Standards encourage meaningful coaching between the manager and employee about performance.

Overall, the use of performance standards produces positive outcomes for all involved.

Creating Performance Standards

Performance standards must be clear and well written. When creating standards, the SMART (Specific, Measurable, Achievable, Relevant, Timely) model should be applied as follows:

Specific

Performance standards must be well written and clearly defined. Clear and specific standards help the manager to communicate performance expectations. Also, clear standards make the process of achieving objectives easier for the employee.

Measurable

Measurable standards describe how the task is to be completed. These standards reduce confusion about the work needed to complete job tasks.

Achievable

Employees must be able to achieve the assigned performance standards. If an employee does not have the skills or ability to achieve a performance standard, the employee must be coached, developed, or reassigned. In some cases, the standard can be rewritten to meet the skills and abilities of the employee. Moreover, it is the responsibility of the manager to ensure that the employee has the resources and tools necessary to meet the performance standards.

Relevant

Each performance standard must be aligned to the strategic goals and objectives of the office, department, and/or organization. Relevant performance objectives allow the employee to understand his or her role in contributing to the strategic goals and objectives of the organization.

Timely

Performance standards should include a schedule for completing tasks. Time schedules clarify expectations for an employee and provide necessary motivation to complete tasks.

Using Performance Standards as a Management Tool

Performance standards provide a framework for managers to lead employees. Standards provide all involved with a common ground for understanding performance. This understanding allows managers to provide employees with coaching and development between performance appraisal periods. During this time, managers should spend quality time with each employee by observing performance. From these observations, the manager documents instances of employee performance to provide continual constructive feedback. Additionally, feedback and coaching based on performance standards reduce conflict because the conversation stays constructive (related directly to performance, not personality). If managers use a constant model for feedback and coaching, employees will never be surprised about ratings on their performance appraisals. Once the appraisal period arrives, the employee and manager will have a productive meeting because continual communication has occurred over time. All in all, using performance standards can produce positive outcomes for the manager, employee, and organization.

Conclusion

Well-written job descriptions contribute to the employee's ability to meet expected performance standards. Standards help the employee to perform job tasks and help the manager to provide feedback and coaching. Furthermore, when used as a management tool, standards encourage productive communication between the employee and manager about performance. Finally, the use of performance standards improves the organizational culture, thus benefiting both the manager and employee.

Resources:

Bates, Gary D. "Employee Performance Standards: What Works Best?" *Journal of Management and Engineering* (1995), 24–26.

Buhler, Patricia M. "Managing in the New Millennium: The Performance Appraisal Process." *Supervision,* 2005.

Gilley, Jerry W., and Ann Maycunich. *Organizational Learning, Performance, and Change: An Introduction to Strategic HRD.* Cambridge, MA: Perseus Publishing, 2000.

NOTE

1. John O. Alexander, "A Performance Plan that Thrives On Change." *Management Review* (1988), 20.

Derrick E. Haynes

PROMOTION

An organization has two options when filling positions. It can select and promote internal candidates, or rely on external hires. Promoting a qualified individual from his or her current position to a higher-level position in an organization's hierarchy, and to a higher salary grade, has many advantages for the organization and the employee.

Advantages

From the organization's perspective, the internal candidate is known—his or her past performance, interactions with coworkers, and capacity for learning and growth have been observed. Internal candidates have knowledge about the organization, the technology, and the operations, and therefore make the transition or orientation faster and smoother compared to hiring from the outside. Further, promotions can be viewed as a motivational or retention strategy. Retaining employees is viewed as a competitive advantage in terms of keeping talent (knowledge, skills, and abilities) within the company. Further, promoting employees perpetuates the culture and values of the organization. In the case of promotions to supervisory positions, the organization will benefit from having supervisors who are coordinating the efforts of people whom they know. This contact provides a social basis of influence.

The use of promotions creates a sense of fairness, workplace justice, and subsequent satisfaction. If employees do outstanding work, but outsiders are brought in over them, there will be a perception of disaffection on the part of the organization and subsequent dissatisfaction on the part of employees. Also, there is a nonmonetary incentive produced by the move, which is status-based. A sense of achievement and pride in terms of career progression is realized. A promotion provides a signal to the internal candidate that he or she is valued. It also suggests to the rest of the organization's workforce that there are opportunities for growth and career advancement, and therefore, employees will be encouraged to stay with the firm.

Advantages notwithstanding, employees may be promoted beyond their competence and may find it difficult to achieve the outcomes expected. Also, some employees may find it hard to earn the respect of peers when they have started in the company at lower-level positions.

Overcoming Obstacles

Overcoming the obstacles to successful promotions is imperative. Given the projected labor shortage in the United States, organizations can not afford to promote internal candidates only to have them fail due to lack of support and resources.

The organization can ensure successful internal promotions by providing employees with training, coaching, mentorship, and sponsorship from higher-level management. Further, meeting with internal candidates not selected for a promotion is an important part of the process of developing employees within an organization. Having a discussion regarding gaps between the internal candidate's skills and the required competencies of the position can lead to a development plan for the employee, prevent wounded feelings, and encourage unsuccessful candidates to remain with the organization.

Other useful strategies for ensuring successful promotions are to develop clear selection criteria and establish procedures for posting available positions. Doing so provides assurance that employees will be made aware of the promotional opportunity and that the most qualified internal candidate is selected. These administrative duties are typically performed by human resources in conjunction with line management.

Resources:

Society for Human Resource Management. http://www.search.shrm.org.

 Workforce Week. http://www.workforce.com

Pamela Dixon and Marie Shanle

RETENTION

Strategic business decisions such as restructuring and downsizing implemented in U.S. organizations have eliminated the notion of job security and, to varying degrees, decreased the commitment level of employees. This has equated to a shift in the psychological contract that exists between an employee and employer. The psychological contract regulates the employee-employer relationship and is supported by the notion of reciprocity. If employees do not believe that their employer is committed to their well-being, they are less likely to be engaged and committed to the organization; moreover, they are more likely to leave that employer.[1]

A new psychological contract requires that employers demonstrate a commitment to their employees through policies and practices that (a) provide equitable pay and recognition; (b) provide opportunities for training and career development; (c) support the individual's performance by establishing and communicating standards, expectations, and feedback; and (d) promoting and championing work-life balance. In return, the organization will be able to retain higher numbers of employees and, at the same time, receive a higher level of commitment and engagement.

Retention is defined as an ongoing employment relationship. Conversely, turnover is defined as the separation from an employment relationship. Retaining talented employees has become an organizational imperative. Human resource management (HRM) policies and practices that address retention in today's competitive workforce will take into consideration broader predictors of employee satisfaction than just monetary incentives.

HRM Practices

Retention is influenced by HRM policies and practices that promote employee recognition, professional growth, mechanisms for successful performance, and personal well-being.[2] Policies and practices include compensation and recognition; promotional, career development, and training opportunities; establishment and communication of performance standards, expectations, and feedback, and work-life balance; all of which have been shown to have an indirect influence on an organization's operational and financial performance.

Compensation and Recognition

In addition to a base salary that is perceived as competitive and equitable, incentive pay is also used as a retention strategy. Incentive pay may consist of bonuses or employee stock ownership.

Retention is not entirely achieved with monetary incentives. Employees rarely leave their jobs because they are not satisfied with their pay. Rather, they choose not to stay with a company if they have a poor relationship with their supervisor; or they do not feel valued for their contributions and recognized for their talent; or there are limited opportunities for promotions and other career growth opportunities.

An effective way to motivate employees and demonstrate appreciation for their contribution is to simply say "thank you" or praise their work in a public forum. In addition, coaching employees is also a motivational factor in that the supervisor is recognizing their strengths and taking the time to help employees improve areas that are weaknesses.

Promotional, Career Development, and Training Opportunities

Providing opportunities for promotions or lateral assignments that offer increased challenge and skill development have been linked to a perception that the organization is making an investment and is encouraging career growth, which in turn has been linked to job satisfaction. A positive relationship has been demonstrated between experiential, career-focused development opportunities and perceived organization support, which has been empirically connected to higher retention.[3] Astute organizations, even those with a flatter structure where potential for promotion is limited, recognize that providing learning and career development opportunities that increase employability can be a powerful mechanism for retention.

Performance Standards, Expectations, and Feedback

Clearly communicating what is expected, and how performance will be measured, enables employees to achieve goals and successfully perform their jobs. Also, providing feedback that is specific, timely, and communicated in a way that is respectful also contributes to ongoing successful performance. Further, feedback that is two-way is also important. When employees know that their supervisor is willing to listen, employees will be more likely to express frustration and issues can be resolved, versus the employees not trusting that their opinion counts or that their issues will be taken seriously.

Work-life Flexibility

The change in workforce composition has played a role in the increase of initiatives geared toward work-life flexibility. Initiatives include flexible work arrangements, long-term saving and profit-sharing programs, and resources to help with day care and/or elder care. Work-life flexibility not only requires the appropriate initiatives, but also a different way of thinking in terms of supporting and managing retention in organizations. No longer can organizations think about getting work done in the traditional sense; employees will physically be at work from 9 to 5, and work 40 hours or more per week, Monday through Friday.

Conclusion

The role of HRM will continue to be critical as organizations continually adapt to a changing workforce and global marketplace. HRM policies and practices will necessarily define and support critical capabilities that organizations must maintain to remain competitive and thrive. A new psychological contract that demonstrates an employer's commitment to their employees' well-being (both career and personal life) will foster an engaged and committed workforce, and positively influence the retention of key talent.

See also Compensation: An Overview; Turnover; Work-life Balance

NOTES

1. Robert G. DelCampo, "The influence of Culture Strength on Person Organization Fit and Turnover," *International Journal of Management* 23 (2006): 465–69.
2. Janet Polach, "HRD's Role in Work-life Integration Issues: Moving the Workforce to a Change in Mindset," *Human Resource Development International* 6 (2003): 57–68.
3. Clayton Glen, "Key Skills Retention and Motivation: The War for Talent Still Rages and Retention Is the High Ground," *Industrial and Commercial Training* 38 (2006): 37–45.

Pamela Dixon

360-DEGREE FEEDBACK

Three-hundred-sixty-degree feedback, also known as multirater assessment, can be a valuable tool for performance management and employee development. Three-hundred-sixty-degree feedback has been defined as "evaluations gathered about a participant from two or more rating sources, including self, supervisor, peers, direct reports, internal customers, external customers, vendors, and suppliers."[1]

Though supervisors are traditionally responsible for providing developmental feedback to employees, many do not have exposure to the true picture of an individual's performance. By using a 360-degree program, employees also receive feedback from those who work most closely with them and who are in a position to provide better input on specific competencies and skills in need of development. While not all-inclusive, examples of competencies include leadership, creativity, integrity and trust, listening, negotiating, strategic agility, and business acumen.

Uses of 360-Degree Feedback

While originally used in leadership-development programs for senior management, 360-degree tools are now being used across all levels of organizations. Most organizations use 360-degree feedback to identify areas in need of improvement and provide developmental opportunities for employees. "The questions used in a good 360-survey used for development purposes rate observable behaviors and skills. The intent is to gather sound and reliable data for feedback with the aim of building a development plan."[2]

Growing in popularity, however, is the use of 360-degree surveys for performance appraisals. The feedback is a supplement to a supervisory review and used to facilitate discussion between the employee and supervisor. "It blends the multisource feedback on behaviors or competencies with the supervisor's assessment of results. Individuals are evaluated both on how they do the job—that is, their behaviors—and what they do—their results or outcomes."[3]

Requirements for an Effective Process

There are no standardized models for 360-degree feedback, and the feedback can be collected via paper-and-pencil or electronic means or simply through dialogue with survey respondents. Many human resource vendors offer companies online tools that make data collection more efficient. Other organizations develop electronic tools through in-house resources. However, whether an employer uses hard copy or computer-based tools, there are several factors and/or features that should be considered to ensure an effective process.

- Determine the purpose of your feedback system before selecting or determining the method to use for data collection. For example, will the feedback be used for employee development or performance appraisal? What do you want to accomplish, and does it support the organization's values, position competencies, etc.?
- If you design your own survey, consult with key stakeholders (e.g., management, employees, customers, etc.) to ensure that it will accurately measure the desired information.
- Determine the minimum and maximum number of evaluators to be surveyed. Results can be skewed if too few people respond. A minimum of four respondents in addition to the manager and employee receiving the feedback is recommended.[4]
- Ensure that raters are trained to provide usable feedback. They should be coached on providing honest, actionable feedback on behaviors or competencies that are important to the person and position being evaluated versus making personal attacks.
- Provide an opportunity for the respondents to provide written comments to provide context for the numerical ratings.
- Limit questions to avoid respondent fatigue. Additionally, larger organizations might want to consider implementing the process over several weeks to ensure that respondents are not asked to complete too many surveys at one time.
- Ensure confidentiality to protect the anonymity of the respondents.
- Ensure that employees are trained how to receive and interpret the feedback as well as provide guidance to employees on how to create a developmental plan.

See also Performance Management: An Overview; Performance Management System; Performance Appraisals; Developmental Evaluations; Feedback

NOTES

1. Michael A. Campion, Frederick P. Morgeson, and Troy V. Mumford, "Coming Full Circle: Using Research and Practice to Address 27 Questions About 360-Degree Feedback Programs." *Consulting Psychology Journal: Practice and Research* 57, no. 3 (Summer, 2005): 196–209.

2. Jane L. Wilson, "Business of Training—360° Appraisals" *Training and Development,* June 1997, 44.

3. Mark R. Edwards and Ann J. Ewan, *360° Feedback: The Powerful New Model for Employee Assessment & Performance Improvement* (New York: AMACOM, 1996), 7.

4. Ibid., 20.

Nancy Svoboda

Chapter 4
Compensation, Benefits, and Insurance

Compensation: An Overview

The primary purpose of any organization is to secure results. This benefits the organization by leading to improved quality, responsiveness, efficiency, and productivity. The responsibility for securing desired results rests with leaders whose sole challenge is to "get results through others." Improving organizational effectiveness remains a difficult undertaking, requiring the cooperation of all represented groups. Therefore, organizations must develop a compensation and reward philosophy, select appropriate compensation and reward strategies, adopt principles of effective compensation and reward programs, and align compensation and rewards with the goals of the organization.

Traditional Compensation and Rewards

Historically, compensation and reward programs merely rewarded employees for showing up and looking busy. Traditional programs attempted to justify individual increases in compensation based on annual performance appraisals. Because of biases, inaccurate or unfair performance measures, and difficulty in assessment, rewarding individual performance was severely compromised. In essence, traditional compensation systems fail to recognize employee performance differences.

Compensation and reward programs also frequently fail to recognize (1) employee growth and development, and (2) organization goals. A compensation and rewards program that fails to link performance improvement to growth and development "will stagnate or even decline."[1] Failure to align compensation and reward programs with strategic organizational goals sabotages their growth and is yet another indicator of outdated, ineffective compensation and reward practices.

Money continues to be a very popular form of reward and a powerful motivator. For example, in a recent survey, 79 percent of salespersons chose cash as their favored reward. Interestingly, as respondents' salary increased, the importance of cash decreased. Of those who make under $50,000 per year, 83 percent chose cash, compared to 66 percent of those who earn between $151,000 and $200,000.[2]

Money remains a status symbol for many people because it represents power and prestige. Money and the things it buys demonstrate our success to the world. Thus, monetary rewards do get results. Effective organizations link monetary rewards to desired performance that supports strategic goals and objectives while encouraging employee learning, reflection, and growth. From the organization's perspective, money is a widely used incentive for three reasons: it is easy to equate with or align to performance, is universal (typically desired and accepted by all), and is thought (erroneously) by supervisors to be the primary motivator of human behavior.

This chapter explores the numerous avenues available to organizations through which to compensate their employees, from cash and bonuses to benefits (including health care insurance) and retirement plans. A firm's overall compensation philosophy and specific strategies draw upon many of the entries that follow.

Compensation and Reward Philosophy

A compensation and reward philosophy should be based on rewarding employees for the "right" performance. In this way, organizations demonstrate their understanding that "the things that get rewarded get done."[3] This approach ensures that the organization will secure its desired outcomes. On the other hand, failure to reward the right behaviors leads to unsatisfactory outcomes.

A compensation and reward philosophy should be flexible enough to take into account the dynamic nature of the organization's change initiatives, and other important system-wide activities. When this occurs, the compensation and reward program remains fluid, subject to review, alteration, or redesign. This approach encourages continuous compensation improvement that reflects the organization's culture, values, guiding principles, and strategic business goals and objectives. Compensation and reward philosophies define who participates in compensation and reward decisions, whether decision making should be centralized with leadership or decentralized within departments, and whether managers should be held accountable for their respective decisions and contributions to the compensation and reward program.

An effective compensation and reward philosophy takes into account each step of the organization's performance management process, enabling organizations to (1) identify constituents' needs and expectations; (2) design jobs that produce maximum results at the highest possible level of quality; (3) encourage leaders to build synergistic relationships with employees; (5) require leaders to conduct formal performance appraisals with employees; and (6) collaboratively create performance growth and development plans designed to enhance performance.[4]

Compensation and Reward Strategies

Compensation and reward programs should be designed to help organizations achieve specific outcomes. As stated previously, compensation and reward programs are often performance-based, with little consideration given to rewarding employees for a variety of other desired behaviors that contribute to achieving results. Therefore, it makes tremendous sense to reward individuals for the "right things," such as (1) creativity, (2) leadership, (3) teamwork and cooperation, (4) commitment and loyalty, (5) long-term solutions, and (6) learning and applying new skills. Rewarding these behaviors works wonders in improving performance and achieving the results needed by the organization.

Rewarding Creativity. Fear of failure or punishment may prevent employees from engaging in creative expression. Organizations that stifle individual creativity neglect the benefits of their employees' experience and talent. Effective organizations encourage risk-taking on the part of their staff, understanding that failures provide experience and insight that often lead to ultimate success. Employee ideas and creativity are often credited with cost savings, new product development, improvement of existing programs, stream-lined processes, or elimination of redundant procedures.

Compensation programs that encourage creativity reward the sharing of ideas, invite risk-taking, and promote free-flowing communication between leaders, managers, and employees. Dynamic organizations build climates of creativity, encourage employees to let their creative juices flow, and include creativity in individual responsibilities. From suggestion boxes to innovation incentives to regular team brainstorming meetings, encouraging creativity is a simple concept that may yield enormous benefits for employees and the organization. Many leaders are beginning to discover the importance of encouraging and rewarding employees who share their innovations.[5] Rewarding innovative ideas serves as an inducement to employees to share their creative insights.

Rewarding Leadership. Although many organizations encourage leadership, they seldom reward it. Consequently, a leadership vacuum exists in many of today's firms. Effective organizations compensate and reward those who take initiative, offer opinions, and make suggestions to better their companies. Leadership characteristics that should be rewarded include idea advocacy, servantship, vision, initiative, risk taking, results orientation, self-sacrifice, long-term focus, dedication, flexibility, responsibility, accountability, and so forth. Skills include creativity, communications, ability to inspire or motivate, build teams, and coaching aptitude. Organizations should reward leadership talents with base compensation, benefits, and incentives commensurate with an individual's effort and results.

To be effective, a leadership reward strategy must closely align with the organization's culture, values, goals, and objectives by integrating leadership attributes into job descriptions, providing opportunities for leadership expression and development, and by assigning mentors to help develop potential among future leaders.

Rewarding Teamwork and Cooperation. Many organizations desire teamwork and cooperation, advocating its importance and value in helping the organization achieve better results. In reality, most organizations continue to compensate and reward employees for their individual efforts. Annual performance appraisals, for example, typically stress individual skills, competencies, and attitudes, while rarely recognizing collaboration and teamwork attributes such as loyalty, support, cooperation, or communication. Dynamic organizations identify desirable, effective collaboration and teamwork components, communicate these to their employees, stress their importance, incorporate teamwork skills into the evaluation process, and reward these talents accordingly. Teams win and lose together, play and struggle together. Members of the team who win together should be rewarded together. Successful teams may be compensated monetarily or with other meaningful incentives or rewards.

Rewarding Commitment and Loyalty. Success is a journey that all organizational members take together. Therefore, leaders need to understand one important principle in order to adopt appropriate reward strategies—the principle of *reciprocity.* Simply stated, employees will reciprocate the behavior they receive from their employers.[6] When individuals are treated with respect, they treat others with respect. Thus, loyalty begets loyalty, and commitment begets commitment.

Although organizations expect, even demand, loyalty and commitment, they rarely examine their compensation and reward programs to determine whether they are practicing hypocrisy. Quite simply, organizations must reward loyalty and commitment in order to get it. Organizations need to determine whether providing job security, appropriate work environments, promotion and growth opportunities, and fair, livable wages are essential in enhancing employee commitment and loyalty. When an organization is willing to invest in and reward commitment and loyalty, it is, in essence, communicating its employees' importance to the execution of the vision and mission.

Rewarding Long-term Solutions. Many organizations and their leaders embrace short-term solutions—convenient quick fixes such as downsizing, layoffs, or reducing employee benefits—that fail to satisfy long-range strategic organizational objectives. Customer, employee, investor, community, and competitive pressures demand immediate results, often undermining the integrity of sound, long-term objectives necessary to maintain organizational viability.

Effective compensation and reward strategies focus on the horizon and rewarding long-term activities for reaching it. The emphasis on organizational effectiveness forces leaders and managers to concentrate on measurable, meaningful initiatives capable of sustaining the organization's indefinite long-term growth. Examples of desirable long-range behaviors include investing in leadership training, mentoring programs, encouraging employee creativity and innovation, enhancing customer service, development of new products, and so forth.

Rewarding the Application of New Skills. "Employees are the organization's greatest asset; therefore, organizations must develop long-term compensation and reward strategies that encourage them to participate in performance growth and development activities that foster continuous learning and skill acquisition."[7] Organizations that encourage employee growth at all stages of career or professional development assess employee needs and potential for growth, providing abundant, pertinent learning opportunities and application in areas of importance such as facilitation skills, computer and Internet competency, communications, current job-related tasks, supervisory skills, and the like.

Employees are encouraged to participate in learning activities *and* apply their knowledge on the job. A long-term compensation and reward strategy should also reward leaders, managers, and supervisors for creating environments instrumental to learning acquisition and transfer.

Linking Compensation and Rewards to Organizational Goals

Employee performance increases dramatically when an organization's compensation and reward strategy is linked to its mission and goals. Linking compensation and reward programs to goals requires working in harmony with other vital systems within the firm. Linkage ensures the consistent allocation of compensation and rewards, helping the organization function in a way that is acceptable to all constituents.

Developing an effective compensation and reward program requires a well-conceived, designed, implemented, and monitored plan, as evidenced by the following nine principles of effective compensation and reward programs:

1. *Align your compensation with the organization's culture, values, and strategic goals and objectives.* Compensation should be integrated with all aspects of the business.
2. *Link compensation to other changes.* Compensation should support and reinforce organizational change initiatives.
3. *Time the compensation program to best support other change initiatives.* Timing is everything. Compensation should not force change or lag behind the process.

4. *Integrate compensation with other employee processes.* Compensation is not a substitute for developing relationships with employees.
5. *Democratize the compensation process.* Incorporate employees' opinions and decisions in compensation and rewards.
6. *Demystify compensation.* Since knowledge is power, communication counts. Clearly articulate aspects of the organization's compensation and reward program so that all understand. Therefore, share the wealth, so to speak, in more than the traditional way.
7. *Measure results.* Performance can and should be measured with fairness and consistency.
8. *Refine. Refine again. Refine some more.* Continually improve the compensation program—analyze and revise. Keep up with the times.
9. *Be selective.* Do not take to heart everything you hear or read about compensation.[8]

Reward Strategies

Rewards have been studied, at length, for years. Historically, efforts to motivate employees and improve organization performance have focused on universal motivators—a one-size-fits-all strategy. This approach ignores individuality, priorities, and degree of motivation due to intrinsic and extrinsic rewards. Recognizing the power and importance of individualism enables firms to offer a variety of unique incentives to reward individual employees along their journey of productivity, growth, and renewal. The following rewards are intended to promote continuous growth and development of the individual and organization: recognition, noncash incentives, group/team incentives, responsibility and authority, professional development, freedom and independence, vacation, leisure time, sabbaticals, and fun.

Recognition

Recognition is second only to cash as a powerful motivator. It is impossible to negate the power of recognition and the genuine pleasure we feel when acknowledged for our efforts. Recognition boosts our self-esteem, places us on a pedestal, and validates our abilities. Recognition proves effective for rewarding stellar performance, professional development, attainment of performance goals, earning of advanced degrees, innovations and creative ideas, teamwork, community involvement, promotions, years of service, cost-savings ideas, and so forth.

Appropriate recognition includes timely praise for a job well done; involvement in major project teams, acquisitions, or strategy sessions; employee -of-the-month or year awards; honors banquets; trophies, certificates, and plaques; publicity in the organizational newsletter; formal and informal announcements by supervisors or leaders; organizational gifts such as pens, rings, watches, etc.; president's club or hall of fame; and so forth.

Noncash Incentives

Noncash incentives such as gift certificates, organizational merchandise and clothing, trophies or plaques, or other prizes are often desirable incentives. These noncash incentives are usually small in value (often less than $50) and are bestowed more frequently, such as when used to promote completion of a special project or going the "extra mile" for the organization or a customer. Noncash incentives may also be distributed and awarded on a peer-to-peer basis.

Group/Team Incentives

Group incentives reward performance of a particular set of employees, often a small group, cross-functional team, unit, or department. If group performance improves or reaches a certain goal, members are rewarded accordingly. This practice bolsters teamwork and cooperation, often resulting in a closeness and camaraderie absent prior to inception of the recognition program. Group incentives are important to those organizations that encourage or demand group or team work of their employees.

Responsibility and Authority

Employees prove themselves every day; from completing small, routine tasks to far exceeding personal and professional expectations. Those who are willing and able to assume greater responsibility should be given opportunities to do so. Many firms take care to balance additional responsibility with correspondingly increased authority. Responsibility without authority is a frustrating, de-motivating phenomenon.

Professional Development

Some organizations treat personal growth and development as a routine function, not an award for doing well. Internal ongoing training and external educational reimbursement send powerful messages—that the employee is valued, and his or her growth and development are critical to organization success.

Freedom and Independence

"Highly enterprising employees will welcome the opportunity to obtain freedom and independence as a reward for a job well done."[9] Freedom takes many forms: the ability to develop a new product or process; casual dress days; opportunities to work on a "special" project; and so forth. Genuine growth and development are by-products of individual creativity set free.

Vacation and Leisure Time

Hardworking employees push themselves to achieve personal and professional growth, often working overtime, evenings, or weekends. Since companies reap the benefits of extra effort and growth, it makes sense to compensate individuals for their efforts. Too much work can cause frustration or burnout; thus, employees need time to relax and reenergize. Extra vacation or leisure time is an appropriate reward for someone who has devoted long hours to business pursuits, and may provide a refreshing "time out" in preparation for the next challenge.

Fun

Laughter is the best medicine. What better way to relieve the tension of challenging work situations than to engage in lighthearted, fun activities, particularly with one's peers? One of the authors worked for an organization that regularly held golf outings, bowling nights, raffles, decorating contests, and the like. These amusements promoted a sense of teamwork, camaraderie, and goodwill while alleviating the stress that accumulates over time. Many organizations encourage and support teams of volunteer employees, occasionally called "sunshine," "excitement," or "fun," committees to coordinate motivational activities. Often, service on the committee itself proves stimulating.

Conclusion

Compensation is designed to reward employees for a job well done or to motivate them to continue or enhance their performance. Organizations that embrace the challenges of the twenty-first century develop a dynamic, responsive compensation and reward philosophy, select appropriate compensation and reward strategies, adopt principles of effective compensation and reward programs, and align compensation and rewards with goals and objectives. Compensation and rewards must be responsive to employees' needs and individual motivators while furthering organizational aims.

NOTES

1. Jerry W. Gilley, Nathaniel W. Boughton, and Ann Maycunich, *The Performance Challenge: Developing Management Systems to Make Employees Your Greatest Asset* (Cambridge, MA: Perseus, 1999), 139.
2. K. Hern and V. Alonzo, "This Is What We Want," *Incentive,* October 1998, 40.
3. Michael LeBoeuf, *Getting Results: The Secret to Motivating Yourself and Others* (New York: Berkeley Books, 1985), 9.
4. Gilley, Boughton, and Maycunich, *The Performance Challenge.*
5. David Ulrich, Jack Zenger, and Norm Smallwood, *Results-based Leadership: How Leaders Build the Business and Improve the Bottom Line* (Boston: Harvard Business School Press, 1999).
6. E.L. Thorndike, *Human Learning* (Cambridge, MA: MIT Press, 1931).
7. Gilley, Boughton, and Maycunich, *The Performance Challenge,* 144.
8. T.P. Flannery, D.A. Hofrichter, & P.E. Platten, *People Performance and Pay: Dynamic Compensation for Changing Organizations* (New York: The Free Press, 1996), 247–50.
9. Jerry W. Gilley and Nathaniel W. Boughton, *Stop Managing, Start Coaching: How Performance Coaching Can Enhance Commitment and Improve Productivity* (New York: McGraw-Hill, 1996), 217.

Ann Gilley and Marisha L. Godek

ABSENCES

An absence is a period of interruption in the continuous work cycle of an employee. The majority of absences are preceded and followed by paid employment. Recently, the increase of absences among employees has been identified as a growing problem for organizations. Unscheduled absences result in reduced production for companies. Most recent survey estimates indicate that unscheduled absences cost companies annually $660 per employee.[1]

Types of Absences

Absences are counted toward a nonproductive time for the organization. Some absences are considered to be legitimate, such as illness of the employee or one of his or her immediate family members, vacation time, jury duty, and so on. These absences have a legitimate justification as to why the employee is not present at work.

The other type of absence is considered absence abuse and considered to be nonlegitimate. Workers who falsely take sick days or time off to which they are not entitled are contributing to the rise of absence abuse.

Reasons for Absence Abuse

The increase in absence abuse among some members of an organization pushes employers to apply more pressure on workers who are present in order to achieve their goals and objectives. This strategy causes some workers to seek stress relief by taking every opportunity not to be present at work, creating the "push back" effect within the organization.

Other factors impacting absence abuse include substance abuse, smoking, obesity among employees, stressful work environments, and family issues, to name a few. Another contributing factor to absence abuse is poor management. Investigating the absence problem among employees often provides management with valuable information with regard to absences, management problems, and other contributions to absence abuse.

Combating Absence Abuse

Many strategies exist to reduce absence abuse, including communicating with employees, enhancing coaching/mentoring activities, improving working conditions, offering better benefits, and involving workers in decision making. Additionally, some companies revise their existing performance evaluation system or develop a new evaluation system. New systems are often based upon the output of the employee and not her working hours. Policies such as these allow workers some flexibility in managing their schedules, lives, and stressors by permitting them to set their own hours. Although some workers abuse this policy as well, it has been shown to alleviate absence abuse in some firms.

Some companies, like Georgia-Pacific and Southwest Airlines, are inventing new ways of tracking the absence abuse among their employees. Southwest Airlines, for example, has new software that tracks the under-the-wing crew and has already saved the company $2 million annually in reduced administrative costs alone."[2]

One of the best ways to deal with the increased number of absences among employees is to keep the employee engaged and involved in processes within the organization. Motivating employees by increasing their awareness of the processes within the organization and showing the vital role they play by doing what they are doing on a daily basis also decreases the number of absences. Personal development plans for employees that specify promotion opportunities and professional growth within a firm may be used to motivate and engage employees, while concurrently reducing absences.

See also PTO (Paid Time Off) Bank

NOTES

1. Statistics Canada, *Absences from Work* (June 2007); "Shrinking Working: The War on Hooky," *Business Week,* November 12, 2007.
2. "Shrinking Working: The War on Hooky," *Business Week,* November 12, 2007.

Igor Golovatyy

BENEFITS

In addition to direct compensation (e.g., base pay), organizations provide employees with indirect compensation, also known as benefits. The use of benefits can be viewed as a strategic approach that enables an organization to recruit and retain highly skilled talent and increase the likelihood of employee commitment. Benefits are a part of an organization's total compensation program and are viewed as a way to promote financial security and overall well-being.

Commonly offered employee benefits include medical/health insurance, dental, vision, vacation and sick days, personal days, life and disability insurance, tuition reimbursement, and discounts on company products. Benefits may comprise 30 percent or more of an employee's total compensation. The basic benefits offered in organizations are highly regulated, and some are legally required.

Benefits Legislation and Statutes

Federal and state governments mandate some benefits, such as:[1]
- Employee Retirement Income Security Act (ERISA)
- Health Insurance Portability and Accountability Act (HIPPA)
- Consolidated Omnibus Budget Reconciliation Act (COBRA)
- Family and Medical Leave Act (FMLA)

ERISA

The Employee Retirement Income Security Act establishes minimum standards for health, life, disability, and retirement plans. Employers are not required to offer health, life or retirement plans, but if they choose to have a plan, it must conform to the guidelines outlined by ERISA.

HIPPA

The purpose of the Health Insurance Portability and Accountability act is to ensure that health plans (1) do not limit or deny coverage for preexisting conditions, (2) are renewable, (3) are portable when individuals change jobs, (4) adhere to antidiscrimination rules, and (5) have established privacy rules for health care plans and providers.

COBRA

Under the provisions of the Consolidated Omnibus Budget Reconciliation Act, organizations that provide health care benefits to their employees, and that employ 20 or more people, must provide for benefits continuation in circumstances such as when employment has been terminated (except when termination is due to gross misconduct).

FMLA

The Family and Medical Leave Act enables eligible employees to take up to 12 weeks of unpaid leave for the birth or adoption of a child, or a serious health condition of the employee or the employee's spouse, child, or parent. The act covers employers with 50 or more full- or part-time employees. To be eligible for this benefit, employees must have worked 12 months and 1,250 hours in the year prior to requesting the leave.

Other benefits required by statute include Social Security, unemployment insurance, and workers' compensation.

Social Security

Social Security has two elements—Social Security and Medicare. The Social Security program provides retirement, disability, death, and survivor's benefits. Medicare covers hospital insurance and supplemental medical insurance. All individuals are eligible for Medicare at the age of 65, regardless of whether they have retired or not. If an individual is retired, Medicare is the primary carrier and the employer's insurance is secondary.

Unemployment Insurance

Unemployment insurance, which is regulated by individual states, provides subsistence pay to individuals who are between jobs.[2] In brief, provisions for eligibility indicate that individuals have to be available and actively seeking employment. Further, they cannot have left their previous job voluntarily or been terminated for misconduct. Other provisions apply, and laws may vary state by state.

Workers' Compensation

The purpose of workers' compensation is to protect employees who have a work-related injury or illness. Under this plan, employers assume all costs regardless of who is at fault for the accident or exposure. Cost control is a goal of management, which is handled by implementing strategies such as prevention programs and training.

Conclusion

Benefits, which make up one part of the total compensation program within an organization, are viewed by employees as a way to protect the financial and physical well-being of themselves and their families. Employers view benefits as a strategic approach to recruit and retain talent. At the same time, employers are continuously focused on controlling the ever-rising costs of benefits—particularly health care benefits.

See also COBRA; ERISA; FMLA; HIPAA; Payroll; Workers' Compensation

Resources:

Milkovich, George T., Jerry Newman, and Carolyn Milkovich. *Compensation* (New York: Irwin/McGraw-Hill, 2007).

Society for Human Resource Management Toolkits, http://www.shrm.org/hrtools/toolkits_published/ (accessed August 18, 2008).

WorldatWork, http://www.worldatwork.org (accessed August 18, 2008).

NOTES

1. David A. DeCenzo and Stephen P. Robbins, *Human Resource Management,* 6th ed. (New York: John Wiley & Sons, Inc., 1999), 77–79.

2. Ibid.

Pamela Dixon

BONUSES

The purpose of bonus programs is to increase performance and reward employees. Bonuses provide employees with extra compensation and are paid out as a lump sum. In other words, an employee's base pay is not adjusted based on the bonus. There are three common types of bonuses, including performance-based bonuses, formula-based bonuses, and discretionary-based bonuses. In addition, holistic approaches to measuring performance levels are becoming more popular. In these instances, bonuses are tied to a larger number of variables, including customer satisfaction and other aspects that are not necessarily a primary function of the job. Regardless of the type of bonus plan utilized, organizations must take care to ensure that performance targets and the timing of bonus payouts do not become disincentives for employees.

Performance-based Bonus

Performance-based bonuses, the most commonly used, are paid out based on the degree of achievement of some preestablished performance criteria, at the individual, group, and/or organization levels.

Formula-based Bonus

Formula-based bonuses are based on a percentage of the company's financial goals. An organization sets targets to meet a minimum gross margin or profit level, and it must meet this target for anyone in the organization to receive a bonus.

Discretionary-based Bonus

Discretionary-based bonuses are given based on the judgment of managers. For example, managers may give employees discretionary bonuses for superior performance or achievement of a goal that was not originally tied to a formal performance goal. Or, a manager may use her discretion to give a bonus at the end of the year to make up for the loss of performance-based bonuses.

Bonuses Based on a Balanced Scorecard

Bonuses may be based on goals that include many variables that are indicative of an employee's primary job responsibilities, as well as how the employee contributes to other facets of organizational performance. In this instance, the bonus grid is structured as a balanced scorecard. The balanced scorecard incorporates financial and nonfinancial goals such as customer satisfaction and learning and development. The movement toward using a balanced scorecard reflects a holistic approach to measuring the success of an organization.

Bonus Targets and Payouts as Disincentives

Annual incentive bonuses are designed to reward employees for achieving performance goals and contributing to the organization's overall results. Bonus targets and the respective payouts are intended to motivate employees to increase and maintain high levels of performance. However, the performance level required and the timing of payouts may become disincentives.

Performance targets that are set at unrealistic levels, and will not likely be met, become disincentives and frustrate employees, rather than motivate higher levels of performance. Further, if the timing is such that rewards are paid out only on a yearly basis (or more), then momentum could be lost during the year. Annual incentive programs that are supplemented with interim rewards to recognize progress toward goals are more likely to maintain momentum and drive the performance desired.

Conclusion

Effective bonus programs increase performance and reward employees. To ensure bonus programs are effective, realistic performance targets are created, employees are rewarded on an annual basis, and their achievement of milestones is also celebrated. When designed appropriately, bonuses provide employees with incentives to continually work toward improving performance and achieving organizational goals.

Resources:

Milkovich, George, T., Jerry Newman, and Carolyn Milkovich, *Compensation* (New York: Irwin/ McGraw-Hill, 2007).

Pamela Dixon

CAFETERIA BENEFIT PLANS

In the competitive labor economy, employers are looking for the best benefit package to lure potential employees into their employment ranks. A cafeteria benefit plan is one tool that employers are turning to with greater frequency due to the flexibility it offers employees with diverse needs. Under this plan, employees select employment benefits from a "cafeteria" list of two or more benefits and cash. Allowable benefits under a cafeteria plan include disability, accident, and sickness benefits; group-term life insurance; dependent care assistance; adoption assistance; 401(k) plans; vacation pay; and health care benefits. This flexible type of benefit allocation allows an employee in need of health care insurance to allocate benefit dollars there, while another employee is able to focus on building retirement savings. The Internal Revenue Code, Section 125, enables employers to offer these plans in combination with other benefits.

Types of Plans

Cafeteria plans provide employees with the opportunity of choosing between two or more employee benefits and cash. Employers may include coverage for group-term life insurance, accident, and health insurance, dependent care assistance, adoption reimbursement, and health care costs. Major types of plans used today include the following:

1. Pretax Conversion Plans, whereby employees are covered by a contributory medical plan.
2. Multiple-Option Pretax Conversion Plans, which consist of one or more HMOs or PPOs with differing amounts of employee contributions.
3. Flexible Spending Accounts (FSA), which are set up by employers to reimburse employees for medical expenses. Employees authorize a deduction of pretax wages to fund the account. The account allows the employee to save both income tax and Social Security tax. Funds withheld for one year must be used within the year.
4. Employer Credit Cafeteria plans, which give the employee a specified number of credits that the employee can "spend" on different employee benefit plans or contribute to a flexible spending account. Usually, there are sufficient employer credits for an employee to choose a low-cost medical plan and a base amount of life insurance coverage without requiring the employee to contribute his own money. To the extent that the employee chooses a more costly benefit package, he will have to make contributions out of his own money, usually through a pretax conversion feature.

Complying with the Code

The Internal Revenue Code specifies that a cafeteria plan must be in writing. The plan can cover only current employees (rather than those who have retired) and must not discriminate among employees.[1] Independent contractors and other agents are not covered. The employer must adopt and promulgate the plan description—so that each employee receives a copy. It is important for the employer to market the plan to employees during times of open enrollment.

There are some benefits that cannot be included in a cafeteria plan. The plan cannot provide for deferred compensation other than a 401(k) plan. Life insurance products that involve the buildup of cash values or investment accounts cannot be included in a cafeteria plan. Further, employers may not use cafeteria plans to cover scholarships or meals and lodging. The terms of a cafeteria plan do not fall under ERISA.

Advantages

Cafeteria plans are an added benefit that assist companies in retaining good employees. Employees are motivated by being able to choose among benefits. At a young age, health insurance might not be as valued to an employee as dependent care assistance. In other workplaces, health care reimbursement might be of the utmost concern. Organizations are perceived as caring about its employees, which is reflected in increased retention and recruiting power.

Cost management is another advantage. Flexible plans are used to better link benefits expenditures with an organization's profitability and true benefits cost. Organizations have the ability to better control and manage the cost of benefits because employees give up some benefits to obtain others. Furthermore, their costs are shared with employees.

The primary advantage for employees is that they have choices and can select benefits that meet their own needs, and they have the option of taking some dollars currently spent on tax-free benefits in the form of taxable cash. Further, employees are able to gain maximum tax advantages, and there is increased satisfaction on the part of employees due to their ability to make their own benefits decisions.

See also Benefits; ERISA

Resources:

"FAQs for Government Entities Regarding Cafeteria Plans," Internal Revenue Service, http://www.irs.gov/govt/fslg/article/0,,id=112720,00.html (accessed August 18, 2008).

NOTES

1. Allen Smith, "IRS Proposes Rule on Cafeteria Plans," *HR Magazine,* (2007): 24.

Laura Dendinger

CHILD AND ELDER CARE

In recent decades (since the early 1980s), child care, whether in the form of on-site care, child care vouchers, company sponsored child care, etc., has often been offered by organizations as a possible benefit for employees. Some contemporary organizations, however, are taking this concept a step further and including elder care as part of the benefits package. In the face of the Family and Medical Leave Act, companies not only are following the law regarding absenteeism to care for children and elderly family members, but they are taking a proactive stance and sending a message to employees that they care. Sometimes called "family-friendly benefits," organizations are using child and elder care programs as part of the strategic plan to recruit and retain good employees.

Provisions for Child and Elder Care

Companies have a multitude of choices to offer employees in the way of child and elder care. Some choices include on-site child care, flexible work schedules, child care vouchers, and in-home care for elderly family members.[1] Many companies are also offering flexible spending plans to pay for child and elder care. Basically, the employer deducts a monthly amount (determined by the employee) from the employee's pay to set aside to pay child and elder care costs. This amount is deducted before taxes, so the employee enjoys significant tax savings.

For some employees, however, peace of mind is much more important than the financial burden. Knowing their children and elderly parents or family members are cared for in a safe environment is benefit above and beyond the financial issue. Today, employees are seeking information from their employers regarding elder care more frequently. Some studies show that as many as 35 percent of workers face daily elder care responsibilities at some point.[2] Used proactively, companies that offer child and elder care options up front can reap the benefits of recruiting and retaining valuable employees.

Using Benefits as a Recruiting/Retention Tool

The Family and Medical Leave Act states that employers *must* give employees (male or female) 12 weeks' unpaid leave for medical or family needs, including paternity and family member illness. This is the minimum employers have to offer, and adherence to this act will keep them out of the courtroom. These days, however, providing the minimum to avoid legal repercussions will not allow organizations to remain competitive.

Today's employees are looking for more than a just a job; they are looking for quality of work life. Companies that offer family-friendly benefits maintain a better position to recruit and retain good employees, especially women.[3] Furthermore, these benefits may improve return-to-work rates. In a one-year study of more than 7,000 employees, organizations that offered expanded dependent care found improvements in employee satisfaction, employee retention, and rate of return to work.[4]

Some companies are leading the way in leveraging child and elder care to recruit and retain the best employees. They offer benefits above and beyond traditional child care, including annual in-home or out-of-town backup care for children, spouses/partners, or parents, providing a nanny for nursing mothers while traveling on business, and extending the care of these dependents to include locations anywhere in the country.[5] These organizations are at the forefront of providing quality of work-life environments to present and future employees.

Conclusion

Traditionally, offering child care to employees emerged with the need to accommodate more women in the workforce. This benefit has transformed into a much more strategic tool to recruit and retain the best talent, male *and* female. By expanding dependent care to include elderly family members, and providing more creative ways to afford flexibility in the financial aspects (flexible spending) as well as work environment (on-site care, flexible hours, etc.), companies may well be leveraging one of the biggest new trends in employee benefits offered today to achieve competitive advantage through one of its most valuable resources, human capital.

NOTES

1. T.S. Bateman and S.A. Snell, *Management: Leading and Collaborating in a Competitive World* (New York: McGraw-Hill Irwin, 2007).

2. "Workplace Flexibility Pivotal to Easing Employees' Elder Care Concerns," *Managing Benefits Plans* (2006), 9–10.

3. Bateman and Snell, *Management.*

4. "Workplace Flexibility Pivotal to Easing Employees' Elder Care Concerns."

5. "Back-Up Care for All: A New Benefit Trend?" *HR Focus* (2007), 12–13.

Brenda E. Ogden

COMPENSATION

Compensation is the total value of an employee's pay and benefits.[1] An organization's compensation strategy is influential in attracting and retaining qualified employees at all levels.

Methods of Pay

The primary methods of employee pay are salary, wages, commission, and incentives. A *salary* is paid regardless of the number of hours one works and is based on results and output. Salaries are typically paid weekly, biweekly, monthly, quarterly, or yearly. Salaried workers are usually considered "exempt," meaning they are exempt from overtime pay.

Wages are paid hourly, and these employees are typically considered "nonexempt," which means they are subject to overtime rules and pay (see FLSA below). Nonexempt employees who work more than 40 hours per week are entitled to overtime pay, which is usually one and one-half times (1.5x) the rate of normal pay, for each hour worked beyond 40 in a standard work week. Some companies, particularly unionized firms, pay double-time for weekends and/or triple-time overtime pay for holidays.

Commission pay is based on sales. Many sales personnel are commissioned; they receive a percentage of their sales as pay. The percentage is based on the value of the item—typically the more expensive the item, the lower the commission rate.

Incentives include pay based on performance and may be paid to hourly, salaried, and commissioned workers. Incentives are paid for production (piece-rate) and/or increases in productivity. Bonuses, a type of incentive, are often tied to objectives in productivity and profitability (profit-sharing), with the intent of rewarding employees who work smarter or harder.

Team-based Pay

Team-based pay links incentive compensation to teamwork behavior and/or team results. Individuals may be rewarded for specific behaviors that exhibit teamwork, and/or members of a team may be rewarded, collectively, for their results as a team. Team-based pay reflects the workplace trend toward teams and group accomplishments.

Pay Grades and Ranges

To determine how much to pay employees, organizations frequently group together jobs that are similar in importance, skill, or outcome, and assign corresponding pay grades. The more important the job, the higher the pay grade and the rate of pay. A pay grade of 5, for example, pays less than a 7. This is a common approach for the government and military, for example.

Another common approach is to assign pay ranges to each job. After evaluating the worth of the job, the firm commonly establishes a low-middle-high range for the job. The company hopes to bring in new hires at the low point, experienced personnel at the midpoint, and promote or transfer those who reach the high end. Employees at the high end of the range are often frustrated when they fail to receive a raise worthy of their performance due to the limitation imposed by the high end of the pay range.

To be competitive within the region or industry, firms may research the pay at other organizations for the same or similar jobs and set their pay accordingly. External resources for pay information include the Department of Labor, online salary surveys, and the many salary comparison reports produced by private/HR firms such as Mercer.

Equal Pay Act

The Equal Pay Act of 1963 requires that men and women be paid the same for equal work. However, the law does not prohibit differences in pay due to education, experience, or skill level.

Fair Labor Standards Act (FLSA) of 1938

The FLSA sets minimum wages, maximum hours, overtime pay provisions, and child labor standards. Exempt, or salaried employees, are not subject to overtime or minimum wage provisions. Nonexempt, or hourly employees, are entitled to additional pay (typically time and a half) for overtime (typically defined as hours worked in excess of 40 per week).

Benefits

Benefits are a critical component of a firm's overall compensation strategy. Traditionally, workers' benefits included health and dental insurance, disability coverage, paid vacations and holidays, paid sick days, and contributions to a pension or 401(k) plan. Although employers and employees often split the cost, the amount of employer reimbursement has been decreasing, due primarily to the rising cost of health care coverage. Benefits often comprise one-third or more of an employee's total compensation.[2]

Life insurance, tuition reimbursement, company discounts, child and elder care benefits, and flextime have been increasing, as employers attempt to meet the work-life-balance needs of employees.

An increasing number of employers are offering cafeteria-style benefit plans, which allow employees to choose the benefits they desire based on their unique needs. Individuals are often given a preset spending limit and may receive cash back if they select benefits that cost less than their allotted dollar value.

Legally Required Benefits

By law, employers are required to provide certain benefits to all employees, including
- Worker's compensation
- Unemployment compensation
- Social Security

Worker's compensation covers job-related injuries. An employee who applies for and receives worker's compensation after being injured on the job may be entitled to monetary compensation for missed work and time off to attend doctor's visits.

If an employee is laid off or terminated, he or she may be entitled to worker's compensation if sufficient days have been worked for a specified span of time (e.g., a year). Worker's compensation benefits are based on the employee's previous rate of pay and are paid for a limited time (commonly a maximum of 26 weeks).

Social Security taxes are deducted from an individual's pay and matched by the employer. Social Security is a tax that pays welfare benefits to certain classes of individuals (e.g., children who have lost one or more parents, retirees, and the disabled).

Conclusion

An organization's compensation strategy is a major determinant of its ability to attract and retain talented employees.

See also 401(k) Plans; Bonuses; Employment Law: An Overview; Pension Plans; Salary Benchmarking

NOTES

1. Robert N. Lussier, *Management Fundamentals,* 3rd ed. (Mason, OH: Thomson South-Western, 2006).

2. R. Lieber and B. Martinez, "Companies Pass the Buck on Benefits," *Wall Street Journal,* November 26, 2002, D1.

Ann Gilley

DEFERRED COMPENSATION

The compensation landscape has changed dramatically over the last 10 years. The global business environment has become increasingly competitive, requiring employer organizations to search out more creative ways to incite high performance throughout employee ranks. HR has responded to this challenge partly through modernized compensation strategies. These contemporary strategies have emphasized a movement away from fixed, entitlement-based pay systems to flexible, performance-based pay systems.[1] Concurrent with this shift has come an increased emphasis on deferred and incentive-based compensation.

Basic Definition and Typical Forms of Deferred Compensation

Employer organizations are increasingly offering compensation flexibility to their employees, including deferred compensation. A deferred compensation plan allows employees to defer some of their earned income to a later date. This, of course, allows the employee to defer tax on that income until it is actually paid out. The following are the most commonly offered forms:

- *Defined benefit pension*—a traditional pension that is typically fully funded by the employer organization and paid out as an annuity upon retirement. Through the 1970s, defined benefit pensions were normative in the United States.

- *Defined contribution pension/retirement account*—a contemporary pension/retirement account that is typically jointly funded by matching contributions from both the employer organization and the employee. These pension/retirement accounts allow for individual employee control regarding investment options and shared costs/risks between employer and employee. The most common form of defined contribution pension/retirement account is a 401(k). Defined contribution pension/retirement plans became normative in the United States in the 1980s.
- *Social Security benefits*—a government-controlled, defined benefit pension plan funded jointly by employer organizations and employee payroll taxes.
- *Employee stock option grants*—an employer-funded plan that bestows to the employee the right to buy a certain number of shares of the employer organization's common stock at a predetermined price within certain time parameters. Typically, these time parameters delineate a vesting schedule of when the options can be exercised.
- *Restricted stock grant*—an employer-funded plan that bestows to the employee a certain number of shares of the employer organization's common stock that are not transferable (e.g., cannot be liquidated) until certain vesting requirements are met. These vesting requirements typically include both performance-based and time-based parameters.

Deferred Compensation as a Long-term Performance Incentive

Employee stock option grant plans and restricted stock grant plans have emerged as the central means of affording employees significant, long-term incentive pay as deferred compensation. Thus, HR must be both knowledgeable of the mechanics of employee stock option and restricted stock plans, and savvy in employing such plans as a means of motivating and retaining high-performing employees. In this way, HR facilitates the accomplishment of strategic objectives via deferred compensation vehicles that align employee performance and retention with organizational priorities, resulting in higher productivity, profitability, and higher total employee compensation.[2]

See also Compensation: An Overview; Pay for Performance; Pension Plans; Retention; HR Strategy

NOTES

1. Edward E. Lawler, *Rewarding Excellence: Pay Strategies for the New Economy* (San Francisco: Jossey-Bass, 2000).
2. James C. Sesil, Maya K. Kroumova, Douglas L. Kruse, and Joseph R. Blasi, "Broad-Based Employee Stock Options in the United States: Company Performance and Characteristics," *Management Revue*, March 2007, 5–22.

Scott A. Quatro

DISABILITY INSURANCE

Disability-income insurance provides income benefits to those insureds who are unable to work due to sickness or injury. Disability insurance policies replace income for those insureds who become disabled from sickness or an accident. Most insurance companies limit the time and amount of benefits. Income is typically replaced for an extended period of time and typically ends after five years or when the disabled person reaches the age of

65. The amount of insurance available is usually limited to no more than 60 to 80 percent of a worker's gross earnings.

Total Disability

Total disability has been defined by insurance companies in several ways, including:
- The inability to perform all duties of one's own occupation
- The inability to perform the duties of any occupation for which the insured is reasonably qualified by experience, training, and education
- The inability to perform the duties of any gainful occupation
- The loss-of-income test

Most insurers use a combination of the first two definitions.

Partial Disability

Some disability-income policies provide for payments due to partial disability, which is the inability of the insured to perform one or more important duties of his or her occupation. Partial disability benefits are usually at a reduced rate for a shorter period of time, and in most policies must follow a period of total disability (as when one returns to work on a part-time basis to assess whether recovery is complete).

Short-term Disability

Short-term disability, often included as a component of one's employee benefits package, provides income payments for the early stage of a disability. Typically, short-term disability policies pay benefits for two weeks up to two years.

Benefit Period

Benefit period is the length of time that disability-income benefits are payable after a specified elimination period has been met. Insureds may choose their desired benefit period, typically two, five, or 10 years, or up to age 65 or 70. The longer the benefit period, the more expensive the disability-income insurance premiums.

Elimination Period

Disability-income benefits are paid after a mandatory waiting period, known as the elimination period. Insureds usually choose their desired elimination period, typically 30, 60, 90, 180, or 365 days. The shorter the elimination period, the more expensive the disability-income insurance premiums. Most employers provide sick leave or short-term disability plans that provide income during elimination periods.

Other Provisions

Most disability policies include a waiver-of-premium provision that pays the disability-income insurance premiums as long as the worker remains disabled. When the insured recovers, premium payments must be resumed. Some policies also provide additional benefits for accidental death or dismemberment, such as for loss of both hands or sight in both eyes.

Conclusion

The financial impact of a disability on one's life can be devastating. Disability-income insurance offers valuable protection to insured workers via monthly income payments after one has been disabled due to sickness or an accident.

Resources:

About-Disability-Insurance.com. http://www.about-disability-insurance.com (accessed August 18, 2008).

Insurance Information Institute. http://www.iii.org (accessed August 18, 2008).

Ann Gilley

DOMESTIC PARTNER BENEFITS

The term "domestic partner benefits" refers to employee benefit plans that offer the same or similar benefits as those provided to married couples or nonmarried couples as well. Although the term "domestic partner" is often associated with gay or lesbian couples, it also includes unmarried couples of the same sex. Employers usually do not offer domestic partnership benefits unless employees ask for them. However, an increasing number of employers, in both the public and private sectors, are starting to offer such benefit plans.[1] Although domestic partner benefits are increasingly popular, the rules that govern the benefit plans are not uniform and vary between states as well as across companies.

The two states that recognize civil unions, Vermont and Connecticut, "require that all state government employers provide benefits to the dependents of a party to a civil union if the government provides those benefits to married couples."[2] Because Canada allows same-sex couples to marry in most provinces under the Canadian Modernization of Benefits and Obligations Act, also known as C-23, the country allows same-sex common-law couples to have the same obligations and benefits as opposite-sex common-law couples; this includes distribution of benefits in the workplace.[3] However, in the United States, private employers who have benefit plans governed under the federal Employee Retirement Income Security Act of 1974 (ERISA) are not required to offer coverage to civil union partners. Accordingly, "insurers are required to offer policies that include civil union coverage to private employers in Vermont and Connecticut, but private employers and employers in other states may decide who will be eligible to enroll in their plans."[4]

Definition of a Domestic Partner

A domestic partnership is usually understood to mean "two unrelated, unmarried adults who share the same household."[5] In order to qualify for domestic partner benefits, employees often need to demonstrate that his or her "eligible partner" meets specific criteria that is defined by the employer.

Participation in domestic partner benefit plans is often limited to those who are in a relationship that is considered to be "committed"—a term that can be defined in many different ways; other domestic partner benefit plans limit participation to same-sex partners. In states that do not recognize civil unions, domestic partners can sometimes have the option to register their partnership. Although this registration does not carry the same legal status as a marriage or a civil union, it can be made a condition of participation in a benefit plan.

Other plans require a waiting period, most often six months to one year, before a partner will be eligible to enroll in the benefits plan.[6] Accordingly, the definition used in many domestic partner benefit plans defines an "eligible partner" as someone who is:

- At least 18 years old
- Not related more closely than would be allowed for a legal marriage under state law
- Sharing a "committed relationship"
- In an exclusive relationship with his or her partner
- Financially interdependent with his or her partner[7]

Covered Benefits

Many domestic partner benefit plans do not offer full health benefits, but offer other minimal and low-cost benefits. Examples include but are not limited to sick leave, relocation expenses, access to company property, and permission to attend company functions.[8]

However, health and medical insurance is often of greater interest to those seeking domestic partner benefits than those benefits that are more commonly offered. An assumption that the cost will be too high is the main hindrance for many employers. However, studies have shown that the increased cost of adding domestic partner coverage to a health insurance plan is often less than many employers anticipate, for many reasons. This is often because participation in domestic partner benefit plans tends to be very low, and the typical employee who participates tends to be younger and healthier than the average employee.[9] Additionally, this population, due to the fact that they are often partners in same-sex relationships, has a decreased risk that a health insurance plan will have to cover the high costs of pregnancy and childbirth.

Tax Consequences

Federal income tax laws treat domestic partner benefits and benefits offered to married couples differently. Ordinarily, an employee whose spouse obtains benefits must include the cost of those benefits as taxable income. The exception to this is when the employed spouse is claiming the covered spouse as a legal dependent by the Internal Revenue Service (IRS). Accordingly, to be considered a legal dependent by the IRS, "a partner must live in the same household as the employee and must receive over half of his or her support from the employee."[10]

NOTES

1. National Gay and Lesbian Task Force, *The Domestic Partnership Organizing Manual for Employee Benefits* (1999), http://thetaskforce.org/reports_and_research/dp_manual (accessed September 20, 2007).

2. D.R. Euben, (2005, August). "Domestic Partner Benefits on Campus," http://www.aaup.org/AAUP/protect/legal/topics/partners.htm (accessed September 24, 2007).

3. Canadian Department of Justice, *Civil Marriage Act* (February 2005), http://www.justice.gc.ca/eng/news-nouv/nr-cp/doc_31376.html (accessed September 8, 2008).

4. Euben, "Domestic Partner Benefits on Campus."

5. "Domestic Partner Benefits," FindLaw for Small Businesses, http://smallbusiness.findlaw.com/employment-employer/employment-employer-benefits/employment-employer-benefits-partner.html (accessed September 25, 2007).

6. Ibid., 4.

7. Ibid., 3.

8. Ibid.

9. Ibid.
10. Ibid., 7.

Lea Hanson

EMPLOYEE ASSISTANCE PROGRAMS

Employee assistance programs (EAP) are increasingly offered by employers to assist employees to manage life issues that could affect their work. Many times, these plans are offered in conjunction with health insurance benefits. A survey of employers in 2007 revealed that 73 percent of employers have some form of EAP.[1]

Benefits to the Employees

Employees can, confidentially, contact the EAP for assistance with workplace stress, marital and family issues, depression or other mental health issues, and substance abuse. At times, employees may need the assistance due to a major life adjustment, such as the birth of a child, an accident, or the death of a loved one. At other times, employees may need assistance due to financial or legal concerns. Usually EAP services are offered free of charge (or in coordination with health insurance benefits). Often the employee's family members are eligible to receive EAP services. Services can often be initiated with a phone call to an 800 number.

Benefits to the Employer

Most employers contract with a third party for this value-added service for employees. The cushion of having a third party offer this service reduces the issues of confidentiality associated with many of the circumstances that employees face in the areas for which they need EAP help.

Estimates in the EAP industry are that employers in the United States lose close to $200 billion per year due to loss of productivity and absenteeism without an EAP.[2] Employees who are stressed by workplace or personal situations are often absent from work and are distracted and less productive when they are present.

When employers introduce and market the availability of EAP services, they will soon see an improvement. Employees often have increased morale and focus for their work. Employers often note a decrease in absenteeism and higher production. EAP could lead to better employee retention and less turnover.

In addition, EAP firms often offer training for member firms. The training may supplement or replace the efforts of HR practitioners on safety and related issues. In addition, EAP firms may be of assistance to the employer in response to crisis situations.

See also Health Care Plans

NOTES

1. Kelley Butler, "EAP Benefits Worth More Than Their Price Tag," *Employee Benefit News*, September 1, 2007, 9.
2. Andy Cohen and John Brewer, "Getting Personal," *Sales and Marketing Management*, 1996, 24.

Laura Dendinger

EMPLOYEE STOCK OPTION PLAN (ESOP)

Employee stock option plans (ESOPs) allow organizations to contribute a limited number of company shares into a trust for the employees' benefits package.[1] The higher the percentage of one's income/salary that an employee is allowed to contribute, the more it directly affects the employee's feeling of ownership in the organization. ESOPs have been thus identified as a way for organizations to attract talented employees and to motivate and retain these employees. According to the literature, there are over 11,000 organizations with ESOPs and more than 10 million participants.[2]

How ESOPs Are Established

Once an employer has decided to establish an ESOP, a trustee or board of trustees is set up to oversee the plan. The organization borrows money to set up a trust for the purchase of stock. Rules are set up to determine how employees are vested into the program. There are also guidelines for when the employees can redeem their shares. When a vested employee leaves the organization, the vested shares are bought out at fair market value. Employees meeting the vesting requirements and reaching a certain age have disbursement options.[3] There are governmental requirements and oversight for ESOPs. "Congress has modified the laws governing ESOPs, most notably in the Tax Reform Acts of 1984 and 1986, the Small Business Job Protection Act of 1996, the Taxpayer Relief Act of 1997, and the Economic Growth and Tax Relief Reconciliation Act of 2001."[4]

Employee ownership can be accomplished in several different ways. Workers can purchase stock directly from the company or receive shares through profit-sharing plans, or stock can be awarded to the employees as bonuses. The most common ESOP usually includes an employer's matching contribution to the employee's contribution into the plan. Contributions made by the company are tax-deductible, and employee contributions are not taxed until the time of distribution to the employee. These shares may or may not have voting rights, depending upon how the ESOP was established.[5]

Stock shares are generally contained within the organization and not sold on the common market. There are currently arguments that ESOPs should be reorganized to be more employee-friendly to assure employees of ethical governance over the management of ESOP funds. Positive correlation found between unionization and ESOP design suggests that "unionized firms tend to have ESOP structures that are more attentive to the equity possession of employee owners."[6] Accordingly, unions may have better communication lines established between the employer and the employee to explain this condition, and are set up to maximize input from employees.

Benefits

ESOPs benefit both the organization and employees, as the employer can utilize ESOP loan funds for capital expansion or to meet other needs within the organization. Employees benefit by being shareholders of the company. These benefits may show up in improved employee performance. ESOPs established by organizations lead principally to increased job satisfaction and lower absenteeism and turnover rates. However, organizations may not realize these retention benefits if the employees are not comfortable with the structure of the plan. Some organizations tailor the provisions of the ESOP to their employees' needs as a way of increasing acceptance of the ESOP and improving employee loyalty to the organization.[7] In other words, ESOPs are used to give the employee a sense of ownership in the organization; therefore, some ESOPs are set up with "participative decision making."[8]

See also Compensation: An Overview; Motivation; Performance Management: An Overview

NOTES

1. "Employee Stock Option Plans," http://www.sec.gov/answers/esops.htm (accessed February 16, 2008).

2. The Menke Group, "ESOP Section Overview." http://www.menke.com/information/about.php (accessed February 16, 2008).

3. National Center for Employee Ownership, "A Comprehensive Overview of Employee Ownership," http://www.nceo.org/library/overview.html (accessed May 9, 2008).

4. National Center for Employee Ownership, "A Short History of the ESOP," http://www.nceo.org/library/history.html (accessed February 16, 2008).

5. National Center for Employee Ownership, "How an Employee Stock Ownership Plan (ESOP) Works." http://www.nceo.org/library/history.html (accessed February 16, 2008).

6. Patrick P. McHugh, Joel Crutcher-Gershenfeld, and Diane L. Bridge. "Examining Structure and Process in ESOP Firms." *Personnel Review* 34, no. 3 (2005): 277–93.

7. Daniel E. Hallock, Ronald J. Salazar, and Sandy Venneman, "Demographic and Attitudinal Correlates of Employee Satisfaction with an ESOP," *British Journal of Management* 15, no. 4 (2004): 321–33.

8. Robert N. Stern, "Employee Ownership Plans. Background Paper No. 34." *Department of Labor, Washington, DC, Commission on Workforce Quality and Labor Market Efficiency* (September 1989): 1777–1829.

Debora A. Montgomery-Colbert

401(K) PLANS

The 401(k) plan is a type of employer-sponsored retirement plan named after the section of the U.S. Internal Revenue (IRS) Code that defines it. It is generally classified as a type of *defined contribution pension plan.* A 401(k) allows both the employee and the employer to contribute to a retirement account held in the employee's name while deferring income taxes on the contributions and earnings until the money is withdrawn.

All 401(k) plans are strictly voluntary in nature but can be an important component of the benefit package offered to employees and can become an integral part of the recruiting process. Therefore, employers need not only understand how 401(k) plans are structured, but they must also be aware of current industry trends in order to remain competitive in the job market.

Plan Design

Employers have the flexibility to design a 401(k) plan tailored for their specific company and the needs of their employees. Within the framework provided by the government, the employer must decide:
• Who can participate in the plan
• When employees are eligible to begin contributing

- Whether the employee is responsible for investment choices
- When and how often contribution amounts and investment choices can change
- Whether a matching contribution will exist, when it will be provided, and how long employees must work to earn those monies
- Whether hardship withdrawals or loans will be permitted
- Whether to accept rollovers from other qualified plans
- Whether to allow employees to remain members of the plan if they leave the company for reasons other than retirement

Contributions

All contributions made to a 401(k) plan are voluntary in nature. Employees may save up to a maximum annual limit determined by the IRS, and increased incrementally every year for inflation. For example, in 2006, this limit was $15,000 and rose to $15,500 for 2007 and 2008.[1]

Employees may choose to contribute either a fixed dollar amount or a certain percentage of their salary, which is deducted from their paycheck each pay period and deposited by their employer into an account in their name. The deposited funds and any earnings on those funds immediately belong to the employee and are considered to be 100 percent vested.

Employers may choose to contribute to an employee's 401(k) fund in a number of ways. They may choose to match the employee's contributions based on a predetermined formula. For example, the employer may offer to match 50 percent of the employees' contributions up to a designated amount. If the employees contribute 5 percent of their salary, the employer would then match 50 percent up to a maximum of 2.5 percent of the employees' salary. This method encourages the employees to save for retirement knowing that they will receive a certain amount of "guaranteed return" on their investment. Another possible alternative is for the employer to contribute based upon a percentage of the profit of the company. The contribution amount can be based on a predetermined formula, or it may represent a lump-sum payout. This method encourages employees to work harder to earn better rewards. Regardless of the method chosen, the total amount contributed by the employee and employer is limited by the IRS. This limit is the lesser of 100 percent of the employee's annual compensation or $44,000 for 2006, $45,000 for 2007, and $46,000 for 2008.[2]

Employers may choose to have their contributions subject to a vesting schedule whereby the percentage of contributions and related earnings to which an employee is entitled is based upon the number of years of employment. Generally, the longer the employment period, the higher the vesting percentage. With cliff vesting, employees go from 0 percent to 100 percent vesting on a specified employment anniversary date. With gradual vesting, employees are entitled to a larger percentage for each year of employment until they have reached the full 100 percent. Generally, if an employee leaves employment prior to reaching full vesting, the unvested funds are distributed among the remaining participants in the plan.

Withdrawals from the Plan

Generally, withdrawals from a 401(k) plan are allowed upon reaching age 59½ but are required beginning on April 1 of the calendar year after reaching age 70½. However, exceptions exist in which an employee may begin taking withdrawals before reaching age 59½ or defer withdrawals beyond the age of 70½. The amount of the withdrawals will be dependent upon such factors as how much money is in the account, how long the employee expects to live, and whether other retirement benefits exist.

Employers may choose to allow employees to withdraw funds for the purpose of paying expenses due to a hardship. Hardships are legally defined in the tax code and include such things as purchase of a primary residence or medical expenses not covered by insurance. Employers may also designate which specific types of hardship withdrawals will be allowed under their particular plan.

Employers may choose to allow employees to take out loans from their accounts and may also establish both minimum and maximum limits for the amount of the loans. The loans are repaid to the employee's account through payroll deduction and include interest at a predetermined rate based upon comparable loan rates in effect at the time. The interest is also paid into the account and represents earnings on the account. In essence, employees are borrowing from, and paying interest to, themselves.

Tax Considerations

Because a 401(k) plan meets certain regulatory requirements, as defined by the Internal Revenue Service, it is considered to be a "qualified" plan. This means that it provides certain tax advantages to both the employee and the employer. Contributions by the employee are deducted pretax, meaning that they are not included in the employee's taxable income for that year, and interest earned on the contribution will also be tax-free. In fact, the employees will not pay tax until they receive distributions from the plan. In addition, employers are able to deduct the 401(k) contributions from their taxable income.

If employees choose to withdraw funds from their accounts for reasons other than hardship or retirement, the funds are subject to a 10 percent penalty as well as taxation as ordinary income. This can become an issue when an employee leaves the company for another position. If the employer does not allow the employee to leave her money in the plan, the employee needs to decide whether to withdraw the funds and incur the penalty or deposit the money into another type of tax-deferred plan.

Other Considerations

All employee contributions and any employer contributions in which the employee is vested belong to the employee. This means that if employees leave the company prior to retirement, they must decide what to do with the money in their account. Employers may allow these employees to leave their money in the plan and may also choose to charge a maintenance fee to the employee for the privilege to do so. The employee also has the choice of rolling the money into another qualified plan such as an IRA or a plan provided by their new employer. Lastly, the employee may choose to withdraw the monies subject to certain tax considerations as described previously.

To help ensure that companies extend their 401(k) plans to all employees, the IRS limits the maximum deferral made by "highly compensated" employees to the average deferral made by the company's non–highly compensated employees. This rule applies even if the highly compensated employees have not deferred more than the maximum limit established by the IRS. Therefore, if low-paid employees save more for retirement, then executives are allowed to save more for retirement. This provision is enforced via "nondiscrimination testing" performed at the end of each plan year. If the plan is found to be "discriminatory" based on this test, the employer will be required to withdraw and return the excess funds by April 15 of the next year.

NOTES

1. Internal Revenue Service, http://www.irs.gov.
2. Ibid.

Teresa K. Cook

GAINSHARING AND PROFIT SHARING

Gainsharing and profit sharing refer to any of a number of plans put into place to improve productivity by offering financial incentives to employees for gains in productivity or profit to the company they work for. Gainsharing and profit-sharing plans are also viewed as core pieces to the implementation of other modern management strategies, such as stakeholder strategies.[1]

While employers clearly benefit from increased profits through increased productivity, a less obvious benefit to employers comes from providing a level of flexibility in labor compensation. When external factors decrease profitability, bonuses automatically decrease. This lowers compensation costs without needing to renegotiate hourly wages or perform layoffs, which would decrease the internal talent pool of the organization.[2]

The most common of the gainsharing and profit-sharing plans are the Scanlon Plan, the Rucker Plan, and Improshare. Although these are the most widely used plans, the customization of gainsharing or profit-sharing plans occurs on a regular basis, and several consulting firms in business exist solely for the purpose of designing and implementing customized plans.

The Structures of the Major Gainsharing and Profit-sharing Plans

The Scanlon Plan focuses on improving company productivity, meaning an improvement in the ratio of inputs to outputs, by means of labor savings. This plan seeks to reduce the amount of time needed to produce an item without increasing the cost of production. A company implementing the Scanlon Plan undergoes a study of current standard work hours and costs. This study is carried out to develop a formula to measure employment costs as a proportion of total sales. A standard ratio of labor costs to sales is determined, and when employment costs fall below the standard ratio, the savings are distributed between the employees and the business.[3] The percentage shared with the employees is negotiated prior to implementation.

The Rucker Plan spreads its focus beyond issues of labor savings, but ties bonuses heavily to the value added by labor, as opposed to total sales. "Value added" is derived by taking the amount of sales and subtracting the cost of materials and supplies. The Rucker Plan ratio is calculated as a comparison of labor costs to value added. Allen Rucker believed the pay proportion of value added holds steady unless the organization suffers from mismanagement or a drastic change of policy.[4] The Rucker Plan focuses solely on providing a ratio for the business to follow, without searching for a means to foster future gains.

Improshare plans focus on reaching a higher number of units produced in fewer person-hours. Any improvements in this area result in a bonus to labor based on a pre-negotiated rate. No other areas of concern are taken into account with Improshare plans, making them the easiest of the major plans to implement.

History of Gainsharing and Profit Sharing

The history of gainsharing and profit sharing can be informally traced back to the development of human economic systems. Any time a business owner gives an employee a raise or bonus based on increased productivity, it is an example of gainsharing or profit sharing.

The first of the major gainsharing models to emerge in modern times was the Scanlon Plan. It was developed by Joe Scanlon in the late 1930s while working as a steelworkers' local labor union president at a small Ohio steel company. Scanlon believed workers could be a great source of ideas for improvements if given the incentive to do so. He had an opportunity to test this theory in 1938 when the aforementioned steel company's management notified him that production had to improve or they would have to halt operations.

Scanlon worked with executives to develop a union-management productivity plan designed to decrease the labor cost per unit of production. His first attempt was a success for the company, saving them $150,000 annually at a cost of only $8,000 for new equipment. Scanlon was quickly called on to work with other ailing companies through the steelworkers' union national headquarters. He worked with dozens of troubled companies and, by 1945, he had developed a program that consisted of discovering the normal labor cost per unit of production, then giving a large portion of savings back to workers for producing at less than the normal labor cost. Rucker Plans and Improshare were both developed later, adding their own twists to gainsharing and profit sharing, as outlined earlier.

Typical Criticisms of Gainsharing and Profit Sharing

Gainsharing and profit-sharing plans are often criticized due to their lack of individual rewards to those who stand out in their achievements. There is often too much room for some individuals to shirk their responsibilities while others go beyond expectations. This, of course, occurs in all other situations involving production of goods. Rewarding the team as a whole creates a scenario of internal peer pressure for all to carry the load equally, minimizing the inequity of work performed by individuals.

Some feel these plans are detrimentally focused on savings in labor. Many believe the focus on labor blinds management to other sources of savings,[5] potentially damaging the company's future.

Another criticism of these plans is they remove too much control from the hands of management. If gains are realized, management cannot simply decide how best to use these gains, as their use is already predetermined through the process of implementing a gainsharing or profit-sharing plan. Members of management must embrace participative management theories to be successful.

Keys to Success with Gainsharing and Profit-sharing Plans

Regardless of the format followed, all gainsharing and profit-sharing plans to date hold the same keys to success:[6]

1. The standard labor cost per unit must be measurable.
2. The ratio of sales value of production or units of production value to the cost of labor must be somewhat stable.
3. There must be a perception of fairness in regard to the distribution of the profits gained through increased productivity to the laborers who produced the increases. This usually means employees should receive the bulk of the increased profits, instead of management.

See also Employee Stock Option Plan (ESOP); Scanlon Plan

NOTES

1. Ann Svendsen, *The Stakeholder Strategy: Profiting from Collaborative Business Relationships* (San Francisco: Berret-Koehler Publishers, Inc., 1998).
2. Douglas Kruse, *Profit Sharing: Does It Make a Difference? The Productivity and Stability Effects of Employee Profit-sharing Plans* (Kalamazoo, MI: Upjohn Institute, 1993).
3. Michael Armstrong, *Reward Management* (London: Kogan Page, Limited, 2004).
4. Ibid.
5. Brian E. Graham-Moore and Timothy L. Ross, *Productivity Gainsharing* (Englewood Cliffs, NJ: Prentice-Hall, Inc., 1983).
6. Ibid.

Adam VanDreumel

GARNISHMENT

The Department of Labor Field Operations Handbook defines the term "garnishment" to mean "any legal or equitable procedure through which the earnings of any individual are required to be withheld for payment of any debt."[1]

A garnishment is both a legal and an emotional issue for HR/payroll and the organization's employee. It is legal in that HR/payroll has a legal responsibility to effectively process the employee garnishment; it is emotional because the employee may believe that his or her job is in jeopardy as a result of the garnishment.

Today, many states dictate employee garnishments for a number of issues, most commonly child support payments. This entry will describe garnishments, HR/payroll's responsibilities, the need for confidentiality, and how to help an employee get back on the right track.

HR/Payroll and the Garnishment

A garnishment is a deduction from an employee's earnings to repay a debt that is court ordered. Because it is a court-ordered legal action, strict rules govern its completion dictated by the state that is issuing the action. Knowing the specifics of a garnishment based on the jurisdiction is important for HR/payroll.

Title III of the Consumer Credit Protection Act (CCPA) limits the amount of an employee's earnings that may be garnished. It also protects an employee from being fired if pay is garnished for only one debt. The amount of withholding subject to garnishment is based on an employee's "disposable earnings," the amount left after legally required deductions are made. There are a number of legally required deductions such as federal, state, and local taxes, the employee's share of state unemployment insurance, and Social

Security. Withholdings for employee retirement systems required by law would also be included in this designation. Deductions not required by law—such as voluntary wage assignments, union dues, health and life insurance, contributions to charitable causes, purchases of savings bonds, retirement plan contributions (some of these can be required by law as stated above), and payments to employers for payroll advances or purchases of merchandise—cannot be subtracted from gross earnings when calculating disposable earnings under the CCPA.

There are legal maximum limits that can be garnished from an employee's pay. For ordinary garnishments (e.g., those not for support, bankruptcy, or any state or federal tax), the weekly amount may not exceed the lesser of two figures:

- 25 percent of the employee's disposable earnings, or
- the amount by which an employee's disposable earnings are greater than 30 times the federal minimum wage.

In cases in which an employee has a garnishment for child support and alimony, the rules are more stringent, with a maximum of 50 percent of a person's disposable earnings if the employee has a spouse to support or 60 percent if the employee does not.

Importance of Confidentiality

Confidentiality is critical for HR/payroll in general; however, in the case of a garnishment, it is paramount. An employee who has a garnishment judgment against him may believe that his job is in jeopardy. Certainly, there are cases in which a garnishment in a certain area raises questions about an employee's ability to perform his job functions; however, many will be purely a function of deducting the garnishment and getting the employee focused on business.

Applying the Rules

Managing garnishments within an organization is important because there are substantial liabilities for employers who do not administer garnishments correctly. Organizations must understand "the importance of having well-trained employee specialists and procedures in place that include every person that may touch the garnishment."[2] This is particularly important under the provisions of Sarbanes-Oxley at publicly held companies. The Office of Child Support Enforcement (OCSE) has established a portal with state-specific links to information that employers can access to determine requirements for their state.[3]

Getting Back on Track

For an employee, a garnishment may represent a very difficult point in life. Some may even consider resigning from the company before having a garnishment exercised. For HR/payroll professionals, handling the garnishment process in a professional, direct manner without making judgments helps the employee traverse this troubled time and get back to the business at hand. Most employees are able to fulfill the garnishment order and continue to be effective workers.

Resources:
Department of Labor, Office of Child Support Enforcement, http://www.acf.hhs.gov/programs/cse/index.html.

NOTES

1. U.S. Department of Labor. Rev. 644 *Field Operations Handbook,* Rev. 644 (February 9, 2001), http://www.dol.gov/esa/whd/FOH/FOH_Ch16.pdf (accessed November 27, 2007).

2. Elaine Stattler, "Tips for Managing Garnishments," *Payroll Manager's Letter* 22, no. 21 (November 7, 2006): 7.

3. Office of Child Support Enforcement (OCSE), http://www.acf.hhs.gov/programs/cse/index.html (accessed February 27, 2008).

Lisa Scott Brinkman

HEALTH CARE PLANS

The 60-plus-years link between employment and health benefits is being examined with increasing skepticism by industry observers, critics, and employers alike, as the demand for and cost of care continues to inhibit profitability in a highly competitive global economy. Some assessments are blunt, such as "The linkage of employment and health-care benefits is a product of another age, when American business was dominant, when it didn't have to worry about global competition, and when unions made up a much larger portion of the work force."[1]

The vicissitudes of global competition are not a new phenomenon: national and multinational employers have long sought incremental advantages on the cost and revenue side of their businesses. This entry examines why employment-based health insurance (EBHI) persists as a major component of U.S. employers' benefit packages and simultaneously looms larger as a disadvantage in companies' ability to compete effectively.

History

EBHI is one of the most enduring and coveted features of the American workplace. Its origins lie in a 1942 War Labor Board decision that encouraged employers to expand fringe benefits to attract and retain scarce workers. EBHI flourished when employers' health insurance benefits and employee contributions to health insurance were excluded from taxable income, as an offset to continuing post–World War II wage and price freezes.[2] In the evolution of the U.S. health care system, EBHI quickly moved from a novel incentive to an entitlement, firmly embedded by life-saving, life-extending medical technology, provider autonomy, and a willing federal and commercial reimbursement system.[3] "For decades, Americans have treated health care as if it exists in a separate economic and political world: when people need care, they should get it; costs should remain out of sight."[4] For these reasons and others, any discussion about altering this link between employment and health benefits quickly has met with resistance.

Demand and cost of care accelerated in the last two decades of the twentieth century. To avoid acrimony as well as strategic inertia, insurers and employers turned to a succession of plan forms, including variations on indemnity plans, and an alphabet soup of managed care (HMOs, PPOs, POSs, etc.). These plan forms are all attempts to manage demand for care.

Health Care Plans

Indemnity Plans: Reimburse an enrollee for all medical expenses, irrespective who the provider is (physician, hospital, etc). Most have caps on the total amount that can be reimbursed within a set time period.

Managed Care Plans: Include HMOs, PPOs, EPOs, and POS. All forms of this coverage include restrictions on providers available to enrollees and some degree of utilization management.

HMO: A health maintenance organization provides a wide range of comprehensive health care services to members who prepay a fixed periodic fee for the service. The choice of physician and hospital (providers) can be made from an "open panel" or group model, which includes providers who are contracted with the HMO, or from a "closed panel" or staff model, with tight limits of choice.

PPO: A preferred provider organization is essentially a more tightly managed version of HMOs, with fewer provider choices for enrollees and tighter utilization management. Enrollees pay a larger share of charges if they receive care from a provider that is not contracted with the PPO provider network.

EPO: An exclusive provider organization is similar to a PPO, although an enrollee's charges for care from an out-of-network provider are not covered by the EPO.

POS: A point of service plan combines characteristics of both the HMO and the PPO. Enrollees choose a primary physician (similar to group model HMOs and PPOs), but also may choose from a larger number of providers. Out-of-network charges are handled similar to PPOs. Members of a POS plan do not make a choice about which system to use until the point at which the service is being used, an arrangement that favors enrollees who travel frequently and need regular access to care.[5]

Organizational Challenges

These multiple plan forms have done little to change the general public's expectations for access to care. The problem for organizations deciding how to provide health insurance for current (and retired) employees is made more difficult by these fragmented delivery and payment mechanisms, even as it also has become a threat to organizations' ability to remain competitive in global markets.

The competitive disadvantage is rooted in a profound economic and social difference between this country and its international business competitors. "U.S. companies now compete in the world market with companies from other industrialized nations that have national health systems. Those countries treat health care as a "societal cost" borne across the economic spectrum, not imposed primarily on employers as an additional cost of their products and services."[6]

Recent declines in the rate of premium increases are good news, but they are modest and unevenly distributed; employers still struggle with the declining affordability of health insurance.[7] Employers of low- and middle-income workers face the most trying circumstances: "premium increases, high administrative costs, the likelihood of increased regulation, and as well as the pressures of increased global competition."[8] These problems loom as serious confounders for those employers who might be open to initiatives to address health care issues.

Current Conditions

Although the rate of health insurance premiums has slowed, premium prices are nevertheless continuing to rise. The share of the premium that is passed on to employees is also increasing, and studies show fewer firms offer coverage to their workers.[9] Other studies suggest the amount of coverage offered is less of a factor than a decline in "*take-up*,"[10] or enrollment, by eligible employees. One consequence of this trend is increasing numbers of under- and uninsured people, and further strains faltering public (government) systems.

"Employers [still] tend to view health benefits as a human resources tool and part of a complex compensation package, rather than as an instrument of health policy. Consequently, they do not have a broad strategy to deal with the explosion of healthcare expenditures."[11] The earliest recognition of accelerating EBHI costs generated several initiatives designed to influence healthier behaviors and informed choice-making among health plan participants, including types of plan options offered, employer-subsidized wellness programs and centers, disease management, and financial rewards for healthy choices. The impact of these initiatives has generally leveled out; they have done little to change demand for care.

Large employers have also self-insured and tried to closely manage utilization; medium and small employers have formed coalitions to "collectively purchase health care, proactively challenge high costs and the inefficient delivery of health care, and share information on quality."[12] Union contracts are being renegotiated, insurance premiums are being linked to salary level to increase worker contributions, and the number of part-time uncovered workers is growing.[13]

The latest responses to this issue are predicated on leveraging consumer education and market forces to rein in demand and cost. They include HDHPs, HSAs, DCHPs, and CDHPs.

HDHP: High Deductible Health Plans are a health insurance plan with lower premiums and higher deductibles than a traditional health plan. They are sometimes referred to as catastrophic health insurance plans.
HSA or HRA: Health Savings Accounts or Health Reimbursement Arrangements are IRS-sanctioned plans that allow an employer, as agreed to in the plan document, allow employees to save pre-tax dollars for later reimbursement for medical expenses paid from their account through their employers. HRAs reimburse only those items (copays, coinsurance, deductibles and services) agreed to by the employer which are not covered by the company's selected standard insurance plan (any health insurance plan, not only high-deductible plans).
DCHP: A Defined Contribution Health Plan allows the employee to choose his own health plan using funds the employer has already allocated for the employee.
CDHP: Consumer-Directed Health Plans are a more precise version of HSAs that give consumers more responsibility for managing their health care spending.[14]

These options have enjoyed mixed success despite considerable attention and publicity, including the IRS's blessing, and the enthusiastic endorsement from the President at the time these options were rolled out. Critics cite several flaws, such as high deductibles, persistently high out-of-pocket costs, and a lack of accessible, transparent information to support consumer choices of quality, cost-effective care options. An October 2006 RAND Corporation study notes that CDHPs can reduce health care use and lower costs, but expresses doubt whether the plans could accomplish this without deterring consumers from seeking needed care.[15]

High-deductible plans may further segment consumer access according to their income, education, and sophistication, and thus marginalize low-deductible plans. A 2004 Commonwealth Fund study notes that, "Employer-based health insurance coverage has been held up as the one place in which risk pools tended to be unified, with costs spread among employees (albeit paid directly in large part by employers). CDHPs have the unappealing potential to unravel this important risk-spreading role, segmenting to the advantage of healthy workers and to the disadvantage of less healthy, lower incomes workers."[16]

Conclusion

Employers have two equally uncertain choices to address health care issues: pursue conventional health insurance plan options, hoping that some other factors will stem the trend of higher premium prices and limited options; or opt for the initiatives that leverage consumerism and market forces. The latter options, however, have not been nearly as predictable factors in the health care arena as they have for employers' products and services.

The least likely option is for employers to completely sever the tie between employment and health insurance, at least for the foreseeable future. The message may be "know your employees" and decide to be part of wider solutions. Perhaps, says a Hewitt Associates report, "If we have any hope of ever truly improving costs and outcomes, we must focus on effectively influencing the interactions between patients and providers. That is where health care happens. We need to move beyond cost sharing, consumerism, and passive health risk management and focus on supporting the necessary behavior changes as people move from being consumers to becoming patients."[17]

The best and most challenging news for employers is the availability of numerous sources of information upon which to base decisions. This may awaken a new force for change, but, as with the case of any activity with which little or no immediate revenue is associated, the efforts to make informed decisions are another cost, at a time when margins for many American companies are tightened by competition and regulation.

NOTES

1. Jeanne Schulte Scott, "Big Business, Where Are You?" Health Care Is Again on the Table in Washington. And the U.S. Business Community Should Be Invited to Dinner," electronic version, *Healthcare Financial Management* 61, no. 1,(January 2007): 36(2).

2. Harry A. Sultz and Kristina M. Young, *Health Care USA* (Gaithersburg, MD: Aspen Publishers, Inc, 1999).

3. Paul Starr, *The Social Transformation of American Medicine* (New York: Basic Books, 1982).

4. Robert J. Samuelson, "Let's Not Hide Health Care Costs," *Newsweek,* February 5, 2007.

5. "Health Insurance: Indemnity vs. Managed Care," http://www.agencyinfo.net/iv/medical/types/indemnity-managed.htm (accessed May 20, 2008).

6. Scott, "Big Business, Where Are You?"

7. Rose M. Rubin, "Declining Employer Sponsored Health Insurance: Tennessee and the U.S.," electronic version, *Business Perspectives* 18, no. 1 (Fall 2006): 26(6).

8. Ibid.

9. Yu-Chu Shen and Sharon K. Long, "What's Driving the Downward Trend in Employer-sponsored Health Insurance?" electronic version, *Health Services Research* 41, no. 6 (December 2006): 2074(23).

10. Ibid.

11. Rubin, "Declining Employer Sponsored Health Insurance."

12. Knowledge Source, "Business Coalitions Market Overview—2006" (October 28, 2006), http://knowsource.ecnext.com/coms2/summary_0233-901_ITM (accessed February 10, 2007).

13. Rubin, "Declining Employer Sponsored Health Insurance."

14. U.S. Office of Personnel Management, "High Deductible Health Plans (HDHP) with Health Savings Accounts (HSA)," http://www.opm.gov/hsa/ (accessed February 2007).

15. "Study Shows Americans Still Not Enthusiastic about CDHPs," electronic version, *Healthcare Financial Management,* 61, no. 1 (January 2007): 14(2).

16. The Commonwealth Fund, "Will Consumer-Directed Health Care Improve System Performance?" (August 2004), http://www.cmwf.org/topics/topics_show.htm?doc_id=235966 (accessed February 10, 2007).

17. Hewitt and Associates, "Hewitt Associates Data Reveals Lowest U.S. Health Care Cost Increases in Eight Years," October 9, 2006, http://www.hewittassociates.com/Intl/NA/en-US/AboutHewitt/Newsroom/PressReleaseDetail.aspx?cid=3113 (accessed February 10, 2007).

Paul M. Rosser

HIPAA

On August 21, 1996, Congress enacted the Health Insurance Portability and Accountability Act of 1996, also known as HIPAA. Contained in this law, the Department of Health and Human Services issued the regulation Standards for Privacy of Individual Identifiable Health Information, which protects patients' privacy rights and governs privileged health information. The Office for Civil Rights is also involved in this law, taking on the role of enforcing this regulation.[1]

What Information Is Protected?

Each time an individual visits a hospital, physician, or health care provider, documentation of that visit is made. This record consists of that person's symptoms, physical examination and any test results, a diagnosis, and treatment plan. This data can be shared among health care providers who play a role in that person's specific treatment. The HIPAA Privacy Rule guards these medical records and health information and creates a national standard of protection. In fact, this law empowers individuals to manage how their records are used and disclosed.[2]

Who Must Observe the HIPAA Privacy Rule?

The Privacy Rule pertains to insurance health plans, health care clearinghouses (e.g., billing service companies) and health care providers.[3] These *covered entities* allow them to contract with their *business associates* to perform some of their essential functions.[4] Health care providers generally use a patient's health information for treatment, payment, and general health care operations (e.g., confirming an appointment). A description of privacy practices should be available from the health care provider.

What Is HR's Role in Enforcing HIPAA?

A *business associate,* as defined by the HIPAA Privacy Rule, includes a third party, such as a benefits administrator,[5] which falls under the HR umbrella. In fact, HR can play a significant role in security compliance. Below are some of the ways in which HR can participate in ensuring HIPAA security compliance:
- *Implementing policies:* It is important for HR to negotiate with their health plans at contract time to ensure that personal health information includes verbiage safeguarding against unauthorized use. Within the organization, it is important for HR to also make sure their own internal policies adhere to the HIPAA Security Rule (e.g., proper handling of terminated employees, identifying security incidents, etc.)

- *Awareness training:* Other actions HR might take are to conduct security awareness training throughout the department to ensure that there is no unauthorized access to personal health information. This can also include limiting access to any electronic records and by choosing a representative in the department as a security agent.
- *Legal help:* It is also important for HR to realize the impact that a security breach might have if personal health information was made public. This would result in costly legal fees and tarnished reputations. Communicating with the organization's legal department when policy making occurs would help guarantee the effectiveness of the internal compliance plan to avoid any security risks.[6]

Conclusion

The HR department plays a significant role in the HIPAA Privacy Rule process for an organization. In understanding not only the law itself, but also the responsibility and function of the role, HR can enhance personal health information security for their employees and protect the organization in the process.

See also Privacy Act; Privacy Rights

NOTES

1. U.S. Department of Health and Human Services, "Medical Privacy—National Standards to Protect the Privacy of Personal Health Information," U.S. Government, http://www.hhs.gov/ocr/hipaa/bkgrnd.html (accessed July 3, 2007).

2. Ibid.

3. Ibid.

4. 45 C.F.R. § 160.103 (2006).

5. U.S. Department of Health and Human Services, "Medical Privacy—National Standards to Protect the Privacy of Personal Health Information."

6. Philip L. Gordon, "HR's Role in 'HIPAA Security Compliance,'" FindLaw, http://library.findlaw.com/2005/May/19/174544.html (accessed July 3, 2007).

Nicole Brown

INSURANCE

Insurance plays a broad role in our economy. It helps to assure that both economic and noneconomic activities can proceed with peace of mind. The concept of insurance is simple. In exchange for the insured's payment of the premium, a relatively small sum of money, the insurer (insurance company) assumes the risk of financial consequences for any loss. The insurer is actually an organization that administers the "sharing" of losses among its members (the insureds), providing financial security for all participants.

Often, as much as 80 percent of a company's total insurance premiums are spent on employee life and health coverage, while a mere 15 to 20 percent is spent on all of the property and liability coverage a company needs.

Life Insurance

There are numerous forms of life insurance coverages available for specialized needs, and numerous insurers are willing to tailor a policy to meet those specific needs. Employee life insurance and accidental death insurance coverages are commonly marketed and sold on a group basis via a master policy to a company or employer.

Insurable Interest

An insured has an insurable interest in his or her own life when the goal is to provide a source of funds and/or continuing income stream for his or her beneficiaries. Therefore, an insured may take out a life insurance policy on his or her own life for the benefit of named beneficiaries (persons or entities).

Disability Income Insurance

Disability income insurance is a type of health insurance that provides coverage to replace a percentage of the insured's income if he or she becomes temporarily or permanently disabled as a result of "nonoccupational" (nonwork-related) illness, accident, or injury. Disability coverages have many variable features:

- Waiting period—the time between the effective date of the disability and the date the insured can start to collect benefits. Common waiting periods are one week, or one, two, three, or six months. The longer the waiting periods, the lower the premiums. Employees usually use vacation time and/or sick leave to maintain a full salary during the waiting period.
- Disability policies vary in the length of time of payment according to the type of disability (e.g., illness or accident).
- Disability policies also vary in the amount payable, which is usually expressed as a percentage of the insured's income in the range of 50 to 60 percent. The intent is to replace the insured's net income loss, not gross. Disability income payments are usually not taxable; therefore, someone not receiving wages is no longer paying Social Security and Medicare taxes.
- Disability policies also vary in their definition of the employee's disability and its impact on the employee's ability to perform the duties of his or her usual occupation or another more restrictive occupation.
- Disability is defined as benefits paid based on partial or total disability.

Health Insurance Policies and Managed Care Plans

Health care coverages, in their present state, are really no longer considered insurance in the traditional sense described earlier. They were formally called hospital room and board, hospital supplies and equipment usages, surgical, physicians' coverages, drugs, and tests.

Most people are members of or subscribe to a service plan under which they receive health care services from a health maintenance organization (HMO) or some other managed care plan. Blue Cross (an association of hospitals) and Blue Shield (an association of doctors) are the backers if not the creators of managed care plans.

Managed care plans include HMOs, preferred provider organizations made up of hospital and doctor members (PPO) and point-of-service plans (POS). The purpose of managed care organizations, according to their enabling statutes, is to transfer the financial risks of health care from the patients to the managed care organizations.

The principal characteristic of managed care organizations is that the organization receives a fixed fee from each person or unit enrolled and provides specified health care if needed (e.g., medical, dental, vision, etc.).

COBRA Rights

The Consolidated Omnibus Budget Reconciliation Act of 1985 (COBRA) established certain duties on the part of employers with respect to continuation of health care coverages under employment-sponsored plans when certain defined triggering or qualifying events occur, including.

o Termination of employment
o Reduction of employee's hours below that eligible for health plans
o Divorce resulting in the ineligibility of a previously covered spouse
o Employee eligibility for Medicare benefits
o Ineligibility of a dependent child because of age or marriage

The previously insured person may remain covered for a maximum of 36 months for all benefits, whether medical, dental, or vision, provided he or she pays the full single-person premiums.

See also Benefits; COBRA; Disability Insurance; Health Care Plans

Resources:

Zevnik, Richard W. *The Complete Book of Insurance.* Naperville, IL: Sphinx Publishing, 2004.

Title 42, *U.S. Code,* Selection 300e (42USC-Sec.300e).

Healthinsuranceinfo.net, Georgetown University Health Policy Institute, http://www.health insuranceinfo.net. Persons wishing to obtain a state-specific summary of their own state laws regulating health care policies and plans, which also includes discussions of applicable federal statutes and regulations, should visit this site.

Douglas G. Heeter

MERIT PAY

Merit pay is the process in which permanent increases in employee compensation are implemented based on the evaluation of an employee's performance. An employee's evaluation is typically conducted using criteria determined by an employer. These evaluations are usually conducted on periodically determined time intervals (e.g., quarterly, biannually, or annually) and involve a review discussion between the supervisor and employee concerning that employee's work performance over a particular period of time.[1]

A salary adjustment under merit pay is measured as a percentage increase to the current base salary, resulting in the adjusted higher salary. Ideally, the increased rate of salary should correspond proportionally with how well an employee performs on the job.[2] Merit pay systems may also have a variable salary rate change structure that rewards excellent individual performance differently, based on salary distribution. For instance, employees in a low pay range who receive an excellent performance rating would receive a higher-percentage salary increase than those employees in a higher pay range who also receive the same excellent rating.[3] In general, annual pay increases of 3 to 4 percent are considered low, while pay increases between 10 and 20 percent are viewed as high.

Merit Pay Structures

Merit pay structures deal with decisions on how to allocate an organization's compensation distribution based on performance, rather than dealing with other factors such as the relative value of a particular position within an organization.[4] Merit pay structures operate under a merit budget, determined by the amount of overall salary spending allocated for distribution among all employees in a department or organization.[5] A credible merit pay structure assesses and measures performance, while appropriately rewarding differences in performance between individuals within a department and/or organization.

Performance Appraisal Management

Performance appraisal systems are used to determine merit pay decisions as well as to clarify job expectations for employees and establish employee objectives that correspond with overall organizational objectives and needs. Appraisals are also utilized to determine promotional, transfer, and termination decisions, while helping to identify organizational training needs.[6] There are a variety of appraisal systems, each of which evaluate a set of parameters that reflect an employee's overall job performance.

In general, appraisal systems measure how well an employee performs at meeting assigned responsibilities and objectives, as well as their quality of work, teamwork, leadership, communication skills, dependability, etc.[7] Appraisal ratings structures vary but typically use a point-scale rating system to measure whether an employee's overall work and/or components of their work are exceptional, above average, average, below average, or poor.

See also Compensation, Gainsharing and Profit Sharing

NOTES

1. U.S. Department of Labor, "Wages: Merit Pay," http://www.dol.gov/dol/topic/wages/meritpay.htm (accessed December 5, 2007).

2. Lance A. Berger and Dorothy R. Berger, ed. *The Compensation Handbook: A State-of-the-Art Guide to Compensation Strategy and Design,* 4th ed. (New York: McGraw-Hill, 1999), 510.

3. Ibid.

4. Robert L. Heneman and Jon M. Werner, *Merit Pay—Linking Pay to Performance in a Changing World,* 2nd ed. (Charlotte, NC: Information Age Publishing, 2005), 6.

5. Berger and Berger, *The Compensation Handbook,* 522.

6. Ibid., 513.

7. Ibid., 514.

Matt Neibauer

PAY FOR PERFORMANCE

Pay for performance is a generic term that encompasses any number of methods of compensation that link some or all of an employee's pay to some measure of individual or group performance. Most of these programs shift labor costs from fixed to variable, providing an automatic control on labor costs during economic downturns, and are at the heart of the trend in compensation today toward less stable and less secure compensation packages.[1]

Programs can either be "success-sharing" or "risk-sharing." Success-sharing is a generic term for programs that permit employees to share in the success of the organization based on some measure of performance (e.g., profits, reduced costs) without penalty when performance is poor. With risk-sharing programs, employees also share in the financial risk, such that in times of poor financial performance, employees' compensation is reduced. In return for sharing the risk, employees generally receive a greater reward when there is good performance than under success-sharing programs.

Pay-for-performance plans help to motivate employees by linking the financial rewards an employee receives to organizationally desired behaviors/outcomes (e.g., production quantity, sales volume, reduced costs, higher profits). Performance targets used in these plans should be tied to the organization's strategic objectives and fit well with the HR strategy and objectives. For example, individual incentives would be inappropriate if the objective is for employees to function as a team. For these programs to be accepted and considered fair by employees, there must be a reliable way to measure performance, the goals must be attainable, the environment must be relatively stable, and the performance must be under the employee's control.

Individual Plans

Individual pay for performance plans reward employees based on their individual performance. Experts agree that individual plans have greater potential for, and better track records in, delivering increased productivity.[2] They may, however, result in competitive behavior among employees and a decrease in cooperation and teamwork.

Piece Rate

An objective method of compensating employees based on production quantity is piece rate. It may represent all of an employee's earnings or be an additional payment over and above a base wage. The most basic plan is referred to as "straight piecework," where the payment per piece is fixed regardless of quantity produced. Other plans vary the payment per piece relative to a standard rate of production. Care must be taken to ensure that the program does not create unintended consequences. For example, a piece rate plan that has no quality requirements may result in the production of a large number of substandard products.

Commission

Used for compensation of salespeople, commission is similar in concept to piece rate, although the employee's compensation is based on a percentage of sales dollar volume. The commission rate may or may not be in addition to base pay and may vary based on product or product line. Typically there is no base pay when the sales involve high priced products such as real estate, capital equipment, vehicles, insurance, or financial services. In retail sales, the commission is often in addition to a relatively small base pay. An employer may also pay a higher commission rate for high margin or new products to encourage salespeople to focus on the sales of those products. Where there are not defined sales territories (e.g., retail), it may encourage competitive behavior between coworkers that may be detrimental to the organization.

Merit Pay

Merit pay is an increase in base pay granted to an employee based on some typically subjective measure of performance, usually identified in an annual performance appraisal (see also the entry on Merit Pay).

Lump-sum Bonus

A lump-sum bonus is a onetime payment to an employee based on his or her performance. Employers are increasingly using this as a substitute for merit pay. Since it is not added into base pay, it essentially freezes employees' pay, thus controlling labor costs. It can also help diminish a sense of entitlement among employees. Lump-sum bonuses are sometimes negotiated in union contracts as a substitute for across-the-board raises that add to base pay.

Individual Spot Awards

A spot award is an add-on bonus awarded to an employee based on exceptional performance, often on a special project or in an unusually difficult situation. Programs vary from organization to organization and tend to be more formal in larger organizations and less formal in smaller organizations. In general, management is alerted to an employee's performance and makes a special onetime payment to reward the employee.

Group Plans

Group pay for performance plans link a portion of employees' compensation to some measure of group performance. They are effective in encouraging cooperation and teamwork but do not hold individuals directly accountable for their performance. Plans that have a time line of one year or less are considered short-term plans, while those over one year (e.g., ESOPs, stock options, BBOPs) are classified as long-term incentives (LTIs).

Team Incentive Plans

Team members receive periodic payments based on the team's performance against predetermined production standards.

Profit Sharing

A portion of an organization's profits over a predetermined minimum level are shared with employees. Payment may be in cash or company stock. Theoretically, it motivates employees to work hard to help the company be more profitable; realistically, most employees do not feel that their individual efforts have a significant impact on the financial success of the organization.

Gainsharing

Payments to employees based on group performance relative to some cost index (labor, scrap/rework) represent gainsharing. Employees essentially share in a portion of the financial returns for gains in productivity. These programs are typically better at motivating employees than profit sharing because employees see a closer connection between their efforts and rewards.

Balanced Scorecard

A balanced scorecard provides bonus payments to employees based on progress toward strategic objectives. A variety of weighted measures in the areas of financial results, process improvements, customer service, and innovation are used to measure performance.

Employee Stock Ownership Plans

Employees receive stock in the company as a portion of their compensation and/or are allowed to purchase shares of company stock without paying a commission to a broker, often through a payroll deduction plan. As with profit sharing, ESOPs are designed to motivate employees to ensure the company is successful. In actuality, the link between an individual employee's performance and the price of the stock is virtually nonexistent.

Stock Option Plans

While there are a number of variations, most stock option plans offer executives the option of purchasing stock for a specified period of time at a predetermined price. Stock options often represent the largest component of executive pay, giving them a substantial financial incentive to make decisions that increase the market price of the stock (e.g., employee layoffs).

Broad-based Option Plans (BBOPs)

A relatively new trend in compensation, stock grants are extended to employees at all levels. Stock grants may be an equal percentage of each employee's earnings, linked to the individual employee's performance, or based on pay-grade level.

See also Bonuses; Compensation; Gainsharing and Profit Sharing; HR Strategy; Merit Pay; Motivation

NOTES

1. George T. Milkovich and Jerry M. Newman, *Compensation,* 9th ed. (New York: McGraw-Hill Irwin, 2008), 269.
2. Ibid., 299.

Beverly J. DeMarr

PAYROLL

A number of things are required in running payroll. These include calculating wages, deducting taxes, printing and distributing checks, and signing checks. Payroll also includes setting up direct deposits, preparing pretax deductions such as health care and 401(k) plans, and distributing W-2s in January. Finally, payroll includes communicating change in the payroll system to employees and complying with all local, state, and federal laws and procedures.

In many organizations, payroll has long been considered a less significant HR practice. However, if mistakes are made in payroll, it becomes an executive- or board-level issue and can have serious fiduciary consequences. Therefore, using payroll as a strategic initiative is becoming more and more imperative. More specifically, payroll can be used as a source of information for decision making that can help executives and managers in human resource planning and to assess the morale of employees so as to determine their levels of motivation and commitment to the firm.

When payroll is used as a strategic tool, it can help by:

- *Driving strategic decision making*—this enables HR professionals and managers to constantly look for efficiencies within the payroll function and analyze alternative strategies such as outsourcing. Activities may include regularly analyzing the in-house vs. outsourcing equation; regularly auditing cost structures; and providing incentives to payroll employees to increase efficiencies in the organization.
- *Striving for operational efficiency*—this applies both to the essential transactional work for which payroll is directly responsible as well as related activities such as time data collection.

Activities include streamlining business processes and developing techniques to improve the quality of data coming into the payroll.

- *Becoming an information provider*—this might take the form of trend analysis, in which HR professionals and managers examine overtime by comparing department to department, for example, or how much is being spent in one department compared to previous years.[1]

Payroll Management

Payroll management generally includes activities in two major areas: (1) payroll accounting, and (2) payroll administration. Payroll accounting consists of calculating the earnings of employees and the related withholding for taxes and other deductions, recording the results of payroll activities, and preparing required tax returns.[2] Payroll accounting also involves reporting the results of payroll activities to the local, state, and federal tax agencies. Payroll administration includes the managerial aspects of maintaining a payroll, which are distinct from the accounting aspects of payroll. Payroll administration includes managing employee personnel and payroll information and compliance with federal, state, and local employment laws.[3]

Outsourcing the Payroll Function

Managing the payroll function is complicated, time-consuming, and costly. For these reasons, many organizations have elected to outsource the function to specialized payroll companies. However, there are several factors to consider when deciding whether to outsource the payroll function. The following questions should help in making this decision:

1. Are wages consistent in that the organization has the same number of employees at the same wage level for a while, with no plans for change? If so, then the payroll function should be fairly automated and a good candidate for outsourcing.
2. Does the organization employ mostly full-time hourly workers rather than a mix of part-time and freelance employees? The latter would make outsourcing very complicated and susceptible to errors and mistakes.
3. Is turnover a serious problem in that the firm expects a lot of turnover? Such a condition is very time-consuming and costly, and outsourcing may be a less expensive alternative.
4. Does the organization pay local, state, and federal taxes quarterly or annually? Outsourcing may be more cost-sensitive, and the service firm may have individuals more qualified to address tax issues.[4]

There are several considerations when selecting an outsourcing organization (service firm).[5] First, select a firm that has experience with similarly sized businesses. Second, determine if the service firm has clients in the same industry and is familiar with the local tax laws that apply accordingly. Third, determine if payroll management is the service firm's primary area of business, or a secondary one. Fourth, ascertain whether the service firm is bonded and insured. Fifth, explore what other services the firm can provide. Sixth, avoid early low-fee offers, which will help avoid additional fees or aggressive sales upgrades. Seventh, examine the service firm's infrastructure to determine whether the firm has adequate human resources to properly manage the payroll function. Eighth, inquire as to possible penalties for late entries, oversights, or fees associated with writing a check as opposed to having the payroll firm make direct deposit. These will help in the selection of an acceptable outsourcing firm.

Salary Grade and Market Range Assignment

Many organizations use salary grade and market range assignment to determine salary levels for exempt employees. The process begins when the payroll administrator assigns each exempt employee a payroll title (job code) in predetermined salary grades (for example, 5–10) to a "market range" within a salary grade. The market ranges are developed from the data gathered in the most recent salary survey provided by survey research firms, adjusted for market trends. A market range normally has a narrower span than the salary grade to which it is assigned. Most payroll systems display the market range minimum and maximum for exempt employees' job codes.[6] Further, the market range midpoint is the pay rate that is halfway between the market range minimum and the market range maximum, which is an established average rate of pay for similar jobs in the regional market.[7] Accordingly, the market range minimum and maximum represent a designated percentage below and above the market range midpoint. The amount of this percentage varies depending on the salary survey results for the targeted market position for a specific job family.[8]

See also Compensation

NOTES

1. Keith Rodgers, "Strategic Payroll" (June 2007), Webster Buchanan Research, http://www.websterb .com/articles.php?ID=ae698fc3637c366b (accessed August 18, 2008).

2. "Payroll 101 Overview," http://payroll.intuit.com/payroll_resources/payroll_101/index.jsp (accessed August 18, 2008).

3. Ibid.

4. Daniel Richards, "Payroll Management—Minding Your Employees' Money," About.com, Entrepreneurs, http://entrepreneurs.about.com/od/beyondstartup/a/payrollmgmt.htm (accessed August 18, 2008).

5. Ibid.

6. "Professional Staff Compensation: Overview," University of Washington, http://www.washington .edu/admin/hr/ocpsp/prostaff/index.html (accessed August 18, 2008).

7. Ibid.

8. Ibid.

Paul Shelton and Jerry W. Gilley

PENSION BENEFIT GUARANTY CORPORATION

The Pension Benefit Guaranty Corporation, or PBGC, is a U.S. government–chartered corporation that was created by the Employee Retirement Income Security Act of 1974 (ERISA) to encourage the appropriate maintenance and continuation of private sector–defined benefit pension plans, to provide timely and uninterrupted payment of pension benefits, and to keep pension insurance premiums at the lowest levels possible.[1] The enactment of ERISA by the U.S. Congress was primarily to protect participants in and beneficiaries of private sector–defined benefit pension plans and to ensure that such plans are adequately funded. The PBGC oversees only defined benefit pension plans (sometimes referred to as "traditional" pensions); it has no authority to either insure or regulate defined contribution plans (sometimes referred to as "contemporary" or "401(k)" plans).

Pension Insurance Programs

The PBGC provides a minimum level of benefits to participants in a qualified defined benefit pension plan in the event the plan is unable to pay benefits. U.S. law does not require employers to provide their employees with such pensions, but if they choose to do so, ERISA requires insurance to be purchased from the PBGC and also establishes funding standards to maintain good standing. Two pension insurance programs are overseen by the PBGC, which are single employer and multiemployer.

Single Employer

The single-employer plan, which is more common, requires a particular employer to pay annual premiums, based upon the number of plan participants, to the PBGC in accordance with federal law. Additionally, for single-employer plans with more than 100 participants, if the funding ratio (value of assets divided by current liabilities) falls below 90 percent, sponsors are required to make additional payments, or deficit contribution reductions, to remove "underfunded" status and to return to an adequate funding level.

Multiemployer

The multiemployer plan, which is less common, allows several employers who are involved in a similar line of business to collectively bargain with a union to provide pension benefits for employees. Multiemployer plans are commonly used in the construction and transportation industries, where employees frequently move from company to company. As such, multiemployer plans are often portable, allowing employees to gain pension credit from work with several different companies, a practice much less common with single-employer plans.[2]

Governance

The PBGC is headed by a director, who reports to a three-member board of directors, consisting of the secretaries of labor, commerce, and treasury. The secretary of labor currently serves as chairperson. The PBGC is further aided by a seven-member Advisory Committee, appointed by the president of the United States, to represent the interests of labor, business, and the general public. ERISA outlines certain responsibilities for the PBGC's Advisory Committee, including investment of assets, trusteeship of terminated plans, and matters as determined by the PBGC.[3]

Operations

The PBGC receives no funds from federal tax revenue, and ERISA explicitly states that obligations are not backed by the full faith and credit of the U.S. government. Operations are currently financed by flat-rate insurance premiums, adjusted each year for inflation, based on changes in the national average wage index,[4] and are paid only by sponsors of defined-benefit plans. Additionally, investment income, assets from distress or involuntarily terminated pensions the PBGC insured, and recoveries from companies formerly responsible for the plans, account for the remainder of revenues.[5] Single-employer plans considered underfunded must also pay a variable-rate premium, which is determined by the degree to which a plan's vested liabilities exceed its assets on a net-present-value (NPV) basis. Additionally, the PBGC has the authority to invest the assets it oversees however it believes appropriate, as long as it acts in the best interests of beneficiaries.

Termination of a Pension Plan

Terminations of single-employer pension plans are categorized as standard, distress, or involuntary. Additional information regarding terminations may be found under Title IV of ERISA.

Standard Termination

Standard, or voluntary termination, is allowed as long as an employer provides 60 days' notice to participants and ensures that the plan has sufficient assets to cover all future liabilities or benefits, and that the termination does not violate any collective bargaining agreements currently in force. The PBGC is not responsible for assuming liabilities under a standard termination, as plan sponsors are required to purchase group annuity contracts for participants, or to provide lump-sum payments for all accrued benefits.

Distress Termination

A distress termination typically occurs when a company has petitioned bankruptcy court for purposes of either liquidation or reorganization. The PBGC may determine that the continuation of the plan will place an unreasonable financial burden on the company, jeopardizing its ability to pay creditors and remain in business unless such a termination takes place.

Involuntary Termination

The PBGC may conduct an involuntary termination if it is determined that, in addition to not adequately funding its pension, a lump-sum payment has occurred to a participant who is a substantial owner of the sponsoring firm, or the eventual financial loss to the PBGC is expected to be unreasonable, unless the plan is terminated.

Multiemployer plans are typically provided direct financial assistance in the form of a loan, which is typically not repaid, to continue to make payments to beneficiaries, even after the PBGC has determined that such a plan is insolvent. These loans will generally continue on an annual basis until the plan no longer needs financial assistance or has paid all promised benefits at the guaranteed level. As such, the PBGC does not become trustee of multiemployer plans.

Benefits Paid

The PBGC pays benefits in accordance with the provisions of those plans for which it has become responsible as a result of either a distress or involuntary termination. While most participants in these plans receive all benefits promised, ERISA caps how much each participant in a terminated plan can receive, unless the PBGC is able to recover sufficient assets during a termination to allow payment of benefits above the maximum guarantee. The maximum guarantee is based upon a retirement age of 65, and this amount is adjusted downward for those retiring early, upward for those retiring later.

The PBGC's Future

The PBGC faces unique risks and obligations that make its long-term financial condition uncertain. Current risks are concentrated in certain industries (such as passenger airlines and steel manufacturing), but the PBGC is not able to decline insurance coverage regardless of the potential risk of loss posed by an insured. Private insurers are capable of tailoring premiums in response to actual or expected claims exposure, but the PBGC must collect premiums according to federal statute, which contains no such provisions. Additionally, other than a $100 million line of credit with the U.S. Treasury, no source of additional funding for the PBGC exists. Should all assets be exhausted, either a drastic reduction of benefits or a bailout enacted by Congress would be necessary to restore solvency. Such variables as the performance of equities markets, long-term interest rates, general economic conditions, the ability of plan sponsors to fulfill pension obligations, and the bankruptcy rates among firms over which the PBGC exercises oversight all will have a material influence in determining its financial outlook.[6]

See also ERISA; Pension Plans

NOTES

1. Pension Benefit Guaranty Corporation, "Mission Statement," http://www.pbgc.gov/about/about.html (accessed December 14, 2007); and U.S. Department of Labor, "Retirement Plans, Benefits and Savings: Employee Retirement Income Security Act (ERISA)," http://www.dol.gov/dol/topic/retirement/erisa.htm (accessed December 14, 2007).

2. Congressional Budget Office, "A Guide to Understanding the Pension Benefit Guaranty Corporation" (September 2005); and U.S. Department of Labor, Bureau of Labor Statistics, "Single- and Multi-employer Defined Benefit Pension Plans Differ," http://www.bls.gov/opub/ted/1999/Apr/wk1/art03.htm (accessed December 15, 2007).

3. Pension Benefit Guaranty Corporation, "Governance" http://www.pbgc.gov/about/about.html (accessed December 14, 2007).

4. Pension Benefit Guaranty Corporation, "Annual Management Report, Fiscal Year 2007" (November 14, 2007).

5. Pension Benefit Guaranty Corporation, "How PBGC Operates." http://www.pbgc.gov/about/operation.html (accessed December 14, 2007), and "Welcome to PBGC." http://www.pbgc.gov/ (accessed December 13, 2007).

6. Congressional Budget Office, "A Guide to Understanding the Pension Benefit Guaranty Corporation"; and Pension Benefit Guaranty Corporation—Annual Management Report, Fiscal Year 2007; and Pension Benefit Guaranty Corporation—Annual Management Report, Fiscal Year 2007 (November 14, 2007).

Steven J. Kerno Jr.

PENSION PLANS

A pension is a fixed sum of money paid by an employer to an employee at regular intervals. The amount and timing of the payments are established by contractual agreement between the employer and the employee and are normally based upon the salary and length of employment of the employee.

Pension payments generally begin when a person retires from employment because of age, disability, or the completion of an agreed-upon length of service to the company.

In essence, they represent a means of rewarding an employee for extended years of service to the company. The payments generally continue for the recipient's natural life and can sometimes be extended to a widow or other survivor.

Pension plans are strictly voluntary in nature but are considered an important component of the benefit package offered to employees and can become an integral part of the recruiting process. Therefore, employers need to understand not only how pension plans are structured, but they must also be aware of current industry trends in order to remain competitive in the job market.

Types of Pension Plans

Pension plans can be divided into two broad categories: defined contribution and defined benefit. Before the 1990s, the defined benefit plan was the most popular and common type of pension plan in the United States. Many of these plans are still in existence and paying benefits. Since that time, the defined contribution plan has become the most common type of plan in the United States for many reasons, some of which include:

- A shift in the economy away from unionized jobs that favor defined benefit plans
- The government making defined contribution plans more available
- The government making defined benefit plans less attractive to employers by imposing stricter requirements for contributions to defined benefit plans and limiting what employers could do with excess funds
- Defined contribution plans being buoyed up by strong economic growth in the 1980s and 1990s, resulting in 401(k) assets, a form of defined contribution plan, to grow at unprecedented rates[1]

Either category of pension plan may have vesting provisions whereby the percentage of pension benefits to which an employee is entitled is based upon the number of years of employment. Generally, the longer the employment period, the higher the vesting percentage. Cliff vesting involves a single jump from 0 percent to 100 percent vesting when the employee reaches a specified employment anniversary date. Gradual vesting is vesting over a period of years; for each year of employment, employees become entitled to a larger vesting percentage until 100 percent vesting is reached.

Defined Benefit Plans

Defined benefit plans are those in which the employee upon retirement receives an annuity, a fixed stream of payments. The amount of the payments is predetermined by a payment formula specified within the plan and is generally based upon years of employment and the final salary of the employee. It may also include other factors such as age at retirement and Social Security payments to be received by the employee. An example of a typical benefit formula is:

Annual Pension = 1.5% x years of service x final salary

With this formula, the more years of service, the greater the percentage of final salary an employee will receive. This implies that benefits are "back-loaded." That is, a significant part of the benefit occurs at the end of an employee's service with the employer.

Employers need to determine the amount of the contribution that must be made today in order to meet the pension benefit commitments that will arise in the future. The calculation is complex and, at best, represents an educated guess based on economic and financial assumptions. The assumptions include, but are not limited to, average retirement age and life span of the employees, the returns earned by the pension plan's investments, and any additional taxes or levies imposed on the pension fund. For this reason, the calculation of required plan contributions is best performed by an actuary using actuarial software. The funds are held in a trust where the primary purpose is to safeguard and invest the monies so that enough money exists to pay the employer's obligation to the employees.

Employers are at risk with defined benefit plans because the amount of current contributions needed to fund future benefits is defined in terms of uncertain future variables, not the least of which is market performance of the pension fund. In addition, because of this, the accounting for defined benefit plans is complex. The amount of the liability is controversial because it is based on uncertain variables. The expense recognized each period is not necessarily equal to the cash contribution.

Within a defined benefit plan, employers bear the risk of spending higher-than-expected amounts of money to fund higher-than-expected benefit payments. On the other hand, retirees do not bear any risk because the amount of the benefit is guaranteed.

Defined Contribution Plans
Defined contribution plans are those in which the employer agrees to contribute a sum of money, based on a formula specified within the plan, into an individual account for each participant. No promise is made regarding the ultimate benefits paid out. The resulting benefits are based solely on the amount contributed to the account, income accumulated in the account, and the treatment of forfeitures of funds caused by early terminations of other employees.

The employer's responsibility in a defined contribution plan is solely to make a contribution each year based on the formula established in the plan. An independent third-party trustee acting on behalf of the beneficiaries, the participating employees, normally handles the funds. As a result, accounting for a defined contribution plan is straightforward. The employer's annual expense is simply the amount that it is obligated to contribute to the pension trust. A liability is recorded only if the contribution has not yet been paid in full.

Generally, the employees are responsible for selecting the types of investments toward which the funds in their retirement funds are allocated. Employees may be allowed, or even required, to invest a certain amount of their fund in company stock. However, employers commonly retain financial advisors to assist the employees in making their choices. By doing so, employers can help employees make better-informed decisions toward reaching their retirement goals. Any fees due to the advisors are typically deducted from the employees' retirement funds.

Within a defined contribution plan, investment risk and reward are assumed by each participant and not by the employer. In addition, retirees bear the risk of their retirement income being limited or underfunded. Employers assume no risk because they are readily able to determine the amount of money needed to cover the benefit.

Other Considerations

If a pension plan meets certain regulatory requirements, as defined by the Internal Revenue Service, it is considered to be a "qualified" plan. This means it provides certain tax advantages to both the employer and the employee. Employers are able to deduct the pension contributions from their taxable income. The contribution is not included in the employees' taxable income for that year, and interest earned on the contribution will also be tax-free. In fact, the employees will not pay tax until they receive distributions from the plan.

Employers can use pension plans as a recruiting tool. Defined contribution plans can be structured as a 401(k) plan, in which employees can elect to take current compensation and defer it, putting it instead into tax-sheltered accounts. In addition, employers can offer to match the employees' contributions or contribute portions of company profits to the plan. Either of these options can prove to be a factor in the recruiting process. In addition, contributions that are tied to company profits can act as an incentive to increase productivity and, therefore, overall company performance.

See also 401(k) Plans; Benefits; Pension Benefit Guaranty Corporation; Simplified Employee Pension (SEP)/Simple Plans

NOTE

1. A. Baker, D. Logue, and J. Rader, *Managing Pension and Retirement Plans: A Guide for Employers, Administrators, and Other Fiduciaries* (Oxford: Oxford University Press, 2005).

Teresa K. Cook

RETIREMENT

Changing Face of Retirement

One of the definitions of retirement in the *Merriam Webster 11th Collegiate Dictionary* is "withdrawal from one's position or occupation or from active working life." This definition was accurate for much of the late twentieth century. However, defining retirement as a terminal act or end point is no longer valid, at least in the United States.

Retirees are increasingly reentering the workforce, in a full- or part-time capacity, starting their own businesses or working as volunteers for social, religious, and community organizations and activities. The traditional retirement–to–old age phase of life is now shifting to a *third age* in which "the workspace becomes a dynamic space for older workers," work "becomes a search for continued meaning and contribution as well as to satisfy a financial need," and "older workers might make the decision to remain in, retire from or return to periods of part-time, full-time or seasonal or holiday work."[1]

Drivers of Retirement Choice

In general, a worker can more easily retire if he or she believes that income in retirement will be adequate to support the lifestyle desired, and/or that working longer will provide increased income sufficient to offset additional years of deferred benefits. In recent years, income has been less and less of a factor in the retirement decision, as retirees' relative wealth has increased along with their ability to migrate to lower-cost areas upon retirement.[2]

The continued availability of health care insurance benefits is also a driver of the choice by employees to retire or stay in the workforce. The recently passed Medicare Modernization Act (2003), which added prescription drug benefits, also contains a provision that allows employers to reduce or eliminate health care coverage for retirees once they are eligible for Medicare. The impact of this change is not yet clear. However, if employers increasingly exercise this option, it could have a dampening effect on the rate of retirement of workers in the future.

Types of Retirement Plans

Social Security

The basic income security program in the United States for those workers who reach the eligible retirement age is Social Security. Social Security benefits are determined on a formula based on quarters of work and paid on a monthly basis. Since the beginning of the Social Security system, the Full Retirement Age (FRA) at which a recipient can begin to receive the maximum amount of benefits has been 65. A change in the Social Security Act in 2000 set a schedule for slowly raising this age to 67 by 2007. The age at which an eligible person can begin receiving a reduced monthly retirement benefit under Social Security remains at age 62 (60 for widows without their own eligibility). Between age 62 and 65, when the recipient reaches FRA, the amount he or she can earn from wages, salary, or income from a self-owned business without a loss of benefits is capped, and rises slowly each year. For those recipients who are at or above the FRA, there is no reduction in benefits based on annual earnings.[3]

Some see a potential for the Social Security system not being able to support a significant increase in the number of retirees drawing on the systems, while others disagree that the aging of the population will necessarily result in a crisis for Social Security.

Private and Public Organization Retirement Plans

Over half of U.S. workers have participated in some type of private- or public-sector pension plan during their working careers.[4] Also, three-fourths of workers over age 55 have some type of pension coverage beyond Social Security. These private-sector and public pension plans are generally of two broad types; "defined benefit" and "defined contribution" plans.

Defined Benefit Plans. From the perspective of the worker, defined benefit plans provide a low-risk incentive for retirement, as the amount of the annuity is fixed, depending on a combination of average pay (often over the last three to five years of employment), length of service in the organization, and age at retirement. These plans are usually set up to pay a fixed monthly amount to an eligible employee during his retirement years. Contributions by both the employee and the employer are based on actuarial projections of age at death minus age at retirement to determine the amount of the required contribution to the retirement fund during working years. Generally, there is a ceiling on the amount of contribution. Most private organizational plans of this type specify a minimum retirement age of 65 or a combination of age and years of service (e.g., total of 85) to receive a full annuity. Some plans also allow for an earlier retirement, at age 62 for example, with a reduced payout. Most plans of this type are mandatory for employees of the organization and are fully managed by the employer either directly or through an independent fund manager. These plans are usually favored more by older workers.

Defined Contribution Plans. Defined contribution plans have a potential for larger or smaller benefits than defined benefit plans, with greater risk of variability in retirement benefits falling on the worker. Because of the often-lower long-term cost and financial risk to them, U.S. employers are increasingly shifting to these types of plans. The amount the employee receives at retirement is not fixed in advance, but is based on the level of contribution by the employee (and sometimes by the employer) and the amount in the employee's account is based on how the funds in the account are invested. This investment is often in mutual funds, company stock, a profit-sharing arrangement, or other investment combinations. Also, the employee usually has a degree of independence in the choice of the mix of investment types in his or her retirement account. For the employee, these plans have greater risk and potential reward than defined benefit plans. In addition, defined contribution plans are voluntary and provide pension portability for workers who change organizations frequently. These types of plans usually favor younger workers who have more time to plan and select investment opportunities which provide retirement benefits in the future.

Because there is more risk placed on employees in defined contribution retirement plans, there is more incentive for them to delay retirement based on growing returns or to await an increase in returns after a market downturn such as the ones experienced in 2000–2001 and 2008. Thus, organizations may also be encouraging older workers to stay in the workforce longer by accelerating the trend of shifting retirement plans from the defined benefit type to the defined contribution type. On the other hand, if returns from the stock market and other investments again accelerate as they did in the late 1990s older workers may retire in greater numbers.

Bridge Employment or Gradual Retirement

The United States leads many countries in the number of people who are involved in some form of bridge employment between their long-term careers and full retirement.[5] However, most of these arrangements seem to be self-directed by the employee and not part of a formal employer system. In addition, many of these arrangements are based on a shift in the ability of organizations to provide partial retirement or bridge retirement. Part-time work for older workers or rehired retirees is currently restricted by tax, age, and retirement laws and regulations.

See also Pension Plans

NOTES

1. Tonette Rocco, David Stein, and Chan Lee, "An Exploratory Examination of the Literature on Age and HRD Policy Development," *Human Resource Development Review,* 2 (2003): 156.

2. Dora L. Costa, "The Evolution of Retirement: Summary of a Research Project," papers of the 110th annual meeting of the American Economic Association, *Journal of Economic Review* 88 no. 2 (1998): 232–36.

3. U.S. Social Security Administration, *How Work Affects Your Benefits,* Publication 05-10069, ICN 467005 (Baltimore, MD: U.S. Social Security Administration, February 2004).

4. Satyendra K. Verma and Jules H. Lichtenstein, "Retirement Plan Coverage of Baby Boomers and Retired Workers: Analysis of 1998 SIPP Data," *AARP Public Policy Institute Paper, 2003-10* (Washington, DC: AARP, 2003).

5. Phillip Taylor, *New Policies for Older Workers* (Bristol, England: The Policy Press, University of Cambridge, 2000).

Donald L. Venneberg

SALARY BENCHMARKING

Organizations utilize many ways to benchmark their salary data, including comparing data to outside sources, internally to existing positions, or a combination of both methods. Whichever method the organization utilizes to maintain its salary structure, it is vital to the health of its compensation system. Organizations that monitor their compensation strategies may improve employee retention, and attract and maintain a competitive workforce.[1]

The Compensation Structure

Organizations determine how to benchmark salary data depending on their compensation structures and procedures. Executives typically decide how to benchmark their data during the compensation structure creation. A job worth hierarchy is created during the compensation structure conception. A job worth hierarchy is "the perceived internal value of jobs in relationship to each other within an organization. The job worth hierarchy forms the basis for arranging similar jobs together and establishing salary ranges."[2]

Job Evaluation

Job evaluation involves building a job worth hierarchy. Two basic approaches of job evaluations and their methods include market data and job content.

Market Data
Market data collects and compares organizational benchmark jobs; job content evaluations are then conducted to place jobs in the job worth hierarchy.

Job Content
Job content evaluations occur before the data collection and analysis. Some job content methods use market data and others do not.

Nonquantitative or Whole Job. During the job content analysis, the whole job is considered via ranking or classification.
- *Ranking:* Every job is compared to another and based on internal value; jobs are placed in the job worth hierarchy from highest to lowest.
- *Classification:* Jobs are compared to the classification description of each job grade and placed in the grade that is a best fit.

Quantitative or Factor. This analysis examines job components or point factors.
- *Job Component:* Compensation analysts use multiple regression of market data plus two or more independent variables collected from a questionnaire, such as education, work experience, and duties and responsibilities, to establish a job worth hierarchy.
- *Point Factor:* Organizational and compensation leaders determine and define weighted factors that are important to the organization. Compensation analysts use the weighted factors to conduct job content analysis, and based on the analysis, points are assigned to jobs. Jobs are placed into the job worth hierarchy accordingly.[3]

Benchmark Jobs

Benchmark jobs can be used by organizations to benchmark salary data using the job evaluation methods applied to internal and external data. The jobs can be used to build or validate an organization's base pay structure. A benchmark job represents many organizational levels and numerous employees, and is important to the internal job worth hierarchy. It is recommended that 50 percent of the jobs within an organization are benchmarked.[4] Depending on the existing internal job hierarchy, benchmark jobs can be used as internal anchor points and comparative marks for non-benchmark jobs.

To determine benchmark jobs:

1. The benchmark jobs should be grouped using a standard guideline.
2. The job titles should be recognizable and found in other organizations and/or industries and classification systems.
3. The job descriptions should be created closely from a well-known classification system such as O*NET or OCSM (Occupational Classification System Manual).

O*NET is a complex online network that offers clients the opportunity to search for occupations, job families, and skills across databases. The database reports provide information on tasks, knowledge, skills, abilities, work activities, work content, work styles, work values, related occupations, and wages.[5]

The U.S Department of Labor Bureau of Labor Statistics utilizes the OCSM (Occupational Classification System Manual) to conduct the National Compensation Survey (NCS).[6] The OCSM is a classifying system that compensation employees can utilize to organize, categorize, and create job descriptions for benchmark jobs. The following are a few examples from the list of the MOGs (Major Occupational Groups).

1. Professional, Technical, and Relational Occupations
2. Executive, Administrative, and Managerial Occupations
3. Sales Occupations

Salary Surveys

Benchmark jobs are crucial for compensation employees who utilize salary surveys to benchmark their organizations' compensation data. If the benchmark jobs are used for salary data, they can help to find data for up to 70 percent of the organization's positions.[7] Once the benchmark jobs have been assigned values based on market pay, other positions can be placed in the job hierarchy around them based on their pay grades and levels.

Companies participate in salary surveys to provide compensation data on positions they match to job descriptions provided to them. Many of the descriptions are provided by the survey organization by industry and type of position. Not all of the positions that companies have are listed on the salary surveys; therefore, they are reliant on the benchmark positions for which they are able to provide and obtain data. It is important for the compensation team to understand the specific industry and geographic regions in which the company is looking for data.

Companies may purchase salary surveys or conduct their own surveys. Companies may purchase several surveys for multiple sources of data. Further, salary surveys may have data on different positions within the same industry. For example, one survey may focus on IT positions and have several positions that other surveys do not.

If the compensation team purchased several market surveys, the team must combine the data or enter it into a software system that combines and analyzes the data. The data is presented to the executive team, and a determination is made where the organization's salary baseline will fall in relation to the market. After the decision, adjustments are made to each benchmark job and non-benchmark job accordingly.

Market pay adjustments are given to individuals if necessary. For instance, if the mechanics position within the organization was 10 to 20 percent under the baseline, the compensation team might decide to increase the employees' salary within the position.

Conclusion

There is no right or wrong way to salary benchmark. The organization's needs are the deciding factors, and the decision often involves the consideration of the complete rewards package. Compensation, its structures, and its practices are reactive to the needs of the organization while complying with relevant laws such as the Fair Labor Standards Act (FLSA) and Equal Pay Act of 1963.[8]

See also Compensation

Resources:

HR-Guide.com, http://www.hr-guide.com.

Occupational Classification System Manual (OCSM), available from the U.S. Bureau of Labor Statistics, http://www.bls.gov.

NOTES

1. G. T. Milkovich and J. Stevens, "Back to the Future: A Century of Compensation," Working Paper 99-08 (Ithaca, NY: Center for Advanced HR Studies, Cornell University, 1999).

2. World at Work, "Course C2: Job Analysis, Documentation and Evaluation, Training Series, 2003.

3. Ibid.

4. Ibid.

5. O*NET Online. Occupational Informational Network. (2003), http://www.online.onetcenter.org (accessed February 20, 2007).

6. The U.S Department of Labor, Bureau of Labor Statistics, utilizes the OCSM (Occupational Classification System Manual) to conduct the National Compensation Survey (NCS). (http://www.bls.gov).

7. World at Work, "Course C2."

8. Milkovich and Stevens, "Back to the Future."

Jen Fullerton

SCANLON PLAN

The Scanlon Plan, sometimes called the Frost-Scanlon Plan, is the oldest and most commonly used gainsharing plan. The term "gainsharing" refers to any of a number of plans put into place to improve productivity by offering financial incentives to employees for gains in productivity to the company as a whole. The Scanlon Plan focuses efforts on improvements in the ratio of total labor costs to sales or market value of production.

Other popular gainsharing plans are the Rucker Plan and Improshare.[1] The Rucker Plan spreads its focus beyond issues of labor savings, but ties bonuses heavily to the ratio of total labor cost to value added, as opposed to total sales. Improshare plans focus on reaching a higher number of units produced in less person-hours. The Scanlon Plan is the only major gainsharing plan that is not copyrighted.[2]

The Goal of the Scanlon Plan

The goal of the Scanlon Plan is to improve company productivity, meaning an improvement in the ratio of inputs to outputs, through means of labor savings. The Scanlon Plan seeks to reduce the amount of time needed to produce an item without increasing the cost of production.

History of the Scanlon Plan

The Scanlon Plan was developed by Joe Scanlon in the 1930s. Scanlon, then a steelworkers' local labor union president at a small Ohio steel company, believed that if workers were motivated financially, they could be a great source of ideas for improvements. In 1938, Scanlon was notified by the steel company's management that they would have to cease operation unless improvements were made in company production; this gave Scanlon an opportunity to test his theory.[3]

Scanlon sought to decrease the company's labor cost per unit of production. Working with company executives he developed a union-management productivity plan that proved successful; as a result, the company saved $150,000 annually, at a cost of only $8,000 for new equipment. This success led Scanlon to work with dozens of other ailing companies through the steelworkers' union national headquarters. In the process, he developed a program that determined the normal labor cost per unit of production, gave workers the opportunity to produce at less than the normal labor cost, and then gave a large portion of those savings back to the workers. Scanlon based everything around the success of the company as a whole, rather than individual units. This alleviated the sense of internal competition and increased employee participation toward the success of the company.

The successes of the Scanlon Plan soon garnered attention from a variety of industries and from companies in a wide array of financial statuses. The plan was found to be just as successful at improving production in healthy companies as it had been in failing companies.

In the late 1940s, Joe Scanlon left the manufacturing world for the Massachusetts Institute of Technology, where he stayed until his death in 1956. During this time, Scanlon worked further on developing his gainsharing concepts. While at MIT, he worked closely with Douglas McGregor, Fred Lesieur, and Carl Frost, each of whom continued development of the Scanlon Plan after Scanlon's death.

The Foundations of the Scanlon Plan

The Scanlon Plan should not be viewed as a short-term plan to help a company get through troubled times. Rather, it is to be viewed as a process through which a company transforms into an organization that accomplishes continuously improved productivity and continued development of its employees. The Scanlon Plan is based on the belief that all human beings hold untapped potential and that employees want to contribute toward the success of their employers. It is the goal of the Scanlon Plan to bring forward this untapped potential to improve productivity and reward the staff for tangible improvements made as a result of employee input.

The principles of the Scanlon Plan were developed and extensively researched at MIT and by Carl Frost at Michigan State University. The four principles consist of Identity, Participation, Equity and Competence.

- *Identity:* Employees must understand the business reality of the organization. The principle of identity covers "who we are" and "where we are going." When employees fully understand the business reality, they are likely to see themselves more as business partners than as cogs in the machine of the organization. This provides incentive for employees to help the organization compete and adapt to change. This principle ties in directly with using open-book management, change management, cooperative labor relations, and lean manufacturing.

- *Participation:* Employees are encouraged to provide advice and recommendations regarding their own areas of competence. Through harnessing the knowledge and efforts of each employee, it is believed the organization will improve productivity.
- *Equity:* All stakeholders in the organization must share in the financial successes and failures of the organization. Gainsharing, goal-sharing, or profit-sharing systems are instituted to ensure all stakeholders gain financially from the organization's productivity improvements.
- *Competence:* Employees should continually increase their knowledge and skills. The employer should provide materials and opportunities for its employees to enhance existing skills, or to learn new ones valued by the organization.

Implementing a Scanlon Plan

Though each Scanlon Plan is customized for a specific organization, there is a general format that should be followed.

1. Meet with executives to develop a clear understanding of what the Scanlon Plan is really about. It should be made clear that its use is not meant to be a short-term fix.
2. Develop models and formulas for use in predicting financial gains and costs associated with improving productivity, as well as sharing those gains.
3. Prepare rules and presentation materials, and then develop a method to notify all employees of the new policy.
4. Retrain management to be supportive of the process.
5. Form a production committee consisting of at least one manager and one peer-elected employee from each organizational unit. This committee should meet regularly to review suggestions on how to increase productivity and implements the suggestions when appropriate.
6. Form a steering committee with a number of managers from different functional areas and an equal number of elected nonmanagerial employees. The committee should meet regularly to determine bonuses paid based on the previously decided formulas when productivity improves.[4]

Typical Criticisms of the Scanlon Plan

The Scanlon Plan is often criticized due to its lack of individual rewards to those who stand out in their achievements. Another criticism is that the plan removes too much control from the hands of management. If gains are realized, management cannot simply decide how best to use these gains, as their use is already predetermined through the process of implementing a Scanlon Plan.

See also Employee Stock Option Plan (ESOP); Gainsharing and Profit Sharing

NOTES

1. Scanlon Consulting Services, "Costs and Benefits of Scanlon," *Scanlon Leader,* http://www.scanlonleader.com/index.php?option=com_content&task=view&id=30&Itemid=51 (accessed January 20, 2008)

2. "The Scanlon Plan," *Time,* http://www.time.com/time/magazine/article/0,9171,807657-2,00.html (accessed January 20, 2008).

3. Hope College—The Frost Research Center, "About the Frost-Scanlon Plan," Hope College, http://www.hope.edu/admin/frost/frost-scanlon.html (accessed January 20, 2008).

4. Ronald J. Recardo and Diane Pricone, "Is Gainsharing for You?" *Quality Digest*, July 1996, http://www.qualitydigest.com/jul/gainshre.html (accessed August 18, 2008).

Adam VanDreumel

SIMPLIFIED EMPLOYEE PENSION (SEP)/SIMPLE PLANS

One of the disadvantages of owning a small business is that many do not have company-matching 401(k) programs in which to invest for their retirement. For this reason, many small business owners choose to open another type of individual retirement account (IRA) for themselves and their employees. Two of the most common are the Simplified Employee Pension (SEP) and the Savings Incentive Match Plan for Employees (SIMPLE).[1] Each plan has unique distinguishing characteristics.

For employees to take part in a SEP plan, they must have worked for the company for three years out of the last five, be at least 21 years of age, and made at least $450 before becoming eligible to participate.[2] Once eligible, an employer can contribute up to 25 percent of an employee's salary, not to exceed $46,000 (in 2008). The contribution rate for all employees must be uniform. Any amount that a small business owner contributes to an employee's SEP is automatically vested.

The employee can take distributions from a SEP plan when he or she reaches the age of 59½ years, and the distributions are taxed as ordinary income. However, if the recipient of the distribution is less than 59½ years old, then a 10 percent penalty is included. Unlike the 401(k)s of larger companies, an individual cannot take out a loan from a SEP. If an employee withdraws money, it will be considered a distribution and, if the person is not 59½ years old, he or she will incur a 10 percent penalty along with the regular amount of taxes.

SIMPLE programs are set up differently from SEP programs but, depending on the small business and its owner, may be just as effective. For employees to contribute to a SIMPLE plan, they must have earned at least $5,000 in the previous two years and must plan on making the same amount in the current year. Employers can contribute to a SIMPLE IRA in one of two ways. The first is a dollar-for-dollar match up to 3 percent of the employee's income, with the employee's contribution being pretax income. This reduces the amount paid in income tax.[3] The second option is for the small business owner to make a contribution of 2 percent of the employee's income whether or not employees elect to make any contributions of their own.[4] In either case, the amount that an employee can contribute to a SIMPLE plan is $10,000. The distribution rules that apply to the SEP plan also apply to the SIMPLE plan.

Depending on the small business owner's situation, both IRA plans may be good vehicles to use in a person's retirement planning. Each small business should take a look at its own situation to decide which plan works best for them. For example, if a small business generates a lot of money, the owner may want to implement a SEP plan for its higher contribution levels. If a small business is a part-time affair, the owner may elect to start a SIMPLE plan. Whatever the case may be, both plans, if managed properly, will go a long way in contributing to a person's retirement future.

NOTES

1. Jeffrey H. Rattiner, "SEPs or SIMPLEs?" *Financial Planning* (September 2002): 105–6.

2. Randy Gardner, Julie Welch, and Brooke Grechus, "Choosing the Right Retirement Plan for a Self-Employed Individual," *Journal of Financial Planning,* (February 2004): 28–32.

3. Internal Revenue Service Web site: http://www.irs.gov/publications/p560/ch02.html#d0e1093 (accessed January 21, 2008).

4. Ibid.

Ryan Skiera

SEVERANCE PAY

Severance pay is intended to bridge the gap between termination and reemployment. It is a voluntary continuation of an employee's salary after termination paid by the company, either in a lump sum or on a salary continuation basis. The amount is typically based on the employee's length of service and/or position in the company. The severance package may also include medical benefits continuation for the employee and/or dependents and outplacement services.

Rationale

Severance is typically provided by companies because it is a moral obligation and is part of their culture. They want to maintain a reputation as a good employer that does not leave former employees without any income when the reason for termination is often no fault of their own. This not only helps with future recruiting, but is important to the morale, productivity, and retention of remaining employees. It also eases the anxiety and psychological burden on the executives who have to make the difficult decisions and notify the employees. Moreover, separations (particularly large layoffs) are subject to potential legal, financial, and public relations risks if not well thought out and planned.

Legal Requirements

Providing a severance pay plan is a common business practice. However, it is not an automatic or vested job right. While many employers provide severance voluntarily, there is no federal law requiring employers to give terminated employees any pay continuation. There is a possibility that a severance plan could be an employee benefit under ERISA.[1] This could be the case if it is included in a union contract, or if it is established by the employer as a formal plan, there is a fund or account set aside, or if past practice creates a reasonable expectation among employees.

While it is beyond the scope of this entry, employers should also be familiar with the provisions of the Older Workers Benefit Protection Act (OWBPA), the Age Discrimination in Employment Act (ADEA) and the Workers Adjustment and Retraining Notification Act (WARN). It is best to consult with legal counsel to determine any requirements.

Practices

Severance policies can vary widely based on the size of the company and industry. Larger companies are more likely to have a formal policy than smaller companies, who may negotiate severance on a case-by-case basis. A standard policy does not mean that everyone has to be treated exactly the same. Certain employees can be excluded, and different formulas can be applied to different job levels as long as employees in protected classes are not discriminated against. For example, policies typically provide greater benefits for exempt employees than for nonexempt employees. Severance for executives is frequently greater and often negotiated on a case-by-case basis.

Key Elements

Who Should Be Eligible for Severance?

Typically, employers will provide some severance payments to full-time employees, with a much smaller percentage providing payments to part-time, contract, or temporary employees.

Under What Circumstances Should Severance Be Paid?

Severance is typically paid to those who are laid off due to economic conditions, or are released for nonperformance, outdated skills, or circumstances beyond their control. Poor performers might also be given severance in lieu of notice if there is a threat to employee morale or sabotage. Few employers will provide payment for employees terminated for "cause," such as illegal or immoral behavior, insubordination, or repeated violations of policy.[2]

How Much Should Be Paid?

Severance payments are generally based on years of service and position in the company, with a typical policy being one week per year of service for nonexempt and hourly employees, one or two weeks per year for exempt salaried employees, and one month per year for executives. There is often a minimum payment of two weeks, and a maximum of 52 weeks.

How Should It Be Paid Out?

Payments are made either in a lump sum or on a salary continuation basis. While some companies might provide a choice, this could result in constructive receipt with immediate tax consequences regardless of the selection. Also, lump sums may be spent indiscriminately, leaving the employee with a financial problem. Many companies prefer salary continuation, which includes deductions for employee benefits coverage and does not require special payroll processing and tax calculations.[3] While some companies provide severance only for the period of unemployment and discontinue it when the employee becomes employed, this serves as a disincentive to seeking employment, and the employee will seldom tell the employer that she has been hired.

What Other Benefits Should Be Considered?

The most common benefits included in a separation package are medical benefits continuation, outplacement or career transition services, and accrued vacation and sick pay if permitted by policy. Employers must offer employees medical coverage for 18 months after leaving the company under COBRA, but the employee must pay the full cost plus a 2 percent administrative charge. Many employers continue coverage through the period of severance, paying the normal employer's percent of the premium. The time period and extent of outplacement services generally depends on the level of position.

Can Severance Provide Protection against Retaliation by the Employee?

Employers typically make severance contingent on the employee signing an agreement not to compete, not to recruit other remaining employees, or not to make slanderous remarks about the company. Also, employers can require the employee to sign a release agreeing not to sue the company in return for additional severance benefits.

How Should Severance Plans Be Communicated?

Large established companies typically have formal policies, while smaller, newer firms tend to handle severance on a case-by-case basis. A formal policy not only spells out to employees what they can expect if they lose their jobs, but it also prevents disparate treatment or favoritism that can create liability.[4] Companies with formal policies do not have to be locked into them in that they can provide a special "event-driven" program if unusual circumstances occur. This can include voluntary termination incentives, early retirement incentives, retention bonuses, or additional incentives to assure loyalty during major changes.

Conclusion

In general, severance policies have not seen much change or creativity over recent years. If anything, they have become less generous. Policies should be reviewed periodically to see how they align with the company's culture, financial condition, business prospects, and competitive position. If the purpose is to bridge the unemployment gap, then factors that contribute to the time required to find new positions, such as age, position level, changing skill requirements, and the job market, should be considered as part of a more practical severance package.

NOTES

1. U.S. Department of Labor, "Severance Pay," http://www.dol.gov/dol/topic/benefits-other/severancepay.htm (accessed October 23, 2007).

2. Charles J. Muhl, "The Employment-at-will Doctrine: Three Major Exceptions," *Monthly Labor Review* 124, no. 1 (January 2001): 3–11.

3. U.S. Department of Labor, "How Is Severance Pay Calculated and When Is It Due?" http://www.dol.gov.el;aws/faq/esa/flsa/oo7.htm (accessed October 23, 2007).

4. Paul R. Dorf and Diana D. Neelman. "Severance Benchmarks: Severance Polices Critical for Transition of Employees, CEOs," http://www.managedhealthcareexecutive.com/mhe/article/articleDetail.jsp?id=170528&sk=&date=&%0A%09%09%09&pageID=2 (accessed October 23, 2007).

Al O'Connor and Douglas Maxwell

SKILL-BASED PAY

Skill-based pay is a type of reward system that promotes workforce flexibility by rewarding employees based on the number, type, and depth of skills mastered.[1] Most employers are familiar with traditional job-based reward systems, which tie an individual's compensation to the job definition established by the organization; however, skill-based pay structures seek to address ones willingness or unwillingness to learn new skills by paying them to gain new skills. This focus on individual incentives for skills creates "a person-based approach that rewards employees for acquiring new skills."[2] Organizations that utilize skill-based pay plans provide pay increases for learning and demonstrating acquired new skills even if the employee does not use the skill in his current duties when the skill is acquired. An organization almost always sees skill-based pay programs as a way to increase return on investment to the organization while gaining greater accountability.[3] Skill-based pay plans can reduce overall compensation costs by creating leaner facilities equipped with broadly skilled employees.[4] There is nothing employees hold dearer to their heart than their pay. Allowing an employee to take command of her future monetary goals through concrete action and concise direction can be very powerful in some organizations.

Types of Skill-based Pay Plans

There are five types of skill-based pay structures that can be implemented; each with a focus on the type of knowledge necessary for a particular environment. Vertical skill plans, horizontal skill plans, depth skill plans, basic skill plans, or a combination of skill plans provides a construct for an organization to define a skill-based pay plan.

Vertical skill plans, or vertical knowledge, determine the actual input/output of skills (e.g., supervisory, coordinating, training, or leading others).[5] Vertical skill plans are most commonly used within labor settings in which individuals are expected to learn from each other in self-managed work teams or self-regulating work teams.[6] Additionally, this type of plan has been traditionally used within the skilled trades areas. For example, "a drill press operator who masters preventative maintenance and in-process inspection within a single job."[7]

In horizontal skill plans, or horizontal knowledge, similar skills or knowledge are gained as employees are trained to perform several types of related tasks. For example, the accounts payable person may rotate to accounts receivable or to benefits administration. The added flexibility of having an employee who can fill multiple roles insures continuation of services. Manufacturing also uses horizontal skill-based pay systems to encourage workers to know more than one area of a plant.

In depth skill plans, or depth knowledge, an employee brings to a particular job a particular depth of understanding or aptitude. Human resource professionals may choose to specialize in one area of HR functions such as compensation, benefits, training, organizational development, or HR strategy. The more skill areas a professional has chosen to master, the greater knowledge or depth in the area of specialization. Teachers are sometimes paid on a depth skill plan based on educational area.

Basic skill systems involve building skills that are basic to functioning in an organization, such as reading, writing, and speaking English. This type of plan would be beneficial to organizations that have a high percentage of English-as-second-language employees and would like to see greater aptitude in basic skills. Basic skills plans are often effective to teach norms and practices when entering new global markets where there is limited understanding of the traditions of both the corporate and host country location.

Combination plans, the most common use of skill-based pay plans, are a combination of two or more of the above types of skill-based pay plans. The plans are always tailored to a particular organization's needs and strategic objectives. The previous example of the drill press operator who masters preventative maintenance might also have a depth of skill level in drill press operation based on the organizational needs for drill press operation.

Benefits

The benefits of skill-based pay include a win-win monetarily for the employee and the employer, greater accountability on the part of employees, management becoming a main factor in employee development, and employees believing that management has an interest in them. Individuals in an organization with skill-based pay generally make more than similar individuals at traditional organizations. Organizationally, however, since skill-based pay organizations are generally leaner and have flatter hierarchy, the total labor costs are lower.[8] This is a win for both the employee and the employer. Employees often see skill-based pay systems as a more equitable, personally driven pay structure. Employees receive monetary and nonmonetary rewards for modeling behaviors management wants to encourage and by demonstrating skill knowledge on the job. Management becomes the facilitator of increased employee development, which leads to a direct positive relationship between management and employees. Skill-based pay leads employees to a greater understanding of the overall business because employees are rotating through job systems, thus allowing them to learn multiple functions. Management is often seen as having a greater commitment to individuals and their development, creating a high-trust environment, greater employee self-esteem, and increased loyalty to the employer.[9]

Conclusion

Skill-based pay systems are not for every organization. For some, the programs can be overwhelming in their creation and administration. However for others, they offer a unique opportunity to create an environment in which learning is encouraged and employees see themselves as vital to the organization because of the value they provide. By valuing what an individual brings initially to an organization and how they grow and develop over time, organizations are better equipped to meet the competitive challenges the future brings. Ensuring a fair and equitable compensation for performance is both people focused and organization focused; a win-win for all.

NOTES

1. R.J. Recardo and D. Pricone, "Is Skill-based Pay for You?" *SAM Advanced Management Journal (07497075)* 61, no. 4 (1996): 16.

2. J.D. Shaw, N. Gupta, A. Mitra, and G.E. Ledford Jr., "Success and Survival of Skill-based Pay Plans," *Journal of Management* 31, no. 1 (2005): 28–49.

3. Ibid., p. 29.

4. Shaw et al., "Success and Survival of Skill-based Pay Plans."

5. Recardo and Pricone, "Is Skill-based Pay for You?"

6. J.J. Martocchio, *Strategic Compensation: A Human Resource Management Approach,* 2nd ed. (Upper Saddle River, NJ: Prentice Hall, 2004).

7. Recardo and Pricone "Is Skill-based Pay for You?" 16.

8. J. McAdams, *The Reward Plan Advantage: A Manager's Guide to Improving Business Performance through People* (San Francisco: Jossey-Bass Publishers, 1996).

9. Recardo and Pricone, "Is Skill-based Pay for You?"

Lisa Scott Brinkman

UNEMPLOYMENT COMPENSATION

Federal and state unemployment compensation insurance programs provide income benefits for unemployed individuals in specific instances. Workers who are unemployed through no fault of their own (e.g., due to layoffs, plant closures, downsizing, and so forth) must meet eligibility requirements of their state.

The Social Security Act of 1935 created the Federal-State Unemployment Compensation (UC) Program, which has two main objectives: (1) to provide temporary, partial wage replacement to involuntarily unemployed workers who were recently employed; and (2) to help stabilize the economy during recessions. Each state has its own UC program within guidelines established by Federal law.

The UC system is founded in the Federal Unemployment Tax Act (FUTA) of 1939, and Titles III, IX, and XII of the Social Security Act. All states finance their own federally approved UC programs via a tax imposed on employers, while three states also collect minimal employee contributions.

Benefits

Unemployment compensation benefits are paid for a maximum of 26 weeks in most states, and are based on a percentage of the worker's earnings over a recent 52-week period, up to the state's allowable maximum amount. Additional weeks of unemployment benefits (called extended benefits) may be available during times of high unemployment. Some states provide extended benefits for certain purposes. Benefits are taxable and must be reported on one's federal income tax return.

Qualification for Unemployment

To qualify for benefits, unemployed individuals must (1) meet their state requirements for eligibility and wages earned or time worked during an established period (typically one year) of time, called the "base period"; and (2) must be determined to be unemployed through no fault of their own (as determined by state law).

Continued eligibility requires claimants to continuously meet eligibility requirements, including filing weekly or biweekly claims for unemployment compensation and reporting any job offers, refusals of work, and earnings from work for the week. Claimants may be required to register for work with their state employment service.

Disqualification

Workers who are unemployed due to some reason other than a "lack of work" face refusal, reduction, cancellation, or postponement of benefits. Common causes for disqualification of benefits include: not being able or available to work; voluntary separation from work without good cause; discharge for work-related misconduct, refusal of suitable work without good cause; and unemployment resulting from a labor dispute. Unemployed workers who have been disqualified or denied benefits have the right to file an appeal subject to their state's appeal rights. Employers may also appeal a UC determination if they disagree with the state's determination regarding a worker's eligibility.

Resources:
U.S. Department of Labor. http://www.dol.gov.
 "Unemployment Compensation." *Almanac of Policy Issues,* http://www.policyalmanac.org/social
_welfare/archive/unemployment_compensation.shtml

Ann Gilley

VACATION AND HOLIDAY POLICIES

Time off from work is an important component of any employee benefits package. Granting paid time off allows employees to conduct personal business, care for loved ones, and enjoy time to relax. A generous and flexible time-off policy acts as a recruiting tool, demonstrating to potential employees that the company cares about their welfare. It also improves employee retention, thereby reducing turnover.

Traditional vacation policies are the most common way to grant time off to employees. Holiday policies vary by employer but normally take into account many nationally observed and some personal holidays. A new trend in time off is the Paid Time Off (PTO) policy, which combines several traditional time-off policies into a single bank of time.

Traditional Vacation Policies

In a traditional vacation policy, a company grants a certain number of paid days per year to each employee. Often, these are in addition to a certain number of sick days also granted each year. The amounts granted normally increase with employee seniority associated with certain anniversary milestones.[1] For example, an employee with five years of service would be granted fewer days than an employee with 10 years of service. This can improve employee retention and encourage longevity. Certain categories of employees, like management, may be granted more vacation.

Vacation days can be granted either on a calendar-year basis or an anniversary-year basis. When using a calendar year, all of the days to be granted to that employee are typically accrued on January 1. This date could also coincide with a fiscal year, such as July 1. On an anniversary-year plan, vacation days are accrued on the service anniversary of that employee. For example, an employee who is hired on September 14 would accrue her vacation days each September 14 during continued employment.

Vacation may normally be taken at the discretion of the employee, with prior approval of his direct supervisor. This allows the supervisor to control production schedules and minimize disruption so that not everyone in their department is off at the same time. Scheduling may be done using either seniority or a first requested, first approved approach.

Holiday Policies

Most companies provide for some form of holiday pay, especially if the business is not open on that holiday. In the United States, the most common holidays to be paid are New Year's Day, Memorial Day, Independence Day, Labor Day, Thanksgiving and Christmas Day.[2] Some companies choose to add holidays for the day after Thanksgiving and Christmas Eve day. Depending on their workforce, their type of business and the states in which they operate, some companies also grant additional holidays, such as Martin Luther King's birthday and Good Friday.

To accommodate the diverse religious holidays and other special employee needs, companies may grant several personal or floating holidays to each employee. This allows for employee flexibility without having to close the business for holidays that may be observed by only a few employees. Personal holidays are typically accrued at the same time as vacation days, sometimes subject to a "use it or lose it" policy.

When an employee incurs an unapproved absence before or after a holiday, unrelated to FMLA, some policies may deny holiday pay.

Paid Time Off (PTO) Policies

PTO plans are becoming increasingly popular in today's business environment.[3] These policies combine one or more traditional time-off policies into one bank of time. Typically, PTO banks combine vacation time, sick time, and personal holidays. They often exclude corporate holidays and other time-off policies, such as jury duty or military leave of absence.

Like a traditional plan, PTO is normally accrued on a calendar-year or anniversary-year basis. It can also be accrued a little at a time, either once each month or once each pay period. This approach keeps banks smaller, since the accrual is spread out over the entire year. PTO accrual normally increases with seniority.

PTO plans can be advantageous for both the employees and the organization. For the employee, these banks provide for greater flexibility because there are no or limited restrictions on when an employee may use her time. For the organization, PTO provides for simplified attendance tracking and easier time-off administration.

Other Considerations

All time-off plans take into account the issue of carryover from one year to the next. It may not be possible for an employee to use all of his time before the next accrual. Most plans allow for two or three weeks to be carried forward into the next accrual period. This may increase with seniority. For example, employees with less than 15 years of service may be restricted to a carryover of 10 days, but employees with 15 years of service or over may carry over 15 days. Before setting any carryover policies, check with state and local laws to determine any restrictions.

Most states require that vacation days and PTO remaining in an employee's bank be paid to the employee upon her voluntary or involuntary termination.[4] There may also be restrictions regarding when the employer must make the payment, typically not less than two pay periods following the termination. Normally, these laws do not apply to sick time. Before setting any payment policy, check with state and local laws to determine any restrictions.

Many companies will institute corrective action or disciplinary policies around the use of time off. Commonly, these policies will require time off to be scheduled in advance and set a limit for the amount of acceptable unscheduled time. Once that threshold has been reached, corrective action may begin, up to and including termination of employment. These policies are often set by line management in cooperation with human resources, taking into account the scheduling needs of the line department.

Finally, unionized organizations must include time off as a mandatory subject for bargaining.[5] Time-off policies will be set forth in the bargaining agreement and are applied according to those rules. Changes cannot be made without the proper negotiations to update the contract language.

See also Absences; PTO (Paid Time Off) Bank

NOTES

1. Robert L. Mathis and John H. Jackson, *Human Resource Management,* 8th ed. (St. Paul, MN: West Publishing Company, 1997).

2. Ibid., 111.

3. Corporate Leadership Council, *Designing Paid Time Off Policies in the U.S.* (Washington, DC: Corporate Executive Board, November 2004).

4. Lewis Jackson, ed., *Managing Human Resources in the New Century: Recruiting, Retaining and Terminating Employees* (Ponte Vedra Beach, FL: American Chamber of Commerce Publishers, 2002).

5. Mathis and Jackson, *Human Resource Management,* 237.

Brad Schroeder

WELLNESS PROGRAMS

Employers are searching for innovative ways to control health care costs, reduce absenteeism, and improve worker productivity. Many are finding that voluntary workplace wellness and health promotion efforts can help accomplish those very objectives. Despite this, the EEOC and some employee advocates question whether employee wellness programs come across as mandatory, and go too far into employees' private lives. What is the right choice for your organization? What are your options for an effective program? And what are some key points to remember when implementing a wellness program at your organization?

Examples of some wellness programs include:

- On-site medical testing
- Weight-management programs
- Smoking-cessation programs
- On-site health clubs and fitness centers
- Health club memberships and/or discounts
- Spiritual and mental health programs
- On site physicians, nurses, dieticians, and physical therapists
- Ergonomic office equipment

Wellness Program Pros

There are many positive reasons to undertake an employee wellness program. One of the strongest reasons is in response to the rising costs of health care. More and more insurance providers are offering incentives such as lower health insurance premiums, lower co-pays, flex credit, cash contributions to health reimbursement arrangements (HRAs), gifts, and so forth for companies who adopt wellness programs. The rationale is that healthier employees make fewer medical claims. Many say that healthier employees are also more productive at work, and less inclined to be absent from work. With billions of dollars lost every year on employee absenteeism, and studies showing 75 percent of employee illnesses relate to lifestyle-related causes, wellness programs have become increasingly popular.[1] According to a United Benefit Advisors' survey released in May 2007, 10.5 percent of U.S. employers have a wellness program in place, with 7.6 percent likely to add in 2008.[2]

In addition to an overall improvement in individual health, effective wellness programs that produce results can boost employee morale, and even be a selling point for prospective hires. Many health insurance programs offer employees discounted premiums for participating in certain wellness programs, and others offer prizes and awards for recognition of top performers in certain programs.

Possible Drawbacks/Legal Implications

Are there any drawbacks to implementing an employee wellness program? What is being done to protect employee privacy? Some employee advocate groups agree that workplace wellness programs can violate employee rights. These advocates say that many employees do not know the programs are voluntary and may feel pressure to participate. Also, some fear that employee medical history and factors could someday affect their health care costs (e.g., charging higher premiums for those with high-risk factors such as smoking, high blood pressure, etc.), or that these programs could become a mandatory term of employment. Since there is little legal framework that exists, and laws tend to vary from state to state, employers must design and implement these wellness plans with extreme care.

Some laws that could affect a workplace wellness program are the Health Insurance Portability and Accountability Act (HIPPA), the Americans with Disabilities Act (ADA), and the Age Discrimination in Employment Act (ADEA).[3] Generally speaking, HIPPA prohibits most group health plans from discriminating based on health factors. Health factors can include things like medical conditions, medical history, prior health claims, etc. To properly consider these laws when designing your wellness program, please consult a legal expert.

Tips for Creating a Successful Wellness Program

1. *Seek senior-level support and buy-in.* Since the perception of the program and subsequent participation is vital, employees must feel that the company has an interest in their well-being. Senior managers should lead by example and create an atmosphere of interest in the program.
2. *Create a wellness team or committee.* Also important to a successful wellness program is a team to promote and administer the plan. Many times, this team is made up of all levels of employment as well as lifestyles. Successful committees meet frequently, and have specific goals to achieve.
3. *Gather data.* Research and consider data on absenteeism, medical claims, company culture, demographics, and employee and management expectations. This step will help identify where opportunities exist to meet employee needs.
4. *Set up an organized plan for implementation.* This critical step will help ensure that the wellness program is set up to meet the needs and interests of your employees and organization. This step should include a budget, a detailed timeline, and a communications strategy. At this point, it might be helpful to have the committee put together an action plan for the next 12 months, highlighting goals and objectives, as well as how you will promote the program. Your marketing strategy will differ based on which wellness activities you chose.
5. *Choose and implement a plan.* Many resources are available to find the appropriate plan for your organization. Check Web sites, articles, your insurance provider, and national forums such as the Society for Human Resource Management.
6. *Evaluate and monitor your chosen plan.* The most effective way to evaluate your program is to make it an integral part of your planning process in step 4. As you move through the launch and promotion of your wellness program, keep records that can be tied to results. These records, such as numbers on absenteeism, health care claims, and injuries, can be used to measure the overall effectiveness of the program.

See also Americans with Disabilities Act (ADA); Age Discrimination in Employment Act (ADEA); HIPAA

Resources:

Mathiason, Garry G. *Employer Mandated Wellness Initiatives: Respecting Workplace Rights While Controlling Healthcare Costs.* San Francisco: Littler Mendelson, P.C., 2007.

NOTES

1. Michael Rosenfeld, *SHRM—Online Compensation & Wellness Forum,* February 2005.
2. Stephen Miller, *SHRM—Online Compensation & Wellness Forum,* May 15, 2007.
3. Garry G. Mathiason, *Employer Mandated Wellness Initiatives: Respecting Workplace Rights While Controlling Healthcare Costs* (Littler Mendelson, P.C., 2007).

Jessica Haas

Chapter 5

Employment Law

Employment Law: An Overview

Organizations face many challenges in today's increasingly complex business environment. Pressure to remain competitive, satisfy shareholder expectations, meet state and federal guidelines, and serve the community combine with technology and an information-based society to blur roles and provide numerous opportunities for miscommunication and mistakes. One arena drawing intermittent attention involves various aspects of the law, from recent court decisions involving harassment and pension protection to employee privacy rights and constant tests of antidiscrimination and other employment laws. This chapter explores the relevant legal issues facing human resource management.

Sources of Employment Law

Employers are bound to abide by a host of laws, including federal, state, and local. Federal law includes the U.S. Constitution, federal statutes, and administrative law. State laws flow from states' constitutions, statutes, and administrative law.

In response to the civil rights movement and President Lyndon B. Johnson's attempt to create the Great Society in the 1960s, Congress passed a host of laws aimed at ensuring equal opportunity in the workplace. *Equal employment opportunity* laws, commonly referred to as EEO, specifically prohibited common forms of discrimination (race, color, creed, national origin, gender, religion). These *protected classifications* (e.g., gender) are further subdivided into *protected groups* (e.g. male, female). The entries in this chapter briefly discuss the EEO laws and other major employment laws.

Equal Employment Opportunity Commission (EEOC)

Congress created the Equal Employment Opportunity Commission, which now enforces numerous employment laws such as the Civil Rights Act of 1964 (Title VII), the Age Discrimination in Employment Act of 1967, the Equal Pay Act of 1963, the Rehabilitation Act of 1973, and the Americans with Disabilities Act of 1990. The EEOC "provides oversight and coordination of all federal regulations, practices, and policies affecting equal employment opportunity."[1]

The EEOC receives and investigates employment discrimination charges against public and private institutions. The Commission's mission is to ensure equality of opportunity by vigorously enforcing federal laws prohibiting employment discrimination through investigation, conciliation, litigation, coordination, education, and technical assistance.[2]

When an investigation of a claim yields reasonable cause to believe that discrimination has occurred, the Commission begins conciliation efforts. When conciliation fails, the charge is considered for litigation. The EEOC strives for remedies that correct the discrimination and prevent recurrence.

Major Employment Laws

Employment law impacts all areas of human resource management, including recruiting, selecting, promoting, and terminating employees. Table 5.1 summarizes the main employment laws.

Uniform Guidelines. The Uniform Guidelines on Employee Selection Procedures (1978) apply to nearly all organizations with 15 or more workers. Specifically, they assist organizations in understanding Title VII of the Civil Rights Act of 1964, and help organizations develop employment practices that comply with the law.

The Uniform Guidelines indicate that if an employment decision (e.g., selection, promotion, transfer, termination) results in disparate impact to a protected group, the institution must (1) eliminate the selection device(s) causing the disparate impact, or (2) demonstration the validity of the selection device(s). The guidelines indicate that justification of validity for selection devices that measure characteristics requiring a large inferential leap are inappropriate. Thus, a thorough job analysis is crucial for proving validity.

Employment Practices

The numerous EEO laws are designed to prevent discrimination in the workplace. Nevertheless, discrimination does occur, as evidenced by thousands of court cases across the nation. In deciding whether discrimination has occurred and which remedies are appropriate, courts consider specific and general individual and organizational behaviors, intent, and impact on the plaintiff.

Disparate Treatment and Disparate Impact

Disparate treatment is *intentional* discrimination that violates the Equal Protection Clause of the Fourteenth Amendment, which specifies that no state shall "deny to any person within its jurisdiction the equal protection of the laws." Disparate treatment occurs as a result of bias or prejudice, and when individuals are treated unfairly due to their membership in a protected group. Occasionally, disparate treatment is meant to protect an individual, such as when an employer refuses to assign a task to a woman for fear that she might be hurt. Although well-meaning, the employer is still guilty of discrimination.

Unintentional discrimination constitutes disparate impact, which causes unequal consequences for individuals of different protected groups. Disparate treatment may occur, for example, when an arbitrary (irrelevant) practice (such as requiring a typing test to gauge speed) results in a disproportionately low number of males being promoted. If the practice were relevant and job-related, it would be legal. The arbitrary nature of such practices leads to discrimination claims.

Table 5.1   Major Employment Laws

Law	Provisions
Equal Pay Act of 1963	Prohibits discrimination in pay based on gender; requires employers to pay males and females the same pay for the same work.
Civil Rights Act of 1964 (Title VII)	Prohibits discrimination in employment based on race, color, religion, gender, and national origin for most employers with 15 or more employees.
Age Discrimination in Employment Act of 1967	Prohibits discrimination in employment on the basis of age; protects individuals age 40 or more; restricts mandatory retirement; covers most employers with 20 or more employees.
Occupational Safety and Health Act of 1970	Establishes mandatory safety and health standards in organizations.
Vocational Rehabilitation Act of 1973	Prohibits discrimination against "otherwise qualified" individuals with physical or mental disabilities.
Pregnancy Discrimination Act of 1978	An amendment to the Civil Rights Act of 1964; prohibits discrimination against women due to a pregnancy-related condition.
Immigration Reform and Control Act of 1986	Prohibits discrimination on the basis of national origin or citizenship; prohibits employers from knowingly hiring aliens not authorized to work in the United States.
Americans with Disabilities Act of 1990 (ADA)	Expands on the Vocational Rehabilitation Act of 1973; prohibits discrimination on the basis of an individual's disability; covers most employers of at least 15 workers.
Civil Rights Act of 1991	An amendment to the Civil Rights Act of 1964; permits jury trials and punitive damages; specifies evidence needed to prove a discrimination claim, shifts burden of proof to employer.
Family and Medical Leave Act of 1993	Allows eligible employees to take up to 12 weeks of unpaid leave per year for certain medical (including childbirth) and immediate/family health care needs.

Recruiting and Selection

Organizational recruiting and selection pose many opportunities for unintentional discrimination. Knowledge of appropriate antidiscrimination law affords protection to managers, human resource professionals, and anyone involved in the recruiting and selection process.

Legally defensible, discrimination-free recruiting begins with a thorough job analysis that identifies the education, knowledge, and skills needed by candidates to successfully perform the functions of the job. Appropriate job postings and announcements are free of biased, potentially discriminatory language. Effective recruiting and selection seeks the most qualified candidate for the position and is, in essence, color blind.

Employee Screening. Common candidate-screening methods include written applications, personal interviews, preemployment examinations, and reference checks. Application forms must be carefully checked to ensure that requests for information comply with antidiscrimination laws.

Most candidates seriously considered for available positions are asked to participate in one or more face-to-face interviews. The interview process, however, is often fraught with potentially discriminatory behavior on the part of interviewers, particularly when they have limited knowledge or experience with the hiring process and antidiscrimination laws. Candidates are often asked illegal questions, usually unintentionally, by individuals or panels of interviewers seeking seemingly harmless yet valuable information. Questions that are not job related are prohibited. Table 5.2 lists a sampling of illegal questions commonly asked in interviews, along with acceptable, appropriate job-related queries. Illegal questions, which are best avoided, deal with issues such as:

- Age and gender
- Health
- Marital status
- Children and family plans
- Race or religion
- Non-job-related topics

A colleague of ours recently interviewed with the president of a medium-size organization and was asked the following questions in rapid succession: How old are you? Are you married? Do you have children? Do you plan to have any more? The human resources manager overheard this exchange, was appalled, and quickly took the president aside and informed him of the error of his ways. He was genuinely surprised that these questions were not appropriate. In his mind, they served a genuine business need (to have a stable workforce). Legal questions ask for information related to a bona fide occupational qualification (BFOQ), that is, something reasonably necessary to perform normal operations of a particular job within a firm.

Employee examinations (physical, mental, drug) are commonplace yet sometimes controversial screening instruments. Physical and mental examinations and drug tests of employees may be required as a condition of employment, and are increasingly required by institutions seeking to protect their workforce provided that the examinee's privacy is not unreasonably violated.

Performance tests (typing tests, curriculum development, and so forth) allow candidates to demonstrate sample skills required of the job. Demonstrations of teaching effectiveness, for example, allow interviewers to observe the candidate's knowledge of the topic, organization and/or facilitation skills.

Table 5.2 Illegal and Legal Questions

Law/Topic	Illegal Questions	Allowable Questions
Civil Rights Acts of 1964 and 1991	Are you married? Do you plan to marry? Do you have children? Do you plan to have children? How many? To what social or religious organizations do you belong? What is your religion? What religious holidays do you observe? What is your maiden name? What country are you from? Where are your parents from?	To which professional or job-related organizations do you belong? Are you able to travel on weekends? What is your current address? These are the normal hours and days of work required of our employees. Are you able to work these hours?
Age Discrimination in Employment Act of 1967	How old are you? In what year did you graduate from high school?	Are you over 18? Do you meet the minimum age requirements as set by law?
Vocational Rehabilitation Act of 1973 and Americans with Disabilities Act of 1990	Do you have a mental or physical disability? How many days were you absent from work due to your disability?	Are you able to perform the essential functions of the position with or without reasonable accommodations? How many days were you absent or late from your previous work for any reason?
Pregnancy Discrimination Act of 1978	Are you pregnant? Do you plan to have children?	Are you able to perform the functions of the position with or without reasonable accommodations?
Immigration Reform and Control Act of 1986	Do you plan to become a citizen of the U.S.?	Are you legally authorized to work in the United States?

Reference checks are another common and increasingly important screening device. Most institutions utilize a character reference or an employment and educational record check to confirm the validity of candidates' stated information. Organizations that fail to conduct reference checks may be held liable if their personnel behave inappropriately and a reference check would have revealed previous similar behavior. Conversely, honest reference information is becoming increasingly difficult to obtain in our litigious society. Providing "negative" information regarding employees has been deemed defamation, or worse, in some lawsuits. Defamation is the "unprivileged publication of a false oral or written statement that harms the reputation of another person." The communication of negative information about an applicant could be unlawful if untrue, malicious, or conveyed to someone who is not a party with a legitimate need to know. As a result, those providing reference information are advised to confine their responses to verifiable facts (employment dates, positions held), and make certain the employee has provided written consent to do so.

More and more institutions run *credit checks* on potential employees, particularly for those candidates who will have access to cash, budgets, or other valuable resources. Candidates must be informed of the institution's intent to conduct a credit check and must provide written consent.

Performance Appraisals

Most institutions engage in some form of regular (e.g., annual, semiannual, quarterly) employee performance evaluation. When these performance assessments provide the basis for personnel decisions (e.g., advancement, salary adjustment, transfer, participation in training, demotion, termination), the development and use of appraisal instruments become important legal concerns. Although it is impossible to design and execute a performance appraisal system that is completely safe from litigation, steps can be taken to reduce the occurrence of discrimination:

1. Thoroughly analyze the job to determine skills and characteristics necessary to successful performance.
2. Observable, verifiable, job-related success characteristics should be incorporated into the rating instrument. These characteristics should be specific, avoiding general personality traits that are difficult to measure.
3. Performance standards and expectations should be communicated, in writing, to all employees.
4. Users of the instrument (e.g., managers, supervisors) should be trained in its proper use.
5. All evaluations, performance appraisal meetings, and reasons for follow-up personnel actions (positive or negative) should be documented.
6. The performance appraisal system should be constantly monitored, evaluated, and modified to ensure its timeliness and relevance, and that performance measures have not become outdated or irrelevant.

Termination

Nontenured employees and managers can be discharged upon expiration of their contracts via simple nonrenewal of the contract. *At will* employees can be fired for any reason, or no reason at all. An improper motive, however, one that violates federal law, state law, or public policy, may result in a finding of wrongful discharge and punishment for the employer.

Tenured employees and those subject to powerful union contracts are difficult to discharge except under extreme circumstances (e.g., violation of the law on the employee's part, elimination of his or her position), and even then are still subject to due process. In all situations, managers should keep accurate and detailed written documentation of the worker's actions.

Conclusion

The legal environment surrounding all organizations represents a complex, constantly changing maze of rules and regulations that must be understood and incorporated into daily working life. Leaders, managers, and supervisors must recognize the potential problems, opportunities, and legal guidelines to which they are subject in the management of human resources. A host of laws, nondiscriminatory and otherwise, provide guidelines for successfully running an organization. Effective organizations and their members understand the relevant laws and demonstrate appropriate behavior.

Resources: Age Discrimination in Employment Act of 1967, 29 U.S.C. § 621 *et seq.* Equal Employment Opportunity Commission. "Information for the Private Sector and State and Local Governments." Family and Medical Leave Act of 1993, 29 U.S.C. §§ 2601–2654. National Labor Relations Act, 29 U.S.C. §§ 151–169. Pregnancy Discrimination Act of 1979, 42 U.S.C. § 2000e(k). Sexual Harassment Charges EEOC & FEPAs Combined: FY 1992–FY 2005. http://www.eeoc.gov/types/sexual_harassment.html (accessed November 20, 2006). Uniform Guidelines on Employee Selection Procedures (1978). 29 Code of Federal Regulations, Part 1607. HRTools.com. http://www.hrtools.com. Provides online information about compliance with EEO/diversity, sexual harassment, ADA, and discipline and termination regulations.

Ann Gilley and Jerry W. Gilley

NOTES

1. U.S. Equal Employment Opportunity Commission, "Information for the Private Sector and State and Local Governments."

2. U.S. Equal Employment Opportunity Commission Web site, http://www.eeoc.gov (accessed October 2, 2007).

AFFIRMATIVE ACTION

Affirmative action is the result of executive orders signed by Presidents Kennedy, Johnson, and Nixon. These orders were intended to facilitate equal employment opportunity as mandated by Title VII of the Civil Rights Act of 1964 and the Equal Employment Opportunity Act of 1972.[1] The orders required that federal contractors take proactive (or "affirmative") action to stop unfair discrimination in hiring and employment due to race, color, religion, sex, or national origin, and as a remedy for past discrimination.[2] Although private industry was not affected by the orders, many companies voluntarily adopted affirmative action programs to ensure that they were in compliance with equal opportunity laws and therefore avoid being sued by employees who felt that they had been discriminated against.[3] Affirmative action is a very controversial topic. It is not clear whether or not affirmative action programs have been effective or efficient in terms of actually providing equal employment opportunity. As it deals with issues of racial and gender discrimination, there are heated debates over issues of fairness as well.

The Case for Affirmative Action

Proponents of affirmative action maintain that without it, discrimination against underrepresented minority groups would be rampant. Many employees who have been discriminated against would not have the resources or even knowledge of being discriminated against to be able to sue under the EEO laws. Generally, affirmative action programs have resulted in greater employment for women and minority groups in the workplace, although these programs may not necessarily have any influence on subsequent promotion or advancement of underrepresented groups.[4] In fact, despite affirmative action, women and people of color are still paid less to the dollar than white males, indicating that affirmative action programs are still necessary.[5]

The Case against Affirmative Action

There have been some challenges lately to affirmative action, arguing that instead of equalizing opportunity, the law actually discriminates against the majority of employees (e.g., white males, known as reverse discrimination), and results in de facto quotas. Affirmative action programs can also result in backlash against employees perceived to be hired as a result of it.[6] The perception is that they have been hired regardless of qualifications and must overcome the bias by other employees that they are unqualified for the job. Simply because of race or gender, an employee's qualifications are immediately questioned because the assumption is that the hire was based solely on race or gender.

There are other problems with affirmative action programs. Potential employees in the majority can react negatively to the presence of affirmative action programs at an organization due to perceptions that the programs are unfair.[7] It has been argued that at the federal level, affirmative action has resulted in preferential hiring of African Americans over Hispanics, such that African Americans are overrepresented in the federal government workforce.[8] This argument calls into question whether or not equal employment opportunity actually exists for every underrepresented group.

Conclusion

Affirmative action is a remedy designed to redress past discrimination and to prevent further discrimination in hiring on the basis of race, color, religion, sex, or national origin. Affirmative action programs have been put in place in both federal and private organizations to ensure equal access to employment for all groups. Both the effectiveness and the efficiency of affirmative action have been called into question, and there is no definitive consensus on whether or not affirmative action programs should be continued.

NOTES

1. Carl A. Kogut and Larry Short, "Affirmative Action in Federal Employment: Good Intentions Run Amok?" *Public Personnel Management,* Fall 2007, 197–206.

2. Caitlin Knowles Myers, "A Cure for Discrimination? Affirmative Action and the Case of California's Proposition 209," *Industrial and Labor Relations Review* 60, no. 3 (April 2006): 379–96.

3. Ward Thomas and Mark Garrett, "U.S. and California Affirmative Action Policies, Laws, and Programs," In *Effects of Affirmative Action: Policies and Consequences in California,* ed. Paul Ong (Walnut Creek, CA: Alta Mira, 1999).

4. Francine D. Blau and Anne E. Winkler, "Does Affirmative Action Work?" *Regional Review* (1st Qtr., 2005): 38–40.

5. Ibid.

6. Lisa M. Zurk, Barbara Simons, Rebecca Parsons, and Dawn Cohen, "When an Advantage Is Not an Advantage," *Communications of the ACM* 38, no. 12 (December 1995): 17–18.

7. H. Jack Walker, Hubert S. Feild, William F. Giles, Jeremy B. Bernerth, and Allison Jones Farmer, "An Assessment of Attraction toward Affirmative Action Organizations: Investigating the Role of Individual Differences," *Journal of Organizational Behavior* 28, no. 4 (June, 2007): 485–507.

8. Carl A. Kogut and Larry Short, "Affirmative Action in Federal Employment: Good Intentions Run Amok?" *Public Personnel Management,* Fall 2007, 197–206.

Barbara A. W. Eversole

AGE DISCRIMINATION IN EMPLOYMENT ACT (ADEA)

In 1967, the U.S. Congress, recognizing the need to protect the employment rights of older workers, enacted the Age Discrimination in Employment Act of 1967 (ADEA). The key provision of the ADEA protects individuals, 40 years of age and older, from employment discrimination based on age. This protection is wide ranging and prohibits discrimination against an individual relative to any term, condition, or privilege of employment including hiring, firing, promotion, layoff, compensation, benefits, job assignments or training. The ADEA applies to employers, employment agencies, and labor organizations with 20 or more employees.

Background

The genesis of the ADEA is linked to the passage of Title VII of the 1964 Civil Rights Act.[1] Title VII bans workplace discrimination based on race, color, sex, national origin, and religion. What was absent, however, was a prohibition against age discrimination. Upon passage of Title VII, Congress directed the U.S. Department of Labor to study whether separate age-bias laws were needed. Three years later, a report was delivered to Congress citing clear confirmation of the pervasiveness of age discrimination. The ADEA was enacted supported by the following findings:

- Older workers were disadvantaged in their efforts to retain or regain employment once displaced from a job.
- Setting arbitrary age limits without regard for potential job performance was commonplace.
- Unemployment correlated with deteriorating skills and morale associated with older workers when compared to younger workers.[1]

Purpose

The stated purpose of the ADEA is as follows: "to promote employment of older persons based on their ability rather than age; to prohibit arbitrary age discrimination in employment; to help employers and workers find ways of meeting problems arising from the impact of age on employment."[2] To this end, the statute calls for an ongoing program of research and education to ascertain the needs and abilities of older workers, their potential for employment, and contribution to the economy. Additionally, the results of this research are provided for use to labor unions, management, and the general public to reduce employment barriers for the older worker.

Prohibitions

The statute stipulates that it is an unlawful employment practice for a covered employer "to fail or refuse to hire or to discharge any individual or otherwise to discriminate against any individual with respect to his compensation, terms, conditions, or privileges of employment, because of such individual's age."[3] Furthermore, it is unlawful for an employer to limit, segregate, or classify employees in ways that would adversely affect their employment because of age. Employers may not reduce the wage rate of an employee in order to comply with the act. Requirements necessary to perform the job must be job-related, and job notices or advertisements cannot indicate a preference, limitation, or specification based on age. Seniority systems and benefit plans containing involuntary requirements due to age are unlawful.

Exemptions

While it appears the ADEA provides comprehensive protection against age-based discrimination, there are some exceptions to the statute's nondiscrimination provisions. The ADEA allows employers to discharge or otherwise discipline an employee for any genuine job-related deficiency or misconduct for good cause. Additionally, it allows employers to observe the terms and conditions of a bona fide seniority system, except where such a system is used to require or permit the involuntary retirement of an employee age 40 or over. In very limited circumstances, an employer can use age-based criteria "where age is a bona fide occupational qualification reasonably necessary to the normal operation of the particular business, or where the differentiation is based on reasonable factors other than age."[4] To prevail in this defense, the employer must successfully demonstrate that the age requirement is necessary to safely and appropriately perform the functions of the position.

Enforcement and Procedural Requirements

The enforcement and administration of the ADEA was originally the province of the secretary of labor. Those responsibilities were transferred to the Equal Employment Opportunity Commission (EEOC) effective January 1, 1979, pursuant to a presidential reorganization plan. The EEOC "may issue such rules and regulations as it may consider necessary or appropriate for carrying out this chapter, and may establish such reasonable exemptions to and from any or all provisions of this chapter as it may find necessary and proper in the public interest."[5] The EEOC may also impose fines or mandate jail time to those resisting or interfering during the scope of an EEOC investigation.

The procedural requirements for an ADEA claim are complex. Simply put, a claimant must first file charges with the EEOC alleging unlawful discrimination before an individual may take civil action. The EEOC may conduct investigations on its own initiative and, even though the claimant withdraws his or her charge, the Commission may continue the investigation to the conclusion of the claim. The statute of limitation is two years from the date of an alleged non-willful violation and three years from the date of an alleged willful violation. The claimant does not need to prove age was the only motivating factor behind the employer's decision, but must make a legally sufficient case in which age was one of the determining factors leading to the adverse employer action. Having done so, the responsibility shifts to the employer to provide a legitimate, nondiscriminatory reason for the employee's demotion or termination.

Conclusion

The Age Discrimination in Employment Act of 1967 has been in existence for more than 40 years. Credit is given to the ADEA for eliminating many forms of age-based discrimination in the workplace that were commonplace before its enactment. With the passage of time, it has almost been forgotten that it was commonplace for companies, before 1967, to have mandatory retirement policies and for employment ads to freely assert age requirements as a condition for employment. Others question whether "the ADEA has done more than address age discrimination in its most blatant manifestations. The notion that older people have had their day and should make room for the next generation continues to be deeply ingrained."[6] Although this difference of opinion may never be resolved to everyone's satisfaction, the courts continue, with each new ruling, to redefine and shape the expectations of both employees and employers alike.

See also Bona Fide Occupational Qualification (BFOQ); Older Workers Benefit Protection Act

NOTES

1. "Fighting Ageism, Through the Ages," *AARP,* July–August 2003, http://www.aarpmagazine.org/lifestyle/Articles/a2003-05-21-mag-agediscrimination.html (accessed July 26, 2007).

2. Age Discrimination in Employment Act of 1967, Pub. L. No. 90-202, § 621, 29 Stat. 1 (1967).

3. Ibid.

4. Ibid.

5. Ibid.

6. Robert Grossman, "The Under-reported Impact of Age Discrimination and Its Threat to Business Vitality," *Business Horizons,* 48, no. 1 (January–February 2005): 71–78.

Linda S. Dorré

AMERICANS WITH DISABILITIES ACT (ADA)

The Americans with Disabilities Act (ADA) of 1990 created many rights for disabled individuals and new responsibilities for employers. The ADA applies to any employer with 15 or more employees, and it prohibits any discrimination against qualified individuals with disabilities. The ADA encompasses all terms and conditions of employment, including the application process, interviewing, hiring, firing, advancement, job training, and compensation.

ADA Provisions and Key Terms

The ADA goes beyond prohibiting discrimination by also requiring employers to take actions to provide reasonable accommodations that would enable a qualified individual with a disability to be considered for the job and perform its essential functions. In order to fully understand the ADA, it is important to have a good understanding of the key terms and how the ADA defines these terms.

Disability

The term "disability" means, with respect to an individual, (1) a physical or mental impairment that substantially limits one or more of the major life activities of such individual; (2) a record of such an impairment; or (3) being regarded as having such an impairment.[1]

Qualified Individual with a Disability

The term "qualified individual with a disability" means an individual with a disability who, with or without reasonable accommodation, can perform the essential functions of the employment position that such individual holds or desires.[2]

Essential Function

The essential functions of a job are the primary job duties that an individual must be able to perform, with or without accommodation. Criteria used when determining if a function is considered essential includes (1) if the job exists in order to perform that particular function, (2) if the function is specialized and requires special training or expertise, and (3) if there are a limited number of other employees who could perform the function.

For the purposes of the ADA, consideration shall be given to the employer's judgment as to what functions of a job are essential, and if an employer has prepared a written description before advertising or interviewing applicants for the job, this description shall be considered evidence of the essential functions of the job.[3]

Reasonable Accommodations

The term "reasonable accommodation" may include (1) making existing facilities used by employees readily accessible to and usable by individuals with disabilities; and (2) job restructuring, part-time or modified work schedules, reassignment to a vacant position, acquisition or modification of equipment or devices, appropriate adjustment or modifications of examinations, training materials or policies, the provision of qualified readers or interpreters, and other similar accommodations for individuals with disabilities.[4]

Undue Hardship

The ADA does allow exception to the reasonable accommodation requirement, if that accommodation would create an undue hardship on the employer. The term "undue hardship" is defined by the ADA as an action requiring significant difficulty or expense, when considered in light of certain factors. The ADA lists certain factors that can be considered when determining if an accommodation creates an undue hardship. These include:

1. The nature and cost of the accommodation needed under this act;
2. The overall financial resources of the facility or facilities involved in the provision of the reasonable accommodation; the number of persons employed at such facility; the effect on expenses and resources, or the impact otherwise of such accommodation upon the operation of the facility;
3. The overall financial resources of the covered entity; the overall size of the business of a covered entity with respect to the number of its employees; the number, type, and location of its facilities; and
4. The type of operation or operations of the covered entity, including the composition, structure, and functions of the workforce of such entity; the geographic separateness, administrative, or fiscal relationship of the facility or facilities in question to the covered entity.

Reasonable Accommodation Process

The process for identifying a reasonable accommodation for a qualified individual with a disability should be an interactive process between the individual and employer. The Society for Human Resource Management (SHRM) has identified a five-step process that may be used for identifying a reasonable accommodation. The steps of this process include:[5]

1. Individual asks for accommodation.
2. Identify the barriers to performance of essential job functions for each individual.
3. Identify possible accommodations that might be helpful in overcoming the barriers.
4. Assess the reasonableness of the accommodations, including whether they are the employer's responsibility and whether they impose any undue hardship.
5. Choose the appropriate accommodation for each individual.

Some reasonable accommodations may include things such as job restructuring, assigning nonessential functions to another person, providing a reader to a blind applicant, modifying a work schedule, or building ramps for wheelchair access to a building. A reasonable accommodation does not include lowering quality or performance standards, or actions that would create an undue hardship.

Enforcement and Penalties for Noncompliance

The ADA is enforced by the Equal Employment Opportunity Commission (EEOC). Individuals who feel their ADA rights have been violated can file a charge of discrimination with the EEOC within 180 days of the date of the alleged violation.

Employers who do not follow the provisions of the ADA are held to the same penalties as violations of Title VII of the Civil Rights Act. In 2006, the EEOC awarded over $48.7 million in monetary benefits to charging parties of ADA claims (this figure does not include any additional monetary awards received through litigation).[6]

See also Reasonable Accommodation; Undue Hardship

NOTES

1. U.S. Department of Labor, "The Americans with Disabilities Act of 1990" U.S. Government, http://www.dol.gov/esa/regs/statutes/ofccp/ada.htm (accessed September 18, 2007).

2. Ibid.

3. Ibid.

4. Ibid.

5. Society for Human Resource Management, *The SHRM Learning System Module 2: Workforce Planning and Employment* (Alexandria, VA: Society for Human Resource Management, 2007), 12–16.

6. U.S. Equal Employment Opportunity Commission, "ADA Charge Data—Monetary Benefits," U.S. Government, http://www.eeoc.gov/stats/ada-monetary.html (accessed September 20, 2007).

Shanan M. Mahoney

BONA FIDE OCCUPATIONAL QUALIFICATION (BFOQ)

The term bona fide occupational qualification (BFOQ) is used to describe a situation when a protected class, such as gender, religion, ethnicity, or age is deemed to be necessary to carry out a particular job function.

BFOQs under Title VII

The Civil Rights Act of 1964 provides allowances for situations when gender, religion, or ethnicity are determined to be "reasonably necessary to the normal operations of the business or enterprise," and states that in these situations, it is permissible to use these factors when making employment decisions.[1] The following are examples of allowable BFOQs:

- A clothing company may require that women be hired as the models for evening gowns.
- To be an ordained minister of a particular church, religion may be used as a qualification.
- A movie company may hire Native Americans for roles in a film documenting American Indian tribes.

Title VII does not provide any allowances for using race or color as a BFOQ.

BFOQs under the ADEA

The Age Discrimination in Employment Act (ADEA) also provides for exceptions in cases where age is determined to be a BFOQ. For example, a clothing company specializing in teenage clothing styles can hire a young person to model their clothes in a magazine. In the case of public safety officers, such as police or firefighters, the ADEA also allows for upper age limits in hiring and mandatory-retirement age BFOQs.

Conclusion

Although BFOQs are allowable exceptions to Title VII and the ADEA, the courts closely scrutinize any defense claims of BFOQ. It is important that a BFOQ be directly related to the job. Human resource professionals can best determine if a BFOQ exists by conducting a thorough job analysis for a position to not only identify the knowledge, skills, and abilities required for a position, but also if there are any BFOQs related to the position.

See also Civil Rights Act of 1964 and 1991; Age Discrimination in Employment Act (ADEA)

Resources:

Society for Human Resource Management. *The SHRM Learning System Module 2: Workforce Planning and Employment.* Alexandria, VA: Society for Human Resource Management, 2007, 26–28.

NOTE

1. David A. DeCenzo and Stephen P. Robbins, *Human Resource Management,* 6th ed. (New York: John Wiley & Sons, Inc., 1999), 77–79.

Shanan M. Mahoney

CHILD LABOR

Child labor, and the laws within the United States that govern the practice, typically apply to individuals under the age of 18. At this age, an individual is legally permitted to work a job of choice for any number of hours, as child labor laws are no longer applicable.[1] Current child labor laws are a result of the passage of the Fair Labor Standards Act of 1938 (FLSA) and the numerous amendments to its language.

Fair Labor Standards Act

The Fair Labor Standards Act, and the child labor provisions contained within it, is intended to protect the educational opportunities of persons younger than 18 years of age, and to prohibit their employment under conditions that may be detrimental or hazardous to their health.[2] The U.S. Department of Labor is the sole federal agency responsible for enforcement of the FLSA, and child labor provisions are handled by the Wage and Hour Division of the department's Employment Standards Administration.[3]

Regulations enacted by the FLSA may be broadly subdivided into agricultural and nonagricultural employment. For nonagricultural jobs, the type of work that may be performed is a function of the age of the youth. Employment permitted may be broken down as follows:

— Persons 18 or older may perform any job, whether hazardous or not.
— Persons 16 or 17 may perform any nonhazardous job (applicable laws, either state or federal, should be consulted for a determination of a hazardous occupation).

— Persons 14 or 15 may work outside of school hours in various nonmanufacturing, nonmining, and nonhazardous jobs, and only under certain conditions that may vary by state. Additional restrictions apply to the number of hours that may be worked in a given day or week, depending upon whether or not school is in session, and to the time of day, regardless of school considerations. Exceptions may apply if the youth is enrolled in an approved Work Experience and Career Exploration Program (WECEP).[4]

— Persons 13 or younger may be employed in such jobs as newspaper delivery; act in television, radio, motion picture, or theatrical productions; and perform babysitting or other such minor chores around a private home or residence. Additionally, youths may work at businesses owned by their parents, as long as such employment complies with statues regarding nonmanufacturing, nonmining, and nonhazardous conditions.[5]

Different age requirements apply to youth employed in agriculture. Consult the appropriate U.S. Department of Labor Wage and Hour Division district office or state department of labor to ensure any youth-related labor practices are in compliance.[6]

International Concerns and Related Issues

The Bureau of International Labor Affairs (ILAB) has among its responsibilities to investigate and report on potentially abusive child labor practices outside the United States.[7] The Office of Child Labor, Forced Labor, and Human Trafficking (OCFT), one of three offices reporting to the ILAB, was created in 1993 in response to a congressional request to handle such activities. In recent years, as both domestic and international concern and awareness regarding exploitive child labor, forced labor, and human trafficking have grown, the OCFT has seen a corresponding increase in matters it oversees. To fulfill its purpose, the OCFT is involved in researching and reporting on international child labor conditions and practices, overseeing cooperative agreements and contracts to groups outside of the United States who are attempting to eliminate the most egregious forms of child labor, and assisting with the development and implementation of government policies related to child labor, forced labor, and human trafficking matters.[8] Among the laws and regulations the ILAB has responsibility for enforcement is Executive Order 13126, titled "Prohibition of Acquisition of Products Produced by Forced or Indentured Child Labor." Under procurement regulations, federal contractors who supply products on a list published by the Department of Labor must provide certification that a good-faith effort has been made to determine if forced or indentured child labor was utilized in the production of such items. This list is subject to periodic updates, and can be accessed by contacting the U.S. Department of Labor.[9]

The United Nations Children's Fund, or UNICEF, uses its global authority and influence to attempt to reduce and eliminate many forms of child labor considered adverse and dangerous to the well-being of children, as well.[10] Although it operates independently of the U.S. government and does not possess any sovereign authority, it can propose economic sanctions be taken by member nations of the United Nations against certain countries, if such actions are deemed necessary and appropriate by both UNICEF and the international community.

Potential Fallout for Employers

Many instances exist of companies that have experienced adverse consequences for failing to conduct the proper due diligence of the manufacture of their products.

This includes, but is not limited to, negative press and other publicity, lawsuits, and consumer boycotts against a firm for utilizing child labor. Additionally, what is legal and customary regarding child labor standards and practices in developing nations, where a firm may contract labor services for the manufacture of its products, may be seen as abusive and exploitative in wealthier ones. Companies must be cognizant of the facilities that bear their name and the workers present within them, especially in countries outside the United States. Several have paid a steep price, financial and otherwise, for failing to do so.

NOTES

1. U.S. Department of Labor, Wage and Hour Division. "Youth Rules!—What Jobs Can Youth Do?" http://www.youthrules.dol.gov/jobs.htm (accessed December 18, 2007).

2. U.S. Department of Labor, OASP/Office of Compliance Assistance Policy. "Child Labor (Nonagricultural Work): Who is Covered," http://www.dol.gov/compliance/guide/childlbr.htm (accessed December 18, 2007).

3. U.S. Department of Labor. "Youth & Labor," http://www.dol.gov/dol/topic/youthlabor/index.htm (accessed December 19, 2007).

4. U.S. Department of Labor, OASP/Office of Compliance Assistance Policy. "Child Labor (Nonagricultural Work): Who is Covered," http://www.dol.gov/compliance/guide/childlbr.htm (accessed December 18, 2007); and U.S. Department of Labor. "Youth & Labor: Work Hours," http://www.dol.gov/dol/topic/youthlabor/workhours.htm (accessed December 19, 2007).

5. U.S. Department of Labor, elaws—Fair Labor Standards Act Advisor, "What Kinds of Work Can Youth Perform?" http://www.dol.gov/elaws/faq/esa/flsa/029.htm (accessed December 19, 2007); and U.S. Department of Labor, Wage and Hour Division. "Youth Rules!—What Jobs Can Youth Do?"

6. U.S. Department of Labor, "Youth & Labor: DOL Web Pages on This Topic," http://www.dol.gov/dol/topic/youthlabor/workhours.htm (accessed December 18, 2007).

7. U.S. Department of Labor, "Youth & Labor: International Child Labor," http://www.dol.gov/dol/topic/youthlabor/intlchildlabor.htm (accessed December 18, 2007).

8. U.S. Department of Labor, Office of Child Labor, Forced Labor, and Human Trafficking (OCFT), "About OCFT," http://www.dol.gov/ilab/programs/ocft/ (accessed December 19, 2007).

9. U.S. Department of Labor, Bureau of International Labor Affairs. "Executive Order 13126" http://www.dol.gov/ilab/regs/eo13126/main.htm (accessed December 21, 2007).

10. UNICEF. "About UNICEF: Who We Are," http://www.unicef.org/about/who/index.html (accessed December 21, 2007).

Steven J. Kerno Jr.

CIVIL RIGHTS ACTS OF 1964 AND 1991

The Civil Rights Acts of 1964 and 1991 were designed to prohibit discrimination in public places. Highlights of each will be discussed.

Civil Rights Act of 1964

The Civil Rights Act (CRA) was signed into law on July 2, 1964, by President Lyndon B. Johnson. The CRA prohibited discrimination in public places, made discrimination in employment illegal, and provided for the integration of schools and other public facilities. A public facility was any place that received any form of federal funding, which ultimately was most places. The CRA

- Prohibited unequal application of voter registration requirements, although it did not abolish literacy tests (occasionally used to disqualify poor white voters and African Americans).
- Barred discrimination in all public accommodations (e.g., hotels, motels, restaurants, theaters) engaged in interstate commerce, yet exempted private clubs.
- Made it illegal for state and municipal governments to deny access to public facilities on the basis of one's race, religion, or ethnicity.
- Prohibited discrimination by government agencies that receive federal funding; if found guilty of discrimination, the offending agency may lose its federal funding.

Title VII

One of the most well-known features of the CRA is found in Title VII, which prohibits discrimination by covered employers on the basis of race, color, religion, sex, or national origin. Covered employers are those who employ 15 or more workers for more than 19 weeks in the current or preceding calendar year. Title VII prohibits sexual harassment (including same-sex harassment), which is a form of sex discrimination, and discrimination against an individual due to his or her association with someone of a particular race, color, religion, sex, or national origin. Further, retaliation against employees who report or oppose such discrimination is unlawful.

In situations where religion, sex, or national origin is a bona fide occupational qualification (BFOQ) that is reasonably necessary to the normal operation of a particular business, covered employers are allowed to discriminate on the basis of religion, sex, or national origin. A BFOQ defense requires employers to prove (1) a direct relationship between gender and the ability to perform the duties of the job, (2) the BFOQ is directly related to the essence or "central mission" of the business, and (3) there is no less-restrictive or reasonable alternative. Exceptions to Title VII exist for Native American tribes, bona fide nonprofit private membership organizations, and certain religious group activities.

Enforcement

Title VII of the CRA is enforced by the Equal Employment Opportunity Commission (EEOC) and some state fair-employment practices agencies, which investigate, mediate, and may file lawsuits on behalf of employees. Individuals must file discrimination complaints with the EEOC within 180 days of learning of the discrimination, or they may lose the right to file a lawsuit.

Civil Rights Act of 1991

The Civil Rights Act of 1991 strengthened the CRA of 1964. Under this act, parties may now obtain jury trials and recover both compensatory and punitive damages in Title VII and ADA lawsuits involving intentional discrimination. Title VII plaintiffs may also recover damages for emotional distress, although the act imposes caps on relief for punitive and emotional distress damages based on size of the employer. Technical changes to the act concern length of time allowed to challenge seniority provisions, to bring age discrimination claims, and the ability to sue the federal government for discrimination. Successful plaintiffs may also recover expert witness fees and collect interest on judgments against the federal government.

The CRA of 1991 added a new subsection to Title VII that clarified the disparate impact theory of discrimination. It provided that an employee could prove disparate impact by showing that an individual or group of practices resulted in "disparate impact on the basis of race, color, religion, sex, or national origin, and the respondent fails to demonstrate that such practice is required by business necessity."

Conclusion

The Civil Rights Acts of 1964 and 1991 strengthen and improve federal civil rights laws, specifically prohibiting numerous forms of discrimination in the public and private sectors.

See also Employment Law: An Overview; Bona Fide Occupational Qualification (BFOQ)

Resources:
Civil Rights Act of 1964 (42 USC 2000).
Civil Rights Act of 1991 (42 USC 1981).
Our Documents. http://www.ourdocuments.gov/..
U.S. Equal Employment Opportunity Commission. "Laws, Regulations and Policy Guidance." http://www.eeoc.gov/policy.

Ann Gilley

COBRA

The Consolidated Omnibus Budget Reconciliation Act, or COBRA, gives workers or their families who lose their health benefits the right to continue to purchase group health insurance that was lost due to certain job-related or life-related circumstances. Job-related circumstances include such things as loss of employment, either voluntary or involuntary, reduction in work hours, and transition between jobs. Life-related circumstances include such things as divorce, and death of the provider. The cost of health insurance under COBRA can be as much as 102 percent of the premium, to be paid by the individual. COBRA applies to companies that have group health insurance plans for 20 or more of their employees. COBRA authorizes only temporary extensions of health coverage.

Background

Prior to Congress passing COBRA in 1986, there was no provision for employees to maintain group health care coverage when there was a change in their employment status or when there was a change in dependant status, such as former spouses just after a divorce. Congress changed this in 1986 by passing COBRA, which allowed the employee, former employee, or family members to obtain temporary group health insurance coverage. COBRA insurance coverage is only a temporary provision, and the entire cost, plus a 2 percent administrative fee, is now payable by the employee, former employee, or dependants.

COBRA General Guidelines

Companies with group health plans for 20 or more employees on more than 50 percent of its typical business days in the previous calendar year are subject to COBRA.

To be eligible for continued health insurance coverage under COBRA, the employee must have been enrolled in the company-provided group health care plan, and that group plan must still be in effect for current employees. Employees and/or their dependants become eligible for coverage under COBRA when a "qualifying event" takes place.

Qualifying Events for the Employee
The following are some of the qualifying events for the employee/former employee:

1. Voluntary or involuntary employment termination except for reasons of gross misconduct
2. Reduction in work hours

Qualifying Events for Spouses

1. Voluntary or involuntary termination of the covered employee's employment for any reason other than gross misconduct
2. Reduction in the hours worked by the covered employee
3. Covered employees becoming entitled to Medicare
4. Divorce or legal separation of the covered employee
5. Death of the covered employee

Qualifying events for dependent children are the same as for spouses with the addition of loss of dependent child status under the plan rules.

Length of COBRA Coverage
COBRA coverage is generally guaranteed for a period of 18 months following the event that allowed for coverage under COBRA. If the employee became eligible for Medicare, then the coverage period for COBRA could be extended to 36 months.

Responsibilities under COBRA

The employer, insurance plan administrator, and individual have responsibilities under COBRA.

Employer Responsibilities
The employer has the responsibility to notify the insurance plan administer within 30 days of the employee's death, termination, eligibility for Medicare, or reduction in work hours.

Insurance Plan Administrator
The insurance plan administrator has the responsibility to send an election notice to the individual. The election notice should be sent not later than 14 days after receipt of the notice from the employer.

Individual Responsibilities
The individual affected, either the employee or his/her dependents, have 60 days to elect to continue medical insurance coverage under COBRA, and 45 days to pay the first premium after election of coverage.

What Is Covered under COBRA

COBRA is a provision to provide health insurance coverage for medical care under a group plan. Medical care covers the following:

1. Inpatient and outpatient hospital care
2. Physician care
3. Surgery and other major medical benefits
4. Prescription drugs
5. Dental and vision care

Note: Life insurance and disability coverage are *not* considered medical care and are not covered under COBRA.

Conclusion

COBRA provides continuing group health insurance coverage to employees, former employees, and their dependents. The entire cost of insurance under COBRA is paid for by the individual. The employer does not have financial responsibility for continued health care coverage under COBRA.

Resource
U.S. Department of Labor Web site. http://www.dol.gov/dol/topic/health-plans/cobra.htm.

Henry H. Luckel Jr.

DEFAMATION

According to *Black's Law Dictionary,* defamation is the act of harming the reputation of another by making a false statement to a third person.[1] It is causing harm to another's good name. Defamation is not a criminal act, but a tort, defined broadly as a civil wrong. There are two types of defamation—libel and slander. Libel is committed by the written publication of matter that tends to injure a person's reputation, while slander is spoken. As noted above, both libelous and slanderous actions "must have been published to some third person and must have been capable of defamatory meaning and understood as referring to the plaintiff in a defamatory sense."[2]

Elements

There are specific elements of a defamation claim that must be met in order for actions to be found to be defamatory. Elements for both libel and slander claims vary from state to state, but are generally as follows:[3]

1. The statement must be false. True statements may be hurtful to one's reputation, but cannot legally be defined as being defamatory. In a pending or potential lawsuit, the burden of proof lies with the defendant; this means that the defendant has the responsibility of proving the statement is true rather than the plaintiff (the alleged defamed) proving the statement to be false.
2. In cases of libel claims, written publication does not literally mean published and printed but, rather, a communication to the public at large.

3. The statement needs to clearly be of and concerning the plaintiff. For example, a statement such as "Managers at this company are embezzlers" cannot be defined as defamatory, as it does not address a specific person, but rather a group of people. In the case that the said company has only one manager, this may be considered to be defamatory.
4. With regard to damages, the person claiming to have been defamed must have been damaged in some way, such as reputation, economic, etc. "The wrongs and correlative rights recognized by the law of slander and libel are in their nature material rather than spiritual."[4] In other words, the law does not compensate for mere injury to one's feelings.

Defenses

The most important defense to an action for defamation is *truth,* which is an absolute defense to an action for defamation.[5]

Another defense to defamation is *privilege.* One example of privilege is statements made by witnesses or attorneys in courtroom proceedings. Statements made in the course of legislative proceedings or federal executive officials while exercising the functions of their office are also ordinarily privileged and cannot support a cause of action for defamation, no matter how false or outrageous.[6] Statements made between spouses are also considered to be privileged.

Another defense recognized in most jurisdictions is *opinion.* "If the person makes a statement of opinion as opposed to fact, the statement may not support a cause of action for defamation."[7] Whether a statement is viewed as fact or opinion can depend upon context; additionally, the law considers whether the person who made the statement would be perceived by an ordinary person as being in a position to know whether or not it is true. For example, if a supervisor calls an employee a thief, it is less likely to be regarded as an opinion than if the same statement were to be made by somebody the employee just met.

A defense similar to opinion is *fair comment on a matter of public interest.*[8] For example, if the CEO of a large company is involved in a corruption scandal, an employee expressing the opinion that he or she believes the allegations are true is not likely to support a cause of action for defamation. Additionally, a defendant may also attempt to show that the plaintiff had a poor reputation in the community to begin with in order to diminish any claim for damages resulting from the defamatory statements. It is very difficult to show damage to the reputation of a person who is already known to have a poor reputation.

Finally, someone who makes a defamatory statement without having awareness of its content may raise the defense of *innocent dissemination.* For example, the post office is not liable for delivering a letter that has defamatory content, as it is not aware of the contents of the letter.[9]

An uncommon defense, but sometimes used, is that the plaintiff consented to the dissemination of the statement.

Public Figures

Public figures cannot generally claim to have been defamed. The definition of a public figure is much broader than, but does include, celebrities and politicians. A person can become an involuntary public figure as the result of publicity, even though that person did not want or invite public attention. Examples of involuntary public figures include those accused of high-profiled crimes, people who appear on television, and partners and family members of politicians and other celebrities. In a typical workplace, a large company's CEO is likely to be a public figure, while a regional supervisor or divisional manager is likely not to be. Under the First Amendment of the U.S. Constitution, as set forth by the U.S. Supreme Court in the 1964 case *New York Times v Sullivan,* where a public figure attempted to bring an action for defamation, "the public figure must prove an additional element: That the statement was made with 'actual malice' [personal ill will]."[10] In other words, if a person is a public figure, another person will not be held liable for defaming him unless the comment was made with "knowledge of its falsity or in reckless disregard of whether it was false or true."[11]

Relevance to HRD

Defamation's presence in the HRD field most often arises in the process of giving reference to former employees. Because the most important, and nonarguable defenses to an action for defamation is *truth,*[12] one must take caution to give only true, factual statements when giving references, especially if the information being shared is negative. To avoid any claim of defamation, it is wisest to operate under the guise that true statements can always be proven. Many believe that it is unlawful to share information that contributes to or causes a former employee not to be hired in a new position; negative information shared that can be proven true cannot be claimed to be defaming.

NOTES

1. Bryan A. Garner, ed., *Black's Law Dictionary,* 8th ed. (St. Paul, MN: Thomson West, 2004).

2. William A. Kaplin and Barbara A. Lee, *A Legal Guide for Student Affairs Professionals* (San Francisco: Jossey-Bass, Inc., 1997), 102.

3. Aaron Larson, "Defamation, Libel, and Slander Law, 2003,"http://www.expertlaw.com/library/personal_injury/defamation.html (accessed February 19, 2007).

4. Samuel Warren and Louis D. Brandeis, "The Right to Privacy," *Harvard Law Review* 193 (1890): 7.

5. Larson, "Defamation, Libel, and Slander Law, 2003."

6. Ibid.

7. Ibid., 11.

8. Ibid.

9. Ibid.

10. Ibid., 15.

11. *Garrison v. Louisiana,* 379 U.S. 64, 71 (1964).

12. Ibid.

Lea Hanson

DISPARATE TREATMENT/DISPARATE IMPACT

Employment discrimination cases are considered either "disparate treatment" or "disparate impact" cases. Title VII of the Civil Rights Act of 1964 prohibits employers from treating applicants or employees differently due to their membership in a protected class. Under *disparate treatment,* an employee claims that the employer treated him or her differently than other employees who were in a similar situation because of his or her membership in a protected class (e.g., due to gender, nationality, religion, etc.) In a *disparate impact* case, the employee claims that some employer practice or practices have a much greater negative impact on one group than another. For example, an employer that refuses to hire laborers who are not high school graduates might have a bigger impact on blacks or Hispanics as a whole than on whites. Practices that may be subject to disparate impact challenges include written tests, height and weight requirements, educational requirements (particularly for blue-collar jobs), and subjective procedures such as interviews.

The disparate impact theory is used when there is a large impact based on race, gender, religion, age, or other unlawful factor. Age discrimination cases are included because the Age Discrimination in Employment Act (ADEA) prohibits discrimination against individuals age 40 and over. Even when not motivated by discriminatory intent, employers are prohibited from engaging in practices that have an unjustified adverse impact on members of a protected class, which may be proven by either direct or circumstantial evidence.

Proving Disparate Treatment or Impact

Under the direct method, a plaintiff offers direct evidence that the employer was motivated by the plaintiff's membership in a protected class. Direct evidence may include the defendant's admission of its discriminatory intent, or written documents such as policy statements, e-mails, memoranda, notes, or letters. Typically, direct evidence is scarce, given that most employers do not admit their discriminatory behaviors.

Plaintiffs must often rely on circumstantial evidence to prove disparate treatment or impact. Circumstantial evidence to prove discrimination may include: statistical comparisons; suspicious timing, ambiguous oral or written statements, behavior toward or comments directed at other employees in the protected group, and other activities or behaviors from which an inference of discriminatory intent might be drawn; evidence that other similarly situated employees not in the protected class received systematically better treatment; or evidence that the plaintiff was qualified for but not given the job, someone not in the protected class was given the job, and the employer's reason for its decision is not believable.

Employers usually reply that the employee was fired for a "legitimate, nondiscriminatory reason," to which employees respond by attempting to prove that the employer's reason was simply a pretext or cover-up for an improper reason. If a plaintiff establishes disparate impact, the employer's burden is to prove that the challenged practice is job-related for the position and consistent with business necessity.

See also Civil Rights Act of 1964 and 1991; Age Discrimination in Employment Act (ADEA); Four-fifths Rule

Resources:
Civil Rights Act of 1964 (42 USC 2000).
Civil Rights Act of 1991 (42 USC 1981).
HR-Guide.com. http://www.hr-guide.com/.
Our Documents. http://www.ourdocuments.gov/.
U.S. Department of Labor Web site. http://www.dol.gov.

U.S. Equal Employment Opportunity Commission. "Laws, Regulations and Policy Guidance." http://www.eeoc.gov/policy.

Ann Gilley

DRUG-FREE WORKPLACE ACT

Enacted in 1988, the Drug-Free Workplace Act (DFWA) mandates that companies and individuals contracting with the U.S. government abide by its terms. The threshold amount for federal contracts under this act is $100,000.[1] Contracting employers must enact and enforce policies to ensure a workplace free from controlled substances.

Requirements of the Law

There are four requirements for companies that are covered by the DFWA.

1. Employers must maintain a policy prohibiting drug use/possession/sales in the workplace. The policy should specify a definition of the substances that the employer includes in the policy: illegal narcotics, alcohol, and prescription drugs without a prescription. Also, the policy should fully inform employees about the company's drug testing policy. Finally, the policy should specify the implications of an employee's use of drugs away from the workplace.
2. Employers must promote an educational program for employees to assist them in maintaining drug-free lives. The effort to inform employees about the Drug-Free Workplace policy must be ongoing—informing employees once, upon hire, is not sufficient. The program must inform employees about the risks of drug use while at work, the policy, any available counseling or assistance, and the sanctions that could be imposed upon a violator.
3. Employees directly working on the federal contract must inform the employer of any drug-related convictions (stemming from workplace conduct) within five days of the court action.
4. If a work-related drug offense occurs, an employer must enforce a system of disciplinary measures for violations.

What Is Not Required

The employer is not obligated to prohibit the use of alcohol or the abuse of prescription drugs in the workplace. A contracting employer is not required to have an employee assistance program to comply with the act. Also, the covered employer need not perform drug testing to comply with the act.

Sanctions and Enforcement

If a contracting company is found to be in violation of the DFWA, the contracting governmental agency will suspend payments under the contract. The contracting agency will investigate to determine whether the act was violated. Firms that violate the terms of the DFWA are barred from entering into further contracts with any agency of the U.S. government.

See also Americans with Disabilities Act (ADA), Employee Assistance Programs
   Resources:
Drug-Free Workplace Kit. http://www.drugfreeworkplace.gov/WPWorkit/legal.html.

NOTE

1. 41 U.S.C. §§ 701-07.

Laura Dendinger

EMPLOYEE POLYGRAPH PROTECTION ACT (EPPA)

The Employee Polygraph Protection Act of 1988 (EPPA) prohibits employers from using lie detector tests for preemployment screening or during the course of employment, with certain exceptions. In general, employers may not require a job applicant or employee to take a lie detector test. Further, an employer may not discharge, discipline, or discriminate against a job applicant or employee for refusal to take to lie detector test.

Employers may not
- Use lie detector tests
- Inquire about the results of a lie detector test
- Discharge or discriminate against a job applicant or employee based on the results of a lie detector test
- Discharge or discriminate against a job applicant or employee for filing a complaint or participate in a proceeding under the EPPA

Employees are entitled to file a lawsuit against employers in violation of the EPPA. Complaints may be filed with the Wage and Hour Division of the Department of Labor's Employment Standards Administration. Employers who violate the law may be held liable to the employee or applicant for relief, including employment, reinstatement, promotion, and lost wages and benefits.

Polygraph Testing

A polygraph is a type of lie detector. The EPPA does permit polygraph testing, subject to restrictions, in certain situations. Polygraph testing of some job applicants of security service firms (e.g., guard, armored car, alarm, etc.), pharmaceutical manufacturers, distributors, and dispensers is permitted. Employees reasonably suspected of involvement in a workplace incident (e.g., embezzlement, theft, etc.) that resulted in specific economic loss or injury to a private firm may also be subject to polygraph testing.

Polygraph tests are subject to strict standards regarding the conduct of the test, including pretest, testing, posttesting, and disclosure of information. Polygraph examiners must be licensed and bonded, or have professional liability coverage.

See also Polygraph Test
Resource:
U.S. Department of Labor Web site. http://www.dol.gov.

Ann Gilley

EMPLOYEE RIGHT-TO-KNOW LAW

The "Access to Information about Hazardous and Toxic Substances Act" is often referred to as the Employee Right-to-Know law (ERTK). The law requires an employer to compile and maintain a chemical information list containing the common name, chemical name, and work area for each hazardous chemical used or stored in the workplace.

Hazard Communication Standard 29 Code of Federal Regulation 1910.1200

The Employee Right-to-Know law is more commonly known as Hazard Communication, or HAZCOM. The Hazard Communication Standard (HCS) sets the guidelines for employer compliance. This standard is based on a simple concept—that employees have both a need and a right to know the identities and hazards of the chemicals they are exposed to when working. Employees also have a need to know what protective measures are available to prevent adverse effects from occurring.

Knowledge acquired under the HCS will help employers provide safer workplaces for their employees. When employers have information about the chemicals being used, they can take steps to reduce exposure, substitute with less hazardous chemicals, and ensure all employees have access to proper personal protective equipment. The Occupational Safety and Health Administration (OSHA) is an organization that falls under the Department of Labor. OSHA is the regulatory agency that oversees and enforces the Hazard Communication Standard.

Employee Training

Employers shall ensure that employees are provided with information and training in accordance with 29 Code of Federal Regulation (CFR) 1910.1200 (b)(4)(iii) to the extent necessary to protect them in the event of a spill or leak of a hazardous chemical from a sealed container. The type and amount of training depends on the type of work being conducted. For example, employers that do not produce or import chemicals need only focus on the parts of the HCS that deal with establishing a workplace program and communicating information to their employees. According to 29 CFR 1910.1200, "*employee*" means a worker who may be exposed to hazardous chemicals under normal operating conditions or in foreseeable emergencies. Workers such as office workers or bank tellers who encounter hazardous chemicals only in nonroutine, isolated instances are not covered.

Elements of a hazard communication training program include:

1. Knowing how to identify hazardous chemicals in the workplace. Employees who work with chemicals on a daily basis are often the subject matter experts regarding certain chemicals.
2. Labels and other forms of warning. Workplace containers of hazardous chemicals must be labeled, tagged or marked with the identity of the material and appropriate hazard warnings.
3. The measures employees can take to protect themselves from hazards, including specific procedures the employer has implemented to protect employees from exposure to hazardous chemicals, such as appropriate work practices, emergency procedures and personal protective equipment to be used.
4. Material Safety Data Sheets (MSDSs). MSDSs are required by OSHA to be maintained in the workplace for each hazardous chemical. The employer must ensure that MSDSs are readily accessible during each work shift to employees when they are in their work area(s).

Written Hazard Communication Plan

Part of the communication process is for employers to develop a written hazard communication plan. This written plan describes how the HCS will be implemented at the workplace. Exemptions to the written hazard communication plan are workplaces that are laboratories and work operations where employees handle only chemicals in sealed containers. The written plan does not have to be lengthy or complicated. It is intended to be a blueprint for implementation of the employer's plan—an assurance that all aspects of the requirements have been addressed. Many trade associations and other such professional groups provide templates for developing written hazard communication plans. Using a generic plan is helpful, but an employer must remember that their written hazard communication plan must reflect what is happening at their workplace. If OSHA inspects a workplace for compliance with the Hazard Communication Standard, the OSHA compliance officer will ask to see the written hazard communication plan at the outset of the inspection.

NOTES

1. 29 Code of Federal Regulation 1910.1200, Hazard Communication, http://www.osha.gov/.
2. Elizabeth A. McCane, *Colorado Army National Guard Written Hazard Communication Program* (2002).

Elizabeth A. McCane

EQUAL EMPLOYMENT OPPORTUNITY COMMISSION (EEOC)

In 1964, Congress passed Title VII of the Civil Rights Act, which prohibited employment discrimination and created the Equal Employment Opportunity Commission (EEOC).[1] An employer cannot use race, color, religion, gender, or national origin as the basis for any decision related to any phase of employment. The EEOC creates regulations to prevent discrimination in employment in the United States. In addition, the EEOC investigates allegations of discrimination made by employees under Title VII (and other antidiscrimination laws).

The Legal Threshold

All private sector employers with 15 or more employees (full or part time) are covered by Title VII. An employer must use the "payroll method" to determine the employment relationship—if the employee appears on the payroll for that day; he or she is an "employee."[2]

EEOC Procedure

When an employee contacts the EEOC to file a complaint, an investigator is assigned to interview both sides. The investigating official may seek documentation from each side, and conduct questioning of the parties and other witnesses (both on site and by other means). The EEOC has the discretion, at every step of the investigation, to settle any case—if the parties voluntarily agree. Also, the EEOC may offer to send the matter to mediation to assist the parties in resolving the dispute.[3]Mediation that occurs as a result of such a referral is free. The EEOC moved to offer mediation at every office in April 1999. Since that time, the number of cases involved in EEOC-referred mediation doubled.[4]

The EEOC has several options at the conclusion of the evidence-gathering phase of the case: close the case, determine that a violation occurred, or bring suit in federal court.

If the case is closed the initiating party has 90 days to file suit—such a lawsuit is independent of EEOC involvement. If the EEOC determines that a violation occurred, the agency might suggest conciliation or mediation to assist the parties in resolving the dispute.

Available Remedies

Employees seeking relief in an action for employment discrimination can request pay (stemming back to the incident), a position/reinstatement with the company, promotion, or a reasonable accommodation. In some cases, the employee seeking relief in court might be awarded punitive damages for intentional discriminatory acts, attorneys' fees, and costs of the suit.

See also Employment Law: An Overview; Civil Rights Act of 1964 and 1991
Resources:
U.S. Equal Employment Opportunity Commission Web site. http://www.eeoc.gov/.

NOTES

1. Pub. L. 88-352.
2. *Walters v. Metropolitan Educ. Enters.,* 519 U. S. 202, 136 L. Ed. 644, 117 S. Ct. 660 (1997).
3. U.S. Equal Employment Opportunity Commission Web site, http://www.eeoc.gov (accessed March 1, 2008).
4. U.S. Equal Employment Opportunity Commission, "EEOC Mediation Statistics FY 1999 through FY 2007," http://www.eeoc.gov/mediate/mediation_stats.html (accessed February 9, 2008).

Laura Dendinger

EQUAL PAY ACT

The Equal Pay Act of 1963 was enacted in order to lessen the pay gap between male and female pay rates. The act prohibits gender-based pay discrimination by requiring organizations to pay men and women doing the same job the same rate of pay.

Equal Pay Act Provisions

The Equal Pay Act has several key provisions that must be taken into account when looking at gender-based pay equity.

Equal Pay for Equal Work

Simply stated, the Equal Pay Act requires equal pay for equal work. The act does help to define and describe what is meant by the terms "equal pay" and "equal work."

Equal pay is more than just the wages that are paid to employees. Equal pay includes all payments as well as benefits such as life and health insurance, retirement plans, severance packages, fringe benefits, profit sharing, stock options, expense accounts, bonuses, travel accommodations, or use of a company car. Employers need to look at the full spectrum of total compensation when analyzing if their pay systems are equitable.

Equal work is determined by looking at the job content and working conditions. For purposes of the Equal Pay Act, employees perform substantially the same work when they are performing jobs that require the same level of skill, effort, and responsibility, and are performing those jobs under similar working conditions. Skill relates to the experience, training, education, and ability required to perform a job. Effort includes consideration for the amount of mental or physical exertion expected in the performance of the job. Responsibility factors look at the degree of authority, accountability, supervisory expectations, and consequences of poor performance. Working conditions of the job are determined by the physical environment where the work is performed as well as the hazards of the job.

Neither the job title nor the job description are enough to determine differences in equal work. An employer must show differences in job content in order to justify differences in pay rates.

Covered Employers

Any employer with two or more employees and who is covered by the Fair Labor Standards Act (FLSA) is also covered by the Equal Pay Act. The act applies to all employees, including those employees who are otherwise considered "exempt" from the most common FLSA exemptions, such as executive, administrative, professional, and outside sales workers. This means that employers need to ensure that they have pay equity at all position levels, including white-collar positions.

Enforcement

The Equal Pay Act is part of the FLSA, and is enforced by the Equal Employment Opportunity Commission (EEOC). The act covers only pay disparities between women and men. It does not cover disparities based on race, color, age, disability, religion, or national origin, which are covered under different laws.

Either men or women can bring a suit claiming violation of the Equal Pay Act. The act allows for compensatory damages equal to two years of back pay, and three years of back pay if the violation was willful. Employers who are not following the Equal Pay Act are not able to reduce the wage rate of any employee in order to comply with the act. This means that if found in violation, the employer must raise the wages of all employees who are being paid less.

Exceptions

There are legitimate reasons where exceptions to the Equal Pay Act are allowed. These include situations where pay difference exist due to seniority or merit-based systems. Pay differences that are based on quantity or quality or production are also allowed. The Equal Pay Act also contains a provision allowing pay differentials based on any factor other than sex.

Resources:

Bland, Timothy S. "Equal Pay Act Basics." July 2002. http://www.shrm.org/rewards/library _published/compensation/IC/CMS_000058.asp (accessed September 29, 2007).

Joinson, Carla. "Equal Pay Act." *SHRM White Paper,* July 2002. http://www.shrm.org/hrresources/ whitepapers_published/CMS_000057.asp (accessed September 29, 2007).

Stites, Janet. "Equal Pay for the Sexes." *HR Magazine,* May 2005. http://www.shrm.org/hrmagazine/ articles/0505/0505stites.asp (accessed September 29, 2007).

Shanan M. Mahoney

ERISA

Employers are not required to provide pension and health care benefits to their employees. The Internal Revenue Service has an incentive for those employers that do offer pensions. In 1974, the Employment Retirement Income Security Act was passed to protect pension and health care benefits that employers elected to offer their employees. There is also an incentive—if an employer complies with the provisions of the Employee Retirement Income Security Act (commonly referred to as ERISA) of 1974, the benefits provided are deductible as a business expense.[1] ERISA added protection for employees (and beneficiaries) covered by employer retirement plans.

Who Is Covered?

Most employers providing pension plans are covered by ERISA. The act covers retirement plans offered by companies engaged in commerce or affecting commerce. Exceptions to coverage exist for church pension plans and government plans.

Types of Plans

There are two general types of benefit plans: defined-benefit plans and defined-contribution plans. An employer's obligation under the ERISA depends on the type of plan. A defined-benefit plan specifies the benefit that the employee will receive upon retirement, but not the contribution. Defined-contribution plans do not specify the benefit, as employees may be allowed to make contributions to increase the benefit at the time of retirement.

Requirements of the Act

Under the ERISA, each employer sponsoring a pension plan must appoint a plan administrator. Employers (or plan administrators in the case of outsourcing) must provide information to participating employees, as follows:

1. The employer should send the participating employee a summary of the plan within 90 days of enrollment. The synopsis should include a thorough description of how the plan works (including the formula for contributions and vesting).
2. A description of any change in the pension plan must be sent to participants within 210 days after the end of plan year.
3. If there are changes to the plan, each participant should receive an updated summary description of the plan every five years. If a pension plan is not changed, each participant should receive a summary plan description every 10 years.
4. Each participant should receive a report of the vested portion of accrued plan benefits as of the date of termination of employment.
5. Each plan administrator must file IRS Form 5500 to document the employee census, plan participants, and summary financial data.

Further, employees are protected by ERISA from mismanagement of plan assets. In addition, ERISA provides protection for defined-benefit plans that are underfunded. Employers cannot retaliate against employees who pursue their rights under ERISA.[2]

Duties upon Termination of a Plan

Employers who terminate pension plans must provide 60 days' notice prior to the termination. Employers can terminate a defined-benefit plan.

See also Pension Plans

Resources:

Business.gov Web site. http://www.business.gov/guides/industries/financial_services/.

NOTES

1. 29 U. S. C. §§ 1001–1453.
2. 29 U. S. C. §§ 1056.

Laura Dendinger

FAIR CREDIT REPORTING ACT

The Fair Credit Reporting Act (FCRA) became effective on April 25, 1971.[1] The FCRA is a major federal law that regulates the "gathering, sharing, and use of information by employers and consumer reporting agencies." In addition, it "distinguishes two types of credit report: consumer reports and investigative reports."[2] The FCRA defines a consumer credit report as:

> [A]ny written, oral, or other communication of any information by a consumer reporting agency bearing on a consumer's credit worthiness, credit standing, credit capacity, character, general reputation, personal characteristics, or mode of living which is used or expected to be used or collected in whole or in part for the purpose of serving as a factor in establishing the consumer's eligibility for credit or insurance to be used primarily for personal, family, or household purposes; employment purposes; or any other purpose authorized under section § 1681b.[3]

The term consumer is used because the law applies to information used in making loan decisions and matters that are not employee-related. The following illustrates the purpose of the FCRA, important provisions, and the information contained therein.

Purpose of the FCRA

The purpose of the FCRA is a response to the problem of inaccurate information being gathered and sold about people. This false information could damage a person's career and/or his financial standings. By having consumer reporting agencies collect and disseminate information about consumers according to FCRA guidelines, the information will have a better chance of being valid.

Important Provisions

The provisions included with the FCRA are beneficial to consumers. Once a year, a consumer can inquire and receive a free copy of his or her credit report (via AnnualCreditReport.com). By allowing the consumer to do so, the consumer reporting agencies allow a consumer to view his or her credit report and, if discrepancies exist, she is able to perform the appropriate process to correct the erroneous entry/entries.

This allows consumers one method of knowing if their credit has been compromised. The importance of this is shown in a study done by the U.S. Public Interest Research Group that found that "79% of the credit reports surveyed contained either serious errors or other mistakes of some kind."[4] This means that there could more than likely be an error on one's credit report. Another provision that will prevent identity theft is the National Fraud Alert System. Any consumer who suspects that he has been victimized by identity theft can contact and alert credit lines, thus forcing creditors to proceed with caution when granting credit. Measures have also been enacted to allow consumers to recover their credit if they have been victims of identity theft.[5]

Information Contained

The information contained in a consumer's credit report can include bankruptcy filings, repayment of loans, background checks, references, lawsuits, and conviction records. While a consumer credit report contains the data, investigative reports are based on personal interviews with friends, neighbors, or other associates, thus the inclusion of references.

Implications for Managers

As the use of credit reports becomes more commonplace in business, managers throughout an organization must be aware of the benefits and consequences. While a credit report or other background check may provide information valuable to a hiring decision, it must be understood that no system is flawless. A large percentage of credit reports contain errors or mistakes.[6] Managers involved in hiring must be cognizant of this fact and be prepared to respond to allegations of incorrect information contained in a credit report. An appropriate response might include collection of additional information or allowing the candidate time to correct errors on the report.

When the information contained within a credit report leads to denial of an applicant, the candidate has certain rights under the FCRA. For example, the candidate must be told which credit reporting agency provided the report, and she is entitled to a free copy of the credit report from the reporting agency.

Conclusion

Under the FCRA, consumers are able to keep better track of their credit history, contact credit companies should they suspect identity theft, and have established procedures by which to restore their credit. The information contained within a credit report consists of repayment of loans and bankruptcy filings, references, and other pertinent credit information. With proper knowledge and application of the provisions, consumers can keep their credit histories free from discrepancies, and managers responsible for hiring have access to a valuable tool.

Resources:
AnnualCreditReport.com. http://www.annualcreditreport.com.

NOTES

1. Federal Deposit Insurance Corporation, "FDIC Compliance Handbook" (June 2006), http://www.fdic.gov/regulations/compliance/handbook/manual (accessed April 9, 2008).

2. David Walsh, *Employment Law For Human Resource Practice* (Mason, OH: Thompson Higher Education, 2007).

3. Federal Trade Commission, "The Fair Credit Reporting Act" (July 30, 2004), http://www.ftc.gov/os/statutes (accessed April 9, 2008).

4. U.S. PIRG, "Mistakes Do Happen: A Look at Errors in Consumer Credit Reports" (June 2004), http://www.uspirg.org/home/reports/report-archives/financial-privacy–security/financial-privacy–security/mistakes-do-happen-a-look-at-errors-in-consumer-credit-reports (accessed April 9, 2008).

5. Federal Trade Commission, "Provisions of New Fair and Accurate Credit Transactions Act Will Help Reduce Identity Theft and Help Victims Recover: FTC" (June 15, 2004), http://www.ftc.gov/opa/2004/06/factaidt.shtm (accessed April 9, 2008).

6. Ibid.

Chris Armstrong

FAIR LABOR STANDARDS ACT

The Fair Labor Standards Act (FLSA), originally passed in 1938, established guidelines for employers and employees engaged in interstate commerce regarding minimum wage, overtime for certain jobs, child labor, and record keeping. The FLSA is administered by the Wage and Hour Division of the United States Department of Labor (DOL), which is responsible for conducting audits and workplace inspections.

Interstate commerce is a broad term that effectively allows almost all businesses to be covered. Ordering supplies from out of state or processing credit cards, for example, satisfy the provisions of the FLSA. Further, in order for the FLSA to apply, there must be an "employment relationship" between the employer and employee. Independent contractors and volunteers are not covered because they are not considered employees.

The law originally contained many special industry exemptions, most of which were subsequently repealed, designed to protect traditional pay practices in small, rural businesses. Current important issues and litigation pertain to "white collar" exemptions for professional, administrative, and executive employees.

"Exempt" employees are those who are not subject to overtime provisions as established by the FLSA. Those employees with job descriptions that include managerial functions are typically classified as "exempt" (from overtime). The 2004 amendment to the FLSA requires that an exemption must be based on actual job function, not title.

The FLSA provides that workers who are underpaid may seek remedy in the courts and recover the wages, including overtime, due them along with liquidated damages and reasonable attorney fees.

Minimum Wage

Individuals covered by the FLSA are entitled to receive at least a minimum wage for their work. The federal minimum wage is $6.55 per hour as of July 24, 2008, and will rise to $7.25 per hour effective July 24, 2009. State laws that require higher minimum wages, however, take precedent. Some states and cities require wages higher than the federal minimum, including, for example, Michigan and New York.

Various minimum wage exceptions apply under specific circumstances to workers with disabilities, tipped employees, student-learners, full-time students, and youth under age 20 in their first 90 days of employment.

The FLSA requires that wages be paid on regular paydays for the pay periods covered. The Portal-to-Portal Act of 1947 amended the FSLA and further defined compensable work time. In general, as long as an employee is engaged in activities that benefit the employer, regardless of when performed, the employer is obligated to pay the employee for his or her time. Travel to and from the work place, however, is not considered paid working time.

Overtime Pay

The FLSA mandates that, unless they are "exempt," individuals who work more than 40 hours in a workweek be paid at a rate of not less than one and one-half times their regular rate of pay for the hours worked in excess of 40. Special rules apply to state and local government employment, volunteer services, compensatory time off (instead of cash overtime pay), and so-called "white-collar" jobs.

Whether paid by the hour or piece rate, overtime pay is required for those employees who work more than 40 hours in a week. Work time includes time spent traveling between job sites, engaging in activities before and after their shift starts, or performing activities to prepare for work that are central to work activities. A workweek is a period of 168 hours during seven 24-hour periods, and may begin on any day of the week established by the employer. If a salary is paid on other than a weekly basis, the rate of pay must be converted to a weekly rate in order to determine overtime compensation.

Child Labor

Child labor provisions of the FLSA are designed to protect the educational opportunities of youth and prohibit their employment in potentially dangerous conditions. The provisions restrict the number of hours of work for youth under 16 years of age and list the prohibited hazardous occupations. The law specifies hours that youth may work in farm and nonfarm jobs, by age.

Fourteen is the minimum age for most nonfarm work. Young people may, however, deliver newspapers, perform in radio, television, and theatrical productions, and work for parents in their businesses (except in manufacturing or hazardous jobs). See FSLA regulations for age-range specifics.

Record Keeping

Employers are required to keep certain records for each employee, including identifying information and wage/hour data such as the employee's:
- Personal information, including full name and complete address (including zip code)
- Social Security number
- Birth date, if younger than 19
- Gender and occupation
- Additions to or deductions from wages
- Total wages paid each pay period
- Date of payment and the pay period covered
  Further, additional data required for nonexempt employees includes:
- Time and day of week when the workweek begins
- Hours worked each day
- Total hours worked each workday and workweek

- Basis on which wages are paid (e.g., hourly rate, weekly rate, or piecework)
- Regular hourly pay rate
- Total daily or weekly straight-time earnings
- Total overtime earnings for the workweek

Payroll records, collective bargaining agreements, sales, and purchase records must be kept for at least three years. Records on wage calculations and additions to or deductions from wages must be retained for at least two years. The FLSA does not mandate any particular record-keeping format, or the use of time clocks.

See also Child Labor Law; Employment Law; Exempt/Nonexempt Employee; Age Discrimination in Employment Act (ADEA); Equal Pay Act; Family and Medical Leave Act (FMLA)

Resources:

Fair Labor Standards Act of 1938 (29 U.S.C. ch. 8).

U.S. Department of Labor Web site. http://www.dol.gov.

Jennifer A. Majkowski and Ann Gilley

FAMILY AND MEDICAL LEAVE ACT (FMLA)

The Family and Medical Leave Act of 1993 (FMLA) grants family and temporary medical leave under certain conditions for workers of employers with 50 or more employees within 75 miles of the work site. Covered employers must provide eligible employees with up to 12 workweeks of unpaid leave during any 12-month period for certain medical conditions, and must protect the employee's position and benefits. Covered medical conditions include one or more of the following:

- Birth and care of the newborn child of the employee;
- Adoption or foster care of a son or daughter;
- Care for an immediate family member (spouse, child, or parent) with a serious health condition; or
- Medical leave when the employee is unable to work due to a serious health condition.

An employer may require that a request for medical leave be supported by documentation issued by the health care provider of the employee in a timely fashion. A serious health condition means an illness, injury, impairment, or physical or mental condition that involves inpatient care in a hospital, hospice, or residential medical care facility, or continuing treatment by a health care provider.

An employer may require, at its own expense, that the employee obtain the opinion of a second health care provider designated or approved by the employer. This provider may not be employed on a regular basis by the employer. If the original and second opinions differ, the employer may require, at its expense, the opinion of a third health care provider jointly approved by the employer and employee. The third health care provider opinion shall be considered final and binding on the employer and employee.

Eligible Employee

An "eligible employee" is one who has been employed (1) for at least 12 months by the employer from whom leave is requested, and (2) for at least 1,250 hours of service with said employer during the previous 12-month period. Certain industries and employees, such as education, civil service, and congressional employees, are subject to different rules.

Expansion to Include Leave to Family Members of Military Personnel

H. R. 4986, the National Defense Authorization Act for FY 2008 (NDAA) was signed into law on January 28, 2008 and includes provisions that expand the FMLA to cover family members of military service personnel. The law provides for new or expanded FMLA leave under two circumstances. First, employers must now provide up to 26 weeks of leave in any 12-month period to an employee who is a spouse, parent, child, or next of kin (nearest blood relative) of an injured or ill service member to care for that person while he or she is undergoing medical treatment, recuperation, or therapy, is in outpatient status, or is otherwise on the temporary disability retired list. A recovering service member is defined as a member of the armed forces who suffered an injury or illness while on active duty that rendered him or her unable to perform the duties of his or her office, grade, rank, or rating.

Second, the NDAA also requires that employers with 50 or more employees must provide up to 12 weeks of unpaid leave during any 12-month period for any "qualifying exigency" arising out of active military duty (or notice of impending call or order to active duty) of an employee's spouse, parent, or child.

Medical Leave Requirement

The entitlement to medical leave for the birth or adoption of a child expires 12 months from the date of the birth or adoption. Medical leave may be taken intermittently or on a reduced leave schedule when medically necessary, or if and when the employer and employee mutually agree. The provisions of the FMLA do not prevent employers from offering paid leave.

Employment and Benefits Protection

Upon return from covered medical leave, an eligible employee shall be entitled to resume the position of employment held when the leave commenced, or a position that is equivalent with equivalent benefits, pay, and other terms and conditions. An employee who takes medical leave does not lose or gain any employment benefits accrued prior to the leave, nor does he accrue seniority or benefits. Employers are required to maintain group health plan coverage for employees on leave under the FMLA. Certain highly paid, salaried employees are exempt from restoration requirements if necessary to prevent substantial economic injury to the employer.

Failure to Return from Leave

If an employee fails to return from medical leave for a reason other than the continuation, recurrence, or onset of a serious health condition, or other circumstances beyond the employee's control, the employer may charge the employee the premium paid for group health insurance during the period of unpaid leave under certain circumstances.

An employer may require that employees submit certification by a health care provider that the employee is unable to perform the functions of his or her position due the continuance, recurrence, or onset of serious health conditions of the employee, or the employee's son, daughter, spouse, or parent for whom the employee must provide care on the date that the medical leave expired.

See also Employment Law; Vocational Rehabilitation Act; Americans with Disabilities Act (ADA)

Resources:

Family and Medical Leave Act of 1993. U.S. Department of Labor Web site, http://www.dol.gov.

Form WH-380. An optional form used to obtain medical certification from a health care provider. U.S. Department of Labor Web site, http://www.dol.gov.

Form WH-381. An optional form for use by an employer to respond to an employee's request for leave. U.S. Department of Labor Web site, http://www.dol.gov.

National Defense Authorization Act for FY 2008 (H.R. 4986).

U.S. Department of Labor, Employment Standards Administration. http://www.dol.gov/esa/regs/statutes/whd/fmla.htm.

Jennifer A. Majkowski and Ann Gilley

FIFTH AMENDMENT

The Fifth Amendment to the U.S. Constitution states that "No person shall be held to answer for a capital, or otherwise infamous crime, unless on a presentment or indictment of a Grand Jury, except in cases arising in the land or naval forces, or in the Militia, when in actual service in time of War or public danger; nor shall any person be subject for the same offence to be twice put in jeopardy of life or limb; nor shall be compelled in any criminal case to be a witness against himself, nor be deprived of life, liberty, or property, without due process of law; nor shall private property be taken for public use, without just compensation."[1]

The Fifth Amendment is commonly thought of as the amendment that protects against self-incrimination. For example, "I plead the fifth" is a commonly heard phrase. This relates directly to the Fifth Amendment protections. However, the Fifth Amendment contains much more than the protection of self-incrimination. This amendment contains the grand jury requirement, prohibits forcing a person to be a witness against himself or herself, forbids double jeopardy, protects against the deprivation of life, liberty, or property without due process, and requires appropriate compensation be provided when private property is taken for public use.[2]

Double Jeopardy

While the Fifth Amendment discusses being put in jeopardy of life and limb twice, the interpretation of the amendment is to retry a person on a previously acquitted case. *Ball v. U.S.* specifically states that an acquittal prevents any subsequent prosecution for the same offense.[3] Mistrials do not fall under this double jeopardy protection. In essence, there must be a decision on the case (acquittal, conviction, etc.). A mistrial is not a decision based upon the facts of the case.

Self-incrimination

The Fifth Amendment also protects against self-incrimination or being forced to testify against oneself. To "plead the fifth" is enacting the right to not self-incriminate.

This protection is a personal right that can be exercised only by individuals and is not available to an organization or corporation. Additionally, this protection is only for self-incrimination. For example, if the answers to questions only hurt a reputation or position, the Fifth Amendment does not apply.[4]

Due Process

Both the Fifth and Fourteenth amendments describe and protect due process. The Due Process Clause ensures that no one shall be deprived of "life liberty and/or property" without following the process as outlined in the law. There are two types of due process. Substantive due process refers to due process with regard to laws, ordinances or other regulations as they are written. These types of legal codes must be written in specificity and not in general terms. The second type of due process relates to procedural process. Procedural process is the requirements of notice and proper steps being followed.[5]

Appropriate Compensation for Property Taken for Public Use

The Fifth Amendment guarantees that fair compensation is afforded if property is taken by the government for public use. Another term for this is "National Eminent Domain." When the Bill of Rights was produced, the British took property without appropriate or sufficient remuneration to the property owner. In response to these actions, the Fifth Amendment attempts to limit federal government authority by ensuring that eminent domain is only exercised with fair compensation.

Additionally, the eminent domain or taking of property must be for public use and cannot be exercised if the use of the property will be for private use. Additionally, fair compensation has been defined by the courts as, "a full and perfect equivalent for the property taken."[6]

HR Practitioner

What does any of this have to do with HR? Most references to the Fifth Amendment refer to self-incrimination. However, there is more depth and applicability to human resources in the Fifth Amendment than simply this. Employer drug testing can also fall under this amendment. For example, termination or failure to hire based on a positive drug test result could create issues with "due process" (also discussed under the Fourteenth Amendment definition). The Fifth Amendment Due Process Clause could permit the employee to challenge the process of testing, including test reliability, and allow the employee to refute the test findings, etc.[7]

Conclusion

The Fifth Amendment is one of the most widely known amendments due to the protection of self-incrimination. This aspect of the Fifth Amendment is very important. However, the Fifth Amendment holds many more protections, such as it includes grand jury requirements, prohibits forcing a person to be a witness against himself or herself, forbids double jeopardy, protects against the deprivation of life, liberty, or property without due process, and requires appropriate compensation be provided when private property is taken for public use.[8] These protections are extremely important to the citizens, residents, and workers of the United States. While some of these protections are reiterated in the Fourteenth Amendment, the causation for each amendment is different. Therefore, the scope of each amendment and importance to human resource management differs.

See also Fourteenth Amendment; Privacy Rights

NOTES

1. FindLaw, "Fourteenth Amendment," http://caselaw.lp.findlaw.com/data/constitution/amendment05/ (accessed January 15, 2008).

2. Constance E. Bagley, *Managers and the Legal Environment,* 4th ed. (Mason, OH: Thomson South-Western, 2006).

3. Henry Cheeseman, *Business Law: Legal Environment, Online Commerce, Business Ethics, and International Issues,* 6th ed. (Upper Saddle River, NJ, Pearson Prentice Hall, 2006); and Bagley, *Managers and the Legal Environment.*

4. FindLaw, "Fourteenth Amendment."

5. Cheeseman, *Business Law,* 2006.

6. Findlaw, "Fourteenth Amendment."

7. "Drug Testing," in *Encyclopedia of Everyday Law,* ed. Shirelle Phelps (Gale Group, Inc., 2003), *eNotes.com.* 2006. May 8, 2008, http://www.enotes.com/everyday-law-encyclopedia/drug-testing (accessed August 18, 2008).

8. Bagley, *Managers and the Legal Environment.*

Paul M. Shelton

FOUR-FIFTHS RULE

The four-fifths rule is a measure to determine whether adverse impact for employees is present. Generally, employment laws, regulations, and guidelines are put into place to prohibit and possibly deflect any and all acts of discrimination, perpetrated either as overt or covert, within the employment arena. Discrimination may occur when decisions are made by employers or hiring agencies concerning employment based upon race, sex, age, religion, or any other class. Fair and equitable employment selection must be made based upon job-specific knowledge, potential, or skill set talent and ability held by the prospective employee. Employment selection practices that unfairly discriminate against any specific category of employee are termed *unlawful* or *discriminatory.* Unlawful or discriminatory hiring practices cause adverse impact to a specific class or group of people.

The Civil Rights Act of 1964 disallows overt acts of discrimination and any practice that is "fair in form, but discriminatory in operation." Basically, the Civil Rights Act of 1964 makes discriminatory any employment or preemployment method and any practice not justifiable as related to the job performance or the job position. Cognitive ability testing, for example, stands out as a popular yet sometimes controversial method used to predict performance.

In 1978, four federal agencies issued the *Uniform Guidelines on Employee Selection Procedures,* which embodied guiding principles outlining the use of methods when selecting employees. The *Uniform Guidelines on Employee Selection Procedures* are legally binding and must satisfy two conditions to be considered legal and legitimate when balanced against the guidelines:

• Must be job-related and valid for the purpose used
• A business necessity must be present for use

It is unlawful to use a test or other selection procedure that will cause negative impact on employees when considering hiring, promotion, and other employment, and cannot work to the disadvantage of individuals or groups based on:

• Race
• Sex
• Ethnic base

Further, the guidelines and procedures also cover all matters concerning:

• Referral
• Disciplinary actions
• Employment termination
• Licensing
• Certification
• Training if tied to an employment decision

Four-fifths Rule Calculations

Several approaches are used to determine if an adverse impact has occurred within the employee group. An adverse impact is generally indicated when a selection rate for one group, such as men or women, is less than 80 percent, or 4/5, of the other. This criteria or measure is commonly called the "four-fifths" rule.

> A selection rate for any race, sex, or ethnic group which is less than four-fifths (4/5) (or eighty percent) of the rate for the group with the highest rate will generally be regarded by the Federal enforcement agencies as evidence of adverse impact.[1]

Calculations using the four-fifths rule constitute evidence of discrimination, but not proof of discrimination. Targeted groups, such as minorities and females, should be balanced with the labor market.

To calculate adverse impact:

• Determine the number of prospects tested and the number of prospects who passed the test by group (e.g., men, women, etc.)
• Divide the number who passed by the total number tested
• Divide the lower pass rate by the higher pass rate

Example of an adverse impact calculation:

Male
• 85 tested; 51 passed
• 51/85 = .60
Female
• 135 tested; 108 passed
• 108/135 = .80
Adverse impact calculation
• .60/.80 = .75

The question is whether the 5 percent difference is important enough to cause an adverse impact in the workplace. The answer is yes, according to the four-fifths rule, because the adverse impact percentage is only three-quarters and less than the 80 percent threshold.

The U.S. Department of Labor (USDOL), Bureau of Labor Statistics, showed the workforce, as of May 2006, for all workers 16 years old and older as:[2]

Available labor market:
- Male = 81.2
- Female = 69.8
- or, 86 percent male

Example of a "No Adverse Impact" calculation:

African American
  - 100 tested; 75 passed
  - 75/100 = .75
White
  - 100 tested; 80 passed
  - 80/100 = .80
Adverse impact calculation
  - .75/.80 = .94

USDOL, Bureau of Labor statistics:
- African American = .57
- White = .43
- or, 75 percent African American

Three points to consider when using the four-fifths rule to evaluate whether an adverse impact situation exists:
- Applying the four-fifths rule may prove to be inaccurate and misrepresent the rates of selections when sample populations are very small or extremely large.
- When no contention of adverse impact is made, the *Guidelines* do not require the employer to reveal the method or style of the assessment procedure(s) used.
- If a situation of adverse impact is found during the assessment process, the employer is required to eliminate the disparity or justify why the adverse impact cannot be eliminated.

See also Civil Rights Act of 1964 and 1991; Disparate Treatment/Disparate Impact; Employment Testing; Harassment

Resources:
Edison Electric Institute, Adverse Impact, Dr. Robert Ramos, and Dr. Wanda Campbell.
 HR-Guide.com. http://www.hr-guide.com.
 U.S. Department of Labor, Bureau of Labor Statistics.http://www.bls.gov.

NOTES

1. Uniform Guidelines on Employee Selection Procedures, Sec 1607.3D
2. U.S. Department of Labor, Bureau of Labor Statistics, 41 CFR 60-3.3, February 2, 2007.

Dean Nelson

FOURTEENTH AMENDMENT

The Fourteenth Amendment was added to the U.S. Constitution in 1868. The initial intent of this amendment was to establish and guarantee equal rights after the Civil War. The Fourteenth Amendment prohibits discriminatory and unfair actions by the government. Three specific areas of the Fourteenth Amendment are applicable to organizations today—the Privileges and Immunities Clause, the Equal Protection Clause, and the Due Process Clause.[1]

Privileges and Immunities Clause

The Privileges and Immunities Clause prohibits individual states from establishing laws that discriminate against citizens of other states. For example, it is unconstitutional for one state to establish a law that would prevent a citizen of another state to establish a business in the state. The purpose of this clause was to promote a national allegiance rather than solely a state allegiance.[2]

Equal Protection Clause

The Equal Protection Clause focuses on equal legal protection of persons within a state. A state cannot discriminate or "deny to any person within its jurisdiction equal protection of the laws." It should be noted that this clause protects against states establishing different laws for "similarly situated" persons. The term similarly situated means people in like situations.[3]

Due Process Clause

Both the Fifth and Fourteenth amendments describe and protect due process. The Due Process Clause ensures that no one shall be deprived of "life, liberty, and/or property" without following the process as outlined in the law. There are two types of due process. Substantive due process refers to due process with regard to laws, ordinances or other regulations as they are written. These types of legal codes must be written in specific, not general, terms. The second type of due process relates to procedural process. Procedural process requires notice and proper steps being followed.[4]

Section 1 of the Fourteenth Amendment

"Section. 1. All persons born or naturalized in the United States and subject to the jurisdiction thereof are citizens of the United States and of the State wherein they reside. No State shall make or enforce any law which shall abridge the privileges or immunities of citizens of the United States; nor shall any State deprive any person of life, liberty, or property, without due process of law; nor deny to any person within its jurisdiction the equal protection of the laws."[5]

Applicability to the Workplace

Section 1 above most directly relates to the workplace and human resources today. The Fourteenth Amendment made it a requirement that states could not deprive any person of "life, liberty, or property without due process of law;" or, deny any person equal protection. While this amendment was initially written as a response to the abolition of slavery, it has come to be a founding principle of many work practices. Under the Liberty of Contract tenet, labor laws were founded and supported with precedent-setting cases. Such laws regulate hours of labor, labor in mines, payment of wages, minimum wage, workers' compensation, and collective bargaining, each of which has its basis in the due process clause of the Fourteenth Amendment.[6] While due process has its origins in the Fifth Amendment, the Fourteenth Amendment actually requires the states to ensure due process.

Conclusion

The Fourteenth Amendment contains multiple foci, as it outlines certain freedoms and restrictions. Specifically, the Fourteenth Amendment was established to protect freedom of individuals after the Civil War. It has been applied, over time, to represent and protect individual freedoms relating to due process, equal protection, and privileges and immunities in the workplace.

See also Fifth Amendment; Privacy Rights

NOTES

1. FindLaw, "Fourteenth Amendment," http://caselaw.lp.findlaw.com/data/constitution/amendment14/ (accessed January 15, 2008).

2. Constance E. Bagley, *Managers and the Legal Environment,* 4th ed. (Mason, OH: Thomson South-Western, 2006).

3. Henry Cheeseman, *Business Law: Legal Environment, Online Commerce, Business Ethics, and International Issues,* 6th ed.; Bagley, *Managers and the Legal Environment.*

4. Ibid.

5. Findlaw, "Fourteenth Amendment."

6. Ibid.

Paul M. Shelton

FOURTH AMENDMENT

The Fourth Amendment guarantees "The right of the people to be secure in their persons, houses, papers, and effects, against unreasonable searches and seizures, shall not be violated, and no Warrants shall issue, but upon probable cause, supported by Oath or affirmation, and particularly describing the place to be searched, and the persons or things to be seized."[1]

The Fourth Amendment is part of the Bill of Rights. It was originally established as a result of colonial Americans being searched and property seized by the British. The Fourth Amendment focuses on reasonable expectations of privacy, searches and seizures, and searches incidental to arrest. It should be noted that searches and seizures relate to government officials, usually peace officers, and are not binding upon other organizations or citizens.

Reasonable Searches and Seizures, and Expectations of Privacy

The Fourth Amendment only applies to criminal law. Civil law is excluded under this amendment (*Murray v. Hoboken Land,* 1855). Reasonable expectation of privacy relates to "what a reasonable person would expect to be kept private." This previous phrase is the litmus test for establishing privacy. For example, would it be reasonable for a person to expect privacy sitting in an open park? Would this person's expectation of privacy be different if he was sitting within his own home? The courts have ruled that a person sitting in an open park would not "reasonably" have an expectation of privacy, while a person sitting in her own home could "reasonably" expect privacy.

Peace officers can and do engage in warrantless searches. The Fourth Amendment requires peace officers to establish probable cause before the warrantless search. The cause to search must be sufficient legally in order for the officer to believe that a search is necessary. The courts have taken a strong stance against officers who conduct warrantless searches without probable cause. The exclusionary rule was the outcome of this judicial emphasis. This rule states that any evidence obtained from an illegal search cannot be used in a court of law. Law enforcement uses the term "fruit of the poisonous tree." An officer cannot "eat" (use the evidence) of the poisonous tree (an illegal search).

Searches Incidental to Arrest

Two particular areas of search are legal without probable cause or warrant. These two areas are a "Terry Frisk" and a "search incidental to arrest." The Terry Frisk was established in *Terry v. Ohio*. The court decided that if a police officer witnesses something "unusual" and it would reasonably lead him to believe that criminal activity is occurring and the person might have a dangerous weapon, the police officer may conduct a pat down. Additionally, a search incidental to arrest can occur without probable cause. If a police officer is affecting an arrest, she can search the detained person prior to the arrest without warrant.[2]

Another warrantless search allowed under the Fourth Amendment is the plain view doctrine. The courts have ruled that an officer who is lawfully present may seize and search any object that is in plain view. For example, if an officer responds to a home and is allowed access, then he is allowed to search and seize anything within plain view. The officer may not open drawers to search, but may look in rooms, on top of furniture, etc.

Employers and Computers

The Fourth Amendment impacts human resource management and organizations, specifically with regard to technology. Within the last 15 years, technology, primarily in the form of computers and other information devices (cell phones, Blackberries, iPhones, etc.), has become ever invasive. The laws as written have been stretched to attempt to work with new and ever changing environments. One such area is related to the Internet and privacy expectations. Most cases in the courts today have ruled that an employee does not have a reasonable expectation of privacy regarding any incriminating evidence stored on a work computer. Additionally, in a recent decision, an employer can consent to a search of an employee's computer without employee consent.[3]

Implications for Managers and HRM Practitioners

How does the Fourth Amendment affect managers and HRM practitioners? The reasonable person can expect privacy, but can privacy be expected in the workplace? The courts have ruled very leniently with employers. The Fourth Amendment only regulates government officials and does not affect private companies. For example, surveillance of computers, Internet viewing, and phone calls by the employer do not constitute a breach of a Fourth Amendment right. It should be noted that the Fourth Amendment is the controlling principle, and individual state laws also regulate privacy issues. An example of a state regulation is the California Public Utilities Commission's General Order 107-B, which states that if two parties on a telephone call are in California, they must be notified they are being monitored. However, if the call is between states, the federal regulation Electronic Communications Privacy Act, 18 USC 2510, *et. seq.,* does allow for monitoring the phone calls without notification. This can be important to HRM professionals in the work place.

HRM policies should clearly explain an organization's approach to and employee responsibility for behaviors and actions that occur in the workplace and/or on company time. Employees should be aware that usage of company computers, the Internet, any Intranet, email, or other company owned technology is not private, nor should there be an expectation of privacy. HRM practitioners add value to their organizations by guiding the formulation and dissemination of policies that protect the company, employees, customers, and other stakeholders.

Conclusion

The Fourth Amendment ensures that our privacy and reasonable expectations of being safe and secure in our homes and possessions is protected. People within the United States can have a reasonable expectation of privacy. With some exceptions, warrants are needed to search and seize property. The "Terry Frisk" and search incidental to arrest are two exceptions.

Within private organizations, however, courts have ruled that employees do not have a reasonable expectation of privacy in their work space, on their work computers, or in work-related e-mails or Internet usage.

See also E-mail/Internet Policy; Fifth Amendment; Fourteenth Amendment; Privacy Rights

NOTES

1. FindLaw, "Fourteenth Amendment," http://caselaw.lp.findlaw.com/data/constitution/amendment04/ (accessed January 15, 2008).
2. Henry Cheeseman, *Business Law: Legal Environment, Online Commerce, Business Ethics, and International Issues,* 6th ed.; Constance E. Bagley, *Managers and the Legal Environment,* 4th ed. (Mason, OH: Thomson South-Western, 2006).
3. Bagley, *Managers and the Legal Environment.*

Paul M. Shelton

FREEDOM OF INFORMATION ACT

The Freedom of Information Act (FOIA) was enacted in 1966 (Title 5 U.S. Code, section 552) and generally provides that any person has the right to request access to federal agency records or information. All agencies of the executive branch of the U.S. government are required to disclose documents upon receiving a written request for them.

A Resource for Organizations

Information available through the FIOA touches virtually every aspect of life in the United States. Journalists, researchers, managers, and HR personnel use government data to enhance their knowledge and understanding of government policies and actions that impact public and private concerns. The wealth of data available is nearly endless and includes, but is not limited to, salary information, environmental reports, worker exposure to disease, violence, and accidents, healthy/dangerous workplaces in the country, safety problems in specific industries or organizations, compliance with antidiscrimination laws in certain industries, and government subsidies to firms and industries.[1]

Through the FOIA, managers and HR personnel have access to an exhaustive list of information with nearly endless possibilities. However, government agencies may withhold information that is protected from disclosure due to nine exemptions and three exclusions.

FOIA Exemptions

Information that is exempt from mandatory disclosure of the FOIA is categorized as follows:
• Federal agency records that are properly classified as secret in the interest of national defense or foreign policy.
• Federal agency records that are related to internal personnel rules and practices.
• Federal agency records specifically exempted by other statutes.
• Information concerning trade secrets and commercial or financial data obtained from a person that is privileged or confidential.
• Privileged interagency or intra-agency memoranda or letters, except under certain circumstances.
• Personnel, medical, and similar files, when the disclosure would constitute a clear invasion of personal privacy.
• Investigatory records compiled for law enforcement purposes.
• Records contained in or related to certain examination, operating, or condition reports concerning financial institutions.
• Geological and geophysical information and data, including maps and concerning wells.[2]

FOIA Exclusions

The three exclusions of the FOIA pertain to federal law enforcement agencies:
• Federal law enforcement agencies are authorized under specified circumstances to shield the very existence of records of ongoing investigations or proceedings by excluding them entirely from the FOIA's reach.
• Informant records maintained by a criminal law enforcement agency that are requested by a third party are not subject to the FOIA unless the informant's status is officially confirmed.
• The exclusion pertains only to certain law enforcement records that are maintained by the Federal Bureau of Investigation.[3]

The FOIA does not provide a right of access to records held by Congress, state, or local government agencies, or private businesses or individuals. Each state has its own public access laws that pertain to state and local records.

There is no central office in the federal government that processes FOIA requests for all the federal agencies; each federal agency determines the process for handling FOIA requests that pertain specifically to them. In some instances (e.g., Department of Defense), all major agency components directly receive and individually handle FOIA requests that pertain to their component (e.g., Army, Navy, Air Force etc.). In other instances (e.g., Department of Education), the agency prefers that all FOIA requests be centrally routed through the agency's main FOIA office.

It is quite possible that the FOIA office (or the FOIA official) may fall under the office of human resource management within either federal or state government. Certain employment information, such as names, sex, race, title, and dates of employment of all employees and officers of public bodies are generally made public information under FOIA. The FOIA allows, but does not require, a public body to exempt from disclosure the following employment information:

- Information of a personal nature that would constitute unreasonable invasion of personal property.
- All compensation, with certain exemptions.
- Information discussed in a public meeting during an executive session.
- Certain materials on not fewer than the final three applicants under consideration for a position (the exceptions being income tax returns, medical records, Social Security numbers, and information otherwise exempt from disclosure).

An employee's salary can be disclosed under the FOIA; however, there are certain categorizations that determine if the exact salary or a salary range can be disclosed. Exact compensation can be disclosed for employees earning $50,000 or more annually; part-time employees; persons paid an honoraria or other compensation for special appearances, performances or the like; and employees at the level of agency/department head. For classified/unclassified employees (not subject to the above) earning $30,001 to $49,000, a compensation level within a range of $4,000 can be disclosed. For classified employees (not subject to the above) earning $30,000 or less annually, the position's salary range can be disclosed. For unclassified employees (not subject to the above) earning $30,000 or less, the compensation level within a range of $4,000 beginning at $2,000 and increasing in increments of $4,000 can be disclosed.[4]

Requesting Information

Under the FOIA, anyone can request an agency record. When making a request about oneself, a person must provide a notarized statement or a statement signed under penalty of perjury stating the person is the person she claims to be. Certain types of records created by federal agencies on or after November 1, 1996, are available electronically via the Internet and do not require a FOIA request. When a written FOIA request is received, federal agencies are required to respond within 20 business days. However, an agency may extend the response time an additional 10 business days when records must be collected from various field offices, when an agency must consult with another agency that has substantial interest in the request, or when the request involves a "voluminous" amount of records that must be located, compiled, or reviewed. Requests are normally expedited only when there is a threat to someone's life or physical safety, when there is substantial loss of due process at stake, or when there is an urgent need to inform the public over actual or alleged government activity.

NOTES

1. Guide to the FOIA, http://www.rcfp.org/foiact/guide_a.html (accessed May 19, 2008).

2. U.S. Department of Defense, Office of Inspector General, "Guide to FOIA Exemptions," http://www.dodig.osd.mil/foia/guide.htm (accessed February 1, 2008).

3. Ibid.

4. South Carolina Budget and Control Board, Office of Human Resources, FOIA, http://www.jobs.sc.gov/OHR/employer/OHR-foia-faqs.htm (accessed May 7, 2008).

Victoria T. Dieringer

GAY PARTNER RIGHTS

Rights for gay, lesbian, bisexual, and transgendered (GLBT) individuals are in heated debate currently in the United States. Due to several factors, including a notable shift in the public's attitude toward sexualities that are different from heterosexuality, more and more Americans are openly gay, lesbian, bisexual, or transgendered. Although many issues are currently in debate regarding the GLBT community, in terms of employment, GLBT workers are most likely to request benefits that are similar to benefits that are offered to same-sex domestic partners (see the entry on Domestic Partner Benefits). In the United States, Massachusetts is the only state that recognizes same-sex marriages; Vermont recognizes civil unions. Outside of these places, currently, the law does not require that employers provide GLBT employees with benefits for their partners, but it is becoming more and more common, especially within the field of higher education.

Although Vermont and Massachusetts recognize formal unions between same-sex couples, these unions are not legally binding in other states.[1] Therefore a couple who is married in Massachusetts may not qualify for domestic partner benefits, or similar, in another state.

See also Domestic Partner Benefits

NOTE

1. Public Agenda, *Gay Rights: Overview* (n.d.), http://www.publicagenda.org/issues/overview.cfm?issue_type=gay_rights (accessed October 3, 2007).

Lea Hanson

GOOD FAITH

Effective interaction of human resources within an organization is a determining factor in the strength and success of the organization. Providing a solid platform for that interaction requires the existence of guiding principles that facilitate good business practice and communication. The doctrine of good faith is no stranger to the business community and seeks to establish a starting point from which effective business practices emerge.

A Brief History

The concept of good faith can be found in writings of law and business that date back to the 1800s. A literal translation from the Latin *"bona fides,"* the words embody the idea of a faith-based approach to honoring the conscience and doing what is "right" by all parties. The doctrine of good faith has been traced back to the Romans, who summarized the principle with the expression *"pacta sunt servanda,"* or, "what is so suitable to the good of mankind as to observe those things that parties have agreed upon." The rise of both

Christianity and the merchant class in the eleventh and twelfth centuries became a determining factor in the evolution of good faith as a practice. Increased commercial trade necessitated a "platform" from which fair and honest business could be conducted. The emerging concept of good faith assumed the premise that man inherently desires to do what is right by others. A long-standing component of business practice in European countries like France, Germany, and Italy, good faith has only recently (in the twentieth century) been defined in the United States and Canada.

Good Faith Defined

As the Romans attempted to place a definition on good faith, it was perceived in part as simply an appeal to common sense. A motive to define the doctrine arose from a common concern for the need for fairness in dealing with others, and protection of the reasonable expectations of all parties. From a modern perspective, the Uniform Commercial Code sets forth the following definition:

"Honesty in fact and the observance of reasonable commercial standards of fair dealing"— Uniform Commercial Code § 1-201(20), UCC § 2-103(j).

West's Encyclopedia of American Law defines good faith as follows:

Honesty; a sincere intention to deal fairly with others. Good faith is an abstract and comprehensive term that encompasses a sincere belief or motive without any malice or the desire to defraud others. It derives from the translation of the Latin term *bona fide,* and courts use the two terms interchangeably.

Good faith requires that people operate in what could easily be accepted as an honest and upright manner that involves the exercising of a clear conscience, producing a fair and reasonable outcome.

Good Faith Applied

Equally important to the understanding of the doctrine of good faith is the ability to apply it effectively. In the legal environment of business, there are commonly two contexts in which the doctrine of good faith is applied. To understand the broader scope of how good faith can be enacted, these two facets will be explored.

Good Faith in Bargaining/Contracting

As two or more parties enter into the process of negotiation, the strength of the contractual relationship is dependant upon the exercising of good faith with respect to both intentions and expected outcomes. Referred to as "good faith purchase," the doctrine asserts that all parties involved in negotiation enter into the process with pure hearts and open minds. This assumption—allowed by the exercising of good faith—establishes the premise that future dealings during this negotiation will be committed in the best interest of all parties (collectively). Consequently, outcomes will be fair and equitable—in spite of the fact that *individuals* may not achieve their desired goals.

Good Faith in Performance/Execution

Once the contract—formal or informal—is in place, the parties involved now assume responsibility for execution of the negotiated agreement. As this process unfolds, diligence is required to maintain the standard and spirit of the contracting phase. This action is referred to as "good faith performance." Good faith performance requires the standard of reasonableness as a guide to attain desired outcomes and enact expected performance requirements. The terms "fair and reasonable" are underlying guides that assist parties in managing the way in which an agreement comes to fruition.

Conclusion

Many writings on the subject of good faith incorporate the idea that it is one's "basic duty" to "act in good faith" in the best interest of "the company" and "for a proper purpose." Whether it is action between individuals, or an individual and an organization, the doctrine of good faith seeks to fill an important gap—that of the understanding of one's "intentions." Interestingly, where most phases of business activity can be influenced by the rule of law, one's intentions are left largely unchecked. The exercising of good faith closes that gap and establishes a foundation of strength upon which business can be executed efficiently.

Resources:

The American Law Institute. *Uniform Commercial Code,* 2001.

Farnsworth, Edward Allan. "Good Faith Performance and Commercial Reasonableness under the Uniform Commercial Code. *University of Chicago Law Review* 30, no. 4 (1963): 666–79.

Farrar, John. *Corporate Governance.* Melbourne: Oxford University Press, 2005.

West's Encyclopedia of American Law, at http://www.enotes.com/wests-law-encyclopedia.

Scott McDonald

HARASSMENT

Harassment is defined as any act or acts done without legitimate purpose and with the intent to intimidate, annoy, or alarm. The cost of workplace harassment to individuals and employers includes:

• Loss of physical health and emotional well-being
• Loss of productivity
• Job and career loss
• Financial losses and legal claims
• Loss of trained personnel
• Increased absenteeism and resignations
• Violence in the workplace
• A poor image for employers

Workplace harassment is extremely disruptive and unpleasant. Everyone in the work environment feels the negative effects.

Hostile Work Environment Harassment

Hostile work environment harassment is a specific form of non-consenting conduct that occurs in the workplace and has the purpose or effect of substantially interfering with an individual's professional performance or creating an intimidating, hostile or offensive employment environment. Hostile work environment harassment is subjectively perceived as abusive by the recipient, but must also be perceived as hostile or abusive by a reasonable person. Additionally, such conduct would have to be sufficiently severe, persistent, or pervasive to meet the legal threshold for hostile work environment harassment.

Severe Conduct

Severe conduct is conduct that inflicts physical discomfort, hardship, pain, or distress, or that carries with it the threat or promise of a tangible employment action. Examples of behaviors that would be considered severe include, but are not limited to, the following:

- Aversive, aggressive and/or unwelcome physical contact
- Abrupt, physically confrontational behavior that implies imminent danger
- Overtly hostile, injurious, or destructive behavior
- Verbal threats of physical harm
- Acts of retaliation against a staff member for filing a complaint or offering testimony during an investigative process

Harassing conduct would also be considered severe in either of the following:

- When submission to such conduct is made directly or indirectly a term or condition of an individual's employment.
- When submission or rejection of such conduct by an individual is used as a basis for employment decisions affecting that individual.

This is often called "quid pro quo" (this for that) harassment. Tangible employment actions include:

- Firing
- Demotion
- Denial of promotion
- Poor/good evaluation
- Hiring
- Promotion
- Special treatment
- Reassignment with significantly different responsibilities
- Significant change in benefits

If the allegation of hostile work environment harassment refers to conduct that does not inflict physical discomfort, pose a safety concern, or threaten an individual's employment, the question becomes whether or not the behavior is either persistent or pervasive in nature.

Persistent Conduct

Persistent conduct is conduct that is continuous or has existed for a long or longer-than-usual period of time. The following conduct, if persistent, could constitute hostile work environment harassment:

- Raising one's voice above conversational tones in anger, frustration, rage or with the intent of intimidating the listener.
- Directing profane, abusive and/or derogatory language at others, including name-calling and personal, direct, and intentional insults.
- Mocking, taunting, or ridiculing others, including the use of offensive remarks.

If the allegation of hostile work environment harassment involves a single instance of conduct or conduct with limited duration that would not be considered sufficiently severe, the question then becomes if the conduct is pervasive.

Pervasive Conduct

Pervasive conduct is conduct that occurs frequently and without sanction in the work environment. Pervasive conduct is diffused throughout the working environment or becomes an accepted part of the culture of the environment.

The following conduct refers to a level of intolerant behavior that has the quality or tendency to be spread throughout the work environment. This conduct could constitute hostile work environment harassment because of its discriminatory impact:

- Comments or actions that humiliate, intimidate, exclude, frighten, and/or isolate another on the basis of sexual orientation.
- Comments or actions that humiliate, intimidate, exclude, frighten, and/or isolate another on the basis of race, ethnicity, color, gender, religion or creed (a system of beliefs or principals), age, disability, or marital status.
- Comments or actions that humiliate, intimidate, exclude, frighten, and/or isolate another on the basis of one's employment status.

If the allegation is neither severe nor persistent, and it involves an isolated incident that does not rise to the level of a pervasively discriminatory work environment, it is unlikely the behaviors would be deemed hostile work environment harassment.

Employer Liability

It is an employer's responsibility to maintain a harassment-free environment. Employers are legally liable for discriminatory harassment. Employers may prevent and eliminate workplace harassment as well as limit their liability in cases in which there are founded complaints of discriminatory harassment by:

- Disseminating the organization's antiharassment and nondiscrimination policies and procedures
- Supporting the policies
- Reviewing the policies annually
- Maintaining an internal complaint process, which promptly investigates complaints brought to the employer's attention
- Addressing substantiated complaints brought to the employer's attention by taking appropriate disciplinary and/or preventive action (conciliation, mediation, instruction, termination, etc.) to eliminate the conduct
- Preventing retaliation against staff members who have filed a complaint or offered testimony during an investigative process
- Providing information to help employees recognize, prevent, and respond effectively to hostile work environment harassment

Resources:

Civil Rights Act of 1964, Title VII. http://www.eeoc.gov.

Amanda Easton

H1B VISAS

Definition: Nonimmigrant versus Immigrant

There are two types of visas. An immigrant visa (IV) is given to those aliens seeking to immigrate or reside permanently within the United States. Examples of immigrant visa classifications are IR1(immediate relative) and EB1 (employment-based worker). Nonim-migrant visas (NIV), on the other hand, are obtained by people choosing to enter the United States for a prescribed period of time and who do not intend to permanently reside within the United States. The H1B classification is considered a nonimmigrant classification.

Description of H1B Nonimmigrant Classification

The H1B nonimmigrant visa is meant for temporary workers who will eventually return to their home country. The length of stay of an H1B is three years and is eligible for one three-year extension. After the six years is complete, the alien must return to his home country or change status to another category. This category is subject to numerical limitations and needs to be closely monitored in order to keep the employer and visa holder in status and compliant with U.S. immigration law.

The H1B classification is an employment-based nonimmigrant visa. The Immigration and Nationality Act (INA) places numerical limitations on some visa classifications. The numbers in parentheses represent the annual limit on H1B visas in each category. Institutions of higher education are exempt from the numerical limitations and can apply for H1B classifications for employees at any time. The category is defined as a "specialty occupation which requires the theoretical and practical application of a body of highly specialized knowledge requiring completion of a specific course of higher educa-tion. This classification requires a labor attestation issued by the Secretary of Labor. This classification also applies to government-to-government research and development, or coproduction projects administered by the Department of Defense."[1]

Application Process for H1B

What Forms Are Required?

A form I-129 must be submitted to the U.S. Citizenship and Immigration Service (CIS). This form is completed by the employer to request a specific employee to enter on an H1B visa. This I-129 must be approved prior to the alien's application at a U.S. embassy or consulate. In support of the I-129 petition, the employer must show evidence that a labor condition application was filed with the Department of Labor, that the employment qualifies, and that the alien has a bachelor's degree or higher, an equivalent foreign degree, or evidence of education and experience equivalent to the required degree. The employer must pay at least the prevailing wage for the required skills and experience.[2] The prevailing wage regulation is in effect so the employer does not attempt to hire non-immigrants at a lower rate than the U.S. labor wage.

Once the I-129 has been approved, persons who reside outside of the United States must complete a form DS-156 and DS-157. An interview will take place at the U.S. embassy or consulate in the country of origin.

Time Line for Application

Due to the numerical limitations, all I-129 petitions can be submitted to the CIS on April 1, but prior to October 1 (the beginning date of the federal fiscal year). The CIS will adjudicate the petitions until the numerical limitations have been reached. Historically, those petitions filed closest to April 1 have the greatest likelihood of being approved prior to reaching the numerical limitation.

"Within the U.S. Applicants" vs. "Abroad" Applicants?

In some cases, aliens who may already reside in the United States are required to apply in a different visa category. F-1 students, F-1 students on optional practical training, J-1 exchange students, or J-1 exchange scholars are examples of individuals who typically change their visa status. They are also examples of other nonimmigrant categories that change status.

Visas are issued only outside of the United States. Therefore, if a beneficiary of an I-129 petition already resides in the United States, the beneficiary changes status rather than obtains a visa. When the person leaves the United States, she will need to obtain a visa from the U.S. embassy or consulate abroad. However, if she does not leave the United States, the change of status is sufficient. Once the petition has been approved, the beneficiary receives a receipt (I-797 form) with a new I-94 (Record of Admission) stating their H1B status. The I-94 form and a passport is sufficient to prove the legal right to remain and work within the United States. It will be important for the H1B holder to obtain a Social Security card or a taxpayer ID in order to pay taxes.

Maintaining Status of H1B

A person who holds an H1B nonimmigrant visa must work for the employer that petitioned for the H1B Visa. The Visa holder is able to attend school and, in some cases, is eligible to petition for in-state tuition at institutions of higher education. The dependent of an H1B (i.e., spouse or child) is classified as H-4 nonimmigrants. The spouse and/or child are not able to work within the United States, but can attend school.

NOTES

1. U.S. Department of State, "Temporary Workers," U.S. Government, http://travel.state.gov/visa/temp/types/types_1271.html (accessed October 16, 2007).
2. U.S. Citizenship and Immigration Service, "I-129 Instructions," U.S. Government, http://www.uscis.gov/files/form/i-129instr.pdf (accessed October 16, 2007).

Paul M. Shelton

I-9 FORMS

The I-9, Employment Eligibility Verification, is a form required by the U.S. government, which the employer must keep on file for all employees. Citizens as well as noncitizens must provide the required information to their employer, who is required to keep the I-9 form on file for a minimum of three years beyond the date of hire or one year after employment termination, whichever comes first.

General Information

The purpose of the I-9 form is to have a record on file of the employee's eligibility to work in the United States. The form is kept with other human resource–related documents on file in the hiring company. The form is required by the Department of Homeland Security, U.S. Citizenship and Immigration Services (USCIS). However, the current version of the form, OMB number 1615-0047, expired in March 2007. USCIS guidelines tell us to continue to use this form, even though it is expired, until the new one is published. There is no set date for publication of the new I-9 form.

I-9 Form

The I-9 form contains three sections, one for the employee, one for the employer, and one for any changes that may occur during the period of employment, such as name change, documentation change, and status change.

Section 1: Employee Information and Verification

Section 1 asks for basic employee information such as name, address, date of birth, maiden name, Social Security number, and status. There is space to provide documentation numbers should the employee not be a U.S. citizen. USCIS provides a space for personal information of a translator if one was used.

Section 2: Employee Review and Verification

This portion of the form is crucial for employers. The review of appropriate documentation must take place prior to the hire date. Section 2 is where the employer must record the information gathered from the respective employee (Section 1). There are three lists referenced in Section 2: List A, List B, and List C. These lists show which documents are acceptable as proof that the prospective employee is authorized to work in the United States. All three lists are available for review on the last page of the I-9 form.

List A. List A contains documents that can be used as proof of eligibility to work in the United States. If the employee produces a valid document from List A, the employer does not need to see any other documentation because it confirms the perspective employee's identity and their employment eligibility. Some of the documents on List A are:

- U.S. passport
- Unexpired Employment Authorization card
- Permanent Resident card or Alien Registration card with Photograph

See the last page of the I-9 form for a complete list of acceptable documents.

Lists B and C. Lists B and C work in tandem to provide acceptable forms of identification and forms of employment eligibility. The prospective employee must produce a valid form from both List B and List C. One document from each list is enough to establish legal authorization to work in the United States. Some of the documents from List B are:

- State-issued driver's license or ID card
- U.S. military ID card or draft record
- U.S. military dependant ID card
- Native American tribal document

Some of the documents from List C are:

- Social Security card
- Original or certified copy of a U.S. birth certificate
- Unexpired employment authorization document from the Department of Homeland Security

See the last page of the I-9 form for a complete list of acceptable documents.

If the employee has lost the required documentation or the documentation is damaged, he can request a replacement. Regardless, the receipt showing that replacement documentation is being requested can be utilized; however, the replacement documentation must be produced within 90 days of hire. Receipts can not be used to show the request of initial documentation; they can be used only to show the request for replacement documentation. Receipts can not be utilized for temporary employment lasting less than three days.

Section 3: Updating and Reverification

This section is to be filled out by the employer. It is used to document changes in the employee's status. Employers are required to record name changes, documentation changes, and the date of rehire if applicable. This is also the section that will be used if the employee's "employment authorization" or "employment authorization documentation" expires and new authorization documentation is issued. In this case, a new I-9 form should be filled out and attached to the previous I-9 form. If the employment authorization or appropriate documentation expires, then the employment must end because the employee is no longer authorized to work in the United States.

Penalties for Noncompliance

Employers who do not comply with the requirement to complete, retain, or present the I-9 form for inspection are subject to fines ranging from $110 to $1,100 per employee. Employers who knowingly hire, recruit, or refer for employment unauthorized aliens are subject to fines ranging from $250 to $2,000 per unauthorized alien (first offense). Second and third offenses are fined beginning at $2,200 and $3,000, respectively.

Conclusion

The I-9 form is a federal requirement designed to protect the employer from penalties resulting from hiring unauthorized or undocumented aliens, and to protect the U.S. workforce from those who would illegally seek employment. Take careful and exact steps when reviewing and documenting the required documentation presented by the perspective employee, or upon receiving updated documentation from current employees.

*See also*Immigration Reform and Control Act (IRCA)

Resources:
Department of Homeland Security. U.S. Citizenship and Immigration Services Web site. http://www.uscis.gov.

Henry H. Luckel Jr.

IMMIGRATION REFORM AND CONTROL ACT (IRCA)

The Immigration Reform and Control Act of 1986 (IRCA), also called the Simpson-Mazzoli Act, was signed into law by President Ronald Regan on November 6, 1986. The IRCA was passed to control unauthorized immigration to the United States. Employers are required to verify that all employees hired after December 1, 1988, are legally eligible to work in the United States.

The IRCA has three provisions; it (1) made it illegal to knowingly hire or recruit undocumented workers (immigrants who do not possess lawful work authorization), (2) required employers to attest to their employees' immigration status, and (3) granted amnesty to undocumented workers who entered the United States prior to January 1, 1982, and had resided there continuously.

Under the IRCA, employers may hire only individuals who are legally authorized to work in the United States, such as citizens, U.S. nationals, and aliens with legal work authorization. The employer must verify the identity and employment eligibility of any person to be hired. This requires completion of the Employment Eligibility Verification form (INS Form I-9), which employers must keep on file for at least three years or one year after employment ends, whichever is longer.

A prospective employee may establish identity and legal employment eligibility by providing certain documents, often called List A, List B, or List C documents. Documents that are acceptable for establishing both identity and employment eligibility, called List A documents, include a (1) U. S. passport, (2) an unexpired foreign passport with attached employment authorization, (3) an Alien Registration Receipt card or Permanent Resident card, (4) an unexpired Temporary Resident Ccard, (5) an unexpired Employment Authorization card, or (6) an unexpired Employment Authorization document issued by the INS that contains a photograph.

List B documents that are acceptable for establishing one's identity include a (1) federal, state, or local government agency or entity identification card containing a photograph or information such as name, date of birth, gender, height, eye color, and address; (2) a driver's license issued by a state or a U.S. possession containing a photograph or information such as name, date of birth, gender, height, eye color, and address; (3) a school identification card with a photograph; (4) a voter registration card; (5) a U.S. military card or draft record; (6) a military dependent identification; (7) a U.S. Coast Guard Merchant Mariner card; 8) Native American tribal documents; or 9) a driver's license issued by a Canadian government authority. Individuals under 18 years of age may establish their identity by producing (1) a school record or report card; (2) a clinic, doctor, or hospital record; or (3) a day care or nursery school record.

List C documents acceptable for establishing employment eligibility include (1) a non-laminated Social Security number card other than one that has printed on its face "not valid for employment purposes in the United States"; (2) an original or certified copy of a birth certificate bearing an official seal issued by a state, county, municipal authority, or possession of the United States; (3) a certification of birth abroad issued by the U.S. Department of State; (4) a Native American tribal document; (5) a U. S. citizen identification card; (6) an identification card for use of a resident citizen of the United States; or (7) an unexpired employment authorization issued by the INS (other than these for identity and employment eligibility.

Section H-2A

Section H-2A of the IRCA authorizes lawful admission of temporary, nonimmigrant workers (H-2A workers) to perform agricultural labor or services of a temporary or seasonal nature. Employers are certified for a certain number of H-2A jobs, yet must initially and continuously engage in recruitment of U.S. workers to fill the positions. Certified employers must agree to accept U.S. workers until half (50 percent) of the contract period has been completed, and may not pay less than the federal minimum wage.

Certified H-2A employers must keep records of actual hours worked by employees, "offered" hours, and "refused" hours and provide wage statements that reveal hours worked and refused, basis of pay, total earnings, and all wage deductions for the period.

Enforcement

The Immigration and Naturalization Service enforces the IRCA, which seeks to preserve jobs for those who are legally entitled to work in the United States. Failure to comply by employers who knowingly hire aliens not authorized to work in the United States may result in both civil and criminal liability, with fines ranging from $250 to $10,000 for each unauthorized alien employee, along with possible imprisonment when a pattern or practice of noncompliance is present.

See also: I-9 Forms; H1B Visas

Resources:

Immigration Reform and Control Act of 1986. U.S. Social Security Administration Web site, https://secure.ssa.gov/apps10/poms.nsf/lnx/0500501440; and Wikipedia, http://en.wikipedia.org /wiki/immigration_reform_and_control_act_of_1986.

U.S. Department of Labor. Employment Standards Association.http://www.dol.gov/esa.

U.S. Department of Labor. Wage and Hour Division.http://www.wagehour.dol.gov.

U.S. Social Security Administration. http://www.ssa.gov.

Ann Gilley and Jennifer A. Majkowski

JURY DUTY LEAVE

Jury duty leave is time, sometimes paid for by the employer, to allow an employee to serve on a jury or grand jury. The Jury Systems Improvement Act, 28 USC 1875, is the federal law that deals with employees serving on a federal jury. States and some localities have their own laws concerning jury duty requirements. A company does not, by federal law, have to provide for paid jury duty leave for their employees who are called to serve on a jury or a grand jury. However, companies must allow their employees to serve on federal, state, or local juries. Employees may take leaves of absence to serve on a jury, without fear of disciplinary action by the employer. Employees who take a leave of absence to serve on a federal jury must be returned to their previous jobs, with the same pay. Employers who violate the Jury Systems Improvement Act are subject to fines of up to $1,000.

Some states require companies to provide for paid jury duty leave. Many companies, in addition, provide for paid jury duty leave regardless of state or local law. The following lists provide an overview of state law.

States Requiring Full Payment DURING Jury Duty

- *Alabama*—The employer is liable for usual pay, minus any compensation the employee received for serving on a jury.
- *Delaware*—Requires companies to pay the employee their normal pay. They are not allowed to deduct any per diem payments.
- *Georgia*—Employees will receive their normal pay while serving.
- *Nebraska*—The employer is liable for usual pay, minus any compensation the employee received for serving on a jury. Expenses are not to be deducted from the pay.
- *Tennessee*—The employer is liable for usual pay, minus any compensation the employee received for serving on a jury. Expenses are not to be deducted from the pay.

States Requiring Partial Payment DURING Jury Duty

— *Connecticut*—Full-time employees, those working 30 hours or more per week, must be compensated their normal pay for the first five days of jury duty.
— *Colorado*—Employers are liable to pay employees serving on jury duty up to $50 per day for the first three days or any part of those first three days.
— *Louisiana*—State law requires employers to pay for one full day of jury duty.
— *Massachusetts*—Employers are liable to pay employees serving on jury duty, up to $50 per day for the first three days or any part of those first three days.
— *New York*—Companies with more than 10 employees are required to pay $40 of the employee's wages per day for the first three days of jury duty.

States That Do Not Require Payment for Jury Duty

Alaska	Arizona	Arkansas
California	District of Columbia	Florida
Hawaii	Idaho	Illinois
Indiana	Iowa	Kansas
Kentucky	Maine	Maryland
Michigan	Minnesota	Mississippi
Missouri	New Hampshire	New Jersey
New Mexico	Nevada	North Carolina
North Dakota	Oklahoma	Ohio
Oregon	Pennsylvania	Puerto Rico
Rhode Island	South Carolina	South Dakota
Texas	Utah	Vermont
Virginia	Washington	West Virginia
Wisconsin	Wyoming	

Resources:

Matthies Law Firm, P.C. "Summary of Employment Laws of the U.S. Federal Government." http://members.aol.com/mattlawfrm/fedlaw.htm.

U.S. Chamber of Commerce. "Jury Duty Leave." http://www.uschamber.com/sb/business/P05/P05_4340.asp.

Henry H. Luckel Jr.

LABOR-MANAGEMENT RELATIONS (TAFT-HARTLEY) ACT

The Labor-Management Relations Act of 1947[1] (also known as the Taft-Hartley Act) is a U.S. federal law regarding the activities and power of labor unions. The act set limits on allowable union activities through amending the National Labor Relations Act of 1935[2] (also known as the Wagner Act, or NLRA). The NLRA set guidelines for fair labor practices, but only addressed the acts of employers. Taft-Hartley addresses fair labor practices primarily through setting guidelines for employees, unions, and collective bargaining.

The Labor-Management Relations Act came about as the culmination of 12 years of battles over fair labor practices, starting immediately after passage of the National Labor Relations Act on July 5, 1935. The purpose of the NLRA was "to protect the rights of employees and employers, to encourage collective bargaining, and to curtail certain private sector labor and management practices, which can harm the general welfare of workers, businesses and the U.S. economy."[3] The NLRA also created the National Labor Relations Board (NLRB) to oversee all issues related to the NLRA.

Employers, with great influence from the National Association of Manufacturers, immediately began pressuring lawmakers to repeal or amend the NLRA, citing increases in union striking activities harming the economy in general. Lawmakers reacted energetically, proposing 232 bills to address this issue between 1935 and 1947 before passing Taft-Hartley.[4]

Unfair Labor Practices by Organized Labor Unions

The amendments in Taft-Hartley detail a list of unfair labor practices, many of which were in use by the unions at the time. The act outlaws the following activities:

- Monetary donations by unions to federal political campaigns
- Forcing an employer to bargain collectively with any representative from any other labor union, other than that which is certified as the representative of their employees
- Closed shops—binding agreements disallowing the employer(s) from hiring individuals who were not already members of a labor union
- Expelling union members from their union for any reason other than nonpayment of dues
- Jurisdictional strikes—a picketing tactic used to pressure employers to assign specific duties to union members
- Causing or attempting to cause an employer to compensate employees or affiliates for services which were not performed
- Secondary boycotts and "common situs" picketing—picketing, striking, or the refusal to handle goods of a business with which the union is trying to gain entry

Strikes

Taft-Hartley requires unions and employers to provide written notice to each other 60 days prior to any striking or other forms of action designed to influence collective bargaining. They are furthermore required to provide notice to the Federal Mediation and Conciliation Service within 30 days after notice of the existence of a dispute. They must also notify any state or territorial agency established to mediate and conciliate disputes within the state or territory where the dispute occurred, provided no agreement has been reached by that time.[5]

If a union is found to participate in a secondary boycott, Taft-Hartley mandates that the General Council of the NLRB seek injunctions against the offending union. The General Council of the NLRB has discretionary rights over the pursuit of injunctions against either unions or employers believed to be in violation of the act in other cases.

Members of Management

Taft-Hartley excludes members of management and other supervisors from coverage under the act. The act states that people in such roles must represent and support their employer's stance in regard to union activity. Failure to do so provides the employer with legal grounds to terminate employment of the manager in question. The act allows union representation for many professional employees, but these professionals are subject to special procedures before being allowed to join a bargaining unit with nonprofessional employees.

Rights of Employers

Taft-Hartley allows employers to express opposition to unionization. However, employers may not make threats to the safety or well-being of employees, nor may they make promises or bribes of any kind to employees in order to persuade them away from organizing. Employers were also given the right to file civil suits against unions to recoup losses due to damages suffered from secondary boycotts.

Union shops, shops where new employees are required to join the union within 30 days of accepting employment (as opposed to joining prior to employment), are still allowed, but they are heavily restricted. Furthermore, states were given the right to pass "right-to-work" laws outlawing union shops. The president of the United States was also given the authority to end striking activities through strikebreaking injunctions in cases in which striking had a significant impact on national health or safety.

Opposition and Criticism

President Harry S. Truman was not in favor of this act. He argued that Taft-Hartley would increase the number of strikes, would deprive workers of vital protection under the law, and would put the general public at risk during major strikes due to ineffective and discriminatory emergency procedures in the act. Truman vetoed the act, but the Senate was able to gather enough votes to overturn the veto, voting 68–25 in favor of passing the act into law on June 23, 1947.[6]

The American Civil Liberties Union pushed Congress to develop a union democracy bill throughout the debates between 1935 and 1947. The goals of the bill were to prohibit union discrimination on the basis of race, sex, opinion, and other factors; require regular and fair union elections; offer NLRB protection to union members criticizing union leadership; and require accounting of funds. None of these issues were addressed by Taft-Hartley.[7]

See also National Labor Relations Acts (NLRA); Labor Unions

NOTES

1. Labor-Management Relations Act of 1947, Public Law 101, 80th Cong., 1st sess. (June 23, 1947).

2. National Labor Relations Act of 1935, Public Law 101, 74th Cong., 1st sess. (July 5, 1935).

3. National Labor Relations Board, "National Labor Relations Act," National Labor Relations Board, http://www.nlrb.gov/about_us/overview/national_labor_relations_act.aspx (accessed October 15, 2007).

4. Ibid.

5. Labor-Management Relations Act of 1947.

6. Harry A. Millis and Emily Clark Brown, *From the Wagner Act to Taft-Hartley* (Chicago: University of Chicago Press, 1950).

7. Michael J. Goldberg, "An Overview and Assessment of the Law Regulating Internal Union Affairs," *Journal of Labor Research* 21, no. 1 (2000): 15–36.

Adam VanDreumel

MILITARY LEAVE

Military leave is a right, not a privilege, granted by Congress to all members of the armed forces under federal law. Leave is paid vacation from active duty for recreation and relief from the pressures of job-related duties; it is also taken for personal reasons and emergency situations. Department of Defense (DoD) Directive 1327.5, *Leave and Liberty,* is the overriding directive that governs all military personnel; however, each of the services (Army, Air Force, Navy, Marines, and Coast Guard) has its own service-specific regulations that detail the authorities, processes, and procedures for military leave.

Generally speaking, military leave accrues at the rate of 2.5 calendar days per month for service members on active duty. However, Congress recognizes that military requirements may prevent members from using their planned leave, so the law permits service members to accrue a maximum of 60 days carried over into the next fiscal year. The expression "use or lose" means that any leave in excess of 60 days is lost if not used by the end of the fiscal year (September 30).

Military leave laws are pretty straightforward with regard to service members on active duty. The complexity usually occurs with National Guard members and reservists who are entitled to military leave due to time spent away from their civilian employers while on active duty. Within the past couple of decades, there has been an increasingly greater reliance on using the Reserve Component to augment a smaller active duty force in support of worldwide contingency operations (e.g., Gulf War I and II) and the Global War on Terror. More and more civilian employers are seeing their employees undergo military training or being recalled to active duty on either a voluntary or an involuntary basis.

The major federal law protecting reservists and Guardsman is the Uniformed Services Employment and Reemployment Rights Act (USERRA) of 1994. USERRA protects the jobs, employment rights, military leave, and benefits of Reserve Component service members who are serving on active duty. Also known as the "military leave law," USERRA covers "absences to perform military duty in a uniformed service" and includes training and weekend drills as well as both voluntary and involuntary recall to active duty.[1] In addition, the law gives employees on military leave the option of using paid vacation time while on leave, but the employer is not allowed to require that they do so. The Veterans' Benefits Improvement act of 2004 requires all employers, regardless of size—public and private—to notify all employees annually of their legal rights under USERRA. Although most states have a military leave law, the federal statute provided under USERRA supersedes state legislation, except in cases when the state statute is more generous to the employee.

USERRA does not require an employer to pay an employee on military leave for the time off; however, federal employees who are members of the National Guard or Reserves are entitled to 15 days (120 hours) of paid military leave each fiscal year for active duty, active duty training, and inactive duty training according to law. 5 US Code 6323 also outlines certain conditions in which workdays of military leave for federal employees may be increased for either "emergency duty" or "contingency operation."[2]

The 2008 National Defense Authorization Act, signed by the president on January 28, 2008, includes the first significant expansion of the Family and Medical Leave Act (FMLA) since it became law in 1993. The most notable changes in the newly revised FMLA are the provisions to assist military service members—active duty, National Guard, and Reserves—and their families:

— *FMLA leave for call to active duty of a service member.* Employees are entitled to 12 weeks of FMLA leave due to a spouse, son, daughter, or parent being on active duty or having been recalled to active duty in the armed forces. Leave may be used for "any qualifying exigency" arising out of the family member's active duty or call to duty.

— *FMLA caregiver leave for injured service members.* Employees are entitled to up to 26 weeks of total FMLA leave in a 12-month period to care for an injured or seriously ill service member who suffered the injury or illness while on active duty. In addition to spouses, children, and parents (already covered under the FMLA), a service member's "nearest blood relative" or "next of kin" is also eligible for this type of leave.

The new FMLA provisions are both confusing and complex, since many provisions are currently unclear. For example, "any qualifying exigency" has yet to be defined by the Department of Labor. Potential situations could include overseas assignments, recalls to active duty, and troop mobilizations. Until then, employers are required to act in good faith in attempting to comply with the law, since some portions take effect immediately.

See also Family Medical Leave Act (FMLA); Uniformed Services Employment and Reemployment Act

NOTES

1. U.S. Department of Labor, Veterans' Employment and Training Service, "A Non-Technical Resource Guide to the Uniformed Employment and Reemployment Rights Act—USERRA" (U.S. Government, April 2005), 1–18.

2. U.S. Office of Personnel Management, "Military Leave," http://www.opm.gov/oca/leave/html/military.asp (accessed February 1, 2008).

Victoria T. Dieringer

MINIMUM WAGE

Minimum wage provisions are outlined as part of the Fair Labor Standards Act and are enforced by the Wage and Hour Division of the Department of Labor. The purpose of minimum wage is to provide an income floor for low-wage earning workers so they may maintain a minimum standard of living that keeps them from poverty.[1] The majority of workers earning minimum wage are in the service industry, where tips are meant to supplement regular pay.[2]

Today, legislation has been enacted at the federal and state levels that works to continuously drive pay rate increases. Congress has the authority to change minimum wage at any time. As of July 24, 2008, the federal minimum wage was $6.55 per hour and will increase to $7.25 on July 24, 2009.[3] Most states and some cities have passed minimum wage laws that exceed federal mandates. For example, as of July 2008, the state of Michigan's minimum wage was $7.40 per hour, $8.00 for California residents, $8.07 for

Washington, and $9.36 in the city of San Francisco.[4] Increases in state minimum wage rates are often tied to inflation or the Consumer Price Index.

The goal of minimum wage legislation is to assist the working poor; however, it has been evidenced that it is has had a detrimental effect on poverty in certain sectors of the workforce, particularly unskilled minority youth. Minimum wage does not impact only the workers earning the wage. It has a direct impact on employers and their costs. As wages at the low end of the range continue to rise, so do wages at the midpoint and higher end.

In some cases, there are exemptions to minimum wage regulations.[5] Some examples include vocational students working in retail; agriculture; higher education institutions; and individuals whose earning capacity is impaired by a disability. In all of these cases, employers must receive a certificate from the Wage and Hour Division of the Department of Labor.

See also Exempt and Nonexempt Employees; Fair Labor Standards Act; Overtime

NOTES

1. George, T. Milkovich, Jerry Newman, and Carolyn Milkovich, *Compensation* (New York: Irwin/McGraw-Hill, 2007).

2. Ibid.

3. U.S. Department of Labor, Wage and Hour Division, http://www.dol.gov/esa/whd (accessed March 29, 2008).

4. Ibid.

5. Ibid.

Pamela Dixon

NATIONAL LABOR RELATIONS ACT (NLRA)

The National Labor Relations Act was created by the National Labor Relations Board (NLRB) in 1935. The *NLRB* is an independent federal agency that was created by Congress to administer the National Labor Relations Act (NLRA), which is the primary law governing relations between unions and employers in the private sector; the main purpose of the act is to encourage healthy relationships between workers and employers. Overall, the NLRA "guarantees the right of employees to organize and to bargain collectively with their employers, and to engage in other protected concerted activity with or without a union, or to refrain from all such activity."[1]

The NLRA was designed to decrease and manage work stoppages, strikes, and general labor strife, which, at the time of conception, were viewed as being harmful to the U.S. economy and to the nation's general well-being. The NLRA extends many rights to workers who wish to form, join, or support unions, also known as labor organizations; to workers who are already represented by unions; and to another group of workers (a group being defined as two or more employees) who collaborate without a union and are seeking to modify their wages or working conditions. This third described group of workers' efforts is often referred to as protected concerted activities, which is further described below.

The NLRA extends rights to employers as well as employees, most often protecting commercial interests against unfair actions committed by labor organizations. It also extends rights to labor organizations; this often comes in the form of "protecting organizational and collective-bargaining representative interests against unfair actions committed by employers."[2]

The National Labor Relations Act outlines basic rights of employees as follows:

- The right to self-organization.
- The right to form, join, or assist labor organizations.
- The right to bargain collectively for wages and working conditions through representatives of their own choosing.
- The right to engage in other protected concerted activities with or without a union, which are usually group activities (two or more employees acting together) attempting to improve working conditions, such as wages and benefits.
- The right to refrain from any of these activities. (However, a union and employer may, in a state where such agreements are permitted, enter into a lawful union-security clause).[3]

Protected Concerted Activities

Protected concerted activities is loosely defined as a group of employees that consists of two or more people who are acting together to improve their wages or working conditions. Protected concerted activities are protected under the NLRA whether or not they are acting with in alliance with a union. Some examples of protected concerted activities include:

- Two or more employees addressing their employer about improving their working conditions and pay.
- One employee speaking to his/her employer on behalf of him/herself and one or more coworkers about improving workplace conditions.
- Two or more employees discussing pay or other work-related issues with each other. The NLRA also protects any individual employee's right to engage in union support, membership, and activities.[4]

Conversely, the NLRA protects an individual employee's right not to engage in union activities or in other protected, concerted activities.[5]

Unions and Labor Organizations

The NRLA addresses employees' rights regarding unions and other labor organizations in Section 7. It advises that employees have the right to self-organization.[6] According to the National Labor Relations Act, they have the right to form, join, or assist labor organizations, to bargain collectively through representatives of their own choosing, and to engage in other concerted activities for the purpose of collective bargaining or other mutual aid or protection.[7] Additionally, employees also have the right to refrain from any or all noted activities except to the extent that their right may be affected by an agreement requiring membership in a labor organization as a condition of employment as authorized in section.[8]

The following are examples of Section 7 rights with regard to unions:

- Forming or attempting to form a union among the employees of a company
- Joining a union whether the union is recognized by the employer or not
- Assisting a union to organize the employees of an employer
- Going on strike to secure better working conditions
- Refraining from activity on behalf of a union[9]

See also Labor-Management Relations (Taft-Hartley) Act; Labor Unions

NOTES

1. National Labor Relations Board, "What We Do," http://www.nlrb.gov/ (accessed September 26, 2007).

2. Ibid.National Labor Relations Board. (n.d.a). *Homepage: What we do.* Retrieved on September 26, 2007 from: http://www.nlrb.gov/.

3. National Labor Relations Board, "What Is the National Labor Relations Act?" http://www.nlrb.gov/Workplace_Rights/i_am_new_to_this_website/what_is_the_national_labor_relations_act.aspx (accessed September 26, 2007).

4. National Labor Relations Board, "What Are Protected Concerted Activities?" http://www.nlrb.gov/Workplace_Rights/i_am_new_to_this_website/what_are_protected_concerted_activities.aspx (accessed September 26, 2007).

5. Ibid.

6. National Labor Relations Board, "Basic Guide to the National Labor Relations Act: General Principles of Law under the Statute and Procedures of the National Labor Relations Board" (1997), http://www.nlrb.gov/nlrb/shared_files/brochures/basicguide.pdf (accessed September 26, 2007).

7. Ibid.

8. Ibid.

9. Ibid.

Lea Hanson

NORRIS-LAGUARDIA ACT

The Norris-LaGuardia Act, 1932 was cosponsored by Nebraska Republican Senator George Norris and Republican Representative Fiorello LaGuardia of New York. The Norris-LaGuardia Act made it illegal for an employer to require a prospective employee to avoid union membership as a condition of employment. Norris-LaGuardia also removed the authority of federal courts to issue injunctions to stop non- violent pickets and other activities of those on strike.

Background

Prior to the passing of the Norris-LaGuardia Act in 1932, employers had the advantage in most labor disputes. Between 1880 and 1930, courts issued approximately 4,300 antistrike decrees. Employees were at the mercy of their employers, who made it difficult for labor unions to be effective. Employers could simply fire employees for activities such as striking. Employees could also be required to agree to not join a labor union as a condition of employment, or to remove their membership in a union in order to keep their jobs. These were known as "yellow dog" contracts or agreements. All of that changed with the passing of the Norris-LaGuardia Act. The law also barred federal courts from issuing restraining orders or injunctions against activities by labor unions and individuals, including the following:

• joining or organizing a union, or assembling for union purposes;
• striking or refusing to work, or advising others to strike or organize;
• Publicizing acts of a Labor dispute; and
• providing lawful legal aid to persons participating in a labor dispute

Conclusion

The Norris-LaGuardia Act of 1932 ushered in a new era in labor relations, moving the advantages of labor disputes from the employer to the employee, and removing the courts' authority to issue injunctions against those engaged in legal union activities. It also ensured the right of one union to support another union in their labor dispute. Now, only the highest courts can issue injunctions against those engaged in legal union activities, and then only under very specific rules, generally to prevent bodily harm or property damage from occurring.

Resources:

Ewonaitis, Katie. "The Norris-LaGuardia Act."http://www.stfrancis.edu/ba/ghkickul/stuwebs/btopics/works/norrislaguardia.htm.

"Federal Labor Laws." http://history.eserver.org/us-labor-law.txt.

Henry H. Luckel Jr.

OCCUPATIONAL SAFETY AND HEALTH ACT

The Occupational Safety and Health Administration (OSHA), instituted in 1971, is a federal regulatory agency within the U.S. Department of Labor designed to protect the safety and health rights of all employees in the work environment. It sets and enforces standards such as the Bloodborne Pathogen Standard, which requires employers to adopt practices and procedures reasonably necessary and appropriate to protect workers against occupational exposure to blood or other potentially infectious materials,[1] and performs investigations and inspections. OSHA's purpose is to provide guidelines and support for employers as they develop, implement, and continuously endeavor to improve effective safety and health programs in the workplace. Workplace fatalities have decreased by 60 percent, and occupational injury and illness rates are down by 40 percent, since the emergence of OSHA.[2]

Compliance with OSHA

The human resources manager is responsible for becoming completely informed of and familiar with all Occupational Safety and Health Act (OSH Act, also known as OSHA) requirements that apply to the organization and working with the employer to keep up to code with current OSHA standards. This involves employee training and education; posting OSHA standards, notices, and obligations; documentation; providing each employee with personal protective equipment (PPE); and maintaining a safe work environment.

In general, an employer is responsible for providing a place of employment that is free from recognized hazards that may cause serious injury or death to employees. Employees, in turn, are responsible for complying with occupational safety and health standards and all rules, regulations, and orders that apply to their own actions and conduct.

An important part of OSHA compliance is posting of a comprehensive safety plan along with compilation of Material Safety Data Sheets (MSDS). Safety plans convey the organization's commitment to safety before, during, and after an injury or accident by detailing expectations of all employees' on-the-job safety-related behaviors, procedures, authority and responsibility, contact information, and the like. An MSDS lists the composition of the materials used in the workplace, health risks involved with use of these materials, safe handling practices, personal protective equipment needed for use, first aid in case of contact, and information identifying the manufacturer. The MSDS needs to be readily and easily available to employees, and a notice of their location has to be visibly posted in the workplace.

Documentation

Documentation/recordkeeping is essential in observing OSHA guidelines. Employee injuries and training, conducted prior to task assignments in which occupational exposure may occur and be updated periodically, must be documented. OSHA provides recording forms, which are available at http://www.osha.gov/recordkeeping/OSHArecordkeeping forms.pdf. In the event of a work-related injury or illness, OSHA Form 301, the Injury and Illness Incident Report, must be completed. This form requires information on the employee, physician or health care provider, and details about the case. OSHA Form 300 is a log used to record all incidents for the year, including case number, employee name and title, date of the injury, description of the injury, classification (death, days away from work, job transfer or restriction, or other), the number of days the worker was transferred, restricted, or away from work, and the type of injury or illness. An annual summary of work-related injuries and illnesses is to be submitted on OSHA Form 300A.

Current OSHA standards need to be posted, as well as citations and appeal decisions. These records verify OSHA compliance in case of inspection.

Training will help to keep employees up to date on safety measures, thus hopefully ensuring a safer work environment. Personal protective equipment (PPE) that is required by OSHA in a given workplace is to be provided, free of charge, by the employer; another defense against injury or exposure to the worker. Depending on the work environment, PPE may include latex or vinyl gloves, utility gloves, fluid-resistant lab coats, surgical gowns, face shields and/or protective eyewear with solid side shields, shoe covers, steel-toed boots, hard helmets, respirator face masks, and high-visibility clothing. The human resources manager will need to make sure that each employee who is required to use PPE is aware of why it is needed, how to properly use it, and the importance of always using it.[3]

Inspections, Penalties, and Further Information

If necessary, OSHA will conduct scheduled or surprise workplace inspections to determine whether safety violations have occurred. The OSHA area director issues citations and determines appropriate penalties, if any. "Serious" violations of OSHA carry a mandatory $7,000 penalty, while "other than serious" violations may be fined up to $7,000. "Willful" violations carry a minimum penalty of $5,000 up to a maximum of $70,000, "repeat" offenses may be fined up to $70,000, and employers whose "failure to correct" previous violations may be fined up to $70,000 per day for each day the condition is uncorrected.[4]

Employees have the right to file a complaint and remain anonymous if they choose. The employer has the right to receive an employee complaint before it goes to OSHA, see identification of and accompany an inspector on an inspection tour, have an inspector return for inspection if in the middle of something work-related, have a conference after the investigation, and appeal the investigation, penalty, fine, or other finding. For further information, log in at the OSHA Web site—http://www.osha.gov—or call 1-800-321-OSHA (6742). For an official agency response, one may write to:

Domestic Only:
U.S. Department of Labor
Occupational Safety and Health Administration
200 Constitution Avenue
Washington, DC 20210
International
U.S. Department of Labor
OSHA Coordinator for International Affairs
Occupational Safety and Health Administration—Room N3641
200 Constitution Avenue
Washington, DC 20210

NOTES

1. Sharon K. Dickinson, Richard D. Bebermeyer, and Karen Ortolano, "Guidelines for Infection Control in Dental Health-Care Settings," http://www.dentalcare.com/soap/ce_prot/ce90/pg04.htm (accessed August 25, 2007).

2. "OSHA Facts," http://www.osha.gov/as/opa/oshafacts.html (accessed October 27, 2007).

3. "A Short Guide to the Personal Protective Equipment at Work Regulations 1992," http://www.hse.gov.uk/pubns/indg174.pdf (accessed January 13, 2008).

4. Ibid.

Julianne Daniels

OLDER WORKERS BENEFIT PROTECTION ACT

The demographics of the workforce in the United States are changing. The number of older workers is growing. According to the U.S. Census Bureau, 35 million Americans were 65 years of age and older in 2000, and the number of older Americans is expected to reach 66 million by 2025. In recognition of this trend, employers should be aware of the Older Worker Benefit Protection Act (OWBPA) signed into law in 1990 by President George H.W. Bush.[2] The act amends the Age Discrimination in Employment Act of 1967. The OWBPA has two major provisions: (1) protection of benefits, and (2) strict requirements for any waiver of age discrimination law protection.

Protection of Benefits

It is against the OWBPA to use an employee's age to differentiate in benefits or target older workers for layoffs. The protection of the OWBPA begins for employees at age 40.[3] For example, an employer cannot cut health insurance benefits for those employees who become eligible for Medicare. Employers must continue to provide benefits, equal to younger employees, as long as the eligible worker continues his employment.

Releases under the OWBPA

Employers who reduce their workforces or terminate employees for legitimate reasons often seek to prevent liability under the OWBPA by asking older employees to sign a waiver of the act's benefits at the time of the severance of their employment.

The act provides the following requirements for such a waiver:

- The waiver must be written in simple terms in plain English (without legal wording).
- The waiver covers only the rights of the employee at the time of discharge, not future rights with the company.
- The waiver must specifically refer to the Age Discrimination in Employment Act.
- The employee must receive something of value—beyond what is owed to her by virtue of the existing employment.
- The employee must be instructed, in writing, to review the waiver with her attorney.
- The employee must be allowed at least 21 days to decide whether to sign the waiver.
- If the waiver is presented to a group of employees, the length of time to consider the agreement must be lengthened to 45 days. Also, each member of the group (of any size) must be informed of the job titles and ages of employees included in the group.[3]
- If an employee signs a waiver under this act, she has seven days to revoke the decision.
- An employer cannot ask an employee to waive her right to pursue a discrimination claim against the company.

Failure to comply with any of the provisions of this act will invalidate the release and may subject the employer to age discrimination claims.

See also Age Discrimination in Employment Act (ADEA); Pension Plans

NOTES

1. United States Census Bureau, http://www.census.gov/ (accessed March 1, 2008).
2. Public Law 101-433.
3. 29 U.S.C. Section 623 *et. seq.*
4. Mary Swanton, "Layoff Liabilities," *Inside Counsel* 17, no. 190 (2007): 28–31.

Laura Dendinger

PENSION PROTECTION ACT OF 2006

The Pension Protection Act of 2006 (PPA) was signed into law by President Bush on August 17, 2006. This sweeping legislation includes a number of significant provisions designed to strengthen the pension insurance system, force employers to shore up their pension plans, and protect workers' retirement savings.

Highlights of the Act

The new law addresses a host of issues related to pensions, savings, and retirement, focusing heavily on defined benefit plan reform. The key provisions will be discussed here; however, please see the law for further details.

EGTRRA Permanence

The PPA repealed the "sunset provision" of the Economic Growth and Tax Relief Reconciliation Act of 2001 (EGTRRA) and made permanent many retirement and savings incentives. The EGTRRA, for example, raised contribution limits for defined contribution plans and IRAs, allowed rollovers among qualified plans, permitted 403(b) and 401(k) plans to accept Roth IRA–style contributions, allowed individuals age 50 and over to make additional "catch-up" contributions to their retirement plans and IRAs, and allowed tax-free withdrawals from Section 529 plans for qualified expenses.

IRA Changes

Adjusted gross income (AGI) limits are subject to cost-of-living adjustments for deductible traditional and Roth IRAs (as of 2007). Taxpayers who meet income eligibility limits are permitted to direct all or a portion of their federal tax refund to an IRA (up to the legal limit) since 2007.

Roth Contributions

The PPA permanently extends the Roth 401(k) and 403(b) features introduced in 2006 that were scheduled to expire in 2010. Employees may now make Roth-style after-tax contributions to employer-sponsored retirement plans, with potentially tax-free earnings and contributions withdrawals if the account has been open for five years and the employee is at least 59½ years old.

Rollover Rules

The act extends and enhances many of the rollover provisions of the EGTRRA. For example, beginning in 2008, workers may convert retirement plan funds directly into a Roth IRA without first rolling the funds into a traditional IRA. Ordinary after-tax balances in any qualified retirement plan may be rolled over to any 403(b) or qualified plan that agrees to accept the funds and track them separately. As of 2007, nonspouse beneficiaries have more retirement and estate planning flexibility as they can roll over inherited 403(b), qualified, or public 457(b) funds into their own IRAs.

New Vesting Schedule

The new law requires employers to vest matching *and* nonmatching employer contributions at 100 percent after completion of three years of service, beginning in plan years after December 31, 2006. Previously, employers were allowed to apply slower vesting schedules to both matching and nonmatching funds.

Benefit Statements

For plan years beginning after December 31, 2006, administrators of defined contribution plans are now required to provide at least quarterly statements to participants and beneficiaries. Benefit statements must include account balances, current vesting balances, investment allocation restrictions, and a cautionary statement with regard to the need to maintain a portfolio that is diversified and well balanced.

In-service Distributions

In-service distributions are withdrawals from retirement plans by active employees. As of 2007, 401(k) and other profit-sharing plans can allow in-service distributions (normally prohibited under federal law) by participants who are at least 62 years of age.

Defined Benefit Plans

The PPA modifies the rules for funding defined benefit plans and, in general, requires employers to increase contributions to their pension plans in order to strengthen them. Employers must fully fund their plans over a seven-year period and ensure sufficient plan assets to satisfy future obligations. The 2006 act also identifies "at risk" plans and requires stricter funding to provide stability and avoid asset shortfalls should the plan terminate. The PPA establishes benchmarks to identify at-risk plans and specifies steps to be taken to enhance stability.

Section 529 College Savings Plans

The PPA eliminates the sunset provision of the Section 529 College Savings Plans and makes the tax advantages permanent. Specifically, the PPA allows tax-free withdrawals for qualified expenses and authorizes the creation of prepaid tuition programs and rollovers from one account to another every 12 months.

Investment Advice

With respect to their own (or an affiliate's) contracts or funds, companies will be allowed to offer investment advice to participants in individually directed defined contribution plans or IRAs, subject to certain conditions.

Charitable/Tax-exempt Organizations

The 2006 act increases penalties on charitable organizations that fail to distribute income, have excess business holdings or investments that jeopardize their charitable purposes, and have certain taxable expenditures. The PPA establishes numerous and significant guidelines regarding charitable donations. It defines household items, disallows tax deductions for clothing or household items that are not in good used condition or better, increases penalties for gross overstatements of valuations of charitable deduction property, establishes definitions relating to appraisers and appraisals, and modifies recordkeeping requirements of monetary gifts, to name a few.

Conclusion

The Pension Protection Act of 2006 is a complex piece of legislation with widespread implications. The above highlights offer a glimpse of the act's provisions; please consult the act itself or your legal advisor for more information.

See also Pension Plans

Resources:
U.S. Department of Labor, http://www.dol.gov

Ann Gilley

PREFERENTIAL TREATMENT

Preferential treatment is a controversial term that is often used by individuals or groups concerned with the outcomes of affirmative action policies. Affirmative action commonly refers to policies undertaken by either private-sector businesses or public-sector governmental agencies to redress past grievances against certain racial and ethnic minorities[1] as well as women, individuals who are handicapped or physically challenged, and veterans. The usage of affirmative action (and, hence, the increased likelihood of preferential treatment being extended to certain individuals) is common within admissions to postsecondary educational institutions, hiring and promotion decisions, and the awarding of contracts for various goods and services. Preferential treatment is often used interchangeably with the term "reverse discrimination."

Civil Rights Act of 1964

Preferential treatment is included within Title VII, Section 703, of the 1964 Civil Rights Act. Title VII provides definitions for equal employment opportunity and explicitly prohibits discrimination against individuals because of "race, color, religion, sex, or national origin."[2] In fact, the text string "race, color, religion, sex, or national origin," and the conditions prohibiting it as a factor in employment decisions, is mentioned 13 times within the body of the 1964 Civil Rights Act. The term "preferential treatment" is mentioned twice within the act, although the context and definition is such that it conflicts with the context and definition of "affirmative action," and the conditions under which such affirmative actions may be offered, which is mentioned once (in Section 706 of Title VII, "Prevention of Unlawful Employment Practices"). Although the terms "preferential treatment" and "reverse discrimination" are often used synonymously in casual speech and other correspondence, the 1964 Civil Rights Act does not define, describe, or otherwise codify the latter term. As such, a person must be very careful when using either of these terms, as only "preferential treatment" receives formal definition within this document.

Landmark Legal Precedents

Even though a distinction between these two terms does exist, employers need to be cognizant of the various legal precedents that have been set, regardless of how the subject is couched. The U.S. Department of Veterans Affairs, within the division of Diversity Management and Equal Employment Opportunity (DM&EEO),[3] maintains lists of cases that have been pivotal in establishing the current legal environment with "reverse" discrimination, as well as other areas. Employers should also be aware of any state, county, and city or municipality laws that, while intended to redress past grievances through affirmative action programs and the like, may have the net effect of providing preferential treatment to certain individuals.

Laws outside the United States

Preferential treatment (or a variation of how it has come to be understood, interpreted, and implemented within the United States) does exist in other nations, as well. In Canada, the Employment Equity Act requires employers to submit annual reports to the federal government that detail representation of women, aboriginal citizens, persons with disabilities, and visible minorities within both federally regulated establishments and private businesses with 100 or more employees.[4] The Canadian Human Rights Commission is responsible for tracking the compliance of employers with the act, and conducts programs designed to reduce or minimize the likelihood of workplace discrimination.[5] Many other nations have similar laws to reduce perceived barriers to individuals who may have been discriminated against in the past, while others have ruled that affirmative action and preferential treatment are illegal or unconstitutional. In these latter instances, equal treatment is often seen as necessary to produce a "color blind" citizenry, where individual merit, ability, and achievement are paramount considerations in employment-related decisions.

Given the current state of preferential treatment (how it has been defined within the United States, U.S. court precedents, and the evolving legal and social environment that exist both within the United States and abroad), employers are advised to involve the appropriate personnel from human resources, legal, and government when considering the potential impact of training, record keeping, and correspondence with others regarding this matter. Otherwise, the possibility exists that even well-intentioned actions may have adverse consequences.

See also Affirmative Action; Civil Rights Acts of 1964 and 1991

NOTES

1. Law.com Law Dictionary, "Affirmative Action," http://dictionary.law.com/ (accessed February 11, 2008).
2. Our Documents, "Transcript of Civil Rights Act (1964)," http://www.ourdocuments.gov/ (accessed February 8, 2008).
3. U.S. Department of Veterans Affairs, Diversity Management and Equal Employment Opportunity, "EEO Cases," http://www.va.gov/dmeeo/eeocases/ (accessed February 11, 2008).
4. Department of Justice—Canada, "Employment Equity Act (1995, c.44)," http://laws.justice.gc.ca/en/ (accessed February 11, 2008).
5. Government of Canada, Canadian Human Rights Commission, "Resources" http://www.chrc-ccdp.ca/ (accessed February 11, 2008).

Steven J. Kerno Jr.

PREGNANCY DISCRIMINATION ACT (PDA)

The Pregnancy Discrimination Act is an amendment to Title VII of the Civil Rights Act of 1964. According to the U.S. Equal Employment Opportunity Commission, discrimination on the basis of pregnancy, childbirth, or any pregnancy related medical conditions "constitutes unlawful sex discrimination under Title VII. Women affected by pregnancy or related conditions must be treated in the same manner as other applicants or employees with similar abilities or limitations."[1]

Pregnancy-related protections include five areas: hiring, pregnancy and maternity leave, health insurance, fringe benefits, and disability due to a pregnancy.

Hiring

It is against the law to refuse to hire a woman because she is pregnant. According to Title VII (1964), "An employer cannot refuse to hire a pregnant woman because of her pregnancy, because of a pregnancy-related condition or because of the prejudices of co-workers, clients, or customers."[2]

Pregnancy and Maternity Related Leave

In determining a pregnant employee's eligibility to use sick leave or benefits, pregnancy related leave must be allowed under the same conditions that any other sick leave or benefits are used. Title VII (1964) states, "an employer may not single out pregnancy-related conditions for special procedures to determine an employee's ability to work."[3] However, if an employer requires its employees to submit a doctor's statement concerning their inability to work before granting leave or paying sick benefits, the employer may require employees affected by pregnancy-related conditions to submit such statements.

Additionally, if an employee is unable to perform her job for a brief amount of time due to pregnancy, the employer must treat her the same that other temporarily disabled employees are treated. For example, if the employer allows for temporarily disabled employees to modify work tasks or roles or take disability leave or leave without pay, that employer also must allow an employee who is temporarily disabled due to pregnancy to do those same options.

Pregnant employees must be permitted to work as long as they are able to perform their jobs. According to Title VII (1964), "if an employee has been absent from work as a result of a pregnancy-related condition and recovers, her employer may not require her to remain on leave until the baby's birth."[4] An employer also may not have a rule that prohibits an employee from returning to work for a predetermined length of time after childbirth.

Finally, Title VII (1964) deems that "employers must hold open a job for a pregnancy-related absence the same length of time jobs are held open for employees on sick or disability leave."[5]

Health Insurance

Any health insurance provided by an employer must cover expenses for pregnancy-related conditions on the same basis as costs for other medical conditions. "Pregnancy-related expenses should be reimbursed exactly as those incurred for other medical conditions, whether payment is on a fixed basis or a percentage of reasonable-and-customary-charge basis."[6] No additional, increased, or larger deductible can ever be imposed on a pregnant employee; the amounts payable by the insurance provider can only be limited to the same extent as amounts payable for any other medical condition.

Medical expenses for abortion, "except where the life of the mother would be endangered if the fetus were carried to term or where medical complications have arisen from an abortion, are not required to be paid by an employer; nothing herein, however, precludes an employer from providing abortion benefits or otherwise affects bargaining agreements in regard to abortion."[7]

Fringe Benefits

Pregnancy-related benefits cannot be limited to married or partnered employees. "Even in an all-female workforce or job classification, benefits must be provided for pregnancy-related conditions if benefits are provided for other medical conditions."[8]

Disability Due to Pregnancy

If employees acquire a short-term disability that is a result or is contributed to by pregnancy, childbirth, or related medical conditions, they must be treated the same as other temporarily disabled employees.[9] These benefits include written and unwritten employment policies and examples include but are not limited to vacation accrual, matters such as the commencement and duration of leave, the availability of extensions, the accrual of seniority and other benefits and privileges, reinstatement, and payment under any health or disability insurance or sick leave plan, formal or informal.[10]

Termination or Retaliation

Employees cannot be terminated due to a pregnancy, even if they do not have leave available. According to Title 29, "such a termination violates the Act if it has a disparate impact on employees of one sex and is not justified by business necessity."[11] It is also unlawful to "retaliate against an individual for opposing employment practices that discriminate based on pregnancy or for filing a discrimination charge, testifying, or participating in any way in an investigation, proceeding, or litigation" under Title VII.[12]

Resources:

Civil Rights Act of 1964, Title VII. *Pregnancy Discrimination.* http://www.eeoc.gov/types/pregnancy.html (accessed July 15, 2007).

Title 29—Labor. Chapter XIV—Equal Employment Opportunity Commission. *Guidelines on Discrimination because of Sex.* July 2006. http://a257.g.akamaitech.net/7/257/2422/01jul20061500/edocket.access.gpo.gov/cfr_2006/julqtr/29cfr1604.10.htm (accessed July 15, 2007).

Lea Hanson

NOTES

1. Civil Rights Act of 1964, Title VII, para. 1.
2. Ibid., para. 3.
3. Ibid., para. 4.
4. Ibid.
5. Ibid., para. 7.
6. Ibid., para. 9.
7. Title 29, para. 2.
8. Title VII, para. 12.
9. Title VII; Title 29.
10. Ibid.
11. Title 29, para. 3.
12. Title VII, para. 15.

PRIMA FACIE

HRM professionals must be knowledgeable about employment-related statutes, and view compliance as both legal mandate and good business. That said, it is important for HRM professionals to understand the complexity and tenuous nature of this component of their mandate as it relates to stakeholder management. In short, HRM professionals involved with championing proactive employment law compliance will often need to strike a delicate balance between protecting the interests and rights of employees versus the interests and rights of the corporation.[1] This balance becomes increasingly delicate as an HRM professional advances to more senior-level leadership roles, particularly as a proxy-named executive. And the tenuous nature of this balance is particularly evident when an HRM professional is facing a *prima facie,* or "at first glance," case of employment discrimination.

EEOC and Prima Facie

Perhaps the most critical and central piece of employment-related federal legislation is the Civil Rights Act of 1964. It is designed to protect employees against unlawful employment discrimination in the workplace. It is important to note here that the courts have long interpreted the designation of "employee" to also include applicants, current employees, and previous employees. Title VII also established the Equal Employment Opportunity Commission (EEOC), which is charged with overseeing Title VII. Essentially, any employer organization with more than 15 employees is beholden to Title VII.

Title VII is rightly regarded as the "cornerstone" of employment law. It specifically identifies the following as "protected classes," thereby forbidding illegal employment-related practices (e.g., selection, promotion, training, termination) based upon:

- Race
- Color
- Religion
- Sex (Gender)
- National origin

Subsequent EEO-related federal statutes have added the following to the original list of protected classes:

- Age
- Disability
- Pregnancy
- Marital status
- Military status

Thus, according to Title VII and the interpretive precedents established by court judgments, if an employer organization (for example, the Hooters restaurant chain) either *intentionally* through disparate treatment (e.g., establishing as a de facto requirement that Hooters waitstaff applicants be female) or *unintentionally* via adverse impact (e.g., the hiring rate for male waitstaff applicants at Hooters is not at least 80 percent of the hiring rate for female waitstaff applicants at Hooters) discriminates against employees relative to their membership in one of the protected classes listed above (in terms of Hooters, obviously gender is the primary protected class of concern), that employer organization is potentially guilty of *illegal discrimination.* In both of these situations, a *prima facie* case of employment discrimination has been established.

However, this does not mean that employer organizations cannot be discriminate in their employment practices.[2] In fact, EEO related statutes are in place to not only protect the rights of employees relative to *illegal discrimination,* but also the rights of employer organizations to *legally discriminate* in their employment practices. The Hooters restaurant chain has successfully done exactly this, on multiple occasions. To be specific, Title VII and the interpretive precedents established by court judgments allow an employer to rebut a *prima facie* case of employment discrimination in the following four ways:

- *Job relatedness*—For example, an organization can demonstrate that an employee must be able to repeatedly lift 75 pounds in order to perform the tasks associated with a position in the firm's distribution center, and justify the use of a physical strength test as part of the selection and screening process. Of course, this necessarily results in legal discrimination in regard to disabled employees, as well as many older or female employees.
- *Bona fide occupational qualification (BFOQ)*—For example, a university with an intentionally religious mission, such as Brigham Young University, can require that all tenure-track, full-time faculty be professing and practicing Mormons on that grounds that such a

requirement is essential to successfully performing the occupation of professor at such an institution, given its unique mission. In this case, applicants for faculty positions that are practicing Buddhists or even atheists would necessarily be subject to legal discrimination and denied tenure-track full-time faculty employment solely on the basis of their religious beliefs. This is the primary defense that the Hooters restaurant chain has successfully employed to demonstrate the legality of their discriminatory employment practices relative to gender. In short, Hooters has successfully demonstrated that it is a legitimate BFOQ for all waitstaff in their restaurants to be female, given the unique business purpose/mission and related business model of the firm.

- *Bona fide seniority system*—In essence, if an organization can demonstrate that an impartial seniority system has long been employed in making employment-related decisions then it may continue to do so, even if such systems unfairly impact members of protected classes. In such a case, it is an unfortunate truth that recent efforts to diversify the employee base of an organization may be "undone" if employee layoffs are necessary, as many recently hired employees may be members of traditionally underrepresented groups (for example, female firefighters).
- *Business necessity*—Lastly, consider the case of commercial airline pilots. The airline transportation industry has successfully demonstrated that a mandatory retirement age of 60 for commercial airline pilots is a business necessity to ensure the efficient and safe operation of the enterprise.

In short, it is the responsibility of the aggrieved employee(s) to demonstrate a *prima facie* case of employment discrimination. Once such a case is established, the burden of proof then shifts to the employer organization to demonstrate a justifiable reason for the discrimination based upon one or more of the four defenses outlined above.

See also Bona Fide Occupational Qualification; Equal Employment Opportunity Commission; Staffing: An Overview; Selection; Four-fifths Rule; Disparate Treatment/ Disparate Impact

NOTES

1. Jeffrey A. Mello, "The Dual Loyalty Dilemma for HR Managers Under Title VII Compliance," *SAM Advanced Management Journal,* Winter 2000, 10–15.

2. J.D. Thorne, *A Concise Guide to Successful Employment Practices* (Chicago: CCH Incorporated, 2000).

Scott A. Quatro

PRIVACY ACT

The Privacy Act of 1974 prevents invasion of privacy through the misuse of records by federal agencies and grants people the right to access information the government maintains on itself. The Privacy Act states, in part, "No agency shall disclose any record which is contained in a system of records by any means of communication to any person, or to another agency, except pursuant to a written request by, or with the prior written consent of, the individual to whom the record pertains."[1]

The Privacy Act allows an individual access to how the federal government uses, collects, maintains, and disseminates government records, as well as how it grants access to personal information maintained by federal agencies. Furthermore, the Privacy Act allows people to amend any incomplete, inaccurate, or irrelevant information, and provides access to information recorded by the executive branch of the federal government.[2] The executive branch includes "cabinet departments, military departments, government corporations, government controlled corporations, independent regulatory agencies, and other establishments in the executive branch."[3] Federal agencies that are subject to the Freedom of Information Act are also subject to the Privacy Act, and each agency administers requests for its records, whereby an individual may:

1. "Request notification of whether the Commission maintains a record pertaining to him or her in any system of records,
2. Request access to such a record or to an accounting of its disclosure,
3. Request that the record be amended or corrected, and
4. Appeal an initial adverse determination of any request."[4]

The Privacy Act grants rights to U.S. citizens and aliens admitted lawfully for permanent residence. Nonresident foreign nationals are not able to access records, except those records pertaining to that specific individual.[5] The Federal Trade Commission (FTC) handles individual record requests by searching a "systems for records," organized by seven categories, which include FTC personnel, FTC financial, law enforcement, mailing lists, correspondence, access requests, and miscellaneous systems.[6] A "system of records" is a group of records an agency identifies by an individual's name, social security number, or other form or identification. The Privacy Act does not typically apply to records kept by local and/or state governments or private organizations.[7]

Computer Matching and Privacy Protection Act of 1988

The Computer Matching and Privacy Protection Act of 1988 amended the Privacy Act of 1974. This amendment includes new provisions that regulate the use of computer matching. Computer matching is an electronic comparison of information about individuals to determine federal benefit program eligibility.[8] Matching programs involving federal records generally fall under a matching agreement between the recipient agency and individual source. Matching programs must outline the procedures and purpose of the matching records, as well as establish protections for matching records.[9]

The Computer Matching and Privacy Protection Act of 1988 requires notification of agency findings must be given to an individual before any adverse action is taken as a result of a computer-matching program. Moreover, opportunities must be granted to an individual to contest and/or independently verify any adverse findings/actions. While state and local agencies generally do not offer access to matching records, individuals must be granted the opportunity to contest any matching records, irregardless if they were performed by a federal, state, or local government.[10] Again, HR departments must account for such guidelines when establishing, managing, and maintaining employee records.

General Implications of the Privacy Act on Organizations

The Privacy Act establishes five basic requirements regarding an individual's access to personal information from a government agency, which organizations and their HR departments must consider when requesting information regarding potential or current employees. These requirements state that an agency must:

1. Allow individuals to view and copy records about themselves
2. Publish notices defining all systems of records
3. Make reasonable efforts to maintain relevant, accurate, complete and timely records about individuals
4. Establish rules governing the disclosure and use of personal information
5. Permit individuals to legally enforce their rights allowed under the act[11]

Many organizations have modeled their internal privacy policies after the Privacy Act, thereby creating rules for disclosure and use of employee information, allowing employees access to their own records, and having procedures for correcting inaccurate information. HR is responsible for disseminating information about internal privacy policies and federal and state privacy laws throughout all levels of the organization to ensure that all supervisors, managers, and leaders understand and support privacy rights.

Current innovations and trends pose challenges for companies and their duties to respect employees' privacy, maintain confidentiality, and provide employees and relevant stakeholders with work-related information. Computers, e-mail, telecommuting, and flexible work arrangements often blur the lines of personal and work-related time, resources, and responsibilities. As a result, public- and private-sector firms must develop security strategies and mechanisms to address the privacy concerns associated with providing personal information to employees, external customers, and other stakeholders.[12] Supervisors, managers, and HR personnel add value to their organizations by understanding and complying with privacy rules and laws, including the Privacy Act.

See also Privacy Rights; Workplace Privacy

NOTES

1. U.S. House of Representatives, *A Citizen's Guide on Using The Freedom of Information Act and The Privacy Act of 1974 to Request Government Records—Second Report by the Committee on Government Reform,* 109th Cong. 1st sess., Union Calendar No. 127, Report 109–226 (Washington, DC: U.S. Government Printing Office, 2005), 65.

2. Ibid., 22–23.

3. Ibid., 65.

4. U.S. Federal Trade Commission, "Freedom of Information Act and Privacy Act Handbook," http://www.ftc.gov/foia/foiahandbook.pdf (accessed December 7, 2007), 14.

5. U.S. House of Representatives, *A Citizen's Guide on Using The Freedom of Information Act,* 22–23.

6. U.S. Federal Trade Commission, "Freedom of Information Act and Privacy Act Handbook," 14.

7. U.S. House of Representatives, *A Citizen's Guide on Using The Freedom of Information Act,* 22–23.

8. Ibid., 23–24.

9. Ibid., 23–24.

10. Ibid., 23–24.

11. Ibid.

12. George R. Milne and Mary E. Gordon, "Direct Mail Privacy-Efficiency Trade-offs within an Implied Social Contract Framework," *Journal of Public Policy and Marketing* 12, no. 2 (Fall 1993): 206–15.

Matt Neibauer

PROTECTED CLASSIFICATION

Equal employment opportunity (EEO) laws prohibit discrimination in recruiting, hiring, or other terms or conditions of employment due to one's race, color, gender, religion, age, disability, or veteran's status. EEO laws provide protection for individuals of these classifications, thus the term *protected classification*. Subcategories of people within each protected classification are *protected groups*. Men and women, for example, are protected groups within the protected classification of gender. Discrimination against anyone within the protected group or all protected groups is prohibited, not just the minority group. As a result, discrimination in employment against a man is equally unlawful as employment discrimination against a woman. Further, harassment of applicants or employees due to their membership in a protected class is unlawful, as it is considered a violation of Title VII of the Civil Rights Act (CRA) of 1964.

Title VII offered the first effective federal legislation banning employment-related discrimination. The CRA of 1964 covers employers of 15 or more workers for at least 20 weeks during the year. Since the passage of the CRA, additional federal and state laws banning employment discrimination have passed. Most state laws extend and strengthen the protections offered by federal law. Some states cover employers that are exempt from federal statutes, while others have expanded the number of groups of individuals deserving protection. For example, some states prohibit employment discrimination based on sexual orientation.

The CRA of 1991 strengthened the CRA of 1964 by expanding the remedies that may be awarded in discrimination cases. The 1991 amendment allows for both punitive and compensatory damages when discrimination has been found, and has identified the evidence necessary to prove discrimination claims, thereby making them easier to prove.

Protected Classes and Corresponding Legislation

The *protected classification/groups* as defined by the various EEO, federal, and state laws include race, color, religion, national origin, gender, age, disability, and veteran status.

Discrimination because of one's race, color, religion, gender, or national origin is prohibited by the Civil Rights Act of 1964, Title VII. Federal law does not currently recognize sexual orientation as a protected classification/group, although some states have enacted legislation affording such protections.

The Age Discrimination in Employment Act (ADEA) applies to nearly all companies with 20 or more employees and prohibits discrimination on the basis of age by protecting individuals who are age 40 and older.

The Americans with Disabilities Act (ADA) of 1990 prohibits discrimination against qualified individuals with disabilities. To prove discrimination, an individual must establish that he or she was denied employment due to a disability that could have been accommodated (Vocational Rehabilitation Act of 1973 requirement) and for which he or she was otherwise qualified to perform in terms of essential functions. Employer defenses include the individual's inability to perform essential job functions even with reasonable accommodation or the undue hardship that accommodation would impose on the employer.

Veterans are former members of the armed forces, including disabled veterans, recently separated veterans, Vietnam War veterans, or other protected veterans entitled to Veterans Administration disability compensation. The Vietnam Veterans' Readjustment Assistant Act of 1974 also requires government contractors to proactively hire veterans of the Vietnam era.

Compliance

Employers are encouraged to proactively comply with EEO antidiscrimination laws by using a multifaceted approach, including
- Engage in ongoing analysis of organizational human resource practices in light of EEO requirements
- Establish appropriate antidiscrimination policies and action plans
- Clearly articulate policies (including complaint filing and dispute resolution) to all employees, including supervisors, managers, and leaders
- Provide regular training on EEO law and requirements and encourage dialogue
- Encourage open communication and feedback
- Document, document, document all HR decisions, policies, and procedures

See also Age Discrimination in Employment Act (ADEA), Americans with Disabilities Act (ADA); Civil Rights Acts of 1964 and 1991

Resources:
Civil Rights Act of 1964, Title VII. http://www.eeoc.gov.

Ann Gilley

RAILWAY LABOR ACT

The Railway Labor Act (RLA) is a U.S. federal law that governs labor relations in the railway and airline industries. The act, passed in 1926 and amended in 1936 to apply to the airline industry, seeks to substitute bargaining, arbitration, and mediation for strikes as a means of resolving labor disputes.[1]

When people think of the Railway Labor Act, they think of railroads. However, the act is one of the most crucial laws passed in our nation's economic history. The RLA was enacted in 1926 as a means to keeping the American economy flowing without the disruption of railway labor disputes. While the act was passed to avoid any interruptions to commerce and operations, it also was a means of protecting employees' rights to join a union. The unionization of the railway workers really was the key factor of creating the act so that there would be minimal shutdowns of business railways.[2]

Antecedents to the Railway Labor Act

After the national railroad strike of 1877, which was put down with the intervention of federal troops, the U.S. Congress passed the Arbitration Act of 1888. This authorized the creation of arbitration panels with the power to investigate the causes of labor disputes and to issue nonbinding arbitration awards. This act was a complete failure. For example, only one panel was ever convened under this act, which was during the Pullman strike, and the government issued its report only after the strike had been obverted via a federal court injunction backed by federal troops.

Congress attempted to correct these shortcomings in the Erdman Act, passed in 1898. This act likewise provided for voluntary arbitration, but made any award issued by the panel binding and enforceable in federal court. It also outlawed discrimination against employees for union activities and prohibited "yellow dog" contracts whereby employees agree not to join a union while employed. It also required both sides to maintain the status quo during any arbitration proceedings and for three months after an award was issued. The arbitration procedures were rarely used. A successor statute, the Newlands Act, passed in 1913, proved more effective, but was largely superseded when the federal government nationalized the railroads in 1917.

The Adamson Act (1916) provided workers with an eight-hour day and gave them the same compensation as they previously received for a ten-hour work day. This act also required time and a half for overtime. Another law passed in the same year gave President Woodrow Wilson the power to take possession and assume control of any system of transportation for transporting troops and war materiel. Accordingly, Wilson exercised that authority on December 26, 1917, when he ordered federal administrators to protect railroad workers' right to organize, which established a number of adjustment boards to settle employment disputes.

While Congress considered nationalizing the railroads on a permanent basis after World War I, the Wilson administration announced that it was returning the railroad system to its original owners. However, the Transportation Act of 1920 did preserve the adjustment boards used in the Adamson Act. This legislation created the Railroad Labor Board (RLB) with the power to issue nonbinding proposals for the resolution of labor disputes.

Unfortunately, the RLB soon destroyed its moral authority when in 1921 it ordered a 12 percent reduction in employees' wages, which the railroads were quick to implement. The following year, the RLB issued a declaration that outlawed a national strike organized by shop employees of the railroads. Accordingly, the Department of Justice obtained an injunction that carried out that declaration. From that point forward, railway unions refused to utilize the RLB.[3]

Overview

The Railway Labor Act has four separate purposes:
- Avoidance of interruptions to commerce and operations
- Protection of employees' rights to join a union
- Providing independence of carriers and employees to self-organization unions
- Settlement of grievances[4]

The RLA imposes a duty on carriers and employees to obtain and maintain collective bargaining agreements, and to settle all disputes. The RLA also provides mandatory procedures to regulate disputes regarding union representation and grievances. The RLA also postpones the ability of the parties to take action in bargaining disputes until they have completed an elaborate, time-consuming process involving negotiation. These negotiations are mediated by the National Mediation Board (NMB), which is an independent agency in the executive branch headed by a three-member board appointed by the president with the advice and consent of the Senate.[5]

See also Labor-Management Relations (Taft-Hartley) Act; National Labor Relations Act

Resources:

"About the Railway Labor Act." http://www.ourworld.compuserve.com.

"Highlights of the Railway Labor Act." http://www.fra.dot.gov.

Leslie, Douglas, ed. *The Railway Labor Act* (Washington, DC: BNA Books 1995).

"Railway Labor Act Outline." http://www.nmbfacts.com.

Wilner, Frank N. "Should the Railway Labor Act Be updated?" 2001, http://www.railwayage.com.

NOTES

1. Wikimedia Foundation, Inc., "Railway Labor Act,"http://en.wikipedia.org/wiki/Railway_Labor_Act

2. Brendan Bank, *Railway Labor Act,* University of St. Francis, http://www.stfrancis.edu/ba/ghkickul/stuwebs/btopics/works/railwaylaboract.htm (accessed August 20, 2008).

3. Air Line Pilots Association, Int'l, "Railway Labor Act," https://www.alpa.org/Default.aspx?tabid=242 (accessed August 20, 2008).

4. "Highlights of the Railway Labor Act," http://www.fra.dot.gov/us/content/955 (accessed August 20, 2008).

5. "The Railway Labor Act," Delta Pilots Web site, http://www.dalpa.com (accessed August 20, 2008).

Roger Odegard

REASONABLE ACCOMMODATION

The term "reasonable accommodation" has become a common word in many businesses with the enactment of the Americans with Disabilities Act (ADA) of 1990. The ADA was enacted to eliminate discrimination against persons with disabilities so that they can enjoy the same privileges and opportunities as those persons without disabilities. Under the act, it is the employer's responsibility to provide a reasonable accommodation for a person with a qualified disability. Since this law was put into place, there have been many questions about when it is necessary to provide a reasonable accommodation. In addition, there has been a lot of controversy about what constitutes a reasonable accommodation.

In 1992, the Rehabilitation Act of 1973 was amended to extend the reasonable accommodation privileges to federal agencies. In addition, Executive Order 13164, issued in 2000, furthered the protection for persons with disabilities by requiring that federal agencies develop written procedures for providing reasonable accommodations.

What is a Reasonable Accommodation?

A "reasonable accommodation" is adapting the job site or job requirements for a qualified person with a disability to enable that individual to enjoy equal employment opportunities. There are three categories of reasonable accommodations:

* *Application process modification or adjustments:* ensuring that the application process allows a person with a disability the same access as a person without a disability (an example would be to have job application forms available in Braille, or using very large print).
* *Essential functions:* making reasonable adjustments to allow a qualified person with disabilities to perform the essential functions of a job (examples may be purchasing particular equipment, or providing a sign language interpreter).
* *Employment benefits:* modification or adjustments ensuring that persons with disabilities can enjoy the same privileges of employment (an example would be facilitating a staff meeting in a location of the building that is accessible to a person in a wheelchair).

When using the term reasonable accommodation, the Americans with Disabilities Act provides several examples in which to accommodate a person with disabilities. These examples include:

* Making existing facilities used by employees readily accessible to and usable by individuals with disabilities
* Job restructuring
* Part-time or modified work schedules
* Reassignment to a vacant position; acquisition or modification of equipment or devices
* Appropriate adjustment or modifications of examinations, training materials or policies

- The provision of qualified readers or interpreters
- Other similar accommodations for individuals with disabilities

For example, if an employee, due to a disability, is required to attend doctor's appointments during regular business hours, it would be a reasonable accommodation to allow him flexible hours or to find another position that has hours that are not affected by these appointments.

Another example would be an employee who has a mental disability that affects the ability to retain information or causes social anxiety. In this case, some examples of reasonable accommodation would include giving all requests in writing, having daily planning meetings, or giving considerate and constant positive feedback.

When Is an Employer Required to Provide a Reasonable Accommodation?

An employer is required to provide a reasonable accommodation to persons with qualified disabilities. A disability, as defined by the ADA is:

- A physical or mental impairment that substantially limits one or more of the major life activities of the individual. A major life activity is a function that the average person can perform with little or no difficulty. Examples would include seeing, hearing, breathing, walking, speaking, sitting, and lifting;
- A record of such an impairment; or
- Being regarded as having such an impairment.

An employer is not required to reasonably accommodate a person who does not disclose a disability to his/her employer if it is not a visible disability. An employer may legally require documented proof, if the disability is not visible, before providing an accommodation.

Limitations to a Reasonable Accommodation

There is a distinction between a reasonable accommodation and an undue hardship. It is not a reasonable accommodation if it imposes an undue hardship. An undue hardship is an action that requires significant difficulty or expense to an employer. The burden of proof is on the employer to show that a specific accommodation causes an undue hardship. Typically, the larger the organization, the more ability the employer has to make a reasonable accommodation in terms of accessibility and cost, so it may be more difficult to prove an undue hardship. Factors to be considered in determining whether an accommodation is an undue hardship include:

- The nature and cost of the accommodation
- The overall financial resources of the facility or covered entity; the number of persons employed; and the effect on expenses and resources
- The type of operation or operations of the covered entity

Requesting a Reasonable Accommodation

A request for a reasonable accommodation must be made only for a reason related to a medical condition. An individual may request an accommodation either verbally or in writing. It is not necessary that the individual sites an "act" or uses the term "reasonable accommodation" in a request. A request can also be made for an individual by a family member, friend, health care provider or other representative.

Alternative Accommodations

If an individual has a qualified disability, the employer has some flexibility in granting an accommodation. The employer has the discretion to identify reasonable and appropriate alternatives. For example, if an employee with a qualified disability requires an ergonomically correct chair and requests a particular brand, the employer may decide if it will provide that particular brand or an alternative brand that is also ergonomically correct.

See also Americans with Disabilities Act (ADA); Undue Hardship

Resources:

The Americans with Disabilities Act of 1990. http://www.ada.gov.

U.S. Office of Personnel Management.http://www.opm.gov.

Elizabeth Wheeler

RECORD RETENTION LAWS

Record retention requirements are unclear at best, and a legal quagmire at worst. Not only do federal and state laws apply, but organization size and federal contractor status also affect retention requirements. Three main categories of employment records exist: general employment files (e.g., applications, employment records, and advertisements); payroll files (e.g., time sheets, tax forms, and withholdings); and medical records (e.g., benefits, Family Medical Leave [FMLA] and workers' compensation information).

Due to the variations in state laws, this entry focuses on federal requirements for organizations covered by each specific employment law, with specifics for government contractors noted. Employers are advised to check applicable state statutes (including common law statutes) for information specific to their state.

General Employment Records

General employment records include employee-specific documentation related to basic demographical information (e.g., name, address, Social Security number, date of birth, and gender), application or resume, position information (e.g., job descriptions and classifications), INS Form I-9, employee mobility (e.g., promotion, demotion, transfer, and termination), training (e.g., selection criteria, training attended, and test results) and performance records. Additionally, general employment records include nonemployee-specific data, including job postings (e.g., internal and external advertisements), applicant records (e.g., nonhired applicant resumes and interview records), applicant demographics, seniority, and merit systems.

Employee-Specific Records

The general rule of thumb is that employee-specific records should be maintained for four years from the date of termination, unless a charge or lawsuit has been filed; then, relevant records should be kept until final disposition of the case.[1] Although some legislation actually requires a shorter time frame for retention due to the overlap of required information between statutes, this four-year blanket covers the requirements for any organization with greater than 15 employees imposed by Title VII of the Civil Rights

Act of 1964, the Age Discrimination in Employment Act (ADEA), the Americans with Disabilities Act (ADA), the Fair Labor Standards Act (FLSA), the Federal Insurance Contribution Act (FICA), the Federal Unemployment Tax Act (FUTA), the Federal Income Tax Withholding Act, the Employee Polygraph Act, and the Immigration Reform and Control Act. Additionally, this time period covers federal-contractor regulations covered by the Davis-Bacon Act, the Service Contract Act, the Walsh-Healy Public Contracts Act, and the Rehabilitation Act of 1973. The only exception to the four-year retention blanket is for organizations that use credit reports in employment decisions. As of June 1, 2005, revisions to the Fair and Accurate Credit Transactions Act require that any information derived from a credit report be shred immediately after use.

Nonemployee-specific Records

Title VII, ADEA, and ADA require that applicant information, including internal and external advertising, applications/resumes received, demographic information of applicants and interview notes for nonhired individuals be retained for one year from submission. Additionally, these statutes maintain that policies and procedures on seniority and merit systems should also be maintained for a minimum of one year. Federal contractors or organizations under legal order are required to maintain affirmative action plans and are required to maintain this data, in addition to the yearly action plan, for two years due to requirements in the Vietnam Era Veterans' Readjustment Assistance Act, Executive Order 11246, Rehabilitation Act of 1973, and Uniform Guidelines on Employee Selection Procedures. It may be advisable for all organizations to keep applicant records for two years to provide evidence of hiring practices in the event of a discrimination suit.[2]

Payroll Records

Payroll records include basic employee demographic data, payroll amounts and dates, time sheets, overtime worked and paid, deductions and federal withholdings, tips, annuities and/or pension payments, and tax withholding forms.

Similar to the requirements for employee-specific records, payroll records should also be subject to a four-year rule of thumb. However, unlike general records that should be maintained from the date of termination, payroll records should be retained on a rolling year based on the record date. Although some statutes require less time, a four-year retention policy will cover all the legal requirements from the Equal Pay Act, FLSA, FICA, FUTA, and Federal Income Tax Withholding Act.

Medical Records

Concern over the use and the privacy of medical records in employment began with the Americans with Disabilities Act, but the implementation of the Health Insurance Portability and Accountability Act made this an even greater concern for employers due to the staggering penalties for violating an employee's medical privacy. All medical records should be maintained separately from general employment records, a process that actually makes retention easier. To be compliant under ADA and FMLA, medical excuses, requests for accommodations, FMLA applications, and FMLA leave records should be maintained for three years after termination of employment. The Occupational Safety and Health Act (OSHA) requires that records relating to on-the-job injury be maintained for a minimum of five years for first-aid injuries, and a maximum of 30 years for any injuries requiring major medical care or exposure to blood-borne pathogens or other toxins.

Finally, the Employee Retirement Income Security Act (ERISA) requires that all medical and retirement summary plan documents, pension reports, and any other insurance-related documentation (employee-specific of not) be retained for a minimum six years from the date of implementation (longer if the plan is still in effect).

Conclusion

After legal compliance, the most critical thing to remember regarding record retention is to follow the policies that your organization has implemented. This should include auditing the process and having a record of when files are scheduled to be destroyed, as well as their destruction date. Early destruction of documents may suggest that there is a desire to eliminate something incriminating, while late destruction, or nondestruction, of documents may increase the organization's liability in the event of legal or government investigation.

See also Affirmative Action

NOTES

1. Wallace Bonapart and Cornelia Gamlem, "Federal Record Retention Requirements for Employers," in *SHRM White Papers* (December, 2002), http://www.shrm.org/hrresources/whitepapers_published/CMS_000270.asp (accessed March 5, 2008).

2. Jonathan A. Segal, "Is It Shredding Time Yet?" *HR Magazine,* February 2003, 109–13.

Heather S. McMillan

RETALIATION

Retaliation is defined as "action taken in return for an injury or offense."[1] In the workplace, retaliation has occurred in the form of (adverse) changes in job duties, harassment, reduction in resources or support, demotion, and firing, to name a few. For example, the Supreme Court has stated that a change in job duties after an employee filed a harassment claim might be retaliation if it is "materially adverse" to a reasonable employee. This interpretation upholds the law "to prevent employers from interfering with employees' efforts to assert their rights under the laws that prohibit discrimination and harassment."[2]

While disciplinary action should be taken if an employee deserves it, retaliation against an employee is illegal and is an offense for which the employee can seek legal remedies in court. Retaliation against an employee has been known to occur when one "blows the whistle" against an employer and highlights wrongdoing or illegal activity, files a complaint (commonly discrimination) against an organization or one of its members, or otherwise engages in behavior or actions that somehow threaten another party.

Retaliation is considered illegal by numerous EEO laws, including Title VII of the Civil Rights Act of 1964, the Americans with Disabilities Act, and the Age Discrimination in Employment Act. Therefore, it is important to understand the causes of retaliation, including reasons why an employee would feel that he or she is being retaliated against and the elements of a potential retaliation claim.

Reasons for a Retaliation Claim

Employees commonly cite two main forms of retaliation; denial of promotion and termination of employment. First, an employee may not have received a desired promotion in spite of his or her qualifications for the position (such as tenure, education, or productivity). Second, retaliation claims sometimes surface after an employee has been fired. Absent clear documentation of a history of performance issues, employees occasionally challenge a termination with claims of unlawful treatment due to their justifiable actions (such as complaints about workplace safety, harassment, or product defects).

Elements of a Retaliation Claim

Should a retaliation case be pursued by an employee, the employee as plaintiff must prove the following to establish a *prima facie* case. The plaintiff must prove that he or she engaged in a protected activity, suffered a loss or limitation of employment opportunity, and that there is a link between engaging in the protected activity and the loss or limitation of employment.

Should the plaintiff establish a *prima facie* case, the employer can still provide evidence that a lawful, non-retaliatory motive (such as poor individual performance, an overall reduction in workforce, etc.) was the reason for the employment decision. Thus, if the employee does build a case, the burden of proof shifts to the employer. Should the employer assert a lawful, non-retaliatory motive, the plaintiff must rebut the employer's claim by (1) providing evidence that sheds doubt on the credibility of the claim, and/or (2) providing other evidence supporting the claim of retaliation as being the most likely motive behind the decision.[3] Therefore, it is important for managers and HR personnel to guarantee that the motive for any disciplinary action against an employee does not adversely impact his or her employment opportunities to an unfair extent.

Implications for Managers

It is important to be aware of retaliation and its consequences, as well as its implications regarding dysfunctional organizational norms and culture. In 2004, the Equal Employment Opportunity Commission received 22,740 charges of retaliation based on all statutes enforced by EEOC, and resolved 24,571 claims.[4] Notably, retaliation cases are frequent—and carry associated fines, penalties, and legal costs. As a result, organizations, HR, and managers must be well schooled in EEO law and ways to prevent retaliation. Training, education, documentation, and continuous review of ever-changing laws are necessary to fully inform all organizational employees of the specifics and nuances of retaliation. Organizations should have well-defined and clearly communicated procedures for filing of complaints by employees, and prevention of retaliation by employers.

Conclusion

Retaliation cases are common. It is important to understand the precursors of a retaliation claim, the elements that constitute a claim, how retaliation cases can be prevented, and the legal and financial consequences to an organization of a retaliation claim. Employees who feel wronged by an employer may seek legal remedies that damage a firm's reputation or impose painful monetary penalties. HR and managers serve their employers well by taking all necessary precautions to ensure that all organizational members comply with the law.

See also Americans with Disabilities Act (ADA); Civil Rights Act of 1964 and 1991; Documentation, Harassment

NOTES

1. Title VII of the Civil Rights Act of 1964, U.S. Equal Employment Opportunity Commission (EEOC) Web site, http://www.eeoc.gov/policy/vii.html (accessed December 1, 2007).

2. "Change in Job Duties Might Be Retaliation, Says Supreme Court," Nolo: Law Books, Legal Forms and Legal Software Web site: http://www.nolo.com/support/detail.cfm/ObjectID/0DA3665D-9424-4CEC-9ED3423E29029AAB (accessed August 20, 2008).

3. David Walsh, *Employment Law For Human Resource Practice* (Mason, OH: Thompson Higher Education, 2007).

4. EEOC, "Retaliation" (May 17, 2007), U.S. Equal Employment Opportunity Commission (EEOC) Web site: http://www.eeoc.gov/types/retaliation.html (accessed August 20, 2008).

Chris Armstrong

SOCIAL SECURITY ACT

The Old Age, Survivors,' Disability, and Health Insurance Program (OASDHI), better known as Social Security, was established by the Social Security Act of 1935. The four major categories of Social Security benefits are retirement, disability income, survivors' income, and Medicare.

Social Security is a type of social insurance funded by tax dollars, not a pension plan. Benefits are financed through a tax on employees and employers. Originally, an employee paid a 1 percent tax on the first $3,000 of annual income earned in covered employment; however, this base has increased gradually (e.g., to 6.2 percent of covered earnings up to $102,000 for 2008). The wage base increases automatically each year as earnings levels rise. The base tax covers all but the Medicare element of Social Security, which is financed by an additional 1.45 percent tax on all earned income. The employee's contribution is matched by an identical contribution from his or her employer. The Medicare tax applies to all earned income; no taxable wage base exists.

Worker Eligibility

Workers may receive Social Security benefits only if they have met certain tests based on the length of service for which OASDHI taxes have been paid. A worker earns a credit for each quarter worked, up to a maximum of four quarters per year. A person is fully insured after having worked in covered employment for 40 quarters (10 years). For individuals born prior to 1929, however, fewer credits are required.

Retirement Benefits

Workers born in 1937 or earlier reach their full retirement age at 65; however, they may receive reduced benefits as early as age 62. To enhance Social Security's financial solvency and account for the increase in life expectancy, the full retirement age will gradually increase to age 67. An eligible worker may receive reduced benefits at age 62 regardless of the worker's required full retirement age.

A worker's monthly retirement benefit is based on his or her average indexed monthly earnings (AIME). The indexing year is the second year before the worker reaches age 62, becomes disabled, or dies, whichever comes first. Social Security benefits will automatically adjust each year for changes in the cost of living (e.g., 2.3 percent in 2008).

Earnings Test. Individuals may lose monthly benefits if their earned income rises above certain limits. Beneficiaries under the full retirement age will lose $1 in benefits for each $2 in earnings above the annual limit (which was $13,560 in 2008). In the calendar year in which the beneficiary attains full retirement age, $1 in benefits will be deducted for each $3 in earnings above the limit (which was $36,120 in 2008). The earnings test is eliminated in and after the month that the beneficiary attains full retirement age. As a result, those who have attained full retirement age or beyond can earn any amount and receive full benefits. The earnings test does not apply to certain non-earned income, such as investment income, interest, dividends, rents or leases, or annuity payments.

Disability Income Benefits

Social Security provides payment of disability benefits to workers who have met minimum work criteria. The benefit amount depends on the disabled person's earnings history and is increased if the worker has dependents. Each eligible dependent may receive one-half of the benefit payable to the disabled worker, subject to a family maximum.

Workers seeking disability benefits must provide proof of the disability, specifically in the form of medical evidence that the insured is unable to engage in gainful work activity. The disability must be expected to last at least 12 months, and is subject to a five-month waiting period.

Survivors' Benefits

Dependents of covered workers who die may receive Social Security survivors' benefits, payable monthly as long as the survivors meet specific eligibility requirements. Widows and widowers are entitled to receive Social Security benefits as long as they have dependent children under the age of 16, and again upon reaching age 60. Surviving spousal benefits may be reduced, however, if he or she earns more than a specified amount ($13,560 in 2008, for those below the normal retirement age). Children of deceased eligible workers may also receive survivors' benefits until they reach age 18 (22 if disabled). The monthly benefit amount depends on the earnings of the deceased worker, subject to specific minimum and maximum levels.

Medicare

Medicare was created by Congress in 1965 to provide health insurance for individuals age 65 or older. Initially, Medicare was comprised of two components: a compulsory hospital plan (Part A) and a voluntary medical insurance plan (Part B). A third part, an optional prescription drug benefit (Part D), became effective in 2006. Medicare's hospital insurance, referred to as Part A, covers inpatient hospital care, skilled nursing home care, home health services, and hospice care. Medicare's supplemental medical insurance, called

Part B, provides coverage for medically necessary doctor bills and related expenses (e.g., diagnostic X-ray and laboratory tests, physical and occupational therapy, medical equipment and supplies, ambulance services, organ replacements, and artificial limbs, to name a few). A monthly premium is charge for each part of Medicare. Persons who are covered under Part A are automatically covered under Part B unless they voluntarily decline the coverage. Individuals and their employers pay a tax of 1.45 percent on unlimited wages (unlimited) to fund Medicare.

See also Payroll

Resources:

Social Security Act of 1935.

Social Security Administration Web site: http://www.ssa.gov.

Jennifer A. Majkowski and Ann Gilley

TRADE ADJUSTMENT ASSISTANCE ACT OF 2002

President George W. Bush signed the Trade Adjustment Assistance Reform Act of 2002 (TAA) into law on August 6, 2002. The TAA is a federally funded employment program that assists workers whose jobs have been lost (or whose hours of work and wages have been reduced) due to foreign imports. Workers may be eligible to receive one or more of the following services: training services, reemployment services, job search allowances, relocation allowances, and a health coverage tax credit (HCTC). Additional weekly trade readjustment allowances (TRA) may be available to eligible workers whose unemployment benefits are exhausted, although benefits are typically paid only if a person is enrolled in or has completed an approved training program. Workers not qualified for TRA may still be eligible for training, job search and relocation allowances, and reemployment services.

Eligibility for TAA

The TAA is funded by the Employment and Training Administration (ETA) of the U.S. Department of Labor (DOL) and administered by each state's employment security agency (or any agency designated by the governor to provide reemployment services under the TAA program). Upon a layoff or work reduction, a petition for TAA must be filed with the DOL and the state TAA coordinator by one of the following: (1) a group of three or more workers, (2) a certified union official or representative, (3) an official of the employer/firm, (4) a one-stop agency or partner agency, or (5) a state dislocated worker unit staff person. A community-based organization may not petition. The DOL has 40 calendar days to complete its investigation and decide on eligibility. The two types of eligibility are group and individual, with a different process applying to each.

Group Eligibility

The DOL reviews a petition on behalf of a group of workers in a particular company and determines whether they are eligible to apply for TAA benefits. If so, the group is "certified."

Individual Eligibility

The local state employment security agency or workforce center reviews applications from individual workers whose group petition has already been certified and determines which TAA program benefits the worker is eligible to receive. Applicants must meet three eligibility requirements; they must (1) have lost their job or been "partially separated" (average weekly work hours and pay reduced by at least 20 percent), (2) belong to a group of employees certified by the DOL as qualifying for TAA benefits, and (3) have been laid off or partially separated on or after the impact date and before the termination or expiration date of the certification.

Resources:

U.S. Department of Labor
Employment and Training Administration
Division of Trade Adjustment Assistance, Room C-5311
200 Constitution Avenue, NW
Washington, DC 20210
1-866-4-USA-DOL
http://www.dol.gov
http://www.doleta.gov/tradeact/2002
http://www.fortress.wa.gov/esd/portal/training/laidoff/taa_html

Ann Gilley

UNDUE HARDSHIP

In 1990, President George H.W. Bush signed the Americans with Disabilities Act (ADA).[1] The law was enacted as a measure to prevent discrimination against individuals with real or perceived disabilities. The law applies to employers with 15 or more employees and covers every aspect of the employment relationship from the advertisement of a position through hiring, training, discharge and discipline. Under the ADA, a disabled employee may request a reasonable accommodation to assist in his/her ability to perform essential job functions. However, employers are not required to supply a reasonable accommodation if it would cause *undue hardship* to the employer.

Undue Hardship—Defined

Under the ADA, an accommodation could cause undue hardship depending on:
- The cost of the requested accommodation
- The potential interference with the functioning of the business
- Whether the accommodation is substantial for the operation

As part of this analysis, one must examine the size, structure, and resources of the company. Also, the employer must carefully document all efforts to make the accommodation, including efforts to seek funding for the measure through an external source, such as a vocational rehabilitation organization. In some situations, one might find a federal or state tax credit to minimize the financial implications of the accommodation. Finally, the employer should consider allowing the employee the opportunity to make the accommodation through an alternative idea or his/her own financial resources.

Practical Implications

An employer's responsibility for the ADA begins at the time of recruiting for a position. Therefore, human resource practitioners must review recruitment procedures to guarantee conformity with the ADA guidelines.

Further, human resources departments must take care to educate employees about their rights under the ADA. Once an accommodation has been requested, one must make a good faith effort to accommodate in the company's best interests.

Whether an accommodation is reasonable or causes an undue hardship for a business is a matter for case-by-case analysis. The employer is well advised to open a dialogue about the accommodation with the requesting employee or applicant. In many situations the employee will have an idea for a reasonable accommodation that will meet the standards of the act.

See also Americans with Disabilities Act (ADA); Reasonable Accommodation

Resources:

Internal Revenue Service (tax credit information), (202) 622-6060. Job Accommodation Network provides technical assistance on making Accommodations. 1-800-526-7234.

 U.S. Department of Labor, ADA Disability and Business Technical Assistance, 1-800-949-4232, http://www.dol.gov/dol/welcome.htm.

 U.S. Equal Employment Opportunity Commission, 1-800-669-3362 (voice) 1-800-800-3302 (TT).

NOTES

1. U.S. Equal Employment Opportunity Commission, "Undue Hardship," http://www.eeoc.gov/policy/docs/accommodation.html#undue (accessed February 14, 2007).

Laura Dendinger

UNIFORMED SERVICES EMPLOYMENT AND REEMPLOYMENT ACT

The Uniformed Services Employment and Reemployment Act (USERRA) is a federal law that provides reemployment rights for veterans and members of the National Guard and Reserve Component following qualifying military service. Enacted in 1994, USERRA prohibits employer discrimination against any person on the basis of that person's past military service, current military status, or obligations or future intent to join one of the country's uniformed services. Although the roots of USERRA can be traced back to World War II, there has been a recent resurgence of USERRA-related activity given the increasing dependence on Reserve and Guard forces in the Global War on Terror, other military operations, and noncombat disaster relief.

USERRA significantly strengthened and expanded protection regarding civilian job rights and benefits for veterans and members of the Reserve Component (to include the National Guard). The law covers all employers, regardless of size. A civilian employer, with few exceptions, is legally required to place the employee in a military leave status and extend reemployment rights upon return. USERRA protects service members' rights and benefits by clarifying the law, improving the enforcement mechanisms, and provides eligibility to receive Department of Labor assistance in processing claims.

As defined in Title 38 U.S. Code, Chapter 43, Sections 4301–4334, Public Law 103-353, those protected under USERRA are employees "in service of the uniformed services"

either in a voluntary or involuntary status and include the following:
- Active duty
- Active duty for training
- Initial active duty for training
- Inactive duty training
- Full-time National Guard or Reserve duty
- Absence from work for an examination to determine a person's fitness for any of the above types of duty
- Funeral honors duty performed by National Guard or Reservists
- Duty performed by intermittent employees of the National Disaster Medical System, which is part of the Department of Homeland Security—Emergency Preparedness and Response Directorate (FEMA), when activated for a public health emergency and approved training to prepare for such service[1]

The "uniformed services" consist of the following:
- Army, Air Force, Navy, Marine Corps, or Coast Guard
- Army Reserve, Air Force Reserve, Naval Reserve, Marine Corps Reserve, or Coast Guard Reserve
- Army National Guard or Air National Guard
- Commissioned Corps of the Public Health Service
- Any other category of persons designated by the president of the United States in times of war or emergency[2]

USERRA expands the cumulative length of time that an individual may be from work for military duty and retain reemployment rights to five years (previously, it was four years). However, there are important exceptions that may lengthen the period of protection, such as initial enlistments lasting more than five years and involuntary active duty extensions, recalls, and mobilizations—especially during a time of national emergency. Reemployment protection does not depend on the timing, frequency, duration, or nature of an individual's service. The law also provides enhanced protection for disabled veterans, requiring employers to make reasonable efforts to accommodate the injury. Service members convalescing from injuries sustained while in military uniform now have two years to return to their job.

USERRA also provides that returning service members are reemployed in the job that they would have attained had they not been absent for military duty (the long-standing "escalator" principle), with the same seniority, status, and pay, as well as other rights and benefits determined by seniority. It also provides that reasonable efforts (e.g., training) be made to returning service members to refresh or upgrade skills to help them qualify for reemployment. The law clearly provides for alternative reemployment positions if the service member cannot qualify for the "escalator" position.

Health and pension plan coverage for service members is also covered by USERRA. For military service of less than 31 days, health care coverage continues as if there was no break in employment. For military service over 30 days, the service member may elect to continue employer sponsored health care for up to 24 months; however, they may be required to pay 102 percent of the required premium. All pension plans are protected under USERRA, and military service must be considered service with an employer for vesting and benefit accrual purposes.

USERRA also requires service members to provide advance written or verbal notice to their employers for all military duty unless giving notice is impossible, unreasonable, or precluded by military necessity. An employee should provide notice as far in advance as is reasonable under the circumstances. Time limits for returning to work depend on the duration of a person's military service. For military service 30 days or under, an employee must report back to work on the first regularly scheduled work period following completion of service. For military service between 31 and 180 days, an employee has 14 days to submit an application for reemployment. For service of 181 or more days, an employee must submit the application for reemployment within 90 days.

See also Military Leave

NOTES

1. U.S. Department of Labor, Veterans' Employment and Training Service, "A Non-Technical Resource Guide to the Uniformed Employment and Reemployment Rights Act—USERRA," (U.S. Government, April 2005), 1–18.
2. Ibid.

Victoria T. Dieringer

VOCATIONAL REHABILITATION ACT

The Vocational Rehabilitation Act is federal legislation that authorizes the "formula grant programs" of vocational rehabilitation, supported employment, independent living, and client assistance, that further authorizes a variety of training and service discretionary grants that are administered by the Rehabilitation Services Administration. Additionally, the act authorizes research activities administered by the National Institute on Disability and Rehabilitation Research along with the work of the National Council on Disability. The act also includes a variety of provisions focused on the rights, advocacy, and protections for individuals with disabilities.[1]

The Vocational Rehabilitation Act of 1973

In 1973, the federal government enacted the Vocational Rehabilitation Act, which required all executive agencies and both contractors and subcontractors who receive more than $2,500 annually from the federal government to engage in affirmative action for individuals with disabilities. The government designed this act to encourage employers to actively recruit qualified individuals with disabilities and to make reasonable accommodation to assist them in becoming active members of the labor market. The Employment Standards Administration of the Department of Labor enforces this act.[2]

Section 503 of the Rehabilitation Act requires that all federal contractors take affirmative action to employ and advance qualified people with disabilities. Under Executive Order 11246, contractors and subcontractors to the federal government are required to develop a written affirmative action plan designed to ensure equal employment opportunities to any qualified person with a disability. These plans are monitored by the Office of Contract Compliance Programs (OFCCP) within the U.S. Department of Labor.

Americans with Disabilities Act (ADA) of 1990

In 1990, Congress passed the Americans with Disabilities Act, which extended the rights and privileges of disabled employees of federal contractors under the Rehabilitation Act of 1973.[3] The ADA stipulates that qualified individuals with disabilities may not be discriminated against by a private-sector organization or a department or agency of a state or local government employing 15 or more employees in terms: *"if the individual can perform the essential functions of the job with or without reasonable accommodation."*

The Equal Employment Opportunity Commission (EEOC) Policy, *Guidance on Reasonable Accommodation Under ADA,* suggests the following process for assessing reasonable accommodations:[4]

1. Look at the particular job involved; determine its purpose and its essential functions.
2. Consult with the individual with the disability to identify potential accommodations.
3. If several accommodations are available, preference should be given to the individual's preferences.

Further clarification stated that public facilities such as restaurants, grocery stores, doctor's offices, shopping centers, hotels, and the like must be made accessible to the disabled unless undue hardship would occur for the business. There have been numerous lawsuits and Supreme Court deliberation on what is and what is not considered "undue hardship" for a business to make the adjustment as ordered. With the addition of the ADA, the Rehabilitation Act now prohibits discrimination based on disability in all employment practices to include job application procedures, hiring, terminating, compensation, training, and promotion. The new ADA defines disability as a physical or mental impairment that substantially limits one or more major life activities, to include having a record of such impairment, or being regarded as having such an impairment to exist.[5]

Therefore, the addition of the ADA covers physiological disabilities such as cosmetic disfigurement and anatomical loss affecting the neurological, musculoskeletal, sensory, respiratory, cardiovascular, reproductive, digestive, hemic, genitourinary, or lymphatic systems. Additionally, it also covers mental and psychological disorders such as mental retardation, organic brain syndrome, emotional or mental illness, and learning disabilities. Situations that are not included are obesity, substance abuse, eye and hair color, and those who are predominately left-handed.

See also Americans with Disabilities Act (ADA); Reasonable Accommodation; Undue Hardship

NOTES

1. Ed.gov, "The Rehabilitation Act," review of Reviewed Item., no. (n.d.), http://www.ed.gov/policy/speced/reg/narrative.html (accessed August 20, 2008).

2. Ibid.

3. Raymond A. Noe, John R. Hollenbeck, Barry Gerhart, and Patrick M. Wright, *Human Resource Management: Gaining a Competitive Advantage,* 4th ed. (Boston: McGraw-Hill Irwin, 2003).

4. H. John Bernardin, *Human Resource Management: An Experiential Approach,* 4th ed. (Boston: McGraw-Hill, Irwin, 2007).

5. The Americans with Disabilities Act of 1990, http://www.ada.gov.

Frank E. Armstrong

WARN ACT

The Worker Adjustment and Retraining Notification (WARN) Act of 1988 created specific requirements for employers who are facing significant organizational downsizing.

This law provides employees with advance time to prepare for the transition between jobs, search for a new job, or seek training opportunities, and it reduces the impact of the layoff or plant closing.

Employers are covered by WARN if they have 100 or more full-time employees, or if they have 100 or more full-time and part-time employees who combined work at least 4,000 hours per week at all employment sites. Part-time employees include those employees who work less than 20 hours per week, or employees who have been employed with the company for less than six months. Employers who are private for-profit, private nonprofit, or quasi-public entities are covered by the WARN guidelines. Federal, state, and local government employers that provide public services are not covered by WARN.

WARN Notice Triggers

The WARN Act requires covered employers to provide written notice at least 60 calendar days prior to an employment loss due to a plant closing or mass layoff. The plant closing or mass layoff may be either permanent or temporary to trigger WARN.

Employment Loss
An employment loss is the involuntary termination of employment, a layoff for more than six months, or a reduction in an employee's hours of more than 50 percent for each month of a six-month period.

Plant Closing
A plant closing occurs when there are at least 50 or more employment losses for full-time employees. Plant closing employment losses may be a result of either a temporary or permanent shutdown of an entire single site, or one or more facilities or operating units within a single employment site.

Mass Layoff
A mass layoff triggering the WARN Act can occur in two possible situations: (1) when there are 50–499 employment losses during any 30-day period for full-time employees, and those employees make up at least 33 percent of the workforce at a single site, or (2) when there is an employment loss of 500 or more full-time workers during any 30-day period at a single employment site.

Exceptions to the Act

The law does acknowledge that there may be instances in which advance notice may not be possible. In the event of unforeseeable business circumstances, natural disasters, or a faltering company, WARN does allow exceptions to the 60-day notice rule. The exception does not remove the employers' obligation to provide notice. The employer is still obligated to give notice as soon as possible and also must provide a statement as to why the notice period was reduced.

Unforeseeable Business Circumstances
WARN defines an unforeseeable business circumstance as a sudden, dramatic, and unexpected action or condition outside the employer's control. Examples include the sudden cancellation of a major contract or a strike at a key materials supplier.

Natural Disasters
When a plant closing or mass layoff is due to a force of nature, such as an earthquake, flood, tornado, or similar event, the natural disaster exception to the 60-day notice may apply.

Faltering Company
The faltering company exception to WARN will apply in circumstances in which the company is actively seeking funding or business capital that would enable the employer to avoid a layoff or shutdown. If these efforts fail and result in a mass layoff or plant shutdown, they may have protection from the 60-day notice period due to the faltering company exception.

Contents of the WARN Notice

Employers impacted by WARN must provide notice to affected nonunion employees, union representatives of affected unionized employees, the appropriate state dislocated worker unit, and the chief elected officer of the local government where the employment site is located.

The WARN notice must be in writing and must contain specific information about the upcoming mass layoff or plant closing. Elements that should be included in the WARN notice are:[1]

1. The name and address of the site where the plant closing or mass layoff will occur.
2. The name, address, title, and phone number of the company official to contact for further information.
3. Information as to whether the planned action is expected to be permanent or temporary, and if the entire facility is to be closed.
4. Information of whether bumping rights, the right to displace other workers, will exist.
5. The date when the plant closing or mass layoff is expected to take place.
6. The number of affected employees.
7. Information about which employees will be affected and the schedule for employment losses.
8. Identification of any union representatives or the affected employees.

Penalties

Employers who fail to give appropriate notice may be subject to a penalty equal to the back pay and benefits to each employee for the length of the violation, up to 60 days. The liability can be reduced for wages paid over the notice period or any voluntary payments the employer made to its employees that was not required by law.

Employers may also be liable for civil penalties of up to $500 per day, when the employer has not provided proper notice to the unit of local government.

Conclusion

The WARN Act is an important law affecting employee rights. Employers who are faced with downsizing are not restricted from taking necessary action needed for the economic stability of their business, but they do need to ensure that any action taken follows the guidelines established by the WARN Act.

Resources:
Ditelberg, Joshua L. *A Practical Guide to Workforce Reductions.* http://www.shrm.org/hrresources/lrpt_published/CMS_000974.asp (accessed July 24, 2007).

Society for Human Resource Management, *The SHRM Learning System Module 2: Workforce Planning and Employment.* Alexandria, VA: Society for Human Resource Management, 2007, 26–28.

U.S. Department of Labor, Employment and Training Administration, *Worker Adjustment and Retraining Notification (WARN) Act: Employer's Guide to Advance Notice of Closings and Layoffs* (Washington DC, 2003).

NOTES

1. U.S. Department of Labor, Employment and Training Administration, *Worker Adjustment and Retraining Notification (WARN) Act: Employer's Guide to Advance Notice of Closings and Layoffs* (Washington DC, 2003).

Shanan M. Mahoney

WHISTLE-BLOWING

Whistle-blowing is defined in its simplest form as the process of telling others, inside or outside the organization, of illegal or unethical behavior. For decades, public, private, and nonprofit organizations have been faced with the dilemma of dealing with whistle-blowers. For those "blowing the whistle," the road is paved with bitterness and possible retaliation from other employees or principals. For the organization, the results may be legal action or major damage to image and reputation. Therefore, it comes as no surprise that whistle-blowing has developed a predominately negative connotation.

There are several internal repercussions from whistle-blowing, and depending on how organizations respond to the employee who divulged the information, there may be external repercussions. Companies can, however, use whistle-blowing as a preventative measure to prevent illegal or unethical behavior that could have even bigger consequences.

Internal Repercussions

The most prevalent point of contention for managers surrounding whistle-blowing is that employees frequently break the chain of command. Many managers believe that by going either to the principals of the organization or to outsiders (the media, special interest groups, authorities, etc.), the employee is undermining their authority.[1] Employees who blow the whistle believe they are acting in good faith in most cases. The challenge here is that "illegal" and "unethical" is sometimes left up to individual perceptions.[2] The final determination must be made upon further investigation. Fortunately, however, under public policy exception to the employment-at-will doctrine, they cannot be fired for the practice.[3]

External Repercussions

Aside from the obvious legal action, organizations can experience great damage to their reputation resulting from allegations of illegal or unethical behavior. To complicate matters further, whistle-blowing is not limited to legal and ethical issues. Contemporary society also views wasting or inappropriate use of resources to be worthy of note to various stakeholders. Nonprofit organizations are accountable to the public, while for-profit organizations are accountable to shareholders first, then other stakeholders (employees, community, etc.)[4] Ironically, Enron could have been saved if they had listened and taken action when a key employee blew the whistle. The conclusion is, therefore, that if companies form a clear policy for whistle-blowing and protect employees from termination and retaliation, they can benefit from this practice.

Whistle-blowing as a Preventative Measure

Organizations can proactively put steps in place to protect whistle-blowers, thereby discovering illegal or unethical behavior before it gets to the point of legal action or becomes damaging to the company's image. Most sources agree on the following steps to develop an effective whistle-blowing policy:[5]

1. Clear definition of individuals to be covered in the policy
2. Nonretaliation provisions for individuals who blow the whistle
3. Confidentiality
4. Clear process for reporting illegal or unethical acts
5. Communication of the policy to all stakeholders

Since today's organizations must put ethics at the forefront of strategic planning and operation, giving employees the courage to report illegal or unethical acts by creating a clear whistle-blowing policy is critical.

NOTES

1. R. Kreitner, *Foundations of Management: Basics and Best Practices* (Boston: Houghton Mifflin, 2005).

2. Thomas S. Bateman and Scott A. Snell, *Management: Leading and Collaborating in a Competitive World* (Boston: McGraw-Hill Irwin, 2007).

3. Ibid.

4. Tim V. Eaton and Michael D. Akers, "Whistleblowing and Good Governance." *CPA Journal,* June 2007, 66–71.

5. Ibid.

Brenda E. Ogden

WORKERS' COMPENSATION

Whether worker, manager, or business owner, worker's compensation is an important topic. Workers' or workmen's compensation can be defined as the system in which employers compensate employees either for duties performed or an injury sustained during the course of employment. Throughout history, employers and employees have been concerned about this topic.

History

Records show workers' compensation systems in ancient civilizations written in the code of Hammurabi around 1800 BC.[1] A few thousand years later, in the late 1800s, the dawning of the Industrial Revolution brought the issue of workers' compensation to the foreground of American life. Workers crowded into factories and toiled long hours in less than ideal conditions. Industrialization and economic growth came at the price of injuries among the workforce. Injured employees lost jobs, incurred medical bills, and, in severe cases, lost the ability to earn a livelihood. Responding to these conditions, workers began suing employers to recover costs and sustain a living.[2] Courts were overrun, resulting in costly and time-consuming trials. Business owners and employees pushed for new laws specifically governing workers' compensation.

State and federal statues followed the public demand. In the early 1900s, most states developed their own workers' compensation laws; however, it was not until 1948 that all states had laws in place.[3] Since 1906, federal statutes oversee government employees, the District of Columbia, and longshoremen. In 1970, the Occupational Health and Safety Act (OSHA) enacted national regulations controlled by each state. While similarities exist in workers' compensation laws and in OSHA standards, each state has unique regulations.

The Basics

Federal and state laws cover major topics, including who is the employee and who is the employer, what constitutes a work-related injury, who will diagnose or treat the injury, in what time frame the injury must be reported, who will pay for work-related injuries, and the rights of the individuals involved.

Terms such as employee and employer must be defined so rights can be assigned. "Employee" is a technical term excluding independent contractors retained by companies. Typically, employees are hired and paid to perform specific supervised job duties, whereas independent contractors work on an informal basis.[4] Usually, an easy distinction is whether the individual is eligible to receive a 1099 form (independent contractor) or a W-2 form (employee) based on federal tax laws. Defining an employer varies by state laws. Generally, an employer is a business that "pays for services rendered"; in other words, one that has supervised employees.[5] Employers can range from a private, family-run business to a multibillion-dollar corporation.

Large and small employers deal with work-related injuries. To be considered work related, the injury must result from or be "in the course of employment."[6] Work-related injuries include lacerations, contusions, amputations, or other major physical trauma, along with repetitive motion injuries (tennis elbow), or injuries relating to ergonomics (improper body positioning). Work-related injuries may occur obviously or subtly over the course of many years.

The Process

Generally, an employee must report a work-related injury immediately after it occurs, or as soon after he knows it has occurred. If an employee fails to report an injury once it is known within the specified time frame, he may not be eligible for compensation.[7] Reporting time frames vary greatly by state. If the injury is not sudden, employees may not know if the injury is work related or not. If it is unclear if the injury is work related, it is important to seek a diagnosis from an occupational health professional.

Occupational health specialists are doctors or other medical professionals who are trained in recognizing and treating work-related injuries. Most have either studied or have experience within a particular industry or range of injuries.[8] Occupational specialists focus on treating employees so they can return to work while avoiding reinjury. These professionals are skilled in treatment options and legal language, making them preferred by employers to diagnose and treat work related injuries. Usually, within the first 10 to 30 days, the employer can choose the provider, although an employee is always free to seek a second medical opinion.[9] Due to the experience and knowledge of an occupational health specialist, fewer questions are left unanswered, which speeds up the compensation process.

Compensation for injuries begins after the employee is diagnosed with a work related injury. Compensation may occur in the form of medical expenses being covered or through lost time earnings. Medical expenses are paid by the employer or the employer's insurance company.[10] Until an employee is able to return to work, he or she is compensated for lost wages due to the injury. Inability to work is defined as not being able to work until fully recovered, hours decreased during recovery, or disability resulting from the injury. Most states require a waiting period before lost wages will be compensated. In Michigan, for example the employee must be off seven consecutive days before wage loss compensation can begin.[11] Lost wages are not paid at 100 percent. The percentage or reimbursement varies by state and typically ranges between 60–80 percent.[12]

Employees are either directly compensated by employers (private funding) or employers' insurance companies. Not all states allow private funding. Those that do allow private funding require companies to prove they can meet financial obligations relating to injuries.[13] Insurance companies, or in some cases state-run insurance programs, have built a safety net into the system. Premiums are driven by how many claims a company makes based on the overall industry.[14] Consequently, companies with above-average injuries pay higher premiums. Unfortunately, this safety net can backfire. Employers that are unsafe do not always report injuries to their insurance providers; instead, they pay out of pocket. While this keeps company premiums low, it does not benefit employees or industries in which injuries are preventable with property safety techniques. Insurance providers have encouraged safety standards across the nation to lower compensation costs.

Rights and Responsibilities

With regards to workers' compensation, employees and employers have rights and responsibilities. When the injury is reported, employers are responsible to fill out an accident or injury report and submit the information to insurance or pay for treatment themselves. Further, an employee is entitled to all medically available and necessary treatment.[15] Under the workers' compensation system, the employee no longer has the right to sue the employer unless he or she can prove the employer willfully caused the injury.[16] If the insurance company denies the claim, or the worker is discriminated against by the employer, the employee may file a claim with her state's office for workers' compensation. A judge usually hears a case and makes a decision.[17] When evidence supports the injury, it is more than likely (above a 51 percent chance) that the judge will find for the employee.[18] Protecting the rights of all parties increases the fairness and accessibility of the system.

In summary, if an employee is injured, he should seek medical treatment and inform his supervisor or employer. The supervisor should submit an accident report, which human resources can provide to the insurance provider and medical professional. The insurance company, if the claim is approved, should begin paying medical bills and, when appropriate, begin compensating employees. In coordination with the medical professional, preferably an occupational health specialist, the employee should continue treatment until returned to work or declared medically disabled. If a claim is denied, or the employee is discriminated against, counsel should be sought from the state's office for workers' compensation and, if necessary, an attorney. If the employer has concerns regarding the claim, it should do the same.

Importance

The process of workers' compensation is both proactive and reactive. Insurance companies encourage preventative programs and safety standards to prevent injuries. Cooperating at all levels in the organization to make these programs successful increases job satisfaction and the bottom line by decreasing risk factors among the workforce. When injuries do occur, prompt reaction by employers and employees helps prevent further injury and allows the workers' compensation process to begin. Employers should document every injury carefully. Someone from human resources should be assigned to gather information on what happened, who witnessed it, and how the injury took place. These investigations should happen immediately and privately, so no witnesses or information are compromised.

Finally, to be successful, the workers' compensation process requires legal cooperation and ethical involvement. Dishonest or unethical behavior is costly and time consuming, and breaks down the compensation process. Ethical responsibilities include providing accurate information, reasonable care, and the Golden Rule. Employers should, to the best of their ability, prevent injuries by providing job and emergency training. In return, if an employee is injured, he or she should provide accurate information to employers, physicians, and legal authorities in a timely manner. Next, employers should take reasonable care to ensure more employees are not injured in the same manner. Similarly, employees should perform job duties carefully to prevent injuring themselves or others. Lastly, both employers and employees should treat each other honestly. Workers' compensation has been and will continue to be an important reality of working life.

Resources:

National Academy of Social Insurance Web site: http://www.nasi.org/.

U.S. Department of Labor, OSHA Web site: http://www.osha.gov/.

Power, Robert D., and Fredrick Y. Fung. *Workers' Compensation Handbook.* San Diego, CA: KW Publications, 1994.

NOTES

1. Robert D. Power and Frederick Y. Fung, *Workers' Compensation Handbook* (San Diego, CA: KWP Publications, 1994).
2. Lewin G. Joel III, *Every Employee's Guide to the Law* (New York: Pantheon Books, 1996).
3. Price Fishback, "Workers' Compensation." *EH.Net Encyclopedia,* ed. Robert Whaples (August 15, 2001), http://eh.net/encyclopedia/article/fishback.workers.compensation (accessed August 20, 2008).
4. Joel, *Every Employee's Guide to the Law.*
5. Power and Fung, *Workers' Compensation Handbook.*
6. Barbara Repa, *Your Rights in the Workplace,* 5th ed. (Berkeley, CA: Nolo.com, 2000).
7. Power and Fung, *Workers' Compensation Handbook.*
8. Ibid.
9. Repa, *Your Rights in the Workplace.*
10. Power and Fung, *Workers' Compensation Handbook.*

11. Ibid.
12. Ibid.
13. Fred S. Steingold, *The Employer's Legal Handbook* (Berkeley, CA: Nolo.com, 2004).
14. Ibid.
15. Power and Fung, *Workers' Compensation Handbook*.
16. Joel, *Every Employee's Guide to the Law*.
17. Power, and Fung, *Workers' Compensation Handbook,* 37.
18. Ibid.

Betsy Nolan

WORKPLACE PRIVACY

Workplace privacy is much more a part of today's work environment than ever before. A number of issues contribute to the definition of workplace privacy. In the course of doing business in today's environment, a prudent company needs to become expert in all facets of workplace privacy. Consequently, organizations are under pressure to draft privacy policies as part of their employee handbooks. Some companies are taking a more proactive stance and dedicating specialized personnel to interpret laws and monitor employee actions related to privacy.

Workplace privacy is an issue related to the rights and reputation of organizations as well as to the rights and privileges of the employee, while at the same time examining where one's rights begin and end in relation to the organization. In a legal context, the courts are coming down on the side of employers. At the same time, organizations are feeling the need to formalize their positions in an effort to protect all concerned parties. This entry will examine key issues that must be spelled out in any privacy policy to protect all affected parties. It is critical to start from the premise that all employees should have an expectation of privacy, but not an explicit guarantee of privacy.

Privacy Expectations

The employee clearly has some expectations related to privacy. An employee must have an office or a safe place to carry out work-related tasks. This might be a place to store and protect files or related work from public view. An employee's access to the company network or Internet is password-protected. Not only does this protect the employee, but it protects the files of clients under the jurisdiction of the employee. It is important to note that the company and its representatives still have access to files even in a password-protected environment. Other exceptions to the employee's right to privacy follow.

Record Keeping/Personal Files

An organization can release confidential information about the employee without expressed permission of the employee to:
- Administration
- Supervisors
- Government entities
- As a support of a legal action

However, the employee has the right to expect confidentiality in a workplace investigation.

Prospective Employees

An integral part of some organizations' hiring processes is to obtain information from the state or federal bureaus of investigation. Even though this information is part of the public record, an employee has the right to expect that this information will be treated in a confidential manner. Information is also gathered through the reference-checking process for the prospective hire, which should remain confidential. The newly obtained information should remain confidential, especially when the employer elects not to make an offer based on the content of the reference check.

Employee Termination

In an effort to protect the organization, a number of employers err on the side of caution when sharing information with a perspective employer—electing to provide information only on dates of employment and title at the time employment was terminated. However, there may be risk to the company if the employee in question has committed an egregious act. If the details of that act remain confidential, is there any legal liability if a similar act is perpetrated in the subsequent work environment? Can the new employer or those parties on the receiving end of an adverse action file a successful suit against the original company if indeed the company fails to reveal aspects of the infraction?

Physical Privacy

An employee should have reasonable expectations of privacy when he or she has to change clothing in the workplace for work. This includes situations when employees would need to shower or other activities of a personal nature while in the workplace.

Employee Monitoring: What to expect?

With the increasing use of the Internet in the workplace, organizations' concern over employee e-mail as well as web browser activities is under scrutiny. The employee's general perception is that a private e-mail is private; another popular belief is that some Internet browsing is okay if it does not interfere with the employee's work. Nothing could be further from the truth. The computer, and all activities carried out on the computer, is under the jurisdiction of the company. A number of employers are monitoring their employees. The American Management Association confirms that workplace monitoring is not only happening, but is quickly becoming the norm. Monitoring is indeed ongoing, in most cases reflecting concerns of litigation or government agency investigations as well as productivity-related issues. This monitoring can take a number of forms:

- Videotaping employees
- Reviewing voice mail
- Listening to telephone conversations
- Checking computer files
- Reviewing e-mail
- Monitoring browser activity

Organizations should establish clear guidelines for monitoring employees. Employee monitoring is also at the discretion of the organization. The policy statement serves as official notification to employees; monitoring will take place as the company deems appropriate.

Privacy Policy and Guidelines

Guidelines for the use of technology (e-mail and Internet) in the workplace are critical. Technology is controlled by the organization, and its proper use and instruction must be communicated by the organization. The organization is obligated to spell out clear expectations and guidelines to promote good practice.

Resources:

Electronic Communications Privacy Act of 1986. 18 U.S.C. 2510, or http://en.wikipedia.org/wiki/ Electronic_communications_privacy_act.

"Perspectives on Privacy Law and Enforcement Activity in the United States" (revised August 15, 2002). http://www.ftc.gov/speeches/swindle/perspectivesonprivacy.htm.

Privacy for Consumers and Workers Act. http://www.loc.gov/law/find/headings/pdf/001612 01005.pdf.

"Workplace Privacy and Employee Monitoring" (revised February 2006). http://www.privacyrights .org/fs/fs7-work.htm.

Carol Miller

WRONGFUL TERMINATION/DISCHARGE

Wrongful termination, also known as wrongful discharge, is a legal doctrine that emerged from the principle of "employment at will." Employment at will states that employers can discharge (fire) an employee for a good reason, a bad reason, or no reason at all. Additionally, employees may *quit* for a good reason, a bad reason, or no reason at all. On the surface, this principle seems like a win-win situation for both parties. Over the years, however, employees began contesting their discharge in court, and the wrongful discharge doctrine was the result. The doctrine requires that employers have a job-related reason to terminate employees.[1] The good news for employees is that organizations can no longer fire them arbitrarily. The implications for organizations are also clear; they must be accountable for keeping accurate employment records, providing job-related performance appraisals, and monitoring employee performance if they have any hopes of making a case against wrongful termination claims. Employers' first defense against these claims is knowledge of basic employment law.

Knowing the Law

Before deciding if an employee can be fired for certain reasons, employers must first know the reasons why he *cannot* be fired. The Civil Rights Act, the Age Discrimination in Employment Act, the Americans with Disabilities Act, and the National Labor Relations Act prohibit employers from firing employees for multiple reasons. A basic listing of these reasons, although not an exhaustive list, includes race, sex, age, religion, physical or mental disability, participation in organized unions, and whistle-blowing.[2] Employers are charged with making a case for legal termination that is so solid, employees cannot claim any of the aforementioned reasons as basis for the firing. For many organizations, especially smaller ones that do not have developed or formal human resources departments, this is not an easy task. Therefore, employers need to be vigilant regarding documentation and employee feedback to stay one step ahead of the legal system.

Avoiding Wrongful Termination Suits

The key to avoiding lawsuits for wrongful termination lies in clear policy communication and documentation. While some policies may present gray areas, most are written to protect both the employer *and* employee, and when they are clearly communicated so everyone has clear expectations, they will go a long way to keep companies out of the courtroom. For example, policies are normally written to address absenteeism, tardiness, fraternizing with other employees or clients and customers, accepting gifts from inside or outside customers, vacation, personal time, sick time, etc. While this is not a comprehensive list of policies typically held by companies, it represents the most common.

Once these policies are clearly communicated to employees, the employer is responsible for (1) holding the employee accountable to the policies, and (2) documenting each violation and keeping accurate records. Most policies are easily documented; it is not complicated to keep track of absenteeism, tardiness, personal time, etc. Beyond keeping good records, employers need to communicate violations, large or small, to employees and remind them of company policy. Performance appraisals provide a prime opportunity to communicate this information. Making sure that (1) feedback is linked directly with performance and (2) communicated violations are linked with clear company policy is critical.

Conclusion

No one can prevent employees from retaliating against organizations by filing legal action out of anger for being discharged. However, with clear policy and documentation, organizations can avoid long court battles and bad press that could have unfavorable results.

While many of today's companies face valid legal claims surrounding wrongful discharge, one recent case involved a high-level marketing employee that Wal-Mart claims fraternized with a subordinate and accepted gifts from a potential business partner; both actions violated Wal-Mart company policy.[3] They may face a minor blow to their reputation when instances like this reach the public, but holding fast to their position based on a clear violation of policy will provide procedural justice in the eyes of employees.

See also Disciplinary Procedures; Documentation; Termination

NOTES

1. C. Williams, *MGMT* (Mason, OH: Thomson South-Western, 2008).

2. R.S. Schuler and S.E. Jackson, *Human Resource Management: Positioning for the 21st Century* (New York: West Publishing Co., 2003).

3. M. Conlin and R. Berner, "Out For Blood? Who You Gonna Call?" *Business Week,* June 25, 2007, 39.

Brenda E. Ogden